SharePoint Online from Scratch

Peter and Kate Kalmström

ISBN: 978-1530761043

SHAREPOINT ONLINE FROM SCRATCH

Welcome to *SharePoint Online from Scratch*! This book is intended for SharePoint administrators, content creators and other power users. In my work as a SharePoint consultant and trainer for IT professionals, I have come to understand what areas are the most important to SharePoint power users. This book focuses on those areas.

The questions I get are most often concrete – "How do I ...? or "Can SharePoint ...?" – and I hope this book will give the answers to the most common of them. Therefore, *SharePoint Online from Scratch* has many images and step by step instructions, and to be even clearer, I sometimes refer to my online video demonstrations.

SharePoint Online from Scratch is not intended to be a full description of everything in SharePoint Online. The topic is huge, and Microsoft has a lot of detailed information on their websites. Instead, I want this book to give hands-on instructions on how to practically make use of a SharePoint tenant for an organization, or parts thereof.

I will start with an overview of the very basics of SharePoint Online. I describe the Microsoft 365 and SharePoint Admin centers, and after that I explain in detail how to manage and use the SharePoint building blocks: site, app and page. The later part of the book has more advanced information.

SharePoint Online from Scratch includes descriptions of both the modern and the classic experience, but the modern experience has a more prominent place than in earlier versions of the book. Microsoft is constantly developing the modern experience, so a lot that earlier required the classic experience can now be achieved in an easier way with the modern experience.

Even if *SharePoint Online from Scratch* primarily is a handbook, explanations on how SharePoint works are mixed into the instructions. I hope they will give you a good understanding and help you to further explore SharePoint Online.

I sometimes give links to articles with video demonstrations on the kalmstrom.com website. Many of these have been recorded with earlier versions of SharePoint Online than the one described in this book, but I have still decided to keep the links. Even if the interface looks different, I hope you will find it interesting to hear my reasoning about different features and their use.

I will of course update the demos eventually, but I did not want to delay the publishing of this version of *SharePoint Online from Scratch* until that has been done. Readers deserve a book that is as up to date as possible, even if the demos are not!

Microsoft has developed SharePoint so that it is possible to get substantial benefit from a SharePoint system without coding experience, and I have made *SharePoint Online from Scratch* as much no-code as possible. None of my instructions and suggestions require knowledge of how to write code, but in a few cases, I have given examples of code that you can use.

I often give several suggestions on how something can be done, so that you can choose the method that suits you and your organization best. When I give recommendations, they are mainly based on user friendliness and scalability.

Your SharePoint becomes what the users make of it, and believe me, it will grow! You and your colleagues will discover more areas where SharePoint is the best option, and Microsoft will continue to give us new features that expand SharePoint further.

The main part of *SharePoint Online from Scratch* is a manual: how to do various things in SharePoint Online and why you should do it. I also give some examples on SharePoint solutions for different information sharing situations, where you can take advantage of what you have learned and see how it can be used in practical applications.

For even more hands-on exercises, I recommend that you study my book *SharePoint Online Exercises* together with this book. *SharePoint Online Exercises* contains 10 chapters with step-by-step instructions on how to build common business solutions in SharePoint Online.

SharePoint Online Exercises has some explanations, but not at all as much as this book. If you are new to SharePoint, you should therefore study at least the first 13 chapters in *SharePoint Online from Scratch*, before you try the first exercises. Then you can work with both books in parallel.

I am a developer and systems designer in the first place, not an author. Therefore, my mother Kate has helped me get the content of *SharePoint Online from Scratch* together, so that it is introduced to you in a way that we hope is easy to read and understand.

Kate is a former teacher and author of textbooks, so she knows how to explain things in a pedagogic way. She has worked with SharePoint Online in our family business for many years and have seen the product develop.

I have had the last word and approved of all the final text in the book, and it is my "voice" you hear. And of course, I take the full responsibility for the technical content and for the correctness of everything said about SharePoint Online in this book.

Besides my mother, I want to thank QA Engineer Ahmed Farouk, who has proofread the book and given valuable input.

Good luck with your studies!

Peter Kalmström

TABLE OF CONTENTS

16

1 INTRODUCTION

SharePoint is Microsoft's platform for enterprise content management and sharing. It is also a place for social networking within organizations. The cloud edition of SharePoint is called SharePoint Online. It is included in most Microsoft 365 and Office 365 subscriptions, and you need such a subscription to use SharePoint Online. Therefore, this book begins with some general information on how to set up Microsoft/Office 365.

After that, I go through the general build and use of SharePoint, before I describe the different parts and usage possibilities more in detail. The chapters about the SharePoint Online start page and OneDrive for Business describe parts of SharePoint that are especially designed for standard users, but the rest of the book is intended for administrators and site owners.

In the first chapters, I describe in detail how to perform certain actions. When these steps are included in other descriptions later, I don't repeat the steps. That would make the book unreasonably long and boring for everyone who has studied the book from the beginning – which I recommend! – and learned the steps. For example, I only explain once how to open the Site settings. If there is no reference, please use the index to find instructions! There I give the page number for the most detailed explanation.

For the same reason, to save space, I don't explain each time that you must save your changes or click OK when you are done with a modification or have filled out a form. Where possible, I have also cut the screenshots horizontally or vertically inside the image, where SharePoint only shows blank areas.

The screenshots are taken from various SharePoint Online sites in different browsers on a computer with the Windows 10 operating system.

SharePoint Online is an ever-changing platform, so some things will change and no longer work as described in this book. That is part of the charm of the product! I would recommend that you not learn by heart how to do things step by step, but instead look at the instructions as a way of getting to know SharePoint better.

I also recommend that you study the book with a computer at hand, so that you can really try everything I describe, not just read about it.

The steps will change, but if you understand why things are done the way they are, you will be able to figure out how to do what I describe in this book anyway. Even more important is that the knowledge I hope you will acquire by studying *SharePoint Online from Scratch* will help you explore SharePoint far beyond the limits of this book!

2   MICROSOFT 365

Microsoft 365, also called Office 365, is Microsoft's brand name for a group of software and services. Much of it is cloud based, but several subscription plans also include desktop editions of common software like Word, Excel, PowerPoint and Outlook.

In this chapter, you will learn how to set up and configure Microsoft 365 in general. After a short introduction, you will see how you can set up a tenant (an "office in the cloud") for an organization, add users to it and assign them roles. All this is needed before you can start working with SharePoint Online.

I have also included some general information about Microsoft 365 navigation and given an overview of the Microsoft 365 Admin center, which is the place where you manage your tenant.

If your organization already has a functioning Microsoft/Office 365 system, you probably don't need this chapter. Instead, you can go directly to chapter 4, where we will start studying SharePoint.

For information about all the 365 apps and services and more details on how to get started with the platform, *refer to* my book *Office 365 from Scratch*.

2.1   OFFICE 365 AND MICROSOFT 365

Office 365 and Microsoft 365 are two brand names that are often confused. Strictly speaking, the Microsoft 365 platform includes Microsoft Azure and Windows 10 together with Office 365.

However, the Office 365 Business plans have been renamed Microsoft 365 Business, and when it comes to the Enterprise plans there are currently both Microsoft 365 Enterprise plans and Office 365 Enterprise plans.

Except for the Trial section below, it does not matter for the understanding of this book which of the product packages your organization uses, or plan to start using. I will refer to them as "Microsoft 365" or just "365".

SharePoint is included in all 365 Business and Enterprise plans.

2.2   APPS

The word "app" is used widely and with different meanings, but in Microsoft 365 an app is generally a web based application that is run in a web browser (most often Edge, Google Chrome or Firefox).

365 comes with various apps, and many third-party apps can be used together with the apps in a tenant – like my own products, the kalmstrom.com SharePoint solutions. When you build your SharePoint platform, you will use templates to create your own apps for various purposes.

There are also apps that must be downloaded and installed by each user:

- Desktop apps – special editions of the cloud-based apps that are run in each user's computer.

- Mobile apps – apps that run in smart phones and tablets.

2.3   SET UP A 365 TRIAL

Microsoft/Office 365 has several different subscription plans for various kinds of businesses and organizations. In Kalmstrom Enterprises we use the Enterprise E3 plan. This plan includes some of my favorite features, like unlimited mailbox archiving in Exchange and unlimited file storage in OneDrive for Business. It also includes several useful apps such as Teams and Power Automate.

For organizations who need advanced voice, analytics, security and compliance services, the E5 plan is a better choice.

It is currently possible to try the Microsoft 365 Business Standard and Premium plans and the Office 365 E3 and E5 plans for one month without any costs.

Note: When you set up a new 365 tenant, the tenant language is set automatically according to the location of the person who sets up the tenant. Even if each user can set a preferred language, this can create problems for an international company and should be considered. When this is written, there is no way to change the global language after the setup.

2.3.1   *Tenant*

When you start a trial of one of the 365 plans, your organization is assigned a tenant, "an office in the cloud". You can keep the same tenant and all the work you have done, if you decide to go from a trial to a paid subscription.

When you set up your 365 trial, you need to specify a name for the tenant, and it should have the form NAME.onmicrosoft.com. The tenant name cannot be changed after you have started your trial, and it must be unique.

2.3.2   *Setup Steps*

The setup steps below refer to the E3 plan. The process is similar for other plans, but if you want to try a Business package you need to start at https://www.microsoft.com/microsoft-365/business/compare-all-microsoft-365-business-products instead.

1. In the web browser, type the web address https://www.microsoft.com/en-us/microsoft-365/enterprise/compare-office-365-plans. The Compare plans page will open.

2. Click on 'Try for free' under the Office 365 E3 option.

Microsoft 365 Apps for enterprise	Office 365 E1	Office 365 E3	Office 365 E5
The enterprise edition of the Office apps plus cloud-based file storage and sharing. Business email not included[1].	Business services such as email, file storage and sharing, Office for the web, meetings and IM, and more. Office apps not included[1].	All the features included in Microsoft 365 Apps for enterprise and Office 365 E1 plus security and compliance[1].	All the features of Office 365 E3 plus advanced security, analytics, and voice capabilities[1].
$12.00 user/month (annual commitment)	$8.00 user/month (annual commitment)	$20.00 user/month (annual commitment)	$35.00 user/month (annual commitment)
Buy now	Buy now	Buy now	Buy now
Learn more >	Learn more >	Try for free > Learn more >	Try for free > Contact sales > Learn more >

3. Enter your work or school e-mail address. This is to check if you need to create a new account for Microsoft 365. If you already have an account, you will be offered to either sign in or create another account.

4. Fill out your name, phone number and company name.

5. Select how many employees your company has. This does not affect which features you will have access to, because that was decided when you selected your subscription plan.

6. Select your country.

7. Now Microsoft wants to verify your identity. Choose if you want to have an automatic call or a text message.

8. Enter the verification code you received in the call or message.

9. Enter a user name and a tenant name (= "Yourcompany"). Note that the tenant name cannot be changed later. All users will have the tenant name you decide on here – unless you create another 365 account with a new tenant name, of course.

Create your user ID

You need a user ID and password to sign in to your account.

| User name | @ | Yourcompany | .onmicrosoft.com |

username@Yourcompany.onmicrosoft.com

10. Enter a password.

11. Check or uncheck boxes to decide if and how you want to be contacted by Microsoft.

Now the trial account will be created, and you will be asked to add users to the new tenant and install the included desktop apps. This can also be done later. When you are finished, you will be directed to the Microsoft 365 Admin center.

Now you can use Microsoft 365 for free and try it as a Global Administrator. When the evaluation period is finished, you need to subscribe to 365 to continue using the platform. This is done in the Microsoft Admin settings under 'Billing', *refer to* chapter 3.

Demo:

https://www.kalmstrom.com/Tips/Office-365-Course/Setting-up-Office-365.htm

2.4 SIGN IN TO 365

When you have created an account, you need to sign in to 365. These are the steps:

1. Open a web browser and type the web address office.com in the address bar.

2. Click on the 'Sign in' button in the middle of the page, or at the top right corner. A Sign in wizard will open.

3. Type the e-mail address of your 365 account.

4. Click on 'Next'. Now your e-mail address will be analyzed. If the service can decide if it is a work or school account or a personal Microsoft account, you will be taken directly to step 6.

5. (If you are asked to select account type, select "Work or school account".)

6. Type your password.

7. Click on 'Log in'.

8. The 365 homepage will open.

2.4.1 Stay Signed In

When you are on a secure computer, that is locked with a password or PIN, it is convenient to not have to log in each time you want to use Microsoft 365.

The most obvious method is to let the browser save the password.

You should also answer Yes when 365 asks if you want to stay signed in, as this reduces the number of login occasions.

Below I describe more ways to avoid the log in procedure.

2.4.2 Connect Windows 10 to 365

Each user can set Windows 10 to handle the 365 login details. This way the user doesn't have to log in so often.

1. In the computer, click on the Windows icon to open the start menu.
2. Click on the Settings icon and then on 'Accounts'.
3. Click on 'Access work or school'.
4. Click on the 'Connect' button and log in to your 365 account.

When the connection has been established, you will see the Windows icon and the account username below the 'Connect' button, as in the image below.

 Connect

 Work or school account
kate@kalmstrom.com

If you no longer want Windows to manage your 365 login, click on the account under the 'Connect' button. Now you can either manage the account or click on the 'Disconnect' button.

 Work or school account
kate@kalmstrom.com
Manage your account

Disconnect

Demo:

https://www.kalmstrom.com/Tips/Office-365-Course/Signing-into-Office-365.htm

2.4.3   *Single Sign-On*

Another way to log into 365 is to use the 365 credentials as log-in for the computer. This feature only works with Windows 10 Pro and the Edge browser, but if you have that, the browser will pick up the log-in details, so that you have access to Office 365 without further log-in as soon as you are logged in to the computer.

2.5   THE 365 NAVIGATION BAR

In this section, we will look at how you find your way around Microsoft 365. The navigation is managed in the navigation bar, which is present in all 365 apps.

⠿ SharePoint	🔎 Search		⚙	? 👤

2.5.1 The Left Navigation Bar

The left 365 navigation bar has two parts: the App launcher or start menu and the name of the current app or service.

2.5.1.1 The App Launcher

:::

Office 365 →

PowerPoint   OneNote

SharePoint   Teams

Yammer   Power Autom...

Admin   Lists

Project   Forms

Delve   To Do

Whiteboard   Power Apps

Planner

All apps →

Documents

New ∨

X1050 Product Roadmap
SharePoint - Contoso > ... > Go to Market P...

More docs →

You can reach all 365 apps you have access to by clicking on the App launcher in the left corner of the navigation bar.

Apps that are relevant to users and much used across 365 are shown with icons in the launcher.

Only administrators will see the Admin tile. When you click on it, you will be directed to the Microsoft 365 Admin center, where you can manage the tenant.

Below the app tiles, there is a link to all apps, a button for document creation and links to the current user's recent documents.

When you click on a tile in the app launcher, the corresponding app will open in the same tab.

When you hover the mouse over an app tile, three dots, a so called ellipsis, will be visible.

Click on the ellipsis at an app icon, if you want to open the app in a new tab, unpin the app from the launcher (so that it is not visible there anymore) or if you want to learn more about the app.

Microsoft 365

Outlook · OneDrive

Word · Open in new tab

PowerPoint · Unpin from launcher

Learn more

SharePoint · Teams

2.5.2   The Search Box

There is often a search box in the middle of the 365 navigation bar. If you have a small screen, the search box is replaced with a magnifying icon that opens a search box over the whole navigation bar.

In section 4.3.2, I will describe how the search is used to find content in SharePoint.

2.5.3   The Right Navigation Bar

On the right side of the 365 navigation bar, there are other icons. All apps have the profile picture of the current user, and most apps also have a  Settings icon and a question mark. On small screens, the settings and help icons are placed under an ellipsis.

Some apps also have app specific icons to the left of the Settings icon. For example, modern SharePoint pages have a megaphone icon that gives users suggestions on next steps, such as add team members and post news. You can see this icon on the image below.

2.5.3.1   Settings Icon

The Settings icon on the right side of the 365 navigation bar opens a right pane with different content in different apps. There are always some personal 365 settings and some app specific settings or commands.

In SharePoint, the 365 Settings icon shows links to add a new app or page, to see site information and content and more.

There are also personal settings for theme, language, time zone (by default, 365 gets the same regional settings as your computer), password and contact preferences.

If you change your 365 theme, your selected theme will only be shown to you, even if you are the admin of the tenant.

(A default theme for the whole tenant can be set in the Microsoft 365 Admin settings, under Settings >Org settings. Each site can also have its own theme.)

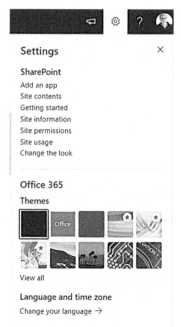

2.5.3.2 Question Mark

Under the question mark icon in the 365 navigation bar, you can find Help on app specific topics. In SharePoint, the topics are gathered under headings.

Help   ✕

← ⌂   🔍 Search help

✓   Get started

♟   Sharing & permissions

▢   Documents & libraries

☰   Data & lists

▭   Pages

⚙   Sites

🔧   Troubleshoot

Explore team sites

2.5.3.3 Profile Picture

When users are new to Microsoft 365, the icon far to the right in the navigation bar has the initials of the current user's name. They are meant to be replaced with the user's photo. The photo (or initials) will be show in many apps and in various contexts within the tenant.

Click on the icon to have more options. It is also under your profile picture that you should sign out when you want to leave Microsoft 365.

In SharePoint, the options under the profile picture are View account and My Office profile, but some other apps have additional options.

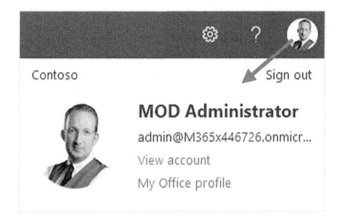

- Click in the icon to add your photo, or to change it.
- Click on 'View account' to find details about your account.

R Overview		
P Security info		
☐ Devices	Peter Kalmström	**Security info** / **Password**
Password		
Organizations	admin@M365x446726.OnMicrosoft.com	
Settings & Privacy		Keep your verification methods and security info up to date. / Make your password stronger, or change it if someone else knows it.
My sign-ins	Why can't I edit? ⓘ	
Office apps		UPDATE INFO > / CHANGE PASSWORD >
Subscriptions		

Devices · **Organizations**

Disable a lost device and review your connected devices. · See all the organizations that you're a part of.

MANAGE DEVICES > · MANAGE ORGANIZATIONS >

Sign out everywhere

Settings & Privacy · **My sign-ins** · **Office apps**

- 'My Office profile', opens the Delve site, where you should add and edit information about yourself that is useful and relevant to your colleagues.

  Here you can also find links to your recent work and to people in the organization that you have cooperated with.

2.6   SUMMARY

Now you have set up your tenant, and you know how you can sign in and navigate in Microsoft/Office 365. Next step is to learn where you can manage the tenant and how you can add user accounts and assign user roles. This is done in the Microsoft 365 Admin center.

If you have created the new tenant, you have automatically become its Global Admin and have full access to the Microsoft 365 Admin center. If you instead are a SharePoint admin or have another admin role, it is still useful to know some about what can be handled in the Microsoft 365 Admin center.

3 THE MICROSOFT 365 ADMIN CENTER

When you click on the Admin tile in the App Launcher or on office.com, you will be directed to the Microsoft 365 Admin center.

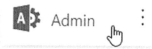

Here, administrators can manage and monitor applications, services, data, devices and users across the organization's tenant. (Of course, only users with administrator roles will see the Admin tile.)

To go through everything in the Microsoft 365 Admin center would require its own book, so I will not do that here. However, I strongly recommend that you explore the Admin center if you have permission to use it, because it is here you find almost everything needed for the management of your organization's tenant.

In this chapter, we will only have a look at how to add users to the tenant and assign administrator roles. I will also explain how to find more Admin centers and point at some other settings in the Microsoft 365 Admin center that I hope you will find interesting.

Most of the SharePoint management is however performed in the SharePoint Admin center, which I will describe in chapter 5, and not in the Microsoft 365 Admin center.

The homepage of Microsoft 365 Admin center has various information about the tenant and messages about updates of Microsoft/Office 365. This information is placed on tiles, and there are often links to pages with more information.

There is also a toggle in the top right corner of the screen for an Essentials view of the homepage, designed specifically for very small organizations with less than 10 users. The Essentials view is *not* what I describe here. If you want to use it in the beginning, it is easy to figure out how to manage the settings.

::: Microsoft 365 admin center
≡
⌂ Home
ⵣ Users ⌄
🖵 Devices ⌄
ᝯ Groups ⌄
▤ Billing ⌄
⌀ Setup
⌀ Customize navigation
⋯ Show all

The full view in the Admin center has a left menu with various entries. The image below shows the default entries. Only Global Admins can change all settings in the Microsoft 365 Admin center.

Via the menu icon on top of the menu, you can collapse the navigation menu to get more space in the main area to the right.

You can customize the left navigation pane by clicking on 'Customize navigation'. When you do that, a right pane will open, where you can check the boxes for the entries you want to show in the navigation.

Admin centers

🛡 Security

🛡 Compliance

🖳 Endpoint Manager

◈ Azure Active Directory

📧 Exchange

📄 SharePoint

📋 Teams

🅰 All admin centers

The other entries can always be reached via 'Show all'. By default, specific Admin centers for various Microsoft 365 apps and services are found here. Among them is the SharePoint Admin center, which of course is important to us.

3.1   SETTINGS

Click on 'Show all' in the left menu to open the Microsoft 365 Admin center Settings tab.

3.1.1   *Search and Intelligence*

Under Search and Intelligence, you can see how people have used Microsoft Search during the last 7, 30 or 90 days. You can also add answers to specific search terms.

By default, users can use Bing with Microsoft Search, but that setting can be disabled here.

×

Microsoft Search in Bing

This will help your users find information specific to your workplace from shared organization sources and the internet.

  Allow your organization to use Microsoft Search in Bing

3.1.2   *Org Settings*

Under the Org settings tab, you can configure many apps and services for the organization.

3.1.2.1 Release Options

Microsoft/Office 365 is continuously updated, and under 'Org settings' you can manage how your tenant receives these updates.

1. Select the Organization profile tab, *see* the image above.
2. Click on 'Release options'.
3. A right pane will open where you can make your choices. The image shows the default setting.

Targeted release means that you get the updates earlier than with the standard release. That way, you can help shape the product by providing feedback on new features.

A good option for a bigger organization is to give only certain people the early updates. These people should be in a position where they can see what each update would mean to the other users and take any actions needed.

When you choose 'Targeted release for select users', you currently need to click on 'Save' to get a possibility to pick the select users. You can also upload a text file with the relevant e-mail addresses.

3.2   USERS

Most user management can be handled in the Microsoft 365 Admin center, under Users >Active users. Here, you can add new users and manage their roles, and you can also delete users, reset passwords, manage product licenses and more.

3.2.1   Administrator Roles

Microsoft 365 comes with a set of administrator roles that can be assigned to users. Each admin role gives permission to perform specific tasks.

The person who signs up for a Microsoft/Office 365 subscription gets the role Global administrator, and he or she is at first the only person who can assign other admin roles. However, one of the roles that can be assigned is Global admin, so there can still be more than one Global administrator for a tenant.

Global admins can modify the settings all over Microsoft 365, so to minimize security risks I recommend that you have more than one Global admin but not more than five.

Instead of Global administrator, you can give the role Global reader to people who need to read settings and administrative information across Microsoft 365 but who not necessarily need to take management actions.

The Global reader role can be combined with a more limited admin role, like SharePoint administrator, to make it easier to get work done without using the Global administrator role.

Make sure that all administrators give a mobile number and an alternate e-mail address in their contact information.

3.2.1.1   Assign Admin Role

By default, new users have no administrator permissions. Global administrators can give administrator permissions when the new user account is created, *see* below, or at any time after creation. People who are License or User administrators are also allowed to set and change permissions for standard users.

To change a user's role, select the user and click on 'Manage roles' above the list of account names to open the right pane. You can also click on the user's name in the list of active users and then select 'Manage roles' in the right pane.

Active users

| | Add a user | Refresh | Delete user | Reset password | Manage product licenses | Manage roles | Export users | ··· |

Display name ↑	Username	Licenses
✓ Adele Vance	AdeleV@M365x446726.OnMicrosoft.com	Microsoft 365 E5 Compliance, Enterpris

In the 'Manage roles' pane, you can assign one or several admin roles. Each permission level has an information icon that opens a pop-up explanation on what the level allows.

Only the most common permission levels are displayed when the pane opens, but you can find them all sorted by category in the collapsed section at the bottom of the pane.

Manage roles

Admin roles give users permission to view data and complete tasks in admin centers. Give users only the access they need by assigning the least-permissive role.

Learn more about admin roles

○ User (no admin center access)

◉ Admin center access

Global readers have read-only access to admin centers, while Global admins have unlimited access to edit all settings. Users assigned other roles are more limited in what they can see and do.

☐ Exchange admin ⓘ

☐ Global admin ⓘ

☐ Global reader ⓘ

☐ Helpdesk admin ⓘ

☐ Service support admin ⓘ

☐ SharePoint admin ⓘ

☐ Teams service admin ⓘ

☐ User admin ⓘ

Show all by category ⌄

3.2.2   *Add Users*

Each 365 user must have his/her own account in the organization's tenant. These accounts are created the Microsoft 365 Admin center >Users >Active Users, and here is also where most of the tenant's user management is handled.

To create user accounts, you need to be Global, License or User administrator. The accounts can be added one by one or in a bulk.

    Add a user   User templates   Add multiple users

3.2.2.1   Create a Single User Account

These are the steps to add a single user to Microsoft 365:

1. In the Microsoft 365 Admin center >Active users, click on the 'Add a user' button.

2. Enter name, display name, username and password settings.

Add a user   ×

- Basics
- Product licenses
- Optional settings
- Finish

Set up the basics

To get started, fill out some basic information about who you're adding as a user.

First name   Last name

Display name *

Username *

@ M365x446726.onmicrosoft.com

Password settings

( ) Auto-generate password

( ) Let me create the password

☑ Require this user to change their password when they first sign in

☐ Send password in email upon completion

Next

3. Click on 'Next'.

4. Select country and assign licenses and apps.

5. Click on 'Next' .

6. If you want to give the user administrator permissions, this is done in the third step, Optional settings.

39

Below the list of permission levels sorted by category, you can fill out additional information about the new user.

7. Click on Next.
8. Review the settings and modify them if necessary.
9. Click on the 'Finish adding' button to add the new user to the tenant.

3.2.2.2   User Templates

To quickly add new users, you can create one or more user templates with a saved configuration. When you have created a template, it will be visible in the dropdown so that you can select it to add a user. Then you only need to enter the name, display name and username for each user in a right pane.

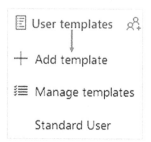

The template creation process reminds of the process to add a single user to the tenant.

Add user template   ✕

○ **Description**

   ○ Basics

   ○ Licenses

   ○ Optional settings

   ○ Finish

Set up your template

User templates allow you to quickly add new users with a saved configuration. To get started, fill out some basic information about the template you're creating.

Name your template *

| Ex: FTE Senior Engineer, New York |

Add a description (recommended)

| Ex: Template for full-time senior engineers in New York office |

Next

3.2.2.3   Import Multiple Users

Instead of adding the users one by one, from scratch or with a template, you can add a group of users or all users at the same time with a CSV file. This is a file with comma separated values that you can create or edit in any text editor or spreadsheet program, for example Excel.

I recommend that you download a CSV file from the 'Import multiple users' pane and enter your user information to it. You may also use another CSV file with the user data, but it must have the same column headings as the downloadable file.

1. In the Microsoft 365 Admin center >Users >Active users, click on 'Add multiple users'.

2. The right pane that opens has two download choices:

   o Download a CSV file with headers.

   o Download a CSV file with headers and sample data.

3. Download one of the CSV files, open it and enter your user information. (Remove the sample data if you use that file.)

4. Click on 'Browse' to upload the CSV file to Office 365.

5. Verify the file.

Add multiple users

● List of users

Upload a CSV file with user info

○ Licenses

Download and save one of the files below. Open the file in Excel or a similar app and add your user info. Save the file as .CSV using commas as delimiters between the 16 columns.
Learn more about importing multiple users

○ Finish

Download a blank CSV file with the required headers

Download a CSV file that includes example user info

Avoid common errors

• You can upload up to 249 users per CSV file.

• Each user must have a unique email address.

• Email addresses may only use letters, numbers, and the following special characters: !#$%&'*+-/=?^_]~.

• Email addresses can't begin or end with a period (.).

• The part of the email address before the @ symbol can have 64 characters or less.

• Save as a CSV (comma delimited) file with 16 columns.

Upload CSV file with your user information

Browse

Next   Cancel

6. Click on Next.

7. Set log-in status and assign product licenses. As this is a bulk creation, all users must be given the same status and licenses.

8. Click on Next to create the user accounts.

9. Now you can download a CSV file with all the usernames, names and temporary passwords. By default, e-mails with login details, in plain text, are sent out to the users.

10. Click on 'Send and close' to finish.

3.2.2.4   Add Users with a PowerShell Script

It is possible to add users to Microsoft 365 with a PowerShell script. Scripts are re-usable and give consistency, but to fully describe the user import PowerShell script is out of scope for this book. Therefore, I will just give a few hints to readers who already know PowerShell and want to try this method.

(If you are new to PowerShell but interested in learning how you can use it with SharePoint, I recommend my book *PowerShell with SharePoint from Scratch*.)

1. Download and install the Azure AD Module, if you don't already have it on your computer.
2. Run PowerShell ISE as an administrator.
3. Run the cmdlet Connect-MsolService to connect to the Azure AD which has the Office 365 user accounts.
4. Create a new user, assign license and add location and user properties.

    Start with the cmdlet New-MsolUser and select the parameter LicenseAssignment and its value. Then select the rest of the required parameters and give their values.
5. Run the script to add the user. The temporary password will be shown in the object.

Demo:

https://www.kalmstrom.com/Tips/PowerShell/Add-Users-PowerShell-Azure-Ad.htm

3.2.2.5   User Actions

When a user has received the account information, he/she can login (and change the password if that is required), install the Office desktop apps and start using the sites, apps and pages that the user has access to.

3.3   SETUP

The Setup tab in the left menu of the Microsoft 365 Admin center is important for organizations that are new to 365, as it gives help with setting everything up.

3.4   ADMIN CENTERS

Under 'Show' more' in the Microsoft 365 Admin center left menu, you can find specific Admin centers for apps and features. Here I will just mention a few of them that are especially interesting for SharePoint usage.

Only Global admins and Global readers can see all Admin center entries. If you, for example, is a SharePoint admin, you will only see the SharePoint and OneDrive Admin centers in the left menu. I will introduce OneDrive in chapter 12, Personal Content.

3.4.1 *Security and Compliance*

The Security and Compliance tabs open centers with a lot of different settings to keep the organization secure. Here I will just mention two of the pages.

3.4.1.1 Policies

Under the Policies tab in the Security center, you can find wizards for several policies that protect your organization and its content.

Select one of the policy wizards and then click on 'Create policy' to create a new policy.

Data loss prevention   ⊣⊐

Policies   Alerts (preview)   Endpoint DLP settings

Use data loss prevention (DLP) policies to help identify and protect your organization's sensitive info. For
exa '   set up policies to help make sure information in email and docs isn't shared with the
wrc Create policy arn more about DLP

+ Create policy   ↓ Export   ○ Refresh   2 items   ⌕ Search

Name		Order	Last modified
U.S. Financial Data	⋮	0	Jul 31, 2020 1:26 PM
General Data Protection Regulation (GDPR)	⋮	1	Jul 31, 2020 1:26 PM

Give the policy a name and set the policy by selecting the preferred options. The image below comes from the ATP safe attachments feature, which automatically scans uploaded files and quarantine files that are found to be unsafe.

3.4.1.2 Audit

Under the Audit tab in the Compliance center, you can search and view user and administrator activity in the whole organization. The only users you cannot monitor here are unauthenticated external users, *refer to* 14.11.1, Authenticated and Anonymous Users.

Audit

Need to find out if a user deleted a document or if an admin reset someone's password? Search the Office 365 audit log to find out what the users and admins in your organization have been doing. You'll be able to find activity related to email, groups, documents, permissions, directory services, and much more. Learn more about searching the audit log

Create audit retention policy

Search

Activities	Users	File, folder, or site ⓘ
Show results for ... ⌄	Search	Add all or part of a ...

View all activities

Start date	Start time
Thu No ...📅	00:00 ⌄

End date	End time
Fri Nov ...📅	00:00 ⌄

Search   Clear all

Sidebar:
- ⌂ Home
- 🏆 Compliance Manager
- ⊘ Data classification
- Data connectors
- ⚠ Alerts
- ⊠ Reports
- ⚌ Policies
- 🔍 Permissions

Solutions
- ⊞ Catalog
- 📖 Audit

3.4.2   Azure AD

Microsoft 365 uses the cloud-based user authentication service Azure Active Directory, or Azure AD, to hold its account information.

Azure AD does not have its own tile in the App Launcher, but Azure AD is one of the specific Admin centers that you can reach from the Microsoft 365 Admin center.

The 365 user accounts are stored in the Azure AD, but normally administrators create and manage users in the Microsoft 365 Admin center, as described above. However, users can be managed in Azure Active Directory too, and Azure AD also gives other possibilities that are out of scope for this book.

In this section, we will just have a look at the LinkedIn Connection, that can be disabled from Azure AD. We will also come back to Azure AD in section 14.10.2, External Guest Access to Group Team Site and 20.2.1, Enable Basic IRM for the Tenant.

3.4.2.1   LinkedIn Connection

By default, users can share SharePoint content with their first level LinkedIn contacts. This setting can be disabled in the Azure AD User settings, or only specific groups can be given this sharing possibility.

Users - User settings
Kalmstrom Enterprises AB - Azure Active Directory

» 🖫 Save   ✕ Discard

🏛 All users

🏛 Deleted users

🔑 Password reset

⚙ User settings

Activity

🔁 Sign-ins

📄 Audit logs

Troubleshooting + Support

✕ Troubleshoot

🖳 New support request

Enterprise applications

Manage how end users launch and view their applications

App registrations

Users can register applications ❶
(**Yes**   No)

Administration portal

Restrict access to Azure AD administration portal ❶
(Yes   **No**)

LinkedIn account connections

Allow users to connect their work or school account with LinkedIn.
Data sharing between Microsoft and LinkedIn is not enabled until users consent to
connect their Microsoft work or school account with their LinkedIn account.
Learn more about LinkedIn account connections ❶
(**Yes**   Selected group   No)

When LinkedIn connection is allowed, users will be prompted to connect their accounts the first time they click to see someone's LinkedIn information on a profile card in Outlook, OneDrive or SharePoint Online. The LinkedIn connection is not fully enabled for each user until the user has agreed to the connection.

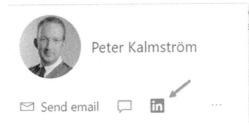

Peter Kalmström

✉ Send email   💬   in   · · ·

3.5   SUMMARY

In this chapter, we have looked at some important parts of the Microsoft 365 Admin center. You now understand how to add user accounts and assign user roles for the tenant, and you know where to find the SharePoint Admin center and many other Admin centers.

It is time to start using SharePoint!

4   GET STARTED WITH SHAREPOINT ONLINE

In this chapter, we will look at how SharePoint is built and describe the two SharePoint Online experiences: modern and classic. I will also give an overview over the search features and give a few tips about content and naming.

4.1   ARCHITECTURE

SharePoint is built as a hierarchy, where the highest level consists of sites. The lowest level contains column values in list and library items.

Each site can have all the lower levels, and things like permissions, navigation and themes can be inherited from higher to lower levels.

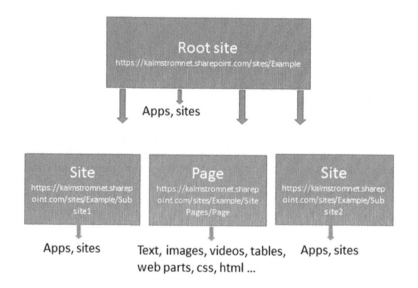

4.1.1   Sites Introduction

The SharePoint sites are the core of the SharePoint tenant. All content is added, and all work is done, within the context of a site. A site can contain apps, pages and subsites. A site and its subsites form a site collection. Often the word "site" refers to a whole site collection.

Each site has a huge number of settings that control how the site works and looks. These settings can be reached from the 365 Settings icon. Sometimes, you must first select 'Site information' and then 'Site settings'.

Settings

SharePoint

Add a page

Add an app

Site contents

Site information

Site permissions

Site usage

Change the look

Site designs

All the contents of a site can be seen and reached in the Site contents. There is a 'Site contents' link under the 365 Settings icon, *see* the image above.

When you need to create a new site, you can create a subsite to an existing site, but Microsoft recommends that you instead create a new site and connect it to a hub. I will describe how to do all that later in this book.

4.1.2   *Apps Introduction*

SharePoint apps can do various things, but here we will focus on lists and libraries. These apps are intended for content sharing and storage.

Apps can be of three different types:

- Lists. A list is very much like a database or Excel table. It contains items such as appointments in a calendar list, contacts in a contact list or tasks in a tasks list.

  You can also create your own custom lists, for example a Cost Center list. Each list has many settings, among others which columns, views and permissions should be used in that list. *Refer to* chapter 8, List Apps.

- Libraries. A library can do almost everything that a list can do, and it has most of the same settings and features. The main difference between a list and a library is what they contain.

  You use list apps to store and share data, while libraries are used to store and share files. Each item in a library contains a file. List items can have attached files, but when the file is the most important content, you should use a library.

  There are several types of SharePoint libraries, but when nothing else is said, I am referring to document libraries when I mention libraries. *Refer to* chapter 9, Library Apps.

- Other apps. These can look and behave in many ways. Your organization can purchase or build them, and they are out of scope for this book. When I talk about apps here, I refer to lists or libraries and not to other apps.

Apps always exist within a site. Each app has its own URL, typically

https://TENANT.sharepoint.com/sites/SITE/Lists/LIST/

or

https://TENANT.sharepoint.com/sites/ SITE/LIBRARY/

Lists and libraries use columns to characterize the content with metadata and keywords. The columns can be filtered, and the apps themselves can have views that display the content in various ways. You will find much more information about this in chapter 7, SharePoint Apps.

4.1.3   *Pages Introduction*

A SharePoint page has a big area in the middle of the SharePoint interface, often delimited by a navigation bar. Each page has its own URL, such as https://TENANT.sharepoint.com/sites/SITE/SitePages/PAGE.aspx

A page can be automatically created and contain settings or an app, but SharePoint also gives a possibility to create custom pages. Such pages can contain text, images, videos, content from apps and much more.

In chapter 13, SharePoint Site Pages, I will describe how pages can be customized.

4.2   MODERN AND CLASSIC EXPERIENCES

In 2016, Microsoft started to roll out a new experience for SharePoint Online. It is called the modern, or new, experience, and it changes the look and features for sites, apps, pages and lately also for admin centers.

There are important differences between the experiences, and one such difference lies in the interface. The modern interface is better adapted to smart devices and more touch friendly than the classic one. It is also more intuitive to use, so it is easier to manage for the average user.

Microsoft is not deprecating the classic experience. Instead, the classic and modern experiences will coexist. The two experiences complement each other. Some things can only be done with the classic experience, as you will notice later in this book.

There are also several features that only exist in the modern experience. Therefore, SharePoint admins and power users should learn to manage both experiences, to be able to judge which experience is best for each purpose. I will describe both in this book.

In almost all SharePoint Online apps, you can switch between the experiences as you prefer. The interface is different, but the app content is the same. Modern SharePoint pages, on the other hand, are different from classic pages, and you cannot switch interface. Modern sites are also different from classic sites.

The two experiences complement each other, but they can also be confusing – and they do complicate things for authors of SharePoint books! I still hope that I have managed to clarify the differences in this book and that you will always understand which experience I am referring to in various parts of the book.

I have sometimes used a smaller font for the classic experience – not because the classic experience is less important to power users, but because you often want to start with the modern experience when you are new to SharePoint Online. Using a smaller font for the classic experience makes it easier for readers to separate the experiences. I have also used bold text in "modern" and "classic" for the same reason.

4.2.1   *Experience = Type*

The modern and classic SharePoint sites and pages are different types of sites and pages.

- Modern pages. New pages are by default modern, while settings pages have the classic experience.

  Modern and classic pages are different kinds of pages with different features, and they are built and managed in different ways. You cannot make a classic page modern – or vice versa.

- Modern sites. Classic and modern sites give different options, and you cannot make a classic site modern – or vice versa.

4.2.2   *Experience = Interface*

Most apps can be viewed in either the modern or the classic experience. It is the same app, just with two different interfaces.

If you make a change in the app contents or settings and then switch experience, you will see the change in the other interface too.

4.3   SEARCH

SharePoint Online has two search experiences, Microsoft Search and SharePoint Search. Both are active, and administrators cannot enable or disable one of them. The experience used depends on where you search from.

- Microsoft Search is used in the modern experience.

- SharePoint Search is used in the classic experience.

The search results are always trimmed by permissions. Therefore, each user will only see results that he or she has permission to open.

4.3.1   The Search Crawler

SharePoint content is automatically crawled based on a schedule. The crawler picks up content that has changed since the last crawl and updates an index. A search schema helps the crawler decide what content and metadata to pick up. In Microsoft/Office 365, we have limited control over that process.

Content cannot be included in search results until it has been crawled and added to the index. Therefore, it may take a few minutes before new additions to SharePoint show up in searches.

Both search experiences use the same search index to find the results, but the with Microsoft Search the results are personalized and based on the user's earlier activity in Microsoft/Office 365. This means, for example, that users will see recent search queries from SharePoint Online and Outlook on the web, when they begin typing in the search box.

An important advantage of search in SharePoint is that the file content is also indexed, not only the file name. This means that you can search for files that have certain words within the text of a document just as quickly and easily as you search based on file names.

4.3.2   Modern Search

The Microsoft Search box in the middle of the 365 navigation bar is present in all 365 apps, not only in SharePoint. It is however not present in the classic SharePoint interface.

The modern search box suggests results even before you start typing, based on your recent activity, and it updates the suggestions as you type. If you don't select one of the suggestions, the process continues in several steps:

1. There is a suggestion to show more results.

Show more results

2. The expanded search takes you to a Search center. It has the verticals All, Files, Sites and News.

Organization > The kalmstrom.com Team Site

All   Files   Sites   News   ▽ Filters

3. You get a chance to search the whole tenant.

We couldn't find any results for zuccini

Search the whole organization for zuccini

4. Now the Search center also gets verticals for People and Power BI.

The Search center 'All' and 'Files' verticals give the possibility to filter by latest modified time: Any time, Past month, Past 3 months and Past year.

When you start the search from an app, and there are hits in that app, the app content is filtered to show only items that matches the search.

4.3.3   *Classic Search*

The SharePoint **classic** interface has a global search in the top right corner. When you use the global search with the default option, This Site, the search results will be shown on a search results page for the current site.

When you use the global search with the options Everything, People and Conversations, the search engine goes through the whole SharePoint tenant, and the results are shown in a Search Center page for the tenant.

Most apps with the classic interface also have a local search field to the right of the view selector. When you enter something in the local search box and press Enter, SharePoint searches only the current app, and the app content is filtered to show only items that matches the search.

4.4   ADD CONTENT

One of the most important reasons for using SharePoint is that you want to share information and documents within a company or organization. You can control the sharing by setting Permissions, *refer to* chapter 14, Permissions and Sharing. Generally, you share the content with either a group of people within the tenant or with everyone in the tenant.

These are the most common methods to add content and share it among colleagues within the same tenant:

- Create a new document directly in SharePoint or upload an existing document to a SharePoint library.
- Add info to a SharePoint list, for example a team tasks list or a team calendar.
- Use the Newsfeed on the homepage of a SharePoint site. Create a new entry or reply to an existing entry or upload an image or even tag someone.
- Add a comments to list items, files or to a modern page.
- Add or edit SharePoint pages. You can fill your pages with text, images, links or videos and insert tables, app parts and web parts.

There will be a lot more information and examples of these ways to share information throughout the book.

Demo:

https://kalmstrom.com/Tips/SharePoint-Online-Course/Share-Info-In-SharePoint.htm

4.4.1   *Naming New Content*

When you create a new site, app, column or page, you need to give it a name. This name can be changed later, but the first name will always be kept in what is called the internal name.

Internal SharePoint names should not have spaces. That is why you sometimes see irritating extra characters in URLs when the name has a space. These characters are added automatically by SharePoint to avoid a space.

kalmstromnet.sharepoi ʌsite/Kick%20Off%20Menus/I

Ideally, internal names should consist of one word or be written in CamelCase style. CamelCase naming is when you write two separate words together without a space and use capital first letters in both words. *SharePoint* is a good example.

Using CamelCase naming give better URLs when a name consists of multiple words:

kalmstromnet.sharepoir site/KickOffMenus/I

When you use the modern experience, SharePoint removes spaces in the internal names for apps and columns and thus in automatically created URLs. In other URLs the spaces can be visible, but spaces might still create problems, for example when you use SharePoint names in programming. We will see an example on that in the last chapter of this book, when we need to use a column name in a flow query.

When you create content from the classic interface, for example from the List settings, you should therefore first name the content you create with a good internal name – one word or CamelCase writing.

Then you can rename the content to a more user friendly name, because even if CamelCase naming has advantages and sometimes is necessary, it can make names more difficult to read for users. The internal name will be kept as it was from the beginning when you rename your content.

Demo:

https://www.kalmstrom.com/Tips/SharePoint-Online-Course/CamelCase-Naming.htm

4.5   SUMMARY

In this chapter, I have given an overview of the SharePoint building blocks that we will look at in more detail later in the book: sites, apps and pages. I have also introduced the two experiences for these building blocks.

I hope you now have an idea on how the search features in SharePoint work and how you can create new content in SharePoint. We will however come back to all this later.

In the next chapter, you will learn how SharePoint, and also some parts of your 365 tenant, can be controlled from the SharePoint Admin center.

5   THE SHAREPOINT ADMIN CENTER

Most administrator settings for SharePoint are handled through the SharePoint Admin center, which you can reach from the Microsoft 365 Admin center.

At the bottom of the left navigation menu in the Microsoft 365 Admin center, you can find the link to the SharePoint Admin center. (You might need to click on 'Show more' to see the Admin centers.)

Note that the settings in the SharePoint Admin center are for the tenant, not for a site. An exception is when one site is selected under Sites >Active sites, as when changing sharing options or permissions for that specific site.

Once you have found your way to the SharePoint Admin center, it is a good idea to bookmark it in your web browser. If you have permission to use the SharePoint Admin center, you will probably want to come back here often.

5.1   EXPERIENCES

The SharePoint Admin center has two experiences, just like apps, and you can control which interface should be displayed by default for all admins that have access to the SharePoint Admin center.

Select 'Settings' in the left menu of the SharePoint Admin center, and then 'Default admin experience'.

≡

⌂ Home

▢ Sites ⌄

⇄ Policies ⌄

⚙ Settings ——————→

🖥 Content services ⌄

⌁ Migration

°₀ Advanced ⌄

⋮ More features

Settings

🔍 Search

Name ↑	Description
Default admin center	Open the new or classic admin center by default
Pages	Allow users to create and comment on modern pages
SharePoint notifications	Allow device notifications about file activity and news
Site creation	Set default settings for new sites
Site storage limits	Use automatic or manual site storage limits

Can't find the setting you're looking for? Go to the classic settings page.

A right pane will open, where you can select if the new (= modern) or classic experience should open by default.

Everything can be managed from the new SharePoint Admin center, both classic and modern sites and features. The new experience is also what Microsoft recommends, so in this chapter I will focus on the new SharePoint Admin center.

As shown in the image above, you can always reach the classic settings page from the new Admin center, and from there the rest of the classic Admin center.

The classic Admin center has no setting for experience selection. Instead, there is a banner on top of each page, where users are urged to open the new Admin center.

Get to everything in the new SharePoint admin center
All the classic features, all the new features, all your sites
[Open it now]

5.2   LEFT NAVIGATION MENU

Below, I will shortly go through the tabs in the left navigation menu of the new SharePoint Admin center in the order they are displayed by default. I will go deeper into several of the settings in the SharePoint Admin center later in the book, in contexts where the different tabs belong.

Via the tab at the bottom, 'Customize navigation', you can hide items you don't use. Other admins will not see your changes, and you can always find the hidden items by selecting 'Show all' in the menu.

When you have learned to find your way around the SharePoint Admin center, you can click on the menu icon in the top left corner of the left menu to collapse the navigation and only see the icons, not the text. That way, you will get more space in the main area to the right.

5.2.1 Homepage

The homepage of the new SharePoint Admin center has statistics on file activity and site usage. To see more, click on 'Details' in the top right corner above each tile.

The homepage also shows messages from Microsoft and service health.

5.2.2 Sites

Under the Sites tab, you can see and edit all active sites, delete and restore sites and create new sites. This subject is expanded in 6.6, Sites in the SharePoint Admin Center.

5.2.3 Policies

Under the Policies tab, you can make some setting that increases the security for the organization's data.

5.2.3.1 Sharing

The organization's policies for external and internal sharing are set in the SharePoint Admin center under Policies >Sharing. These settings apply to the whole tenant.

In most sites, SharePoint gives users a possibility to share items via Share buttons, and sharing with these buttons breaks the default, inherited permissions. This may lead to a situation where you have a lot of broken permissions and no real control over how SharePoint content is distributed. Administrators should be aware of this problem.

Under the Policies tab, you can restrict the sharing options in various ways, both for SharePoint and for each user's OneDrive for Business site. If you want to allow unauthenticated sharing of files and folders, choose the default 'Anyone'. (Sites can never be shared with unauthenticated people.)

If you want to ensure that all people outside your organization have to authenticate, choose 'New and existing guests'.

You can limit external sharing even more, and on this page, you can also change the default permission for shared contents and links and make other settings that might be necessary for your organization's security.

Sharing

Use these settings to control sharing at the organization level in SharePoint and OneDrive. Learn more

External sharing

Content can be shared with:

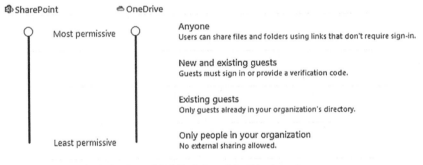

SharePoint   OneDrive

Most permissive

Anyone
Users can share files and folders using links that don't require sign-in.

New and existing guests
Guests must sign in or provide a verification code.

Existing guests
Only guests already in your organization's directory.

Only people in your organization
No external sharing allowed.

Least permissive

You can further restrict sharing for each individual site and OneDrive. Learn how

More external sharing settings ∨

File and folder links

I recommend that you consider carefully which sharing permissions would work best for your organization. The sharing permissions of a single site can never go beyond the maximum allowed level for the tenant. Therefore, in the SharePoint Admin center, you must choose the most permissive setting that is needed by any site in the tenant.

The sharing setting can always be restricted at a lower level:

- Administrators can set the external sharing policy for a single site under the Active sites tab in the SharePoint Admin center, *refer to* 6.6.2.1, Edit an Active Site.

- Site owners can limit the sharing from the site's permission settings, *refer to* 14.4, Share a Site.

This is useful when the organization has confidential information that should never be shared externally but external sharing still needs to be allowed for the tenant. In those cases, the sensitive information can be stored in one or more sites that have external sharing turned off.

As mentioned above, you can never make it the other way around – allow external sharing in some sites when it is disabled for the tenant. Sharing settings for individual sites can never be more allowing than the policy set for the tenant in the SharePoint Admin center. They can only be more restrictive.

5.2.3.2   Access Control

The Access control tab under 'Polices' lets admins restrict how users can access SharePoint content. You can for example only allow access from certain IP addresses or sign out users automatically from inactive browser sessions.

5.2.4   *Settings*

As we have already seen, it is under the Settings tab that you can decide which experience the Admin center should be used with by default. The new experience is default.

Here, you can also disable some default permissions. You can, for example remove the permission for users to create sites and modern pages and to turn on notifications about SharePoint content in mobile apps.

5.2.5   *Content Services*

Under the Content services tab in the SharePoint admin center, you can find the Term store and the Content type gallery. These are meant for more advanced use of SharePoint Online, and we will come back to both later in this book.

5.2.6   *Migration and Advanced*

The Migration tab is useful when you need to migrate content from another cloud platform or from SharePoint on-premises to SharePoint Online.

The 'Advanced' tab is for management of Azure AD-secured API access.

5.2.7   *More Features*

Under the More features tab, you can find settings from the classic experience. Some of these features are interesting even if you use the modern experience.

5.2.7.1   Apps – App Catalog

The SharePoint App Store is a Microsoft operated service that contains apps you can use with SharePoint. Some of the apps are from Microsoft, but many come from third-party publishers like our own kalmstrom.com Business Solutions.

Under 'Apps' in the SharePoint Admin center >More features, you can configure the SharePoint App Store and manage the app licenses in various ways.

Here is also where you create an App Catalog site for the tenant. When you add and update custom or third-party apps to the App Catalog, users can easily install them in sites and embed them in pages.

Apps, or APP files, are also called add-ins. The modern, client-side web parts, which are SPPKG files, can also be added to the App Catalog.

1. Under Apps, click on 'App Catalog'.

2. Keep the default option, 'Create a new app catalog site' and click OK.

3. Fill out the details.

4. Click on the address book icon at 'Administrator' and search for an administrator name. Select the correct name and click OK.

Apps

Create App Catalog Site Collection

Title	Contoso App Catalog
Web Site Address	https://m365x446726.sharepoint.com
	/sites/ AppCatalog
Language Selection	Select a language: English
Time Zone	(UTC-08:00) Pacific Time (US and Canada)
Administrator	MOD Administrator;
Storage Quota	10 GB
Server Resource Quota	300 resources of 13200 resources available

OK   Cancel

Now you can find the App Catalog under 'Active sites' in the SharePoint Admin center.

The App Catalog is a special kind of site, but it reminds of the classic Team site that I will describe later in this book.

Click on 'Apps for SharePoint' to get to a library where you can upload APP or SPPKG files that you want to have available in the tenant. You can also drag files from your computer to the Apps for SharePoint library.

Be careful when you upload files to the App Catalog. Only add files from trusted sites and suppliers.

Uploaded APP and SPPKG files will be displayed under 'From Your Organization' when users 'Add an app'. Such files may also show up among the available web parts in modern pages.

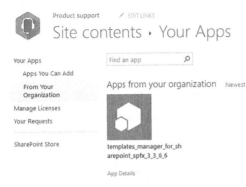

Demo:

https://kalmstrom.com/Tips/SharePoint-Online-Course/App-Catalog.htm

5.2.7.2   Search

As we saw in section 4.3, Search, SharePoint has two search experiences that work on different content. Under More features >Search, in the SharePoint Admin center, you can find many settings for the classic search. (The modern search is managed in the Microsoft 365 Admin center, *refer to* 3.1.1, Search and Intelligence.)

As both search experiences use the same index, most customizations in the classic experience affect the modern search, but there is an important exception:

Some Microsoft Search features might not work if the classic global Search Center URL is set to something else than "yourcompanyname.sharepoint.com/search/pages". Therefore, I recommend that you don't make any changes to the Search Center URL here.

5.2.8   *OneDrive Admin Center*

OneDrive for Business is each users personal SharePoint site. We will have a closer look at OneDrive for Business in chapter 12, Personal Content, and in that chapter, I have also included a section about the OneDrive Admin center.

5.3   SUMMARY

We have now had a first look at the SharePoint Admin center, but we will have reason to come back here later in this book. This chapter has just given an overview of the SharePoint Admin center.

In the next chapter, I will describe the most important SharePoint building block: the site. I will explain what is common for all sites and what is the difference between the most used SharePoint sites.

6 SHAREPOINT SITES

The sites are the core of SharePoint. All content is added, and all work is done, within the context of a site. A site nearly always contains apps and pages that users have created, and the site might also have subsites with its own apps and pages.

One tenant can have from a few up to two million sites. I would recommend that you have many, instead of gathering too much data in the same site.

SharePoint Online has several different kinds of sites, and in this chapter, will describe the commonly used site types. These are the sites that you most likely want to create when you are new to SharePoint, and for most businesses and organizations they are sufficient as they can be highly customized for different needs.

In addition to the classic Team site, which I will describe below, there are, some other classic site types. Should your organization need to use one of these sites, I am sure that you can explore them on your own when you have been used to working with the common site types. The differences are not that extensive.

SharePoint sites can be customized in many ways. You can modify the site's homepage and add different kinds of apps, pages and subsites to it. And all these additions can in turn be customized, so how a SharePoint site looks and how it is used is very flexible.

Three of the site types I will describe here are called modern sites, and one is a classic site. The site types are:

- The modern Communication site

- The modern Group Team site

- The modern Team site without a group

- The classic Team site

Even if three of the site types are modern and one is classic, the three Team site types have common features that are not present in the Communication site. On the other hand, the Communication site has some features that are not present in any of the other site types.

Team sites and Communication sites also look different. All SharePoint Team sites by default have a navigation panel to the left on the page. It is called Site navigation, as it usually shows links to content within the current site. Communication sites instead have the Site navigation on top of the page. You will learn more about the navigation in chapter 11.

I will start with clarifying a few terms and introducing some features that are common for all kinds of sites, before I describe the site types and explain how they are created and how they can be managed.

At the end of the chapter, I will go through two ways of connecting sites, and I will also explain how to delete and restore sites.

6.1   SITE TERMS

Before we go into the different site types, there are some terms that you need to understand.

6.1.1   *Root Site and Homepage*

Each site has its own URL, and by default sites that users can create have the URL https://[tenant name].sharepoint.com/sites/[site name].

---

https://m365x446726.sharepoint.com/sites/ContosoNews

(The 'sites' part can be changed, *refer to* 6.6.1, Settings, but if you are new to SharePoint, I recommend that you keep the default.)

The site is called "root site", as opposed to any potential subsites, and the landing page of the root site is called the site's "homepage".

When you add content to the site, the name and storage place of that content will be added to the root site URL.

Modern sites get a modern homepage that is customized with dedicated web parts, which you can add, remove or reorder as needed. Classic sites get another kind of homepage, which also can be highly customized. I describe all page customization in chapter 13, SharePoint Site Pages.

6.1.2   *Site and Site Collection*

A root site and its subsites, and all their content, can be called a "site collection", but often the word "site" is also used to indicate a root site *and* any subsites and all content.

Microsoft has recently announced that the usage of the label "site collection" will go away. Instead, the word site will always be used for a root site and all its content. I will use the "site" in that meaning here, but you will meet the word "site collection" in many of the SharePoint settings and in documentation online.

In retrospect, it would perhaps have been better to never have introduced the concept of subsites, but that design choice was made by Microsoft more than 20 years ago. Subsite creation is still supported, and I will explain how to create subsites below – but I will also explain how to create the recommended hub families!

6.2   SITE CONTENTS

To see all the contents of a site, click on the 'Site contents' link in the Site navigation, or open the 365 Settings icon and select 'Site contents'.

A page with links to all content in the site will open. In all Team sites, this page can be viewed in both the modern and the classic experience (in contrast to other SharePoint pages). There is a switch link under the Site navigation to the left.

Modern interface link:

Return to classic SharePoint

Classic interface link:

Exit classic experience

The Communication site can only show the modern interface in the Site contents.

Both interfaces have links to the site's statistics, workflows, settings and recycle bin above the actual contents of the site.

📈 Site usage   ⟳ Site workflows   ⚙ Site settings   🗑 Recycle bin (7)

6.2.1   *The Modern Site Contents*

The modern Site contents interface looks like the document library interface, but it has two tabs: one for subsites and one for other content.

To the right of each app name in the Site contents, an ellipsis becomes visible when you hover the mouse over the item.

Click on the ellipsis to reach more information about the app.

Under the Contents tab, the app ellipses let you delete the app, reach the app settings and see details.

When you select the 'Details' option under the ellipsis, you will have a description of the app. You can also create another app of the same type by clicking on the ADD IT button.

DESCRIPTION
Use a document library to store, organize, sync, and share documents with people. You can use co-authoring, versioning, and check out to work on documents together. With your documents in one place, everybody can get the latest versions whenever they need them. You can also sync your documents to your local computer for offline access.

ADD IT

Under the Subsites tab, the ellipsis gives a link to the Site contents of the subsite. The subsite Site contents is built in the same way as the Site contents of the root site.

Contents   **Subsites**

      Name   Description

      Sales
                        Site contents

In the Site contents command bar, there is a 'New' button to create new apps, pages and subsites. We will come back to apps and pages in later chapters.

+ New ∨

List

Page

Document library

App

Subsite

6.2.2   *The Classic Site Contents*

The **classic** Site contents interface shows the items as tiles and gives a possibility to add an app.

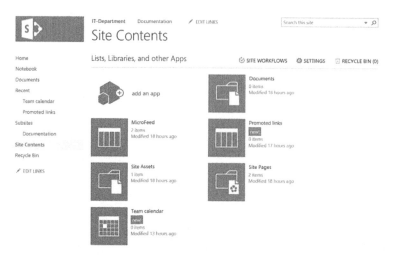

Click on the ellipsis in the top right corner of a tile to reach the same three options as under the ellipsis in the modern experience, here called Settings, About and Remove.

6.3 SITE SETTINGS

The administration of a site is most often done in the Site settings. You can reach the settings for the current site via the settings button in the Site contents, *see* above, and from the 365 Settings icon.

The image to the right comes from a page with the classic interface. In the modern experience, the 365 Settings icon has a 'Site information' link instead of 'Site settings'. Click on that link and then on 'View all site settings' to reach the full site settings page.

Settings   ×

SharePoint

Shared with...

Edit page

Add a page

Add an app

Site contents

Change the look

Site settings

The Site settings has links to site control pages, grouped under headings to be easier to find. Which controls you can find depend on the site type.

Root sites have more controls than subsites, and settings that are only available in the root site apply to the subsites too. The image below comes from a root site built on the classic team site, which is the one that gives most options.

Home   Sales   Development   ✏ EDIT LINKS

Site Settings

Users and Permissions
People and groups
Site permissions
Access requests and invitations
Site collection administrators
Site app permissions

Web Designer Galleries
Site columns
Site content types
Web parts
List templates
Master pages
Themes
Solutions
Composed looks

Site Administration
Regional settings
Language settings
Site libraries and lists
User alerts
RSS
Sites and workspaces
Workflow settings
Site Closure and Deletion
Term store management
Popularity Trends
Translation Status

Search
Result Sources
Result Types
Query Rules
Schema
Search Settings
Search and offline availability
Configuration Import
Configuration Export

Look and Feel
Title, description, and logo
Quick launch
Top link bar
Navigation Elements
Change the look

Site Actions
Manage site features
Enable search configuration export
Reset to site definition
Delete this site

Site Collection Administration
Recycle bin
Search Result Sources
Search Result Types
Search Query Rules
Search Schema
Search Settings
Search Configuration Import
Search Configuration Export
Site collection features
Site hierarchy
Site collection audit settings
Audit log reports
Portal site connection
Content Type Policy Templates
Storage Metrics
Site collection app permissions
Record declaration settings
Site Policies
Content type publishing
Popularity and Search Reports
Translatable columns
HTML Field Security
SharePoint Designer Settings
Site collection health checks
Site collection upgrade

We will come back to the Site settings many times in this book. Here I will just mention a few of the controls, while others will be introduced later.

6.3.1   Change the Look

Under the Site settings 'Look and Feel' heading, see the image above, you can change the name and description of the site and replace the default SharePoint logo with a custom image.

You can also change the site's colors and fonts under 'Change the look'. The default theme is called Office, but there are various other themes to choose from.

The default Team site layout, 'Seattle', has the Site navigation panel to the left. Communication sites use the 'Oslo' layout, which has the Site navigation on top of each page.

The modern experience has additional 'Change the look' settings, *see* below.

6.3.1.1   Modern 'Change the Look' Pane

In addition to the settings under 'Look and Feel', in the Site settings, the modern experience has a 'Change the look' setting under the 365 Settings icon, which gives more options than the Site settings entry with the same name.

When you click on the modern 'Change the look' a right pane will open where you can select a theme and customize the site's header with an image, background color and more.

Communication sites, *see* below, also have choices for the navigation and the footer.

(There is also a 'Site designs' setting where users can apply a design JSON script uploaded by an administrator.)

Settings   ✕

SharePoint

Add a page

Add an app

Site contents

Site information

Site permissions

Site usage

Change the look

Site designs

6.3.2   Site Collection Administration

The links under the Site Collection Administration heading can only be reached from the root site of the site collection, and the controls in this group apply to all sites in the collection, the root site as well as the subsites.

This group can only be seen and used by Site admins, but by default the person who creates a site becomes both Site owner and Site admin.

6.3.2.1   Site Collection Features

One of the links under Site Collection Administration is 'Site collection features', and here site admins can activate features that are not enabled by default.

One such feature is 'SharePoint Server Standard Site Collection features', that adds multiple web parts to classic pages. The Business Data, Filters, Outlook Web App and Search web part categories are added, and each category includes several web parts that can be added to a classic page.

Site Collection Administration

Recycle bin

Search Configuration Import
Search Configuration Export
Site collection features
Site hierarchy
Site collection audit settings

There is also a 'SharePoint Server Enterprise Site Collection features' for the Enterprise subscriptions, and it gives classic web parts for InfoPath Forms Services, Visio Services, Access Services, and Excel Services.

Another site collection feature is 'SharePoint Server Publishing Infrastructure', which we will come back to in chapter 27.

6.3.3   *Site Actions*

Under the Site Actions heading, Site owners can manage what features should be available on the site. It is also here site owners can delete the site, and in site types where it is possible, the site can be saved as a template.

6.3.3.1   Manage Site Features

The 'Manage site features' link under the Site Actions heading, takes you to a page where site owners can activate various extra SharePoint features for the current site.

Site owners can also deactivate features that are activated by default, such as users' possibility to create site pages or follow sites and documents.

6.4   SITE USAGE

The Site usage page shows various statistics on the site usage and sharing of site contents. Pages with the modern interface have a link to the Site usage page under the 365 Settings icon, and the modern Site contents experience has a 'Site usage' button in the command bar.

Pages with the classic interface do not have this link under the Settings icon, but if you open an app with the modern interface you will see site usage for classic sites too.

At the bottom of the Site usage page, site owners can generate a CSV file that shows how the site's content has been shared inside and (if external sharing is allowed) outside the organization.

The report is saved to a new or existing folder in the default document library, and an e-mail with a link is sent to the person who generated the file.

6.5   SITE PERMISSION LEVELS

By default, there are four permission levels on a site:

- Site admin. In bigger organizations, the Site admins are the link to the IT department. Site admins are the only people who can manage the search, the recycle bin, the web designer galleries and the site collection features.

- Site owner. The site owners have full control over all the site's content, but they cannot handle the more technical sides of the site management.

- Site members have edit permissions on the SharePoint site and can add, change and remove apps and items and create pages.

- Site visitors can only view content, not change or add anything on the site, but they can download files.

The person who creates a site automatically becomes Site admin as well as Site owner, but Global and SharePoint administrators can edit these permissions under 'Active Sites' in the SharePoint Admin center.

Refer to chapter 14, Permissions and Sharing, for more information about site permissions.

6.6   SITES IN THE SHAREPOINT ADMIN CENTER

There are settings for sites in two places in the SharePoint Admin center. Some general settings for all sites are found under 'Settings', but most of the site management is handled under 'Sites'.

6.6.1   *Settings*

Under the Settings tab in the SharePoint Admin center, you can disable the default permission for users to create sites. Furthermore, you can select where Microsoft 365 group-connected team sites should be stored.

If your organization just started to use SharePoint, you might want to disable the standard users' possibility to create sites until you all feel more comfortable with SharePoint.

Settings

Site creation

Name ↑

Default admin center
Pages
SharePoint notifications
Site creation
Site storage limits

Can't find the setting you're looking

Select settings for new sites. Learn more

☑ Let users create sites from the SharePoint start page and OneDrive

Create team sites under

https://m365x446726.sharepoint.com | /sites/ ⌄

Default time zone

(UTC-08:00) Pacific Time (US and Canada) ⌄

Default storage limit for new sites

25600   GB

Save   Cancel

Note that even if you uncheck the box for modern sites, all users by default are allowed to create Microsoft 365 groups. When such a group is created, a SharePoint Group Team site will be created automatically, even if site creation is disabled in the SharePoint Admin center. (Microsoft 365 groups are out of scope for this book, but they are described in my book *Office 365 from Scratch*.)

Under 'Settings', you can finally decide how the site storage limits should be handled. The default option is that this is set manually for each site, as done in the image above. There is also an automatic option where each site can use as much storage as it needs.

6.6.2   *Sites*

Under 'Sites' in the SharePoint Admin center, you can select to show either active or deleted sites. Under 'Deleted sites' you can see and restore deleted sites, *refer to* 6.16, Delete and Restore Sites.

Under 'Active sites', you can reach all active sites, create new sites, register hub sites and associate sites with a hub site. Note that only root sites are displayed under 'Active sites', not subsites.

Active sites

Use this page to manage all your sites. Learn more

2.48 GB used of 1.70 TB

+ Create   ↓ Export

↻   🔍 Search sites

≡ All sites • ∨

Site name ∨	URL ∨	Storage used (GB) ∨	Primary admin ∨	Hub ∨	Template ∨	Last activity (UT... ∨	Date created ↓ ∨	Created by ∨
Contoso App Catalog	.../sites/AppCatalog	0.01	MOD Administrator	-	App Catalog Site	-	11/11/20, 3:06 AM	MOD Administrator
Enterprise Search Center	.../sites/enterprisesearch	0.03	MOD Administrator	-	Enterprise Search Center	-	11/10/20, 4:12 AM	MOD Administrator
Custom Search Center	.../sites/customsearchcenter	0.03	MOD Administrator	-	Enterprise Search Center	-	10/30/20, 9:24 AM	MOD Administrator
Project Web App	.../sites/pwa	0.17	Company Administrator	-	Project Web App Site	10/28/20	10/27/20, 9:51 AM	Company Administrator

You can also select multiple sites and edit or delete them in bulk, and you can bulk edit the external sharing and hub site association settings.

The list of sites under 'Active sites' gives a lot of information in the many columns, but the presentation can be customized. The dropdown at each column has a 'Customize columns' command that opens a right pane, where you can uncheck columns to hide them from the view. The dropdowns also have sort or filter options.

There are multiple built-in views for Active sites, in addition to the default "All sites".

≡ All sites ∨

Built-in views

✓ All sites

Classic sites

Microsoft 365 Group sites

Sites without a group

Largest sites

Least active sites

Most popular shared sites

When no site is selected, the command bar above the list of sites only gives the options to create a new site, export the site information to a CSV file, search the sites and select another view.

Except for the Export feature, these controls in the command bar are present also when one or multiple sites have been selected.

When one site is selected under Active sites, the command bar gives multiple options for how to manage that site.

6.6.2.1   Edit an Active Site

Under 'Active sites', you can manage administrators for the site, set rules for sharing and storage and delete the site. When you click on a site name in the list, or of you select a site and click on the information icon to the right in the command bar, an Information pane for the site will open to the right.

Green restaurant

×

General   Activity   Permissions   Policies

Site name

Green restaurant

Edit

URL

.../sites/Greenrestaurant

Edit

Hub association

Restaurants

Edit

Storage limit

1.00 TB

Edit

Template

Team site

Microsoft 365 Group connected

Yes

Domain

kalmstromnet.sharepoint.com

Description

None

The first tab gives general information and a link to open the site. (You can also open the site directly by clicking on the URL in the list of sites.)

As you see in the image above, it is possible to edit the site name part of the URL for many sites. For example, if you have a site named https://contoso.sharepoint.com/sites/Develpment, you can rename the site to correct the incorrect spelling of "development".

A redirect will be generated automatically, to ensure that links do not break, but an URL change can still create problems so you should not change a site URL unless it is necessary.

Depending on the size of the site, it can take up to ten minutes to change the site address. During this time, the site will be read-only, so if you need to change a site URL you should do it when site usage is low.

Under the Activity tab, you can see statistics for the site.

General   **Activity**   Permissions   Policies

As of October 4, 2020 (UTC)

Last site activity	Files stored
October 4, 2020 (UTC)	45 files
Page views in the last 30 days	Page visits in the last 30 days
46 page views	14 page visits
Files viewed/edited in the last 30 days	Storage usage
11 files	1017.38 MB
	10% (1017.38 MB of 10.00 GB)

Under the Permissions tab, you can set the permissions for the site.

Under the 'Policies' tab, you can edit the site's settings for external sharing and sensitivity. It is here you restrict external sharing for the site when it is allowed in the tenant.

General   Activity   Permissions   **Policies**

External sharing

Files and folders on this site can be shared with anyone

Edit

Sensitivity

None

Edit

6.7   COMMUNICATION SITE

Just as the name suggests, a Communication site is used to communicate information, not for collaboration in the first place. Usually, a Communication site has only a few authors but a larger number of readers.

The Communication site has the Site navigation on top of the page, not to the left as other site types.

Below the Site navigation, the homepage of the Communication site has a command bar. Here, site members with edit permissions will see a "New" button that allows them to add content to the site. The command bar also has a button for Site details. It opens a right pane with a site description and version history information.

6.7.1   Templates

When you create a new Communication site, you can either give it a blank homepage and add the web parts you want to use to it or select one of the two available templates.

The templates come with a set of web parts that are especially suitable for information sharing, so that you only need to modify them to get a good-looking homepage. But you can also add, reorder and remove web parts as you like, just as you can change the layout of the page. I have described how to do that in chapter 13.

- Topic – this is the template that is used for the default Home site Communication site, *see* 6.11.1, The Home Site, below. Use the Topic template when you want to share information about events, news and similar content.

- Showcase – a template that makes it easy to show photos and images.

6.7.2   Classic Compatibility

Communication sites are meant to be modern. The only content with the classic iexperience in Communication sites are some apps that only have the classic interface and settings pages and other pages that are created automatically.

It is not possible to add a classic page to a Communication site, and apps only have the modern interface. There is no possibility to switch to the classic interface.

Compared to Team sites, only a few apps can be created in a Communication site. For example, the Tasks list template, a commonly used template that only has the classic interface, cannot be added to a Communication site by default.

There is a setting that gives more app options, among them the Tasks list, *refer to* 7.4.1.1, Apps in Communication Sites. You should however be aware that the Communication site is primarily intended for information, not for cooperation.

6.7.3 Navigation

Communication sites are often used as hub sites, *see* below, and the default Home site for the whole organization is also a Communication site. Therefore, they need to have more navigation options that other site types.

You can either use a mega menu, which allows you to create three levels of hierarchy, or select the traditional cascading menu where links come in a row. The mega menu is default.

In the mega menu in the image below, 'Events' and 'Join the conversation' are labels under 'Happenings', and the third level has links to the different happenings.

Happenings ⌄	
Events	**Join the conversation**
Town Halls	Global Marketing Yammer
Events Calendar	Product Yammer
Ignite	Leadership Yammer
FlySafe	@constosoinc

The mega menu is edited just like other navigation, as described in chapter 11, SharePoint Navigation.

6.7.4 Footer

By default, the Communication site has a footer that can be customized with links, text and a logo. You can also disable the footer.

The footer is edited in the 'Change the look', right pane, which you can reach from the 365 Settings icon, *see* above.

Note that the footer is only shown in the homepage and modern pages. It is not displayed if you switch to an app.

If you want to use the footer and enhance it further, click on 'Edit' in the bottom right corner of the footer and add links or text in the left menu that opens.

Text will automatically be placed to the left and links to the right in the footer.

6.7.5   *Page Translations*

Organizations with staff in different countries will benefit from having their intranet sites available in multiple languages. The Site settings for Communication sites take this into regard under 'Language settings' in the Site Administration group.

Site languages

The default language for this site is English. You can choose options for using multiple languages on this site.

Enable pages and news to be translated into multiple languages

🔘 On

Add or remove site languages

Language	Translators ⓘ	
English	Not applicable for site default language	
Swedish	🔵 kate@kalmstrom.com ✕ Select or type a translator	Remove language
Spanish	👤 MOD Administrator ✕ Select or type a translator	Remove language

Select or type a language ⌄

Here, site owners can enable translation of pages and news and assign translators for each language. The translators will be notified by e-mail when a page has been created or updated in the default language, so that they can translate the content.

When the translation has been enabled, there will be two new links under Site Administration, to export and import translation files. These files are in the .resx format, and translators can for example work with them in Visual Studio.

Site Administration
Regional settings
Language settings
Export Translations
Import Translations

Site visitors will automatically see pages and news in their preferred user language, if it is available. Otherwise, the default language will be used.

6.8   TEAM SITES

In this section, I will describe the three types of Team sites available in SharePoint. Two are modern and one is classic, but you can add classic pages to modern sites and vice versa, and you can use the modern as well as the classic app interface in all Team site types.

A Team site is a place for collaboration, so it is a site where many people both add and view the content. The Team site has the Site navigation to the left.

When you create a Team site, there are no templates and no "blank" option. You get only one option for the homepage, but it is meant to be customized.

6.8.1   Modern Team Site

By default, the homepage of the modern Team site has web parts for News, Activity, Quick links and Documents. Above these web parts, there is a command bar of the same kind as in the Communication site, but the Site navigation is placed to the left, not on top.

Modern Team sites have controls for Theme and Header under the 365 Settings icon >Change the look.

The modern Team site can be connected to a Microsoft 365 group. In those cases, it is called a Group Team site.

6.8.1.1   Classic Compatibility

The modern Team sites are fully compatible with the classic experience. You can create classic pages in modern Team sites, and you can switch to the classic interface and use apps that only have the classic interface without problems.

The only issue is that a few classic web parts do not work well in classic pages in modern Team sites. The examples I give in this book are not among those!

6.8.1.2 Group Team Site

The modern Group Team site is connected to a Microsoft 365 group, that will be created automatically together with the site. A Microsoft 365 group is a group of colleagues that share resources. The site owner will also be the group owner, and all users that are added as site members in the site creation process will be members of the group.

In addition to the Group Team site, the Microsoft 365 group also has other shared apps and services. There is always a shared e-mail inbox, and the group e-mail name is by default the same as the Group Team site name.

The Group's inbox, settings and other shared resources can be reached via the 'Conversations' link in the Group Team site's Site navigation.

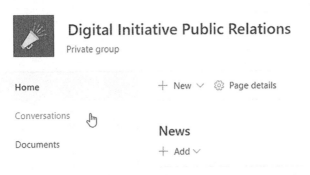

Microsoft 365 groups often cooperate via Microsoft Teams. When the group is not connected to Teams, a team can easily be created via a prompt below the Site navigation in the Group Team site.

When the group has been connected to Teams, a link to Teams will be added in the Site navigation in the Group Team site.

When the Microsoft 365 group is connected to both a SharePoint Group Team site and Microsoft Teams, the group can also be managed in Teams. The apps and pages in the Group Team site can easily be added to Teams, so that people work with the SharePoint content in Teams instead of going to the SharePoint site.

Microsoft Teams

Communicate with your colleagues in real time by creating a Team for your Office 365 Group. ⓘ

Create a Team

Refer to my book *Microsoft Teams from Scratch* for more information about Teams.

6.8.1.3 Team Site without a Group

A modern Team site can also be created without being connected to a Microsoft 365 group. This is suitable when the collaboration is broader and involves people who should not form a Microsoft 365 group.

While all users with Edit permission can create Group Team sites, a modern Team site without a group can only be created from the SharePoint Admin center and as a subsite.

However, if the possibility to create a Microsoft 365 group has been disabled for users without admin privileges, these users can still create a modern Team site – but now without a group.

Modern Team sites without a group have some originally classic features that do not exist in other modern sites, like the full Web Designer Galleries and the possibility to save a site as a template.

6.8.2   Classic Team Site

The classic Team site is intended for collaboration, just as the modern Team sites. It is not connected to a Microsoft 365 group by default, but after the site has been created, you can add such a group to a classic Team site, *see* below.

The classic Team site has a classic homepage, a so called wiki page. It can be customized in many ways and not only with web parts. The image below shows the default homepage of a classic Team site.

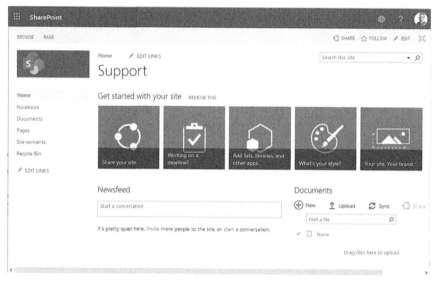

The default homepage does not have the Microsoft Search, but apps with the modern interface and modern pages added to a classic site have that search feature. You can create a modern page and make it homepage in the classic site if you so prefer, *refer to* 13.1.7, Set a Page as Homepage.

The classic homepage has three web parts:

- The Get Started tiles give links that may be important when you are new to SharePoint. These tiles are often removed after a while, when the team site is customized. They are easy to remove by clicking on REMOVE THIS.

- The Newsfeed is intended for sharing information and ideas among the people who use the team site. The content is stored in an automatically created "MicroFeed" list in the site.

- The default Documents web part displays the files in the automatically created "Documents" library, so that users can work with the files directly on the homepage.

Just like the other Team sites, the classic Team site has a Site navigation panel to the left. It also has a Top link bar, sometimes called Global navigation.

The Top link bar usually shows links to other sites within the same collection, but you can add any links you want, also links to external content, outside your SharePoint tenant. The current site is displayed with a distinct color, depending on theme.

kalmstrom.com demos   Sales   Development   ✎ EDIT LINKS

The classic Team site has no command bar. Instead, it has a ribbon with two or three tabs, similar to the ribbon you can find in Office apps. Which buttons are active depend on what you have selected in the page and which object you are working with.

The image below shows the PAGE tab in the ribbon on the homepage above.

On the page, below the ribbon, you can find various commands:

- The SHARE command is used to share the site.

- Each user can use the FOLLOW command to follow the site. The user can find all his/her followed sites in the SharePoint Online start page; refer to 12.1.

- The EDIT command opens the page in edit mode, so that you can customize it. When a page is open in edit mode the EDIT command is replaced by a SAVE command.

- The 'Focus on Content' command shows the page without the navigation parts. Click on the icon again to show the navigation.

- The Search box, by default searches the current site, but the search can be filtered, or you can search in all content of the tenant, see 4.3.3, Classic Search.

6.8.2.1 Modern Compatibility

Apps that are added to a classic team site can be viewed in the modern experience as well as in the classic, and you can add modern pages to a classic team site.

You can also add a modern Team site without a Microsoft 365 group as a subsite to a classic Team site.

6.8.2.2 Save Site as a Template

Under the Site Actions heading in the Site settings, you can save a classic site as a template, to be used when you create subsites in the same or another site.

The template will be saved to the Solutions gallery in the site where you created the template. From there, it can be downloaded and then uploaded to Solutions galleries in other sites.

Site Settings ▸ Save as Template ⓘ

File Name

Enter the name for this template file.

File name:

KTMDevTemplate

Name and Description

The name and description of this template will be displayed on the Web site template picker page when users create new Web sites.

Template name:

KTM Development

Template description:

Include Content

Include content in your template if you want new Web sites created from this template to include the contents of all lists and document libraries in this Web site. Some customizations, such as custom workflows, are present in the template only if you choose to include content. Including content can increase the size of your template.

Caution: Item security is not maintained in a template. If you have private content in this Web site, enabling this option is not recommended.

☐ Include Content

To create a new subsite from the template, open the 'Custom' tab when you create a new site and select the template.

Template Selection

Select a language:

English ▾

Select a template:

| Collaboration | Enterprise | Duet Enterprise | Custom |

KTM Development

6.8.2.3　Add Microsoft 365 Group

A link under the 365 Settings icon, makes it possible for site administrators to associate a classic Team site with a Microsoft 365 Group.

When you use this command, a new modern homepage will be created for the site, but the rest of the site will remain the same. A new Microsoft 365 group with some shared resources will also be created and associated with the site.

The name of the Microsoft 365 group will by default be the same as the name of the site, but when you click on 'Let's get started' you can change the name. You can also decide if the group should be private or public (for the whole organization).

Now you only need to add members to the group and click on 'Finish'. Members can also be added later.

Add additional owners

    Adele Vance   ×

Add members

    Alex Wilber   ×   Nestor Wilke   ×

    Christie Cline   ×   Allan Deyoung   ×

Finish

When this is done, you have a Team site connected to a Microsoft 365 group but with more options in the site settings that the modern Group Team site!

Note, however, that classic sites can only be created in the SharePoint Admin center, so you need to be a SharePoint or Global administrator to manage this workaround.

6.8.3   OneNote

Each SharePoint Team site comes with a Notebook link in the Site navigation. It opens the Online version of OneNote, Microsoft's note-taking tool that is part of the Office package.

OneNote Online works well in the browser, and by having it in SharePoint you can easily share it with other team members. The default OneNote notebook and all other notebooks you create are stored in each team site's Site Assets library.

When you open OneNote Online via the Notebook link in the Site navigation, you will have various options to insert text, images and links.

OneNote Online	Sales ▸ Sales Notebook		Sales Notebook
File Home Insert Draw View Print 💡 Tell me what you want to do		Open In OneNote Give Feedback To Microsoft	
≡ Sales Notebook 🔎			
Untitled Section Untitled Page		Tuesday, December 12, 2017 5:04 PM	

You can reach all the Team site's notebooks by clicking on the menu icon at the top left in the current notebook. The notebooks are stored in the Site Assets library and can be deleted there.

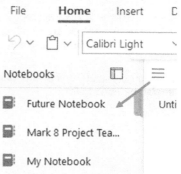

6.8.3.1   OneNote in SharePoint Libraries

The notebook file type is one of the file types you are offered when you create a new file in a document library that has the default content type.

If you don't want users to have access to OneNote, you can edit the '+New' menu in the **modern** interface and uncheck the box for OneNote, *refer to* 9.13.2, Edit the '+New' Menu.

You should also remove the link in the Site navigation, *refer to* 11.4, Edit Navigation.

Demo:

https://www.kalmstrom.com/Tips/SharePoint-Online-Course/OneNote.htm

6.9   SITE COMPARISON

The table below gives a summary of the differences between the commonly used SharePoint sites.

Feature	Communi-cation	Group Team	Team, no Group	Classic	Classic with Group
Solutions gallery			X	X	X
Save site as template			X	X	X
Save app as template			X	X	X
Oslo layout	X				
Seattle layout		X	X	X	X
Modern homepage	X	X	X		X
MS 365 Group		X			X
Admin created			X	X	X
Compatible with classic/modern		X	X	X	X

6.10　Get More Features in Modern Sites

When you create a new classic site, the Web Designer Galleries section in the Site settings will have some features that are not available in Communication and Group Team sites, like the possibility to upload sandboxed solutions. These sites, by default only have the two first features in the image from a classic site below.

Web Designer Galleries

Site columns
Site content types
Web parts
List templates
Master pages
Themes
Solutions
Composed looks

Classic Team sites and modern Team sites without a group, also have the possibility to save the site as well as an app as a template. These features are also missing by default in Communication and Group Team sites.

Most of these differences depend on that custom script is enabled by default in classic sites and Team sites without a group, but not in Communication and Group Team sites.

This can be helped if you enable scripting in sites where it is needed, but you should be aware that allowing custom scripts might be a security risk. If you need a Group Team site with the full Web Designer Galleries and the site and app templates option, there is an alternative: add a Microsoft 365 group to a classic site, *refer to* 6.8.2.3, Add Microsoft 365 Group.

Earlier, it was possible to enable scripting in all sites in the SharePoint Admin center, but I have found that this no longer works. Instead, you can use a PowerShell script and allow custom script where you need the extra features. You need to be a Global or SharePoint Admin to change the scripting.

To describe the whole process of scripting enabling is out of scope for this book, but I show it in the demo I refer to below. If you are used to PowerShell, you can just run this script: Set-SPOsite <SiteURL> -DenyAddAndCustomizePages 0

For more information, refer to Microsoft: https://docs.microsoft.com/en-us/sharepoint/allow-or-prevent-custom-script

If you want to learn about how to use PowerShell with SharePoint, please refer to my book *PowerShell with SharePoint from Scratch*.

When you have run this script on a site, you will have the following result:

- Group Team sites get galleries, site template and app template.

- Communication sites get galleries and app template.

Demo:

https://kalmstrom.com/Tips/SharePoint-Online-Course/Allow-Custom-Script-In-SharePoint.htm

6.11   DEFAULT SITES

When you open the SharePoint Admin center >Active sites for the first time, you will notice that two SharePoint sites are there already. These sites have been created automatically during the 365 setup: the "Communication site" Home site and the "All Company" public Group Team site.

6.11.1   *The Home Site*

The homepage of the Home site is the top SharePoint landing page for your organization's tenant. It usually has links to all Hub sites and other important information, and news that concerns the whole organization should be published here.

The Home site is based on the Communication site template, but it has certain specific characteristics:

- The URL of the Home site is the tenant domain + .sharepoint.com (for example https://kalmstromnet.sharepoint.com). (All other sites by default have the addition of "/sites/[site name]".)
- All the tenant's users are by default added to the Home site.
- All the tenant's users have Edit permission on the Home site. (Note that this is a very high permission level for everyone to have. Most SharePoint administrators want to change that, *refer to* chapter 14, Permissions and Sharing.)
- External sharing is enabled. (Again, this is something that most SharePoint administrators want to change, *refer to* chapter 14.)
- Microsoft Search always searches the whole tenant from the Home site.
- The Home button in the SharePoint Online mobile app directs the user to the Home site.
- The title of the default Communication site is "Communication site", but I recommend that you rename it into something more descriptive.

Currently a tenant can only have one Home site, but Microsoft is planning to make it possible to have multiple Home sites in the future.

6.11.1.1   Switch Home Site

If you want another Communication site to be the Home site, you can execute this PowerShell command in the latest version of the SharePoint Online Management Shell: Set-SPOHomeSite -HomeSiteUrl <the URL of the site>.

Note that the site cannot be connected to a Microsoft 365 group, and neither the current site nor the new site can be hub sites or associated with a hub site when the replacement is performed.

(Refer to my book *PowerShell with SharePoint from Scratch* if you want to learn more about how you can automate SharePoint with PowerShell.)

6.11.2   *The All Company Site*

The All Company site is intended for cooperation between all users in the tenant. It is based on the Group Team site template and connected to a public Microsoft 365 group called All Company.

Everyone in the tenant automatically becomes a member of the All Company group, which means that all the tenant's users have Edit permission on the All Company site. (This is a high permission level for everyone to have, and most SharePoint administrators will want to change it, *refer to* chapter 14, Permissions and Sharing.)

The URL of the All Company site is the tenant domain + sharepoint.com/sites/allcompany

6.12   CREATE A SITE

By default, all users can create Group Team sites and Communication sites. Global and SharePoint admins can also create the other site types.

When you create a new site – not a subsite – it is a totally new site collection. It will not inherit permission settings or navigation from other sites. It is however possible to associate a site to other sites via a hub site, *see* below.

When the site has been created, you can create apps, pages and subsites. They will all belong to the same site, and their URLs will all begin in the same way as the root site.

By default, everything in a site shares the same permissions, because lower levels, like apps and items, inherit the same permissions as the higher level. It is possible, but seldom recommended, to break the inheritance. *Refer to* chapter 14, Permissions and Sharing, for more info.

6.12.1   *Auto-Created Apps*

When you create a new site, SharePoint also creates the default document libraries. Your choice of site template decides which default apps are included in the root site and which features are enabled by default.

When you create one of the common site types, these libraries will be created automatically with the site:

- A document library called "Documents".
- A "Form" document library for forms used in the site.
- A "Styles" document library for styles used in the site.
- A "Site Pages" page library for pages that users create in the site.
- A "Site Assets" document library for other content that is used in the site, for example images that are added to pages. (In Communication sites, this library is not created until you actually add some content that needs to be saved there.)

In Communication sites a calendar is also created automatically, and classic Team sites gets a "MicroFeed" list app for news comments.

6.12.2   *User Site Creation*

By default, all users can create Communication and Group Team sites from the SharePoint Online start page. This is the page that users land on when they click on 'SharePoint' in the 365 navigation bar or on the SharePoint icon under the 365 App launcher.

Users can also create Group Team sites from their OneDrive for Business, *refer to* chapter 12. Personal Content.

As mentioned above in 6.6.1, Settings, Administrators can disable the users' possibility to create sites in the SharePoint Admin center >Settings >Site creation.

The creator will automatically follow the new site, so it will appear among the user's followed sites on the SharePoint Online start page.

Here, I will describe the site creation from the SharePoint Online start page. The first creation steps are the same for the two site types.

1. Click on the 'Create site' button in the top left corner of the SharePoint Online start page.

2. Select the site type you want to use.

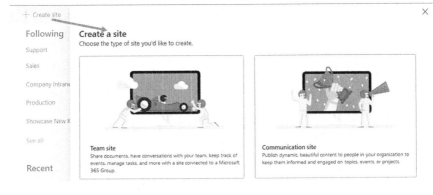

6.12.2.1   Communication site

When you select to create a Communication site, you must first select one of the homepage templates. They have different default web parts, but all can be customized, and the rest of the Communication site is the same.

*   Select 'Topic' to share information such as news, events, and other content.

*   Select 'Showcase' to showcase a product, team or event with photos or images.

*   Select 'Blank' to start with a modern homepage that does not have any default web parts.

89

← Back

Communication Site

Choose a design

Topic	⌄

Topic
Showcase
Blank

Then you only need to give the site a name and a description and click on 'Finish' to create the new site.

6.12.2.2 Group Team Site

When you create a Group Team site, fill out the site name and description. The group e-mail address and the site address will be added automatically when you have entered the name. Any spaces in the name will be removed.

←

Get a team site connected to Microsoft 365 Groups

Use this design to collaborate with your team. Share documents, track events in a shared calendar, and manage project tasks.

Site name

QA Recriutment

The site name is available.

Group email address

QARecriutment	✎

The group alias is available.

Site address

QARecriutment	✎

https://m365x446726.sharepoint.com/sites/QARecriutment
The site address is available.

Site description

Tell people the purpose of this site

Privacy settings

Private - only members can access this site	⌄

Select a language

English	⌄

Select the default site language for your site. You can't change this later.

[Next] [Cancel]

By default, the Group Team site is private, and if you keep that setting you must add the group members manually. (An alternative is to not add any members but keep the site to yourself, also *refer to* 12.2.5, Create a Site.)

When you select the other option, public, all users in the tenant will have access to the new Group Team site. This is not recommended unless the organization is very small.

When you create a Group Team site, you will automatically be its owner and administrator, but you can add additional owners.

Add group members

Group members will receive an email welcoming them to the new site and Microsoft 365 Group

QR   **QA Recruitment**
      Private group

Who do you want to add?
You can also add more people later

Add additional owners

Enter a name or email address

Add members

Enter a name or email address

Finish

The new site will open automatically, and all members will receive an e-mail where they are welcomed to the site.

6.12.3   *Admin Site Creation*

The SharePoint Admin center >Active sites has a '+ Create' button in the command bar.

Active sites

The 'Create' button opens a right pane that has some more options than what is given to standard users.

Create a site ₌ to manage all yc

When a modern site has been created in the SharePoint Admin center, it will show up at once under 'Active sites'.

+ Create   ⅋ Permissions

For classic sites, it may take a few minutes before the site has been created and can be reached from 'Active sites'.

6.12.3.1   Modern Sites

When administrators start creating a site from the SharePoint Admin center, they will have the options Group Team and Communication site, just like standard users.

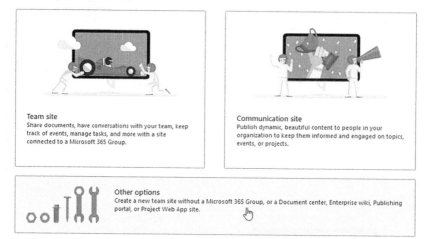

Create a site

Choose the type of site you'd like to create.

Team site
Share documents, have conversations with your team, keep track of events, manage tasks, and more with a site connected to a Microsoft 365 Group.

Communication site
Publish dynamic, beautiful content to people in your organization to keep them informed and engaged on topics, events, or projects.

Other options
Create a new team site without a Microsoft 365 Group, or a Document center, Enterprise wiki, Publishing portal, or Project Web App site.

Admins however have some more options for these site types. Under the Advanced settings, they can set the time zone and storage limit.

Site name

Site owner

Enter a name or email address

Select a language

English

Select the default site language for your site. You can't change this later.

Advanced settings ∧

Time zone

(UTC-08:00) Pacific Time (US and Canada)

Site description

Tell people the purpose of this site

Storage limit

25600   GB

Finish   Cancel

Admins do not automatically become site owners and administrators for the site they create from the SharePoint Admin center. Instead, they must assign one or more Site owners, who will also become Site administrators. If you want to assign another Site administrator, that can be done when the site has been created, *refer to* 6.6.2.1, Edit an Active Site.

The 'Other options' tile below the Group Team and Communication tiles gives a choice of templates. The default option is a modern Team site without a Microsoft 365 group.

6.12.3.2   Classic Team Site

Classic Team sites can only be created from the SharePoint Admin center.

1. Click on '+Create' and select 'Other options' in the right pane.

2. Select the option 'More templates' at the bottom of the dropdown. Do *not* fill out anything in the fields to the right.

3. Select the default option, 'Team site (classic experience)', and specify the details of the classic site. Click on the book icon to search for a site admin.

   The site admin does not become the site owner automatically, so if you want another person for that role, you can set it under 'Permissions' in the site's Information pane under 'Active sites'.

Create Site Collection

Title	Support Cases
Web Site Address	https://m365x446726.sharepoint.com ⌄
	/sites/ ⌄ SupportCases
Template Selection	2013 experience version will be used

Select a language:

English ⌄

Select a template:

Collaboration	Enterprise	Publishing	Custom

Team site (classic experience)
Blog
Developer Site
Project Site
Community Site

A site with a classic experience on the home page and no connection to an Office 365 Group.

Time Zone	(UTC-08:00) Pacific Time (US and Canada) ⌄
Administrator	Nestor Wilke;
Storage Quota	2000 GB
Server Resource Quota	30 resources of 5000 resources available

OK

6.13 ADD MEMBERS

All users get access to the automatically created Home site, but when a new site has been created it is only accessible by the creator, when the site is created from the SharePoint Online start page.

When the site is created from the SharePoint Admin center, a site owner/admin is appointed at creation, and it can very well be another person than the site creator, *see* above.

If you have created a Group Team site, site members might have been added when the site was created. In other cases, you must share the site manually. *Refer to* chapter 14, Permissions and Sharing.

6.14   HUB FAMILIES

As mentioned before, SharePoint sites (site collections) have no connection with each other. Each site is a separate unit with its own permissions and management. You can link to other sites but that is all – unless you register a hub site and create a hub family.

A hub family consists of one hub site and several other sites that are associated with the hub site. This way, related sites can be connected based on project, department, division, region or anything else. Within a hub family, it is easy for users to discover related content, news and site activity across all associated sites.

When you associate a site with a hub site, this will happen to the associated site:

- Content like news and activity from your site will be visible on the hub site homepage.
- You can no longer edit the theme of your site, as it will use the hub site theme.
- Your site will inherit the specific Hub navigation from the hub site.
- You can choose to sync site permissions with hub permissions to increase site access for viewers.
- Content from this and other associated sites will be prioritized in searches from the hub site.

I recommend that you use modern sites for the hub family. In classic sites, the hub navigation and hub settings are only visible in modern pages.

The relationship between the sites in a hub family is not hierarchical. Therefore, you can govern each site independently. If you stop associating a site with a hub site, it does not affect any of the other sites in the hub family.

Hub sites is something that Microsoft recommends instead of subsites, at least when you use the modern experience. All sites can be registered as hub sites and associated with a hub site. A site can only be associated with one hub site.

In a small business, you might want to use the Home Site as a hub and associate all or most of the other sites to it. In a bigger organization, you need to have more hubs.

In a hub site, you can display content that is common to a larger group, while the associated sites can be intended for smaller sections of that group. A small organization can for example have hub sites for HR, Finance, Marketing, Legal and IT. Big organizations should of course have many more hub sites, and there can be up to 2000 hub sites in a tenant.

Global and SharePoint admins can convert any site to a hub site, but I recommend that you first plan how your organization's intranet should be organized and that you then create new Communication sites to use as hub sites. The Communication site type is best suited for these kinds of informative sites.

6.14.1 Register as Hub Site

A hub site is created just like any other site, but it must be registered as a hub site in the SharePoint Admin center.

When you select a site that is not already a hub site or associated with a hub site, you can register the site as a hub site via the 'Hub' button in the 'Active sites' command bar.

∨ 🖧 Hub ∨   ᯆ Sharing   ▯

↓

Register as hub site

Associate with a hub

When you choose the option 'Register as hub site', a right pane will open, where you can give the site a hub name. This name will show up in a dropdown when people associate sites, so choose a name that explains what kind of sites should be associated with this hub.

×

Register as hub site ⊙

Make this site into a hub site to connect related sites and give them a shared experience.

Hub name *

| Leadership Hub |

People who can associate sites with this hub

| |

| Save | Cancel

You can also enter people who should have permission to associate sites with the hub site. If you leave the 'People who can associate sites with this hub' box empty, any site owner who have access to the hub site can associate their site with the hub.

🖧 Hub ∨   ᯆ Sharing   ▯

Edit hub site settings

Unregister as hub site

When a hub site is selected, the dropdown under the 'Hub' command instead give the options to edit the hub site settings or unregister the site as hub site.

If you want to change the hub site display name or the list of people who can associate sites with the hub, you can do that in the hub site settings.

When a modern site has been registered as a hub site, it gets a new navigation bar on top, below the 365 navigation bar.

At first, the hub navigation only has the hub site and an 'Add link' command, but when sites are associated, you should add them here. The same hub navigation bar

Leadership Hub   Add link

will be displayed on modern pages in all the associated sites.

The hub site also gets a new link under the 365 Settings icon: 'Hub site settings'. Here you can upload an image to be used as a hub site icon and create an approval flow.

6.14.2   Associate with a Hub Site

There is no limit to the number of sites that can be associated with a hub site, but you can only associate a site with one hub site.

6.14.2.1   Associate in the SharePoint Admin Center

Global and SharePoint administrators can associate sites with a hub site from the SharePoint Admin center >Active sites. Select the site, click on the 'Hub' button in the command bar and select 'Associate with a hub'.

In the right pane that opens, you can select the hub you want to associate the site with.

The association can be performed in bulk if you select multiple sites under 'Active sites'.

All hub sites and associations are shown in the 'Hub' column in the SharePoint Admin center >Active sites.

In the image below, "Development" means that the site is associated with the "Development" hub site.

Hub ⌄

Development

Development (Hub site)

Development
////////

6.14.2.2   Associate from a Site

By default, all site owners can associate their sites with a hub site, but as we have seen above, that permission can be restricted in the SharePoint Admin center to only allow specific people.

To associate a site with a hub site from inside the site, open the 365 Settings icon and select 'Site information'. There, you can select a hub site from a dropdown.

When you have selected the hub site and clicked on 'Save', the site will be associated immediately or after approval.

When you see the hub site navigation bar in the top right corner of the site, your will know that the site has been (approved and) associated.

Note that the associated site will inherit theme of the hub site, so you cannot edit the look of your site once you've associated it with a hub site.

Site Information   ✕

Site logo

🖼 Change

Site name *

| Contoso Team |

Site description

| A collaboration area for the Contoso Team. |

Hub site association

| None | ⌄ |

None

Contoso News

Development

HQ

Leadership Hub

Save   Cancel

6.14.2.3   Create Associated Sites from a Hub Site

The hub site owner can create a new site from the hub site. It will then be automatically associated with that hub site.

+ Create site   ★ Following   ↩ Share

When you click on 'Create site', a right pane with the options Group Team site and Communication site will be displayed, in the same way as when users create sites from the SharePoint Online start page.

6.14.2.4   Request Association Approval

Hub site owners can create an approval flow, so that sites cannot be associated with the hub site until after approval. In the hub site, click on the 365 Settings icon and select 'Hub site settings'.

A right pane will open, where you can enable 'Require approval for associated sites to join'. When that toggle is on, a 'Create' button will be visible.

Click on the 'Create' button, enter the person(s) who should approve and click on 'Create flow'.

Now an approval flow is created. It can be seen and edited on the Power Automate site, under 'My flows', *refer to* chapter 24, SharePoint Automation. Any requests can be viewed from the Hub site settings right pane.

Edit hub site settings   ✕

Hub name *

Development

🔘 Shown in navigation

Require approval for associated sites to join

🔘 Required   1

Create a flow to require approval

 Create   2

Save   Cancel

6.14.3   *Hub Permissions*

In a hub family, each associated site has its own permissions, just as the hub site has. Hub site owners can however give visitor permission to people and groups, and these permissions can be synchronized to the associated sites. This will increase access for viewers across all sites in the hub, but it will not override or change any site permissions.

The hub permission setting is Off by default, both in the hub site and in the associated sites, and it must be activated in both places to work.

1. When a site is registered as hub site, there will be a new 'Hub' tab under the 'Site permissions'. Here you can enable hub permissions and enter visitor names.

2. When 'Sync hub permissions' has been turned on in the hub site, the associated sites will also have a 'Hub' tab under 'Site permissions', and here site owners can set the synchronization to On.

Permissions   ✕

This site   **Hub**
—————

Sync hub permissions to associated sites

⬤◯ On

Enter the names of individuals or groups to
grant visitor access to the hub and associated
sites. Existing site permissions will not change.
Learn more

Hub visitors

| Enter a name or group |

The synchronization can be turned off anytime, and you should not sync the
hub permissions if your site contains sensitive information.

6.15   CREATE A SUBSITE

The hub family is one way of linking sites together. Another way is to create
subsites and use shared navigation for all sites in the collection. This is the best
way if you prefer the classic experience, because the hub navigation and settings
will only appear in the modern experience.

It is possible to create subsites in sites that belong to a hub family, but Microsoft
recommends that you instead create a new site.

The subsite method to link sites creates a hierarchy, and that gives some
drawbacks:

• Subsite URLs reflect that they are subsites to another site, so if you reorganize
  relationships you will break the links.

• Some features, like policies, apply to the root site and all subsites in a
  collection, whether you want it or not.

All site types have a possibility to nest sites within sites by creating subsites to
the root site or even to another subsite.

The possibility to create subsites can be disabled
in the SharePoint Admin center >Settings >classic
settings page >Subsite Creation. The image below
shows the default setting.

To create a new SharePoint subsite, open the Site
contents of an existing site, click on 'New' and
select 'Subsite'.

＋ New ⌄

List

Page

Document library

App

Subsite

When you create a new subsite, there are different kinds of site templates to select from. The default option is a modern Team site without a group, but you can also create a classic Team site.

Template Selection

Select a language:

English   ∨

Select a template:

Collaboration | Enterprise   Duet Enterprise

Team site (no Office 365 group)
Team site (classic experience)
Blog
Project Site

A site with no connection to an Office 365 Group.

Communication sites and Group Team sites cannot be created as subsites.

There are choices for the navigation but remember that only classic Team sites have a Top navigation. If you select to display the subsite in the Top link bar of a modern parent, the link will be there, but on the place for the Hub navigation. *Refer to* chapter 11, SharePoint Navigation, for more info.

By default, subsites inherit the parent permissions, but you can also create unique permissions for the subsite. The image below shows the default option.

Permissions

You can give permission to access your new site to the same users who have access to this parent site, or you can give permission to a unique set of users.

User Permissions:

◉ Use same permissions as parent site
○ Use unique permissions

When you select unique permissions, a new page will open when you have clicked on 'Create'. Here you can add people or groups to the main groups Owner, Member and Visitor. Also refer to chapter 14, Permissions and Sharing.

6.16   DELETE AND RESTORE SITES

The tenant's automatically created Home site cannot be deleted, but all other sites can be deleted – and also restored within a certain time. The removal is performed in the same way for all sites, but the restoration process is different for root sites and subsites.

6.16.1   Delete a Site

All site types can be deleted under the site's Site settings >Site Actions >Delete this site.

Site Actions
Manage site features
Reset to site definition
Delete this site   ⬅

To delete a **modern** site, you can also click on the 365 Settings icon and then on 'Site information'. Now you can delete the site directly from the right pane.

Site Information   ✕

View all site settings

🗑 Delete site   ⬅

Save   Cancel

Global and SharePoint admins can delete root sites (and thereby any subsites too) in the SharePoint Admin center >Active sites. Select the site you want to remove and click on 'Delete' in the command bar. To just delete a subsite is not possible here, as the Admin center does not show subsites.

In all cases, you will be asked to confirm the removal.

6.16.2   Restore a Subsite

Subsites go directly to the second-stage recycle bin, where they are kept for 93 days. The link to the second-stage bin is found in the recycle bin page.

Can't find what you're looking for? Check the Second-stage recycle bin

The site admin can either restore or permanently delete the subsite from the second-stage bin.

6.16.3   Restore a Root Site

If the site you are deleting is a root site, you are in fact deleting the whole site collection together with the root site. In that case, the site can be restored from the SharePoint Admin center >Deleted sites. Here, sites are retained for 93 days before they are permanently deleted.

↺ Restore   🗑 Permanently delete

When you restore a modern Group Team site, the group and all its resources are also restored. The group resources are however only retained for 30 days.

If you want to permanently delete a site before the 93 days have passed, you can do that too under 'Deleted sites'.

6.17   SUMMARY

In this long chapter, you have learned about the main building block of SharePoint: the site. Now you should know what is common for all sites and what is the difference between the commonly used site types.

You understand how to create different types of sites, and you can connect them in a hub family or by creating subsites.

SharePoint has several kinds of groups, and in this chapter, we have met the Microsoft 365 group. This is a group that share resources, among them a SharePoint Group Team site. You will encounter other groups later in this book.

We will of course come back to sites many times in this book, as it is in the sites everything is contained. In chapter 12, you will learn about each user's personal SharePoint site, OneDrive for Business, and in chapter 14 we will go through site permissions and sharing.

Before that, I will however explain how you can build and customize SharePoint apps and pages. We will start with the apps, and in the next chapter, I will describe features that are the same in both list and library apps.

7 SHAREPOINT APPS

Within SharePoint sites, content can be stored and shared in apps. Document libraries, picture libraries, contact lists and calendars are all examples of apps, and all app types have common features.

SharePoint apps can be either lists or libraries. Libraries are used when the most important content is a file. In other cases, we use a list app.

A SharePoint app is like a database table or spreadsheet. Data is distributed in rows, and each row is known as an item. The image below shows part of a list app, where you can see four items.

Department Name ⌄	Manager ⌄	Staff ⌄
South	Peter Kalmström	15
North	Peter Kalmström	200
East	Kate Kalmström	50
West	Kate Kalmström	4

Each row, or item, has various columns where you can enter metadata, called values or properties, that describes the item. This information is used by the search crawler to update the search index, so metadata plays an important role to make content easy to find.

The value in one of the columns, usually the first column from the left, becomes underlined when you hover the mouse over it. Click on this value to open the item in a list app and the file in a library app. The image below comes from a library.

🗋	Name ⌄			Modified ⌄	Modified... ⌄
📊	Consultants.xlsx	↪	⋮	October 23, 20...	Kate Kalmström
📊	statements_2020-09-01_20...			November 6, 2...	Kate Kalmström

In this chapter, I will explain what is common for both app types:

- The app settings page
- The Standard and Grid/Quick Edit view modes
- Columns, filter and sort
- Views

- Alerts

- Version history

I will also describe the two interfaces, how to create apps, the template options and permission settings.

In the next two chapters, we will have a closer look at first list apps and then library apps.

If you create your own apps to test the features I describe in this chapter – which is something I strongly recommend! – I advise you to create custom list apps via the 'Add an app' command, as described in section 7.4. These have all the features described in this chapter but no other features that might disturb your learning process. It will be time to create other apps later in this book.

When you create a new item in an app, the metadata is filled out in a form. This is done a bit differently for list apps and library apps, so I will describe the item creation in the following two chapters.

I recommend that you create many apps instead of trying to get too much data into one app. You should not have more than 5000 items in any app, as that is the limit for what SharePoint can display.

Microsoft is working on removing that limit, but it is no doubt still there when this is written. You will be able to add much more than 5000 items in an app, but it will create many different problems. Therefore, I strongly recommend that you avoid pushing that limit.

Apps can be embedded in SharePoint pages, and that is something I will describe later in the book.

Note that SharePoint apps are normally shared within a group of people – that is the main point of SharePoint, after all! – so use them for information that should be shared, not for personal data. An exception to that is apps in your personal OneDrive for Business site, which is described in chapter 12, Personal Content.

7.1   BENEFITS

SharePoint apps have many benefits:

- SharePoint apps give a good overview over data.

- Use the powerful Search engine to find information. You can start with searching just the current app, and if there are hits, the app content will be filtered to show only the hits.

- The version history feature lets you see earlier versions of each item and what exactly was changed in each version. If needed, you can also restore an earlier version. The version history is on by default in libraries and off in list apps, but I recommend to have it on in lists too.

- You can filter and sort items to study the information in different ways.

- You can create different views to permanently filter or display items in a preferred way.

- With the Totals feature you can summarize values with sum, average etc.
- You can connect and export SharePoint data to Excel. In the classic experience you can also connect and export to Access, Outlook and Project.
- You can set permissions on a singular item or folder, so that only some people can view or edit it.
- You can let SharePoint send alerts when items have been added, changed or deleted.

7.2   MODERN AND CLASSIC APP INTERFACE

Most apps can be viewed in both the classic and the modern interface. Below are images from the upper part of a document library, and I hope they will give an idea about the differences between the two experiences.

The modern experience:

The classic experience:

With a few exceptions, apps in Communication sites can only have the modern interface. The classic app interface cannot be displayed.

7.2.1   *Differences*

The most obvious difference between the modern and classic interface is that the classic interface has a ribbon, with the commands grouped under tabs. The modern app interface, instead have a command bar, also called "quick actions pane".

Generally, both interfaces have the same commands. However, while the classic ribbon shows all commands all the time, even if some may be greyed out, the modern command bar shows different controls depending on what has been selected in the list of items below. The command bar looks different when no item is selected, compared to when one item or multiple items have been selected.

Another difference between the app interfaces is that much of the settings and editing in the modern interface is performed in a right pane, like the Information pane below.

The right pane opens on various commands, and to close it you can either click on the 'Save' button to save your changes or on the X in the top right corner to close the pane without saving.

The classic interface opens a dialog or a new page in these situations.

When you can switch between the interfaces, which is possible in almost all apps, you can use all features by switching to the interface that is most suitable for each occasion.

7.2.1.1   Modern Command Bar Controls

The command bar in the modern app interface has three features that are not available in the classic ribbon:

- The 'Power Apps' command lets you create a powerapp from the app and also customize the app form in an advanced manner. This is described in chapter 21. To just decide which columns should be visible in the form, *refer to* 7.8. The 'Power Apps' option does not exist at all in the classic interface.

- The 'Automate' command lets you create a flow connected to the app and reach all flows saved in the current user account. *Refer to* chapter 24, SharePoint Automation. The 'Automate' option does not exist at all in the classic interface.

- The information icon in the right part of the command bar opens a right Information pane.

When no item has been selected in the app, the Information pane for list apps shows who has access to the list. The Information pane for library apps shows the latest activity in the library.

When an item is selected in the app, you can see and edit details about the item, such as the item properties and who has access to the item. You can also see recent activity for the item and more. 'Details', under the item ellipsis, shows the same information.

In library apps, there is a preview of the file in the item on top of the Information pane, like in the image to the right.

If you have not made any changes, click on the X in the top right corner of the pane to close it.

If you have made changes that needs to be saved, there is a 'Save' button. It can be placed on top or at the bottom, or in both places.

Except for recent activity, the classic interface gives the same information, but it is not gathered in one place.

When you click on 'Edit all' in the 'Properties' section of the Information pane, a new right pane with a small command bar will open.

In this command bar, see the image below, you can copy a link to the file, and under 'Edit form' you can hide or show columns in the app form or customize it in Power Apps. This will be described later in the book.

7.2.2 Switch Interface

Almost all apps give a possibility to use either the modern or the classic interface. When that is possible, there is a switch link under the Site navigation.

Modern interface link:

Return to classic SharePoint

Classic interface link:

Exit classic experience

App owners and administrators can set the default experience for each app in the List/Library settings:

1. Open the settings, *see* the section below, and click on the link 'Advanced settings' under the General Settings heading.

2. Set the 'List experience' at the bottom of the page to the interface that should be default.

List experience

Select the experience you want to use for this list. The new experience is faster, has more features, and works better across different devices.

Display this list using the new or classic experience?

○ Default experience set by my administrator
◉ New experience
○ Classic experience

Note that this setting only decides which experience the app should open with. Individual users can always switch app interface by clicking on the links 'Return to classic SharePoint' in the modern experience and 'Exit classic experience' in the classic interface, in apps where such links exist.

Demo:

https://www.kalmstrom.com/Tips/SharePoint-Online-Course/Library-Interface.htm

7.3 LIST SETTINGS

Each app has a settings page where you can find many kinds of settings, including settings for permissions, columns and views.

You can reach the settings for all app types from the Site contents. Click on the ellipsis to the right of the app name or title and select Settings.

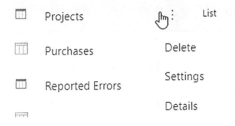

109

When you have the app open, the **modern** interface has a List settings link in the right pane that opens when you click on the 365 Settings icon.

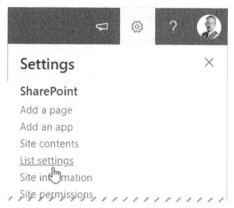

In library apps, the link is instead 'Library settings'.

In the continuation, I will use the word "List settings" also for library settings, when the text is applicable to all kinds of apps.

The **classic** interface has the settings link in the ribbon:

List Settings

- In most lists, the List Settings button is found under the LIST tab in the ribbon.

- In calendars, the List Settings button is found under the CALENDAR tab in the ribbon.

- In document libraries, you can find the Library Settings button under the LIBRARY tab in the ribbon.

In the continuation, I will use the word "List settings" also for library and calendar settings, when the text is applicable to all kinds of apps.

The settings pages are a bit different depending on app type, but all app settings show the app's columns and views and give a possibility to open and customize them.

List Information

Name: Documents

Web Address: https://m365x446726.sharepoint.com/sites/DigitalInitiativePublicRelations/Shared Documents/Forms/AllItems.asp:

Description:

General Settings	Permissions and Management	Communications
▫ List name, description and navigation	▫ Permissions for this document library	▫ RSS settings
▫ Versioning settings	▫ Manage files which have no checked in version	
▫ Advanced settings	▫ Information Rights Management	
▫ Validation settings	▫ Workflow Settings	
▫ Column default value settings	▫ Apply label to items in this list or library	
▫ Audience targeting settings	▫ Enterprise Metadata and Keywords Settings	
▫ Rating settings		
▫ Form settings		

Columns

A column stores information about each document in the document library. The following columns are currently available in this document library:

Column (click to edit)	Type	Required
Title	Single line of text	
Modified	Date and Time	
Created	Date and Time	
Created By	Person or Group	
Modified By	Person or Group	
Checked Out To	Person or Group	

▫ Create column

▫ Add from existing site columns

▫ Column ordering

▫ Indexed columns

Views

A view of a document library allows you to see a particular selection of items or to see the items sorted in a particular order. Views currently configured for this document library:

View (click to edit)	Default View	Mobile View	Default Mobile View
All Documents	✓	✓	✓

▫ Create view

7.4 CREATE AN APP

Microsoft has made it easy to create new apps in SharePoint Online, because you can use a template and modify it to suit your needs. Each new app will be placed inside the SharePoint site where you created it.

Below, I will describe general app creation. There are also specific creation options for lists and libraries, and I will come back to them in the chapters about specific features for these apps.

7.4.1 Create an App from a Template

SharePoint Online offers many templates that you can build a new app on.

1. Open the 365 Settings icon and select 'Add an app'. You can also click on '+ New' and then 'App' on a modern homepage or in a Site contents with the modern interface.

2. The "Your Apps" page will open. Search for a template that is similar to the app you want to create. Click on the icon to create the new app.

3. Give the app a name and click on 'Create'. If you click on the 'Advanced Options' link, you can give a description of the new app. Some app templates also have a few settings under 'Advanced Options'.

When the new app has been created in this way, it will not be opened automatically. Instead, you will be directed to the Site contents, where you can open the app or its settings.

You can also use existing list apps as templates, *refer to* 7.14, Template Options.

7.4.1.1 Apps in Communication Sites

As Communication sites are primarily intended for information and not for collaboration, they by default only give a few options in the "Your Apps" page.

To have the same app options in a Communication site as in Team sites, open the Site settings and click on 'Manage site features' under the Site Actions heading. When a new page opens, scroll down to the Team Collaboration Lists feature and activate it.

 Team Collaboration Lists

Provides team collaboration capabilities for a site by making standard lists, such as document libraries and issues, available.
Activate

In Team sites, this feature is activated by default.

7.4.2 *Custom Apps*

Custom list apps only have a "Title" column in the default "All items" view, and custom library apps have the columns "Name", "Modified" and "Modified by". These columns are visible in the default view. There are also "Created" and "Created by" columns in both app types. The rest of the columns must be added by the creator.

You can create a custom app by following the template steps above and selecting the 'Custom List' or 'Document Library' template.

Another way to create a custom app is to use the 'List' or 'Document library' option in the dropdown under the '+ New' button in **modern** Site contents and homepages.

In that case, you will not be directed to the "Your Apps" page. Instead, a right pane will open, where you can enter the app name and a description. An app created in this way will open when you have clicked on 'Create'.

7.5 APP LINK IN THE SITE NAVIGATION

When you create a new custom app from a **modern** home page or Site contents, as described above, a checkbox for 'Show in site navigation' is checked by default.

When you create an app in another way, or if you want to change the setting, open the app's List settings and then 'List name, description and navigation'. Now you can select the 'Yes' radio button for display in the Site navigation – here called Quick launch. (Note that the newly created app at first shows up in the Site navigation anyway, under Recent.)

Navigation

Specify whether a link to this list appears in the Quick Launch. Note: it only appears if Quick Launch is used for navigation on your site.

Display this list on the Quick Launch?

◉ Yes   ○ No

7.6   DISPLAY MODES

Apps can be displayed in Standard or Grid view mode. You can create new items and edit items in both modes.

7.6.1   *Standard*

The Standard view mode is displayed by default when you open an app. You cannot edit the items directly on the page when an app is displayed in Standard view mode. Instead, you need to open the item in edit mode. (How to do that, will be described later.)

In the Standard view mode, each item has an ellipsis (...) to the right in the Title column in lists and the Name column in libraries. That is normally the first column from the left.

In the modern interface, the ellipsis is only visible when you hover the mouse cursor over the item.

When you click on the ellipsis, you can see options for what to do with the item and information about it. The options are different, depending on what kind of app it is. The image to the right comes from a list app in the modern interface.

Open

Edit

Share

Get a link

Copy field to clipboard

Delete

Alert me

More   >   Workflow

Details   Compliance details

7.6.2   *Grid*

When an app is displayed in the Grid (modern) or Quick Edit (classic) view mode, it looks like a spreadsheet, and you can edit items directly in the cells. Your changes will be saved when you move to the next row or when you leave the Grid view.

Phone Messages

○	Who called? ∨	Callback Number ∨	Called Person ∨	+
○	Kalle Kula	8796 234 976	ade	
+	Add new item			

Adele Vance
Retail Manager

The Grid view mode is very popular and powerful for all who have knowledge of working in Excel lists. Copy and paste as well as some fill commands work in this view. With the little handle in the bottom right corner of the cell you can drag values down, just like you can do in Excel.

The modern Grid view shows 100 items on each page, while the classic Quick Edit only shows 30 by default. If the app has more

‹ 401 - 500 ›

items, there is a "next page" arrow below the last item on the page in both interfaces.

To change the mode in **modern** apps, use the 'Edit in grid view' button in the command bar.

⊞ Edit in grid view

In apps with the **classic** interface, the 'Quick Edit' button is found under the LIST or LIBRARY tab. Lists also have an 'edit this list' button.

| BROWSE | ITEMS | LIST |

View   Quick   Create
        Edit   View

View Format

When you select an item in the **modern** grid interface, an 'Edit' button will be displayed in the command bar. It opens the item's Information pane to the right.

The modern grid interface also has 'Undo' and 'Redo' buttons. Ctrl + Z and Ctrl + Y (Windows) and Command + Z and Command + Shift + Z (Mac OS) will work as well.

⊞ Exit grid view   ✎ Edit   ↺ Undo

In modern apps, the command bar has an 'Exit grid view' button in the Grid view mode. Click on that button when you are finished with the editing, and the list will go back to the Standard view mode.

Classic apps instead have a "Stop editing" command above the grid.

Stop editing this list

7.7 COLUMNS

Information about each app item is kept in columns. The column content is often referred to as values, metadata or properties. Another popular name for column is field, and that term is used behind the scenes when automating SharePoint with programming languages.

When users add a new item to an app, they fill out the metadata in a form where each column is represented by a field. In this book, I will therefore use the term "column" when talking about the app interface and the different types of metadata and "field" when I refer to the form where the metadata is filled out.

The columns are generally the same for each item in the app, even if each field does not have to be filled out for each item. (An exception to this is when you use several content types in an app; *refer to* 25.11.1, Create an Entry Content Type.)

When you create a column, you must select column type depending on what kind of metadata the column should contain, like names, dates or hyperlinks. The default column type is 'Single line of text', but there are many other options.

7.7.1 *List Columns and Site Columns*

Columns can be created just for an app or for the whole tenant.

In the List settings, below the names of the existing columns, there are three options for adding a new column: create a list column, add from existing site columns and indexed columns.

(There is also a link to a page where you can decide in which order the columns should be displayed as fields in the app form.)

Columns

- Create column
- Add from existing site columns
- Column ordering
- Indexed columns

List columns, created with the 'Create column' command, are the easiest column type to create. They can only be used in the app where they were created.

Even if list columns are a bit easier to create the first time, I recommend that you for the long run use site columns as much as possible. They are reusable and more available to the Search engine. From the app settings, you can only add existing site columns to the app, but below I will describe how you can create new site columns.

Indexed columns can be valuable for very large lists, with more than 5000 items, but I recommend that you instead archive items or split lists and don't let them grow that big. Therefore, I will not go into indexed columns in this book.

7.7.2   Create List Columns

The 'Create column' option in the List settings, opens a "Create Column" page. The column you create here, will only be available for the current app.

Give the column a name and select column type.

Then you will have different options depending on what type of column you selected.

The image to the right shows the options for the default column type, Single line of text.

Settings › Create Column ⓘ

Name and Type

Type a name for this column, and select the type of information you want to store in the column.

Column name:

The type of information in this column is:
- ◉ Single line of text
- ○ Multiple lines of text
- ○ Choice (menu to choose from)
- ○ Number (1, 1.0, 100)
- ○ Currency ($, ¥, €)
- ○ Date and Time
- ○ Lookup (information already on this site)
- ○ Yes/No (check box)
- ○ Person or Group
- ○ Hyperlink or Picture
- ○ Calculated (calculation based on other columns)
- ○ Task Outcome
- ○ External Data
- ○ Managed Metadata

Additional Column Settings

Specify detailed options for the type of information you selected.

Description:

Require that this column contains information:
- ○ Yes ◉ No

Enforce unique values:
- ○ Yes ◉ No

Maximum number of characters:

255

Default value:
- ◉ Text ○ Calculated Value

☑ Add to all content types
☑ Add to default view

App columns can also be created in other ways:

- Click on the plus sign in the Grid view of the modern or classic interface.

  When you click on one of the options, a new cell will be created where you can add the column name. You can also add values for the existing items in the cells below the column name, but you must go to the Standard view mode and edit the column to make any column settings.

117

'More Column Types...' directs you to the Create Column page.

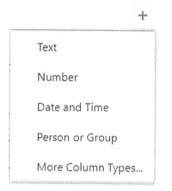

- In the **classic** experience, click on the Create column button under the LIST/LIBRARY/CALENDAR tab. It will take you to the Create Column page.

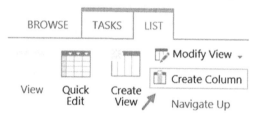

Demo:

https://www.kalmstrom.com//Tips/SharePoint-Online-Course/Categorization-Columns.htm

7.7.2.1   Modern Column Creation Options

The modern interface has more options for column creation than the List settings and Grid methods mentioned above.

The column creation methods described below, open a right pane when you create a new column, instead of opening the Create Column page. It has the most common settings, and you can find more when you expand 'More options'.

In apps with the modern interface, you can create new columns in these ways, in addition to the options mentioned above:

- Click on '+ Add column' in the app's Standard view mode. When you click on 'More...' in the dropdown, you will be directed to in the "Create Column" page.

Single line of text	+ Add column
Multiple lines of text	
Location	
Number	
Yes/No	
Person	
Date	
Choice	
Hyperlink	
Picture	
Currency	
More...	
Show/hide columns	

- In Standard view mode, open the dropdown at one of the existing columns and select 'Column settings' >'Add a column'.

TotalCost ⌄   TestCollectFeedback ⌄   Phase ⌄   Numbers1 ⌄

50,00 kr

Smaller to larger		Single line of text
Larger to smaller		Multiple lines of text
Filter by		Location
Group by TotalCost		Number
Column settings >	Edit	Yes/No
In Progress	Move left	Person
In Progress	Move right	Date
In Progress	Hide this column	Choice
In Progress	Pin to filters pane	Hyperlink
	Show/hide columns	Picture
	Add a column >	Currency
		More...

7.7.2.2   The Modern Location List Column

The Location list column type makes it possible to have location data from Bing Maps, or from your organization's directory, filled out automatically when a new item is created.

This column is currently only possible to create from the '+ Add column' command in the **modern** interface, Standard view mode.

When you create a Location column, you can select which other location data columns should be filled out automatically. (By default, no boxes are checked.)

Think twice when you choose a name for the column, because if you change the column name, the connected location data columns will still have the original name.

Create a column   ✕

Learn more about column creation.

Name *

> Where?

Type

> Location   ⌄

Show linked columns in the current view

☑ Street Address

☑ City

☐ State

☑ Country or Region

☐ Postal Code

☐ Coordinates

☐ Name

More options ⌄

[Save]   Cancel

When a new item is created, users only need to select the location.

The other location details will be filled out automatically according to the column settings.

Where? ⌄	Where?: Street ⌄	Where?: City ⌄	Where?: Countr... ⌄
Eriksberg Hotel & Nature Reserve	Guöviksvägen 353	Trensum	SE

Note: If you select the "Location" *site* column, it will not be of the Location type. Instead, it will be a single line of text column with no extra features.

7.7.3   *Create Site Columns*

A site column is a reusable column that you can assign to multiple apps in a site or even in the whole tenant. Site columns are useful for establishing consistency across lists and libraries, and its values are automatically indexed by the Search engine.

You can use the settings for a site column in multiple apps, so that you don't have to recreate them each time. For example, if you create a site column named Consultants, users can add that column to other apps, and it will have the same settings in the whole site collection or tenant. Only the column values will be different in each case.

Site columns are always used in the reusable sets of columns and settings called Content Types; *refer to* chapter 25.

When you select the second option for adding a column in the List settings, 'Add from existing site columns', you will have many different columns to choose from.

Microsoft gives a huge number of built-in site columns, but any site columns that you create will also show up here and can be selected.

Settings ▸ Add Columns from Site Columns ⓘ

Select Columns

Select which site columns to add to this list.

Select site columns from:

All Groups	∨

Available site columns:

Active	
Actual Work	∧
Address	
Aliases	**Add >**
Anniversary	
Append-Only Comments	
Assistant's Name	
Assistant's Phone	∨
Author	

Columns to add:

Description:
None

Group: Document and Record Management Columns

Options

☑ Add to all content types
☑ Add to default view

OK	Cancel

You can create custom site columns from the Site Settings >Site columns:

Web Designer Galleries
Site columns ⬅
Site content types
Web parts

When you open the Site columns page and click on the 'Create' button, a "Create Column" page will open with the same kind of choices as when you create a list column, *see* above.

7.7.4   Column Types

As you have seen in the images above there are many column types. Here, I will just mention some of them that I think might need some extra explanations. These column types can be created as list columns as well as site columns.

The images below mainly come from Create Column pages, but in the modern app interface most of these settings can be found in the right pane also.

7.7.4.1   Calculated Column

When you create a column of the type Calculated, you can set the values of that column to be a calculation of the item's values in other columns in the app. The calculated values are filled out automatically.

In the image below, I am setting the Total cost column value to be the value in the Hardware Cost column plus the value in the Setup Cost column in the same item.

Name and Type

Type a name for this column.

Column name:

> Total Cost

The type of information in this column is:

Calculated (calculation based on other columns)

Additional Column Settings

Specify detailed options for the type of information you selected.

Description:

Formula:

> =[Hardware Cost]+

Insert Column:

> Location: Country/Re... ▲
> Location: Name
> Modified
> Position
> Setup Cost
> Title
> Year ▼

Add to formula

The data type returned from this formula is:

○ Single line of text
○ Number (1, 1.0, 100)
◉ Currency ($, ¥, €)
○ Date and Time

The Calculated column type is not visible in the dropdown when you create a new column from the modern interface. When you select 'More', you will be directed to the "Create Column" page, where you can select the Calculated column and create the formula for it.

Note: The modern Column settings pane gives the option 'Calculated value' for some column types, but this is a validation feature. You can find the same feature in the 'Column Validation' section of the "Create Column" page.

7.7.4.2   Choice Column

When a column is of the Choice type, users are asked to make a choice among several alternatives.

At the bottom of the "Create Column" page, you should fill out the choices in the order you want them to be shown and select display method for the choices. If you choose to have a default value, it will be filled out if no other value is selected.

It is usually recommended to enter the choices alphabetically, but another option is to add figures before the options, to indicate a proper order.

When there are only a few options, it is nice to have radio buttons for the choice.

Require that this column contains information:

○ Yes ◉ No

Enforce unique values:

○ Yes ◉ No

Type each choice on a separate line:

```
1. Undecided
2. Yes
3. No
```

Display choices using:

○ Drop-Down Menu

◉ Radio Buttons

○ Checkboxes (allow multiple selections)

Allow 'Fill-in' choices:

○ Yes ◉ No

Default value:

◉ Choice ○ Calculated Value

```
1. Undecided
```

In the modern right pane, you can give different colors to the options.

Create a column   ✕

Learn more about column creation.

Name *

> Quote Status

Description

>

Type

> Choice   ⌄

Choices *

1 Undecided	🎨	✕
2. Yes	🎨	✕
3. No	🎨	✕

╋ Add Choice

7.7.4.3   Date and Time Column

Columns of the type Date and Time have a DateTimePicker at the Date field.

🗓 Decision Date

> Enter a date   🗓

When you create a column of the type Date and Time, you will have some options that are only available for this column type.

Date and Time Format:

◉ Date Only   ○ Date & Time

Display Format:

◉ Standard   ○ Friendly

Default value:

◉ (None)

○ Today's Date

○ [   ] [12 AM ▾] [00 ▾]

Enter date in M/D/YYYY format.

○ Calculated Value:

[   ]

If you change the Display Format from Standard to Friendly, the selected date will be shown like this:

Quote Date

Tomorrow

Thursday

7.7.5   *Character Limits in Text Columns*

SharePoint apps have two text columns: Single line of text and Multiple lines of text. One line can only have 255 characters, so the Single line of text column is limited to that.

For the 'Multiple lines of text' there are two ways to give more space.

- When the column is created in the List settings 'Create column' dialog, there is a setting for number of rows. The default number is 6.

Number of lines for editing:

[6   ]

This option is available for all apps, experiences and modes.

- When then column is created with the '+ Add column' command in the **modern** interface, Standard view mode, **document libraries** have a setting for unlimited length in the right pane. This option is disabled by default.

More options ∨

Require that this column contains information

⬤) No

Allow unlimited length in document libraries

(⚪ Yes ⟵

7.7.6   *Filter, Sort and Group*

SharePoint app items can be filtered by the various column values they contain. The column values can also be sorted ascending or descending, and you can combine filtering and sorting of several columns.

In general, app filtering works in the same way as in Excel and Access. A funnel icon to the right of the column name shows that a column has been filtered, so that it does not show all items.

Department ▽ ∨

In the **modern** experience, the options to filter on are selected with check boxes in a right pane. It works in the same way in Standard and Grid view. In the image below, the Department column is ready to be filtered.

Department ∨

	Filter by 'Department' ✕
Ascending	☐ (Empty)
Descending	☐ East
Filter by 🖑 ⟶	☐ North
Group by Department	☐ South
Column settings ›	☐ West
Totals ›	Apply Clear all

Check the boxes for the values you want to show and click on 'Apply'.

Uncheck boxes or click on 'Clear all' and then 'Apply' to remove the filter.

The **modern** experience also gives a possibility to filter multiple columns in an app at the same time, via the funnel icon in the right part of the command bar.

≡ All Items* ∨   ▽ ⓘ ↗

Filters   ▽ₓ ✕

Manager   ...

☐ 🔵 Kate Kalmström
☐ 🔵 Peter Kalmström

Staff   ...

☐ 15
☐ 50
☐ 200
See All

Department Name   ...

The images below show the **classic** experience. To the left is a Product column in the Quick Edit mode. Here you can select one of the values and sort the column by it. 'Clear Filter' will be active when the column is filtered.

The image to the right is from the Standard view mode. Here you can filter by more than one value, just as in the modern interface.

Product ▾

✎ Rename Column ⌃
A↓ Sort Ascending
Z↓ Sort Descending

  Clear Filter

  CB
  CB, TCWG
  FHD
  FHD, CB
  FHD, HOSP
  FHD, KBase

Product ▾

A↓ A on Top ⌃
Z↓ Z on Top

  Clear Filters from Product

☐ CB
☐ CB, TCWG
☐ FHD
☐ FHD, CB
☐ FHD, HOSP
☐ FHD, KBase

The **modern** Standard view mode also lets you group items. In the image to the right, the "Manager" column has been grouped, so there is an icon to the right of the column name. Click on the 'Group by' entry in the dropdown to remove the grouping.

Manager
A to Z
Z to A
Filter by
✓ Group by Manager

(It is possible to group items in the classic interface too, but then you need to create a grouped view in the List settings, *refer to* 7.9.8, Grouped View below.)

Note that there is no Grid view mode when you have grouped items, either you have done it in the modern interface or via the List settings.

The filter, sorting or grouping is dynamically added to the URL, so you can link directly to a specific filter or sort option. You can see this at the end of the URL. For example, "FilterField1%3D**Country**-FilterValue1%3D**Canada**" at the end of a URL shows that the Country column is filtered to only show items with the value Canada.

Demo:

https://www.kalmstrom.com//Tips/SharePoint-Online-Course/Categorization-Column-Filtering.htm

7.7.7   Edit List Columns

Columns can be edited in different ways, depending on if they are list columns or site columns. For list columns and for site columns that you want to use as list columns, you can use the methods described in the sections below. Also *refer to* Edit Site Columns below.

7.7.7.1   Edit via the List Settings

To edit a list column, open the List settings and find the Columns group.

Click on the column you want to edit, and the 'Edit Column' page for that column will open. Here you will have the same options as in the "Create Column" page, except for the full column type selection.

That is because switch of column type, can only be done under certain circumstances. For some column types it is not possible to switch type at all. Other column types give such a possibility, but you cannot switch to any other type. For example, you can switch from a Single line of text to a Choice column type, but not to a Person or Group-column type.

Columns

A column stores information

Column (click to edit)

Title

Created

Modified

Created By

Modified By

Checked Out To

128

You cannot change column type for the "Title" column. It must always be a Single line of text column. You can however rename this column and in many cases, it is highly recommended. Often the name "Title" is too generic.

7.7.7.2   Edit in the Modern Interface

In apps with the **modern** interface in Standard view mode, columns can be moved, hidden and edited in other ways directly from the dropdown at the column. Select first 'Column settings' and then the modification you want to perform.

Some options open an Edit column right pane, where you can make your changes. Options like 'Move' and 'Hide' are performed immediately.

7.7.7.3   Format a Modern Column

Apps with the **modern** interface have a possibility to format columns with data bars and conditional formatting via Column settings >Format this column, *see* the image above. You can also reach the column formatting options from the View selector, *refer to* 7.9.1, Modern App Views.

Number columns have the two options you can see in the image below, Data bars and Conditional formatting.

Date and Time columns have a Format dates option instead of Data bars.

Other column types only have the Conditional formatting option.

The column formatting will not be visible if you switch to the classic interface.

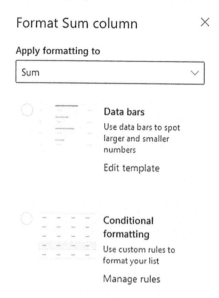

Format Sum column   X

Apply formatting to

Sum   ∨

Data bars

Use data bars to spot larger and smaller numbers

Edit template

Conditional formatting

Use custom rules to format your list

Manage rules

- The Data bars option can show different colors for positive and negative numbers, and the bar size adapts to the number value. You can also set a minimum and maximum number to format.

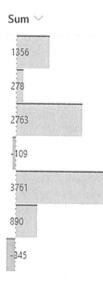

Sum ∨

1356

278

2763

-109

3761

890

-345

- The Conditional formatting option lets you create a rule – or a combination of rules. In the image below I have selected to mark all values greater than 1000 with green color.

In the Advanced mode, you can use JSON code for the formatting. That is out of scope for this book, but you can see some examples at https://docs.microsoft.com/en-us/sharepoint/dev/declarative-customization/column-formatting.

7.7.7.4 Rename a Column

You can rename all columns via the List settings. Just click on the column name to open the 'Edit Column' page and write another name in the 'Column name' field. Note that the internal name for the column will not be changed.

In **modern** apps, it is possible to rename columns directly in the app interface, via the column settings dropdown or in the Edit column right pane. I have however found that when I use Power Automate to create flows for a SharePoint app, new column names are only displayed in the flow's dynamic content if I rename the column in the List settings.

7.7.8 *Edit Site Columns*

Site columns can be edited as described above, that is, just like list columns. Site columns can also be edited at Site Settings >Site columns.

Which method you choose, depends on if you want to continue using the column as a site column or not:

- When a site column is added to an app, a copy is made of the column settings. When those column settings are edited as described in 'Edit the Column' sections above, the link to the site column is broken, and the edited column will become a list column instead.

- If you want to keep the column as a site column, you should go to Site Settings >Site columns and edit the column there. Now the changes will be propagated to all apps that use this column.

7.7.9   Edit Column Values

In the Grid view mode, you can edit the metadata of all app items by simply changing the values in the cells. In the Grid view mode, you can also drag a value in a cell down to the cells below, like you can do in Excel.

The metadata in app columns are often called properties, and properties is the word you should look for in the interface when you want to modify metadata in Standard view mode.

I will come back to item editing in the next two chapters, about list and library apps, but here I will just mention some ways that are available for all apps.

7.7.9.1   Edit Column Values in the Modern Interface

In the modern app interface, the properties can be edited in the Information pane. To open it, select the item and click on the information icon to the right in the command bar, or click on the item ellipsis and select 'Details'.

When the Information pane opens, click on 'Edit all' to edit the properties.

7.7.9.2   Edit Column Values in the Classic Interface

To reach the properties dialog in the **classic** library interface, select the item and click on 'Edit Properties' under the FILES tab in the ribbon.

Check Out

Check In

nt Discard Check Out

Open & Check Out

View Properties

Edit Properties

Man:

⊕ New   ⬆ Upload   ⟳ Sync

All Documents ⋯   Find a file

✓ ☐ Name

✓ 🔲 127-Site-Collection-Navigation

In list apps, Select the 'Edit Item' button in the ribbon instead.

7.7.9.3   Edit Multiple Items

There are two ways to edit multiple items at the same time. This is convenient when you want to give multiple items the same value in one or more columns.

- In the Grid/Quick edit view mode, drag the value in a cell down to the cells below, like you can do in Excel.

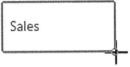

- The 'Edit' button in the **modern** command bar is visible when you select multiple items too. This means, that you can edit multiple items in the right pane. The values you enter in the right pane will be applied to all selected items.

All columns that can be edited in the app are displayed in the right pane when you select multiple items and click on 'Edit' in the command bar. Of course, you only need to add a value in one of them – or in those columns that you want to change. The other columns will keep their current values.

☐   5 items selected   ✕

Bulk edit properties

⩸ Enterprise Keywords

Type term to tag

🔡 Department

Enter value here

The bulk edit feature is especially useful if you cannot sort them in a way that makes it possible to drag down a value in the Grid view mode.

7.8   EDIT THE FORM

The **modern** interface gives a possibility to decide which columns are displayed in the app form – that is, which fields users see when they fill out the properties of an item.

1. The first step depends on if you want to modify the form in a list or library app:

   o In a library app, select an item and click on 'Properties' in the command bar (under the ellipsis).

   o In a list app, click on '+New'. (In most lists, you can also open the Information pane for a selected item and click on 'Edit columns' at the bottom of the pane. That takes you directly to step 3 below.)

2. Open the dropdown in the top right corner of the right pane and select 'Edit columns'.

(Configure layout is out of scope for this book, and Power Apps is covered in chapter 21.)

3. Uncheck the boxes for the columns you don't want to show in the form.

4. Move columns if needed, so that you get the fields in the preferred order.

5. Click on 'Save'.

Now all new and existing items will show only the checked columns as fields in the form, in the modern as well as in the classic interface.

Use views instead, *see* below, if you want to change how the columns are shown in the app interface.

7.9   VIEWS

All apps can show the data stored in the app in different views. A view is a permanent way to display app items and properties, as opposed to a temporary ad-hoc filtering or grouping.

Each view is a separate .aspx page that can be linked to, opened in a new tab, customized and so on.

There are two kinds of views: personal and public. The personal view is only shown to the person who created the view, while public views are shown to all users. The public view is the one we are referring to below.

The default view, created by SharePoint, is called "All Items" in lists, "All Documents" in libraries and "Calendar" in calendars. These are basic views that show all items in the app.

I would recommend that you create new views and arrange data in ways that suit your organization. When doing so, you should combine meaningful views with the use of columns for relevant metadata. This way the information can be sliced and diced in many ways, and your SharePoint apps will be very informative.

A view should not show more columns than necessary, but you can still use the columns you select to hide from the users in each view.

When you have many views for a list or library, you can create a Views landing page, *refer to* 13.8.

7.9.1   *Modern App Views*

In modern apps, you can find all views in the View selector to the right in the command bar. Only the name of the current view is displayed in the command bar. To see the other views, you must open the dropdown at the View selector.

Layout options:

Above the views, there are layout options. The 'List' option is default, but both list and library apps also have a 'Compact List' layout.

The third layout option is 'Gallery' in lists and 'Tiles' in libraries.

hidden under an ellipsis, where you also can find the links to modify the view and create a new view.

All Items	30DayDownloads	Big Four Datasheet	•••	Find an item

Big430Days

Modify this View

Create View

✓   Edit   DownloadDate   DownloadEmail

Demo:

https://www.kalmstrom.com/Tips/SharePoint-Online-Course/View-Intro.htm

7.9.3   *Edit a View*

These are the ways to start modifying an existing view:

- In the List settings, click on the view name under 'Views'.

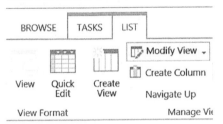

Views

A view of a document library allows you to see a particular selection of items or to see the items sorted in a particular order. Views currently configured for this document library:

View (click to edit)	Show In	Default View	Mobile View	Default Mobile View
All Documents	All	✓	✓	✓
Open Quotes	All		✓	
Quotes, Gantt	All			

- In a **modern** app, select 'Edit current view' in the View selector.

- In a **classic** app, click on the ellipsis after the view name(s) and select 'Modify this View', or click on the 'Modify View' button under the LIBRARY/LIST/CALENDAR tab.

BROWSE	TASKS	LIST

Modify View ▾

Create Column

View   Quick   Create
         Edit   View   Navigate Up

View Format   Manage Vie

In all cases, a new page will open where you can include/exclude and order columns, sort, filter and group the content and much more. (By default, the 'Columns', 'Sort' and 'Filter' sections are expanded when the page opens.)

▸ Edit View ⓘ

| OK | Cancel |

Name

Type a name for this view of the list. Make the name descriptive, such as 'Sorted by Author', so that site visitors will know what to expect when they click this link.

View Name:

All Items

Web address of this view:

https://m365x446726.sharepoint.com/sites /SalesAndMarketing/Lists/Product List/

All Items .aspx 🔊

This view appears by default when visitors follow a link to this list. If you want to delete this view, first make another view the default.

⊞ Columns

⊞ Sort

⊞ Filter

⊞ Tabular View

⊞ Group By

⊞ Totals

⊞ Style

⊞ Folders

⊞ Item Limit

⊞ Mobile

| OK | Cancel |

The image below shows the upper part of the 'Columns' section. Of course, the column names are different in each app, depending on app type and how the columns have been created and modified.

Check the box for the columns you wish to show in the view and put them in the preferred order.

When you change the order number of one column, the others will adapt automatically.

Display	Column Name	Position from Left
☑	Title (linked to item with edit menu)	1 ∨
☑	Code Name	2 ∨
☑	Product Line	3 ∨
☑	Product Type	4 ∨
☑	Color	5 ∨
☑	Notes	6 ∨
☑	Enterprise Keywords	7 ∨
☐	App Created By	8 ∨
☐	App Modified By	9 ∨
☐	Attachments	10 ∨

7.9.4   Create a New View

You can create new views in all SharePoint apps (except for the OneDrive for Business default library; *refer to* 12.2.1). You can either start from scratch or save a filtered or grouped view as a new view.

In the List settings, you can always click on the "Create View'" link under the list of existing views to create a new view from scratch. That will direct you to a 'View Type' Page, *see* below.

View (click to edit)

All Items

Entry

Grouped

No

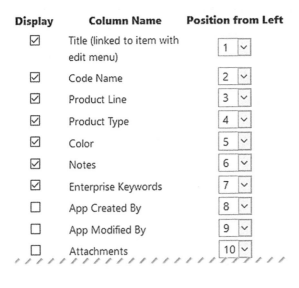

□ Create view

7.9.4.1   Modern "New View" Options

In an app with the modern interface, you can filter and group the 'All items' view, or any other suitable view, as you like and then open the View selector and select 'Save view as'. Give the view a new name, and it will be added to the View selector.

≡ All Items ∨   ▽   ⓘ

✓ ≡ List

Another modern option is to use the 'Create new view' link under the View selector. This opens a dialog with a choice to show the data in the default list view or in a calendar view.

Create new view

The 'List' option, works well in the classic experience too, and it can be edited from under 'Views' in the List settings, as described above.

Save view as

When you select to show the view as a calendar, you will have some options to fill out. SharePoint needs to know which dates should be the start and end

139

dates of the calendar and which column name should be displayed on the calendar "event".

The calendar view is of course most suitable for lists where you actually want to show dates, but it is possible to use it for all apps. The calendar view might be a modern alternative to the classic Calendar app, *refer to* 8.9, even if the classic Calendar app has more views and features adapted for a calendar.

The calendar option is very new when this is written, and the app data is only shown in a calendar if you use the modern interface.

Moreover, the calendar view cannot be edited under the List settings and sorted, filtered and so on. I get an error message when I try to save such modifications to the view.

7.9.4.2 Classic "New View" Options

In the classic app interface, you can create a new view by modifying an existing view and then clicking on 'SAVE THIS VIEW' above the list of items. Now you will be asked to give a name to the new view, and it will be saved.

To create a new view, click on the ellipsis to the left of the view name(s) and select "Create View'".

All Documents   ••• | Find a file

✓   🗋   Name   Modify this View

    Taxi ✳   Create View

There is also a "Create View'" button in the ribbon, under the LIBRARY/LIST/CALENDAR tab. In both cases, you will be directed to the View Type Page.

7.9.4.3 View Types

When you create a new view from the List settings or via the classic new view command, you will be directed to a View Type page. Here you can select what kind of view you want to create. You can also start from a view that already exists for the app and modify it.

Choose a view type

Standard View
View data on a Web page. You can choose from a list of display styles.

Datasheet View
View data in an editable spreadsheet format that is convenient for bulk editing and quick customization.

Calendar View
View data as a daily, weekly, or monthly calendar.

Gantt View
View list items in a Gantt chart to see a graphical representation of how a team's tasks relate over time.

Start from an existing view

▫ All Items
▫ Entry
▫ Grouped

When you choose one of the four view type options, a Create View page will open. It has similar options as in the Edit View page shown above, but it is a bit different for each view type.

When you modify an existing view by clicking on one of the views under 'Start from an existing view', the Create View page will also open, but with the settings from the selected view.

Classic sites also give an option to open SharePoint Designer and create a view there.

(There is also a Map View that requires a column of the type Geolocation, which is not displayed as an option by default. Instead, this column type must be added to SharePoint with a process that is out of scope for this book. Please *refer to* https://docs.microsoft.com/en-us/sharepoint/dev/general-development/how-to-add-a-geolocation-column-to-a-list-programmatically-in-sharepoint for more info.)

7.9.5   *Classic Views*

SharePoint has two classic views that are suitable when an app has dates that together describes a period of time: the Calendar view and the Gantt view.

The Calendar view:

The Gantt view:

Currently these two views look like they do above only in the classic experience, and that will create a problem when you open the Calendar or Gantt view from a view with the modern interface.

If you create a new Calendar or Gantt View, SharePoint creates a new page, with an URL that ends with the view name, like "Calendar.aspx". When you switch from another view to a classic view, SharePoint opens their pages.

When you switch from one view to another in the modern experience, SharePoint just adds the view ID to the 'All items' URL and renders the new view on same page, like "AllItems.aspx?viewid=2d0130a6-451a-45d1-9fea-5cfe88f08b77"

This means that SharePoint wants to use a view ID when you switch to a Calendar or Gantt view. What happens is that these views open like lists on the same page, without their special view characteristics. They look like any other view, but with only the columns included in the Calendar or Gantt view. You need to switch to the classic experience to see the views that I show in the images above.

To avoid this problem, you can set the app to use only the classic experience, under List settings >Advanced settings.

7.9.6 Calendar View

When you have dates information in an app , it is often easier to overview it in a Calendar view. This kind of view is also suitable for Tasks and Issue Tracking lists to visualize creation and due dates, *refer to* chapter 23, Issue Tracking Tips.

Create a new view from the List settings and select the Calendar View Type.

Specify what columns should be used for the dates in the calendar.

Specify what columns should be used as titles and sub headings. (Here, the item name is used as title and the quote value as sub heading. I hope you can see that in the calendar image above.)

⊟ Time Interval

Specify the columns used to place items in the calendar.

Begin:

    Quote Date   ∨

End:

    Decision Date   ∨

⊟ Calendar Columns

Specify columns to be represented in the Calendar Views. The Title fields are required fields. The Sub Heading fields are optional fields.

Month View Title:

    Name (for use in forms)   ∨

Week View Title:

    Name (for use in forms)   ∨

Week View Sub Heading:

    Quote Value   ∨

Day View Title:

    Name (for use in forms)   ∨

Day View Sub Heading:

    Quote Value   ∨

Make other settings as you prefer.

Note that even if you get a link to the calendar view in the other app views, there are no links to the other views in the Calendar view.

To leave the Calendar view, you must either click on the library in the Site navigation, use the browser's back arrow or open the ribbon and switch view there.

Demo:

https://kalmstrom.com/Tips/SharePoint-Online-Course/Quotes-Calendar.htm

7.9.7 Gantt View

A Gantt view is a type of bar chart that illustrates start and end dates.

Create a new view from the List settings and select the Gantt View Type.

Uncheck the 'Name' box and instead select the check box for 'Title' under 'Columns'. I have found that it works better that way.

Make other changes to what columns should be displayed as you prefer. It is often best to just have a few columns in the Gantt view.

Specify which columns should be Gantt columns.

⊟ Gantt Columns

Specify columns to be represented in the Gantt chart. Start Date and Due Date are required date fields. Title is a required text field. Percent Complete is an optional number field. If no fields appear in a list, they must be created to support this view.

Title:
Title

Start Date:
Quote Date

Due Date:
Decision Date

Percent Complete:
Optional

Predecessors:
Optional

Note that the "Name" column is not possible to select as Title. You must use the '"Title", which by default is empty in document libraries. This problem can be solved with a flow or workflow, *refer to* chapter 24, SharePoint Automation.

Demo:

https://kalmstrom.com/Tips/SharePoint-Online-Course/Quotes-Gantt.htm

7.9.8 *Default View*

When you make a custom view default, all users will reach that view first, regardless of how they open the app. Make a view default by checking the default box in the Create View/Edit View page.

View Name:
Sales Issues

☑ Make this the default view
(Applies to public views only)

If you check the default box for another view, that view will become default instead. If you just uncheck the box in the default view, the 'All documents' or 'All items' view will become default, as it was from the beginning.

In **modern** apps, you can also set the default view in the View Selector, as described above.

Demo:

https://www.kalmstrom.com/Tips/SharePoint-Online-Course/View-Default.htm

7.9.9   Grouped View

As we have seen above, the modern interface has a possibility to group items directly from the column dropdown. If you use the classic experience, or if you want a more advanced grouping, you should open the List settings and use the 'Group By' section in the Create View/Edit View page.

Click on the plus sign to expand the accordion. Here you can select what columns to group by on a first and second level and how data in them should be displayed.

The image below shows the default, before any grouping has been made. Not all types of columns can be used for grouping, so only columns suitable for grouping are shown in the dropdowns.

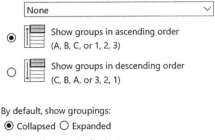

⊟ Group By

Select up to two columns to determine what type of group and subgroup the items in the view will be displayed in. Learn about grouping items.

First group by the column:

| None | ⌄ |

○ Show groups in ascending order (A, B, C, or 1, 2, 3)

○ Show groups in descending order (C, B, A, or 3, 2, 1)

Then group by the column:

| None | ⌄ |

○ Show groups in ascending order (A, B, C, or 1, 2, 3)

○ Show groups in descending order (C, B, A, or 3, 2, 1)

By default, show groupings:
◉ Collapsed ○ Expanded

Number of groups to display per page:
30

The Grid view mode does not work in grouped views, which might be a reason for not making a grouped view default.

Demo:

https://www.kalmstrom.com/Tips/SharePoint-Online-Course/View-Grouped.htm

7.9.10   Totals

The 'Totals' section in the Create View/Edit View page can be used to summarize the values in an app column. The feature works best on number and currency columns, somewhat less on text-based columns and not at all on Calculated and Multiple lines of text columns.

Computers

Title ∨	Hardware Cost ∨	Setup Cost ∨
Kalle's laptop	$500	$100
Stina's tablet	$400	$50
Bert's desktop	$800	$200
	Sum	Sum
	$1,700	$350

In number and currency columns, the SharePoint 'Totals' can calculate sum and other numeric values, like average, maximum and minimum. In columns of other types, the 'Totals' feature can be used to count the number of items in a column.

To add a Total to a column, scroll down to 'Totals' in the Create/Edit View page and click on the plus sign to expand the section. Select the value you want to calculate from the dropdown to the right of the column that should have the Total.

⊟ Totals

Select one or more totals to display.

Column Name	Total
Code Name	None ∨
Color	None ∨
Cost	None ∨
Notes	None
Product Line	Count
Product Type	Average
Title	Maximum
	Minimum
⊞ Style	Sum
⊞ Folders	Std Deviation
⊞ Item Limit	Variance

The result of the calculation is shown below (modern) or above (classic) the column that is calculated.

Totals can only be displayed in the Standard view mode. When this is written, the Total is not visible in the Grid view mode.

Demo:

https://www.kalmstrom.com//Tips/SharePoint-Online-Course/View-Total.htm

7.10   ALERTS

SharePoint apps have an alert feature that sends e-mail notifications on changes in the app. It is possible to set alerts for changes in single items and files. You can also set an alert for changes in a whole list or library.

The 'Alert Me' link can be found under the ellipsis in the modern command bar. The classic experience has buttons under the ITEMS and LIST tabs in the ribbon.

Both buttons have a 'Manage my alerts' option, where you can edit or stop the alert and reach other apps you have access to and set alerts for them.

Both interfaces also have 'Alert me' links for single items under the item ellipsis.

Each user can set and manage his/her own alerts. Site admins can also set alerts to be sent to other users and manage those alerts under Site Settings >Site Administration >User alerts.

The alerts can be somewhat customized, because you can decide at what time they should be sent and for what changes.

1. Change the title (= e-mail subject) if you don't want to use the default: app name (+ item).

2. If you are a Site administrator, add people who should get the alert.

3. If you have text messaging service set up, you can choose between having the alert by SMS or by e-mail. (This is not possible in all countries.) Otherwise e-mail is the only option.

4. Select at what changes you want to receive alerts.

5. Select when you want to receive alerts.

Only send me alerts when:

- ● All changes
- ○ New items are added
- ○ Existing items are modified
- ○ Items are deleted

Send me an alert when:

- ○ Anything changes
- ○ Someone else changes an item
- ○ Someone else changes an item created by me
- ○ Someone else changes an item last modified by me

- ● Send notification immediately
- ○ Send a daily summary
- ○ Send a weekly summary

Time:

6. Click OK.

You will now receive an e-mail confirming that your alert has been set up.

Demo:

https://kalmstrom.com/Tips/SharePoint-Online-Course/HelpDesk-Alerts.htm

To have customized notifications, you should create a flow or workflow, *refer to* chapter 24, SharePoint Automation.

7.11 DELETE CONTENT

User can delete and restore content that they have created. Site admins and owners can delete and restore other content too. Only apps and items can be restored – not columns and views.

7.11.1   *Delete an Item*

It is a bit easier to delete items in apps with the modern interface than it is in the classic, but in both experiences, you can delete an item via the item ellipsis when the app is in Standard view mode.

Open

Edit

Share

Get a link

Copy field to clipboard

Delete

7.11.1.1   Modern Experience

In apps with the modern interface, you can use the 'Delete' button in the command bar, in both Standard and Grid view. This option can be used for several selected items at the same time.

7.11.1.2   Classic Experience

The classic experience has a delete button under the ITEMS/FILES/EVENTS tab. Hold down the Shift or Ctrl key when you select the items, to select and delete several items at the same time.

In the Quick Edit mode, you can also select and delete several rows at a time:

1. Hold down the Ctrl or Shift key and click in the first cell to the left at the items you want to delete.

2. Right-click and click on Delete.

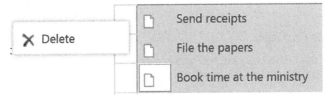

7.11.2   Delete a List Column

To delete a list column, open the List settings and find the list of columns. Click on the column you want to delete to open the 'Edit Column' page. Then click on the 'Delete' button at the bottom of the page.

Delete		OK		Cancel

In the modern interface, you can also open the column settings, *refer to 7.7.7, Edit a List Column*, and select 'Edit'. A right pane will open, and it has a 'Delete' button at the bottom.

Note that some default columns are required and cannot be deleted, for example the "Title" column in list apps. If you don't need such a column, you can rename it and use it for something else that requires the same column type. (The "Title" column is a Single line of text column.)

7.11.3   Delete a Site Column

Site columns are deleted from the place where they were created, that is in the site or in the Content Type Gallery. Open a content type that has the site column and delete the site column under its ellipsis. This will remove the column from this content type. Existing items in lists will not be affected, but new items will not have the deleted column.

7.11.4   Delete a View

The Delete button for views is found in the "Edit View'" page for views that are not default. If the view is default, you cannot delete it until you have set another view as default.

Settings › Edit View ⓘ

	Delete		OK		Cancel

Name

Type a name for this view of the list. Make the name descriptive, such as "Sorted by Author" so that site visitors will know what to expect when they click this link.

View Name:

Due Today	×

Web address of this view:

https://kalmstromnet.sharepoint.com/sites/kalmstrom.comdemos/Lists/KTM Tasks/

duetoday	.aspx

7.11.5   Delete an App

To delete an app, open the List settings and click on the link 'Delete this list' or 'Delete this document library' under the 'Permissions and Management' heading.

Permissions and Management

□ Delete this list

You can also open the Site contents, click on the ellipsis at the app you want to delete and select Delete.

In both cases, you will be asked to confirm that you want to delete the app.

7.11.6   *Restore Deleted Content*

Deleted apps and items are stored in the 'Recycle bin' library for 93 days. All users can see and restore content they have deleted themselves, and the Site admin can see and restore all deleted content.

🗑 Recycle bin (1)

Open the recycle bin from the Site navigation or the Site contents.

In the recycle bin, you can either restore the selected content or delete it. There is also a button to empty the recycle bin of all content.

🗑 Delete   ↺ Restore

If a larger number than usual of document library files are deleted within one hour, SharePoint will send an e-mail to the user who deleted them, with an option to restore the files.

7.11.6.1   Second-Stage Bin

Content that is deleted from the recycle bin, and content that has been in the recycle bin for 93 days, is not permanently deleted. Instead, it is moved to the second-stage recycle bin, where it is kept for another 93 days.

The link to the second-stage bin is found in the recycle bin page, but only the Site admin can see the link and restore or permanently delete content from the second-stage bin.

Can't find what you're looking for? Check the Second-stage recycle bin

7.12   VERSION HISTORY

The SharePoint Version history, or versioning, feature makes it possible to see and restore earlier versions of items in a list app and files in a library app. Version history is always set for the whole app, so that it applies to all the items contained in the app.

Version history is enabled by default when a new SharePoint document library is created. In other SharePoint apps the Version history is disabled by default, but I recommend that you make it a habit to always enable the Version history when you have created a new list app.

The versions do not have any effect on the number of items in the app, so you don't have to worry that you increase the number of items by enabling Version history.

General Settings

☐ List name, description and navigation

The Version history settings are managed in the List settings >Versioning settings.

☐ Versioning settings ◄——

☐ Advanced settings

7.12.1   *See Version History*

To see the version history, select the item, click on the item ellipsis and select 'Version history'.

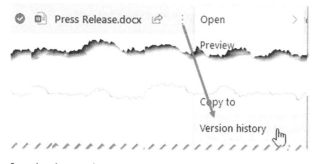

In calendars, select or open an event and click on the 'Version History' button under the EVENTS tab.

Other apps with the classic interface also have a 'Version History' button in the ribbon.

The Version history commands open a page that looks the same for library files and list items. Here, each version has a number and a date and time when the item was modified.

From the dropdown at the date, you can view the item properties, restore the item or delete it. (The current version cannot be deleted here.)

The image below shows the version history for a document that has six versions.

No. ↓   Modified

2.0   2019-03-03 21:57

     Title   tes'

1.0

   View

         tes'

   Restore   Ha

   Delete

Delete All Versions

No. ↓	Modified		Modified By
6.0	2016-03-30 08:38		Kate Kalmström
	Description	Update the slideshow for the new version	
	Comments	It looks fine now. Thanks!	
5.0	2016-03-29 14:10		Rituka Rimza
	Comments	I added two slides about TimeCard Mobile and one about the Summary web part. Please have a look.	
4.0	2016-03-29 11:53		Kate Kalmström
	Comments	Yes, you are right. Please add them.	
3.0	2016-03-29 11:36		Rituka Rimza
	Comments	Done. How about TimeCard Mobile? Shouldn't we have 1-2 slides for the app too?	
2.0	2016-03-26 17:35		Kate Kalmström
	Task Name	TimeCard for SharePoint Slideshow	
	Description	Update the slideshow for the new version	
	Start Date	2016-03-26	
	Responsible	Rituka	
	Project	Other	
	Comments	Remember to include one slide with the TimeCard Summary web part.	
1.0	2014-11-13 12:40		Sales, kalmstrom.com
	Task Name	Slideshow	
	Priority	(2) Normal	
	Status	Not Started	
	Description	Update the slideshow with new images	
	Start Date	2014-10-20	

7.12.2 *Version History in Library Apps*

Office, image and PDF files are opened in the earlier version when you click on the date and time on the Version History page in a document library. Files that cannot be opened are downloaded.

To see the properties of an earlier version, click on the arrow at the date and select 'View'.

When you open an earlier version of an Office file, it has a Restore button below the ribbon.

Word files can be both restored and compared to other versions.

These are the options and the default Version history settings for document libraries:

Create a version each time you edit a file in this document library?

◉ Create major versions
    Example: 1, 2, 3, 4

○ Create major and minor (draft) versions
    Example: 1.0, 1.1, 1.2, 2.0

Optionally limit the number of versions to retain:

☑ Keep the following number of major
    versions:

    500

☐ Keep drafts for the following number of
    major versions:

7.12.3 *Version History in List Apps*

When you click on the date and time on the Version History page in a list app, or if you select 'View' under the dropdown, the item properties are shown and the item can be directly restored or deleted.

These are the options and the default settings for Version history in list apps:

Create a version each time you edit an item in this list?
○ Yes   ◉ No
Optionally limit the number of versions to retain:
  ◌ Keep the following number of versions:

  ◌ Keep drafts for the following number of approved versions:

Demo:

https://www.kalmstrom.com/Tips/SharePoint-Online-Course/Version-History.htm

7.13   INTERNAL NAMES

As mentioned in 4.4.1. Naming New Content, SharePoint content can have different internal and user interface names. If you for example want to create a query in a flow, which we will do at the end of this book, you need to know the internal name.

You can see the internal names in the URL for an open app, for libraries after the site name and for list apps after /Lists/.

🔒 kalmstromnet.sharepoint.com/sites/ ·/Lists/Employees/,

To see the internal name for a column, open the app settings and then the column. The internal column name comes after Field=, last in the URL.

kalmstromnet.sharepoint.com/ &Field=Department

7.14   TEMPLATE OPTIONS

Sometimes you want to use an existing app as a template for a new app, instead of creating the new app from scratch. This can be done in different ways depending on what kind of site the original app is stored in and if the app is a list or a library.

Before you start using a new app that you have created from a template, remember to change any default column values that are set to suit the original site but maybe not the new one.

7.14.1   Create from Existing List

In homepages and Site contents with the **modern** interface, you can use existing list apps as templates for new apps via Microsoft Lists, *refer to 8.2.*

This option has both advantages and drawbacks:

- You can create new lists from lists in any site in the tenant.
- You can only create new lists from existing lists that you have access too.
- You cannot create a document library from another library.
- You cannot create a new list from a list that only has the classic interface, for example a Tasks list.

7.14.2   Save as Template

When you want to use a custom app several times, you can save it as a template. Then it will be available to select when you use the 'Add an app' command.

By default, apps can only be saved as templates in classic sites and modern Team sites without a group, but in those sites, both list and library apps can be saved as templates.

Permissions and Management

1. In theList settings, click on the link 'Save list as template' or 'Save document library as template' under the 'Permissions and Management' heading.

   - Delete this list
   - Save list as template
   - Permissions for this list

2. Give the template a file name, a template name and a description and save it. Most often you want to save the template without content, which is default.

3. A page with a success message and a link to the Templates gallery will be displayed. Click OK.

The template is stored as an STP file in the List Templates gallery of the site where you created it, and it will show up among the other app templates and be available for the site. To create a new list from the template, just add an app as described in section 7.4, Add an App, and select your template.

Demo:

https://kalmstrom.com/Tips/SharePoint-Online-Course/Content-Types-Library-Template.htm

7.14.2.1   Use a Template in Another Site

If you want to create an app from the template in another site, you can download the template from the List Templates gallery to your computer and then upload the template to the List Templates gallery in the other site.

Web Designer Galleries

Site columns

Site content types

Web parts

List templates

By default, you can find the List Templates gallery in the Site settings in classic sites and modern Team sites without a group. It is a kind of classic library.

Demo:

https://kalmstrom.com/Tips/SharePoint-Online-Course/SharePoint-Meetings-Upload-Templates.htm

7.15   PERMISSIONS

By default, apps and items inherit the same permissions as the site where they are created, but it is possible to set unique permissions on both apps and items. Here I will only mention the permissions shortly, because you will have more info in chapter 14, Permissions and Sharing.

7.15.1   *Reach the Permissions Pages for Apps*

Apps have a link to their permissions page in the List settings >'Permissions for this list/document library'.

Permissions and Management

□ Permissions for this list

7.15.2   *Reach the Permissions Pages for Items*

To manage the permissions for a single item in an app with the **modern** interface, click on the item ellipsis and select 'Manage access'. Now a right pane opens where you can see and edit all permissions for the item.

For the **classic** interface, select 'Share' under the item ellipsis and then 'Shared with' in the dialog that opens.

7.16   SUMMARY

With this chapter, I wanted to give an overview on how you can create and edit SharePoint apps and use them to share information in an efficient and user-friendly way. You have also learned how to use existing apps as templates.

I hope you now understand how important it is to create suitable columns for metadata in apps and how you can filter and sort data in various ways and create different views. You should also know how to use versioning and alerts and how to delete and restore SharePoint apps.

There is more to learn about SharePoint apps. In this chapter, I have not included the 'Automate' button and the Approvals feature that is only available in the modern experience. It is described in chapter 24, SharePoint Automation.

Another SharePoint feature that will be explained later in the book is the content type, which I have only mentioned briefly in this chapter. With content types, you can help users create library and list items with a consistent look and valuable metadata.

In the next chapter, we will take a closer look at the features that are specific for list apps. I will also describe two app types that are a bit different: the Tasks list and the Calendar.

8   List Apps

In the previous chapter, we looked at features that are common for all SharePoint Online apps. Now, we will go into features that only exist in list apps, and in the next chapter, we will do the same with library apps.

The main difference between list apps and library apps is that you use library apps to store and share files. List apps are used to store and share other data (even if you can attach files to them), for example data about departments, issues, staff or tasks.

When new list items are created, metadata info is added to fields in a form. Each field represent a column. When the form is saved, the values added to the form fields are displayed under the column headings in the app interface.

In this chapter, we will have a look at the modern and classic list experience, and I will describe the new Microsoft 365 app for lists. I will also show how to use the 'List' command to create list items, and I will introduce two classic lists that have special features: the Tasks list and the Calendar.

8.1   List Experiences

As you know, most apps can have two interfaces, modern and classic. A notable exception is lists built on the Tasks template, which only can be used with the classic experience.

Here, I will describe how the upper part of a list app can look and work in the two experiences.

8.1.1   Modern List Experience

The buttons in the modern experience command bar varies depending on the selection in the list of items below, so that only relevant buttons are shown to the users.

The image below shows the modern command bar in Standard view mode. The Grid view looks the same, except that 'Edit in grid view' is replaced by 'Exit grid view'.

8.1.1.1   No Item Selected

When no item has been selected in the list, the command bar shows buttons to create new items, edit the list in grid view, share the list, export the list to Excel, create a powerapp from the list or create a flow that automates a process in the list.

Under the ellipsis, you can find the controls for alerts on the list, *refer to* 7.10, Alerts.

159

The '+ New' button opens a right pane where you can fill out metadata, or values, in the different column fields of the new item.

The 'Edit columns' command in the 'New item' right pane, lets you hide and show columns in the form, while the Power Apps entry here helps you customize the list form in Power Apps.

I will come back to the 'Share' command as well as Power Apps and automation in later chapters.

8.1.1.2 One Item Selected

When one item has been selected, the command bar has no 'Export to Excel' or 'Power Apps' commands.

Instead, there are new commands for Edit, Copy link, Comment and Delete, and under the ellipsis we can now also find a command for Version history, if that has been enabled for the list.

The 'Edit' command opens a right pane where the values in the various columns can be edited. To the right of the edit form, there is a comments field, *refer to* 8.6.1.1, Comments.

8.1.1.3 Multiple Items Selected

When multiple items have been selected, there are only commands for Edit, Edit in grid view and Delete.

Note that the 'Edit' option is still visible. This means that you can edit multiple items at the same time, which is convenient when you want to give multiple items the same value in one or more columns. The values you enter in the right pane will be applied to all selected items.

8.1.2 Classic List Experience

The classic experience has a ribbon with three tabs: BROWSE, ITEMS and LIST. The 'BROWSE' tab shows no ribbon buttons, but 'ITEMS' and 'LIST' show all available commands even if some of them are greyed out.

When the 'ITEMS' tab is selected, you can recognize some of the commands from the modern interface.

Declare Record, Workflows and Approve/Reject can be found under the item ellipsis in the modern interface, while attachments are added in the right Edit pane in the modern lists.

BROWSE	ITEMS	LIST

New Item ▾	New Folder		View Item	Edit Item	Declare Record	Version History / Shared With / Delete Item	Attach File	Alert Me ▾	Tags & Notes	Workflows	Approve/Reject
New					Manage		Actions	Share & Track	Tags and Notes	Workflows	

Under the LISTS tab, most of the other commands are displayed, among them the List settings.

Here you can find 'Export to Excel' but also some other features that cannot be found at all in the modern interface. They connect SharePoint lists to various other platforms and can only be used with lists that do not have the option to be displayed in the modern interface. I will come back to these features later in the book.

BROWSE	ITEMS	LIST

View	Quick Edit	Create View	Modify View ▾ Current View: / Create Column All Items / Navigate Up Current Page	Tags & Notes	E-mail a Link	Alert Me ▾	RSS Feed	Connect to Outlook	Export to Excel	Open with Access / Open with Project	Customize in InfoPath	Form Web Parts ▾ / Edit List New Quick Step	List Settings	Shared With	Workflow Settings ▾
View Format			Manage Views	Tags and Notes		Share & Track		Connect & Export				Customize List		Settings	

Below the ribbon, the classic interface has commands for new item and edit this list, which opens the Quick Edit/Grid view mode.

⊕ new item or edit this list

All Items   ••• | Find an item 🔍 |

Here you can also find the views and a search box for the list. Up to three views can be displayed to the left of the search box. If there are more views, they are found under the ellipsis, from where you also can modify the view and create a new view.

8.2   MICROSOFT LISTS

The Microsoft Lists app is part of the SharePoint based OneDrive for Business service, that each 365 user has access to for personal use.

You can open Lists via the App Launcher in the top right corner of all Microsoft 365 apps. There is also a mobile app, currently only for iOS.

In Microsoft Lists, each user can find all lists in the tenant that he/she has access to and has used recently – except for lists that only have the classic interface. There is a limit on 100 lists, and I have found that "recent" can be six months back if that limit is not exceeded.

The lists can be opened directly in Microsoft Lists, and except for the possibility to show the classic interface they have the same functionality as in SharePoint.

In Microsoft Lists, users can also create new list apps and add them to any site they have access to. The "new list" options from Microsoft Lists are also found within SharePoint, *see* below.

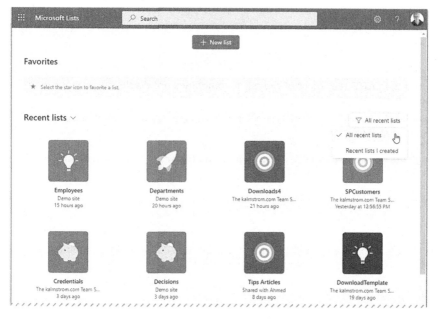

8.2.1   *New List*

When users click on the '+ New list' button in Microsoft Lists, users can create new list apps and add them to any site they have access to. There are four options for the creation: a blank list, a list from an Excel file, a list created from an existing list and a list created from a template.

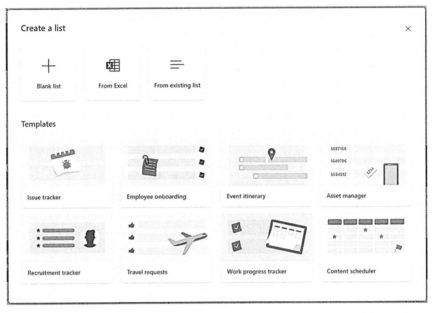

Common for all options is that you can save the list to any site that you have access to, but the default option is to save the new list in Microsoft Lists and use it as a personal app. These personal lists are stored in the user's OneDrive for Business and only displayed in Microsoft Lists.

The new list will open after creation, and when you have added it to a site it will have a link to the site above the list name.

8.2.1.1 Blank list

When you select the 'Blank list' option, a custom list with only a "Title" column will be created in the site you select, or in the default 'My lists'.

You will have a possibility to select a theme color and icon for the list, in addition to giving it a name and a description.

Note that when the list app is added to a site in a hub family, the hub theme will override the list theme.

Name *   ✕

Ideas
_____

Description

What is your list about?
_____

Choose a color

[■] [■] [■] [■] [■] [■] [✓] [■] [■] [■]

Choose an icon

🐞 📅 ◎ 📋 ✈ 🚀 🎨 💡 📦 ⚗ 🤖 🐷

Save to *

┌───┐
│ 🏠   My lists   ⌄ │
└───┘

‹ Back   [Create]   [Cancel]

8.2.1.2   From Excel

Before you create a list from data in an Excel file, I recommend that you
format the data you want to use as a table with no empty rows or columns.
That will make the list creation easy.

The Excel file can be uploaded from your computer or selected from
OneDrive for Business. I have found that selection from OneDrive for
Business works very well, while uploading from the computer has given
errors. This feature is very new when this is written, and it probably has
some bugs.

After upload/selection of the file, you will have a possibility to change table –
in case the file has multiple tables – and column types. You can also select to
not include a column.

Customize

Select a table from this file.

| Products | ⌄ |

Check the column types below and choose a new type if the current selection is incorrect.

Title ⌄	Single line of text ⌄	Single line of text ⌄	Number ⌄
ProductCategory	ProductName	Color	Number
			Currency
Bib-Shorts	Men's Bib-Shorts, L	Multi	Date and time
			Single line of text
Bib-Shorts	Men's Bib-Shorts, M	Multi	Multiple lines of text
			Choice
			Title
Bib-Shorts	Men's Bib-Shorts, S	Multi	Do not import

⟨ Back   [Next] [Cancel]

When you click on 'Next' you will have the same options as when you create a list from blank.

Note that the new list is independent from Excel. There is no synchronization, so changes in one of the apps are not reflected in the other app. *Refer to* 22.2, Connect SharePoint and Excel, if you need updates to be displayed in both apps.

8.2.1.3   From Existing List

When you create a list from an existing list, you can create a new list from any list that can have the modern interface and that you have access to. The new list will have the same columns, views and formatting as the original list.

Select an existing list   ✕

Select a list to use as a template for a new empty list on this site.

Columns, views and formatting will copy over to the new list.

Select a Team or site	Choose a list from Contoso

	Contoso		Name	Type	Last modified
	Contoso Brand	⊘	Content and Structure Reports	List	1/8/2021 6:33 AM
	Contoso News	◯	Marketing	List	11/21/2020 9:25 AM
	Contoso Works	◯	Reusable Content	List	1/8/2021 6:34 AM

Select first site and then list app. When you have selected a list to create a new list from, you will have the same options as when you create a blank list.

8.2.1.4   From Template

Microsoft Lists gives some templates that you can create new lists from, but not at all as many templates as the "Your Apps" page. However, all the Lists templates take advantage of the 'Format this column' feature, which is not the case with the templates you can create from the "Your Apps" page.

When you click on a template, a preview will open. If you change your mind after seeing the preview, you can select another template in the menu to the left.

When you click on 'Use template', you will have the same options as when you create a blank list, but the new list will of course have all the columns, views and formatting of the template.

8.2.2   *Views and Filters*

The default view option in Microsoft Lists is to show 'Recent lists' in the selector to the left. The other option, 'My lists' only shows personal lists.

If 'Recent lists' is selected, the lists can be filtered to show all recently used list and lists that the user created recently.

If 'My lists' is selected, the lists can be filtered alphabetically or by created time.

8.2.3 Tile Options

When you hover the mouse cursor over a list icon in Microsoft Lists, a star and an ellipsis become visible on the tile.

Click on the star to add the list to the Favorites section on top of Microsoft Lists.

Via the ellipsis, you can modify the list's color and icon and change the list name, and you can also share the list.

In the 'Recent list' view, the ellipsis on each tile gives the option to remove the list from the recent lists.

In the 'My lists' view, the option is instead to delete the list.

Decisions
Demo site
13 hours ago

···

Customize

Share

Remove from recent lists

8.3 CREATE A LIST

You can always create a new list with the 'Add an app' command that I described in the previous chapter. I also mentioned that you can click on the 'New' button in a modern SharePoint homepage or Site contents and select 'App', to be directed to the same "Your Apps" page as when you select 'Add an app' under the 365 Settings icon.

Here, we will have a look at another option to create a list, that makes use of Microsoft Lists.

The 'New' button in a modern SharePoint homepage or Site contents also gives the option 'List'. When you click on the 'List' link, you will be directed to a limited version of Microsoft Lists.

You cannot see all your other lists here, but you will have the same four list creation options as in the full version:

+ New ∨

List

Page

Document library

App

Subsite

- a blank list
- a list from an Excel file
- a list created from an existing list
- a list created from a template.

The new list will be created in the current site, and it will open after creation. By default, a link to the app is added to the site's Site navigation.

The 'from blank' dialog gives less options than if you create the list from within Microsoft Lists.

Name *	×

Phone Messages

Description

What is your list about?

Site navigation

☑ Show in site navigation

< Back   [Create] [Cancel]

8.4   CREATE A NEW LIST ITEM

There are several ways to create a new item in a list, depending on what which interface and mode you are using.

8.4.1   Standard Mode

To create a new item in Standard view mode, click on the '+New' button in the command bar (modern) or above the list of items (classic).

+ New   ⊕ new item

8.4.2   Quick Edit Mode

Lists in Grid/Quick Edit mode have a blank row at the bottom. Here, you can create a new item by entering or selecting values for each column.

	Testing environment on VM. ...	Russian
		▼

In the **modern** interface, this last row is marked with '+ Add new item', and when you click in it, the cells become visible.

The modern Grid also has a '+New' button in the command bar, just like in the Standard view mode.

The **classic** SharePoint interface has a "New" button in the left corner of the 'Items' tab in both view modes.

8.4.3   *Mandatory Title*

When you create a new item in a list app, a form will be displayed, where you can fill out metadata. The "Title" field is by default mandatory in list items, so list items cannot be saved until a "Title" value has been filled out.

You can very well rename the "Title" column to give it a more descriptive name.

8.5   VIEW LIST ITEMS

To view an item, click on the value in the "Title" column in Standard view mode. This value gets underlined when you hover the mouse cursor over it, and normally it is found in the column far to the left.

8.6   EDIT LIST ITEMS

When a list item is created, the metadata info is added to a form. To edit the data in such a form, you can open the item and then select to edit the item. This can be done in both interfaces.

You can also click on the ellipsis at the item you want to edit and select 'Edit' (modern) or 'Edit Item' (classic). In the modern interface, you can also select 'Details' and then 'Edit all' at 'Properties' in the right pane.

Both interfaces also have edit buttons in the command bar (modern) or in the ribbon (classic) that you can click on after selecting the item you want to edit.

In the Grid/Quick edit view mode, you can edit the metadata of all app items by simply changing the values in the cells.

8.6.1   *Modern List Interface*

In **modern** lists, the 'Edit' button in the command bar opens a right pane where the list form is placed to the left and a 'Comments' panel to the right. The 'Comments' panel is open by default, but you can hide it by clicking on the comment icon above the 'Comments' field.

Warehouse 1   Comments ∨

🔲 Content Type   Add a comment

Rental Agreement   ∨

🔤 Location Name *

Warehouse 1

ⓘ Square Meters

2,000

🗓 Start Date

12/1/2019   🗓

Be the first one to add a comment

Instead of comments, you can open the dropdown at 'Comments' and select to show all activity for the item.

Comments ∨

　　All activity 🖑

✓　Comments

8.6.1.1　　Comments

The comment icon in the command bar opens the same Edit item pane as shown in the image above, but the form is not in edit mode. Instead of the 'Save' button, there is an 'Edit all' button.

The comment icon is also displayed to the right of the first column in a selected item. If there is a comment on the item, the icon has three  dots. If there is no comment, the icon is empty and has a plus sign. When you click on the icon, the same right pane opens as when you click on the 'Comment' button in the command bar.

If you need formatting, you can instead use a Multiple lines of text "Comment" column with the feature 'Append changes to existing text' *see* below. With that option, you can however not see from the icon on the selected item that the item has a comment.

8.7　　THE MULTI-LINE COLUMN

The column type Multiple lines of text (also called "multi-line column") has some features that are only available in list apps: rich text and append changes to existing text.

When you combine these two features, you can have a comments field with formatting that you can use instead of the 'Comment' command described above in 8.6.1.1. It gives you formatting, but you cannot see in the app interface if the item has a comment or not.

8.7.1   Rich Text

When rich text is enabled in the 'Multiple lines of text' column, it is possible to add formatting, tables, hyperlinks and images to the field when you create or edit the item.

In the **modern** interface, a pen icon to the right of the column name in the edit pane shows that rich text is enabled.

☰ Description   🖉

When you click on the pen icon, a new right pane will open where you can format the text.

Edit Description   ✕

| Calibri   ∨ | 11 ∨ | ■ A ∨ | ☐▽∨ | **B** | *I* | U̲ | ⋯ |

☰ Alignment   >

☰ List   >

ↄ Add or edit hyperlink

→☰ Increase indent

←☰ Decrease indent

✎ Clear format

🖾 Insert image

Save   Cancel

Return to classic experience

Should you need more options, click on the link to the classic experience. That opens yet another right pane, and when you click in the text field more options will open in the ribbon.

In the **classic** interface, a ribbon with rich text controls opens when you click in a rich text field.

Remember to save your changes, under the EDIT tab in the classic ribbon or with the button at the bottom of the modern pane.

If the rich text feature is enabled by default or not depends on how you create the column:

More options ∨

- When you create a multi-line column from the '+ Add column' command in the modern interface, rich text is not enabled by default, but you can enable it under 'More options'.

Use enhanced rich text (Rich text with pictures, tables, and hyperlinks)

(⚫) No

- When you create a multi-line column from the List settings 'Create column' dialog, rich text is enabled by default. If you only want users to add plain text, you must change the setting.

Specify the type of text to allow:

○ Plain text

◉ Enhanced rich text (Rich text with pictures, tables, and hyperlinks)

8.7.2   *Append Changes to Existing Text*

In list apps, columns of the type 'Multiple lines of text' have a feature called 'Append changes to existing text'. It reminds of the Version history feature described in 7.11, and to use this feature you must first enable Version history in the list.

There is however an important difference between Version history and Append changes: you cannot see the version history when you open an item – you must open the Version history to see it.

If you want to see the history for a 'Multiple lines of text' column as soon as you open the item, you should enable the 'Append changes to existing text' for that column. When you do that, all changes are shown as a thread in the 'Multiple lines of text' field.

The earlier text cannot be changed, but new text is shown above the earlier text in the field. The image below shows the same item as in the Version history section, *see* 7.12, but here comments from different versions are shown in the "Comments" field (which is of the type 'Multiple lines of text') as a part of the open item.

Comments   ☐ Kate Kalmström (2016-03-30 08:38):

It looks fine now. Thanks!

☐ Rituka Rimza (2016-03-29 14:10):

I added two slides about TimeCard Mobile and one about the Summary web part. Please have a look.

☐ Kate Kalmström (2016-03-29 11:53):

Yes, you are right. Please add them.

☐ Rituka Rimza (2016-03-29 11:36):

Done. How about TimeCard Mobile? Shouldn't we have 1-2 slides for the app too?

☐ Kate Kalmström (2016-03-26 17:35):

Remember to include one slide with the TimeCard Summary web part.

The Append feature is especially useful for discussions and issue tracking. It is only available for 'Multiple lines of text' columns in list apps.

8.7.2.1   Enable Append

To enable the Append feature, you need to edit the column where you want to append changes.

In the List settings, open the column and select the 'Yes' radio button for 'Append changes to existing text'.

Append Changes to Existing Text
◉ Yes   ○ No

In the **modern** experience, you can also edit the column directly from the list interface and set the toggler to 'Yes' under 'More options' in the right pane.

More options

Use enhanced rich text (Rich text with pictures, tables, and hyperlinks)
 Yes

Append changes to existing text
 Yes

Demo:

https://www.kalmstrom.com/Tips/SharePoint-Online-Course/Append-Changes-to-Existing-Text.htm

8.8 TASKS AND ISSUE TRACKING

When you create a list that builds on the Tasks list template, the new list has some special features:

- A timeline above the list of tasks.

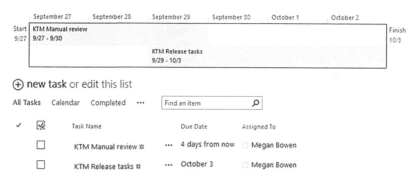

- Time related commands in a TIMELINE tab in the ribbon. Click on the timeline to show this tab.

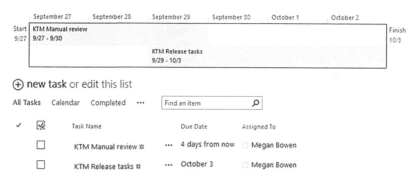

- A TASKS tab instead of the ITEMS tab.

- The default view is called 'All tasks'.

When this is written, the Tasks list can only be used with the classic experience, and because of that, it can only be created from the "Your Apps" page.

If you want to use the modern interface, I recommend the Issue tracker or Work progress tracker template instead. These templates are available in Microsoft Lists. You should be aware, though, that they don't have a timeline and not as many other task tracking features as the Tasks list.

8.8.1 Tasks and Issues Alerts

SharePoint lists that build on the Tasks and Issue Tracking templates have two alert possibilities that are not present in other apps:

- The Alert settings has a view selector under "Send me an alert when'.

  ◉ Someone changes an item that appears in the following view:

  | My Issues ▼ |

- Under 'Advanced settings' in the List settings there is a choice to send an e-mail to the person to whom a task is assigned. The default value is 'No'.

E-Mail Notification

Send e-mail when ownership is assigned or when an item has been changed.

Send e-mail when ownership is assigned?

○ Yes ● No

Demo:

https://kalmstrom.com/Tips/SharePoint-Online-Course/HelpDesk-Email-Notification.htm

8.9   CALENDAR

The calendar is a list type that has its own, classic interface. Use a SharePoint calendar to share event information like holidays, leaves, delivery dates and other information that is of common interest to the users who have access to the calendar.

A very common question is how SharePoint calendars relate/connect/interact with Outlook calendars. The short answer is that they do not. They are stored in totally different places, and SharePoint calendars lack a range of important features that Outlook calendars have, such as invites, reminders and integration with Microsoft Teams.

On the other hand, the SharePoint Calendar app has more features than the calendar list view that I described in section 7.9.4.1, Modern "New View" Options.

To create a SharePoint calendar, add an app built on the Calendar template from the "Your Apps" page.

8.9.1   Calendar Views

By default, a calendar list displays a "Calendar" view that shows all events in a calendar-like interface. The "Calendar" view can display the events for a Day, Week or Month.

In the "Calendar" view, you can switch between periods with arrows.

There are two more built-in views, "All Events" and "Current Events". Both these views show the events in the classic SharePoint list interface. These views are suitable for editing of many events at the same time, as they have the 'Quick Edit' button that is missing in the "Calendar" view.

You can create more views in the same way as for other apps, and when you do that, you are given the "Calendar" view as one of the options.

8.9.2 Create a New Event

In the default "Calendar" view, new events are created with a '+ Add' link that is displayed when you hover the mouse cursor over a calendar date in the Month view or over an hour section in the Week and Day views.

You can also use the 'New Event' button under the EVENTS tab in the ribbon.

In other views than the calendar views, new items are created like in other classic lists.

8.9.3 Edit an Event

Use the 'Edit Event' button in the ribbon to open a selected event in edit mode.

You can also double-click on the event to open it and then click on the 'Edit Item' in the ribbon of the open event.

8.9.4 See Multiple Calendars in One

With the Calendar overlay feature you can merge multiple calendars and display all the events in one single view. All calendars must be in the same site, except if you use the Exchange option and add your own Outlook calendar to a calendar overlay.

176

1. Open one of the calendars.
2. Click on 'Calendars Overlay' under the CALENDAR tab.

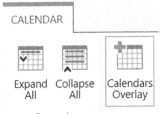

CALENDAR

Expand All   Collapse All   Calendars Overlay

3. Add another calendar to the Calendars Overlay:

   a. Click on 'New Calendar'.

Settings ▸

🖼 New Calendar

   b. Fill out the Calendar name.
   c. In this example, we keep the SharePoint option.
   d. Select color.

e. The site URL should be filled out automatically. Click on 'Resolve'.

f. Select the calendar and the calendar view from the dropdowns.

g. Check 'Always show' if you want the overlay calendar to always be shown. If you not check the box, you will be able to turn different overlay calendars on and off.

h. Click OK.

‹ Calendar Overlay Settings ⓘ

Name and Type

Type a name for this calendar, and select the type of calendar you want to store in the view.

Calendar Name:

USA

The type of calendar is:

◉ SharePoint
◯ Exchange

Calendar Overlay Settings

Specify detailed options for the type of information you selected.

Description:

Color:

Red, #ed0033 ⌄

Web URL:

https://m365x446726.sharepoint.com/sites/   Resolve

List:

USA ⌄

List View:

Calendar ⌄

☑ Always show

Delete   OK   Cancel

When you select to overlay your personal Exchange calendar, you need to give the Outlook Web Access UR and the Exchange Web Service URL.

8.10   SUMMARY

In this chapter, we have studied some features that are specific for list apps. You have been introduced to Microsoft Lists, and you know how to create a list app with the 'List' command.

SharePoint lists also can be created with a PowerShell script. How to do that is described in my book *PowerShell with SharePoint from Scratch*, but it is out of scope for this book.

On the kalmstrom.com website there is a tool that helps you create a list using PowerShell. You can use this tool even if you don't know how to write

PowerShell scripts. Please *refer to*: https://www.kalmstrom.com/Tools/PnP-enerator.html

In this chapter, I have also described how to create and manage list items, and I have introduced the list features 'Rich text' and 'Append to existing text'. Finally, we looked at a few lists with special features: Tasks, Issue Tracking and Calendar.

We will come back to Tasks and Issue Tracking lists in chapter 23, but now it is time to have a look at the library apps.

9 LIBRARY APPS

A SharePoint library is an app with some unique qualities and features, and in this chapter, we will have a look at these.

What distinguishes libraries from other apps, is that each library item has a column that contains a file, and the other columns has metadata related to that file.

Some of the columns are built-in, such as 'Created' and 'Modified By', and their metadata is filled out automatically. You can also create your own, custom columns.

There are several types of SharePoint libraries, for example:

- Document libraries, mostly used for Office documents but can be used for other files as well
- Form libraries, used for forms
- Page libraries, used for custom SharePoint pages
- Picture libraries. used for images

These and more library types can be created from the "Your Apps" page.

8 apps match your search   Newest   Name

Record Library
App Details

Document Library
App Details

Form Library
App Details

Wiki Page Library
App Details

Picture Library
App Details

Asset Library
App Details

Data Connection Library
App Details

Report Library
App Details

As we saw in section 6.12.1, Auto-Created Apps, a document library called "Documents" is created automatically when a new site is created, along with some other libraries.

Here, I will focus on SharePoint document libraries, and when I write "library" in this book, I refer to a document library if nothing else is mentioned.

In this chapter, I will explain why using SharePoint document libraries is a good way to store and share information. You will also learn how to:

- Create content directly in document libraries
- Upload files to document libraries in various ways
- Use – or rather not use! – folders
- Check out and check in documents
- Manage file properties
- Copy and move files
- Use Word Online and OneNote
- Create a Word template for a document library

9.1   WHY DOCUMENT LIBRARIES?

Document libraries are often the best way to share files within an organization, and it is certainly much better than sending e-mail attachments. When you use SharePoint document libraries for file sharing you have everything in one place, and all who have been given permission can reach the files.

A SharePoint document library is however more than a place for file storage and sharing – it is also a place where you can work with the files and even create new files.

I would recommend that you use many document libraries, as a way of categorizing files. For example, if your site is made for sharing information about a new product, you could have these libraries:

- Suggested Specifications
- Supplier Contracts
- Design Sketches
- Radio Commercials

In these libraries you would of course have files. Those files are sometimes referred to as documents in the SharePoint user interface. You can download files from a document library to your computer and vice versa.

9.2   LIBRARY UNIQUE FEATURES

When you click on the ellipsis to the right of the file name in a document library in Standard view mode, you will have many options for what to do with the file.

You can work with the file online or open it in a desktop application. You can also download the file, share it, rename it and much more.

The most used of these options are also displayed in the modern command bar and in the classic ribbon.

SharePoint document libraries have the same features as lists, like alerts, Version history and filtering, but libraries also have some specific features that I will describe below.

Document libraries can be used with both the modern and the classic interface. I will show the library unique features with images from the modern experience, because some of these features are only available there. I will mention which ones they are.

Most of these library specific commands affect the file that is stored in the library item – not the whole item.

There are no specific library commands when multiple items are selected.

9.2.1   No Item Selected

When no item is selected in the library, the command bar has three specific buttons, in addition to the buttons that are available in all apps:

$\bar{\top}$ Upload $\vee$ ⁝ $\widehat{\mathbb{G}}$ Sync $\widehat{\mathbb{G}}$ Add shortcut to OneDrive

- Upload, for uploading files to the library. A new item for the file will be created automatically.

- Sync, to synchronize the library files with a folder on your computer.

- Add shortcut to OneDrive, to add a shortcut to this library in the left menu of your default OneDrive for Business library, *refer to* 12.2.1. This button is only available in the modern experience.

We will come back to all these features later in the book.

9.2.2   One Item Selected

When one item is selected, there are more library specific features. We will come back to most of them later.

| ⊞ Open ∨ | ↓ Download | ⊡ Pin to top | ⊡ Rename | ⊡ Move to | ⎙ Copy to | ⋯ |

Document   ⌀ Properties

                                                                           ⬚ Version history

✔ ▯   :ified ∨   Modified By   column ∨   ⏰ Alert me

✔ ⊞ l.docx ⇧   :'s ago   MOD Administr   ⬚ Manage my alerts

                                                               ⬊ Check out

- Open the file. Office files have two options: open in the desktop app or open in the browser. This button is not visible for all file types.

- Download the file to your computer.

- Pin a thumbnail of the file or folder above the list of items. This feature is only available in the modern experience.

182

Documents

| Local Resource Guide.docx | Employee Sentiment Analysis.xlsx | Product info |
| July 31 | November 3 | About a minute ago |

☐	Name ⌄		Modified ⌄	Modified By ⌄	Titles from Na...
📄	⤴Product info		About a minute ago	MOD Administrator	Stage 1

When an item has been pinned, the command is changed into 'Edit pin' when the same item is selected again. Now you can unpin or change the position of the pin.

- Rename, opens a dialog where you can give the file a new name. This feature is only available in the modern experience.

- Move to, moves the item into or out of a subfolder in the current library, to another library that you have access to or to your OneDrive for Business. This feature is only available in the modern experience.

- Copy to, copies the item to a subfolder in the current library, to another library that you have access to or to your OneDrive for Business. This feature is only available in the modern experience.

- Properties, opens a right pane that shows the values in all columns and gives the option to edit them. In the classic experience, use the 'Edit Properties' button in the ribbon for this.

- Check out a file when you don't want other users to see your changes, or you don't want the changes to be visible in the version history yet.

9.2.3   *Other Unique Features*

When you hover the mouse cursor over the file name in a document library with the **modern** interface, a tile will be visible. It shows the share icon and a 'See details' link that opens the file's Information pane. Several file types also have views information.

When the file is an Office file, there is an 'Inside look' section with information about average reading time for the document and a part of the text.

The **classic** library interface gives different results when you click on the ellipsis at a selected item.

Right-click gives a dropdown similar to the one in lists and the modern interface.

Left-click gives dialog with the options open and share and an ellipsis at the bottom. The ellipsis gives the same dropdown as right-click on the item ellipsis.

The dialog also has a preview of the file, and PowerPoint and Word files have a menu where you can print to PDF and get the embed code to the file.

(The modern interface has a preview in the Information pane, but no easy possibility to print to PDF or get the embed code.)

9.3   CREATE A LIBRARY APP

You can create a new library app from the "Your Apps" page, that you can reach with the "Add an app" command under the 365 Settings icon or with the 'App' command under the 'New' button in a modern SharePoint homepage or Site contents. This was described in chapter 7.

The 'New' button in a modern SharePoint homepage or Site contents also gives the option 'Document library'.

$+$ New $\vee$ $\boxtimes$ Se

When you use this option to create a document library, you will not be directed to the "Your Apps" page.

List

Instead, a right pane will open, where you can enter a name and a description for the new library.

Document library

A document library created with the 'Document library' option from the homepage or Site contents, will open when you have filled out the details and clicked on 'Create'.

9.3.1   *Auto-Created Columns*

When you create a new document library app, several columns will be added automatically. You can see all of them in the Library settings.

The automatically created columns "Name", "Modified" and "Modified by" are visible in the default "All Documents" view.

The "Name" column is for the file name and should of course always be visible, but you can very well hide the other two columns from a view. They are filled out automatically.

The columns "Created", "Created by", "Title" and "Checked out to" are also created automatically, but they are not displayed in the "All Documents" view. "Created" and "Created by" are filled out automatically.

Only the "Name" and the "Title" columns are by default visible in the item form.

9.4   ADD CONTENT TO DOCUMENT LIBRARIES

You can add content to a SharePoint document library either by creating a new Office document directly in SharePoint or by uploading any existing file to the library.

The upload of existing files can be done in several different ways, and I will mention them below. Another way, to synchronize SharePoint libraries with folders in the File Explorer, is described in section 12.5, Synchronize with Local Folder.

9.4.1 *Create an Office File in a Library*

A good way to get content into a SharePoint library, is to create a new file from the library. Click on the '+ New' button in the command bar or above the list of files, to start the creation.

The menu in the **classic** interface, by default gives a choice of creating an Office file or a folder. When you select one of the files, a blank template will open. (Classic libraries also have a 'New Document' button under the FILES tab. This button by default only gives the Word document option.)

The **modern** interface has the same default Office file options as the classic, but here you can also add a link as an item in the library.

As you see from the image to the right, the modern interface gives two more options. I will describe them below in this chapter.

Additionally, Group Team sites have an option to create a Forms survey, and when external sharing is enabled for other sites, the 'New' button in the modern interface gives an Excel survey option. *Refer to* chapter 19 to learn more about the different kinds of surveys available in SharePoint.

It is however quite possible that a document library gives only one, or a few, options. The '+New' menu can be edited, and document libraries may have a custom content type that restricts the file type options when you create a new document. Later in this book, you will learn how to create such content types.

There might also be more options than the default ones.

Follow these steps to create a new Office file in a SharePoint library:

1. Open the library where you want to create the new file and click on the '+New' button.

2. Click on one of the template options.

3. Click 'Yes' to the warning message.

Microsoft Word   ×

⚠ The document you are trying to open is a template. Would you like to open and edit as a standard document?

                                              [Yes]   [No]

---

4. A new document will open, by default in the online version of the document type you selected. If you create the file from the modern

interface, it opens in a new tab. (When you create an OneNote file, you will be asked to give it a name before it opens.)

5. Now you can start working with the document. Changes are saved automatically.

To work in the desktop version instead, click on 'Open in ...' on top of the ribbon. In Word, this command is found under the 'Editing' button.

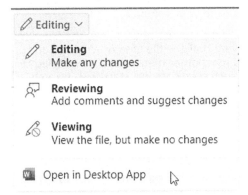

9.4.1.1 Naming

When new files are created inside a SharePoint library, they get a default name: Document, Book or Presentation, depending on file type.

If the creator does not change the default name, the library will eventually contain many documents with different content but with the same, non-descriptive names. That will of course make it difficult to find the correct file on each occasion.

Therefore, users should be taught to name their files consistently and well.

Click on the default name – 'Book, 'Document' or 'Presentation' – above the ribbon. Now you can give the file a new name, and there are links to the site, to the document library and to the Version history (which of course only is interesting for old files, not for new ones).

See 9.8.2, Edit Office files, below to learn more about how you can work with Office files in a SharePoint library.

9.4.2   *Upload Files*

All file types can be uploaded to SharePoint libraries. When you add files to SharePoint by the methods described below, they will be copied to items in the library. They will not be removed from your computer.

When you copy files to a SharePoint library as described below, the file name is always kept. But you should be aware that the file creator, creation and modified dates, security settings and most other metadata is NOT copied to SharePoint. Instead, the addition of such metadata will start from scratch after the upload. The only way to include metadata like Date modified and Permissions is to write code or use third-party software.

9.4.2.1   Select Multiple Files

Use one of these methods to select multiple files in your File Explorer:

- To select any files, hold down the Ctrl key and click on the files you want to add.

- To select files that are sorted together, hold down the Shift key while you click on the first file and then on the last file.

- To select all files in a folder, hold down the Ctrl key and press the A key.

9.4.2.2   Upload Button

In the **modern** experience, click on the 'Upload' button in the command bar to upload one or several files to a SharePoint library.

↑ Upload ⌄

Select 'Files' or 'Folder'. Then you can browse to the item(s) on your computer that you want to upload and click OK. Now the file(s) or folder(s) will be uploaded.

Files

Here, you can also upload a folder and a file that should be used as a template, *refer to* 9.13.1, Upload Office Template.

Folder

Template

In the **classic** experience, you can either click on the 'Upload' button above the existing items or on the 'Upload Document' button under the FILES tab in the ribbon. Here you can only upload files, not folders.

On the other hand, in the **classic** interface, you can add a file as a new version to an existing file and give a version comment, and you can also select to place the file in a folder. (With the modern interface, you must open the folder and upload the file there or move the file to the folder after upload.)

Add a document ✕

Choose a file   [Choose File] No file chosen

           ☑ Add as a new version to existing files

Destination Folder   /Slideshows/   [Choose Folder...]

Version Comments

                                       [OK]   [Cancel]

When you upload a file that has the same name as an existing file in a **modern** library, you will get a question about replacing the file, but the modern interface has no field for a version comment.

9.4.2.3   Save a File to SharePoint

There are two ways to save an open Office file from a computer to a SharePoint library. In both cases, start by opening the Files tab in Excel, PowerPoint or Word and selecting 'Save as'.

- Use the Sites button.

This will open a choice of sites that you have access to, and you can select first the site and then the document library.

- Use the Browse button.

a. Copy the path to the SharePoint library where you want to save the file. Leave out the last part, which should look like this: Forms/AllItems.aspx.

b. Click on 'Browse'.

c. Paste the path you copied into the address field.

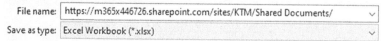

| File name: | https://m365x446726.sharepoint.com/sites/KTM/Shared Documents/ | ∨ |
| Save as type: | Excel Workbook (*.xlsx) | ∨ |

d. Click on 'Save. You will now also have a chance to rename the file.

e. (You must log in to SharePoint, if you have not saved your log in information.)

Demo:

https://kalmstrom.com/Tips/SharePoint-Online-Course/Upload-File.htm

9.4.2.4   Drag and Drop

It is possible to drag and drop files from a computer to a SharePoint Online library. This can be done with one file or with multiple files at the same time, so drag and drop is a fast and convenient way to add files to SharePoint document libraries.

1. Open the File Explorer on your computer in a small window over the SharePoint library window or put the two windows side by side using the Windows button + the left/right keys.

2. Select the file(s) you want to copy to the library.

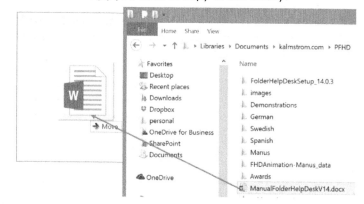

3. Drag the files to the box that becomes visible in the library and drop them there.

You may also drag the files to the browser icon. The browser will then open in the latest visited window, and if that is the SharePoint library you can drop the file as described in point 3 above.

9.4.2.5   Other Methods

In section 12.3, I describe another way to move files to a SharePoint library: synchronize a SharePoint or OneDrive document library with a folder in your File Explorer.

When you want to move a lot of files and folders into SharePoint, I would recommend using SharePoint Designer, as described in chapter 10. This is the most stable no-code method.

To move many files on one occasion, or move files automatically on regular basis, you can use a PowerShell script. In my book *PowerShell with SharePoint from Scratch*, I have described how to write a script that copies all files in a local folder to a SharePoint library and then moves the copied files to a subfolder.

Demo:

https://www.kalmstrom.com/Tips/SharePoint-Online-Course/Upload-Multiple-Files-Drag.htm

9.5   RENAME A FILE

If you want to rename any file type in a document library, you can change the name in already saved or uploaded files in several ways:

- Switch the library to Grid view mode. Select the cell that has the name of the new file and change the name.

- In the **modern** interface, select the item and click on 'Rename' in the command bar or under the ellipsis. Now a dialog will open where you can change the name of the file.

- Edit the Properties of the file:

  o In the **modern** experience, click on 'Properties in the command bar or open the Information pane and click on 'Edit all', to change the file name and any other properties.

o In the classic experience, use the 'Edit Properties' button under the FILES tab in the ribbon, or select 'Properties' under the item ellipsis.

Office documents can also be renamed from the open file:

- Click on the name to change it, as described in 9.4.1.1, Naming, above.
- Open the document and click on 'Save as' under the File tab. Then select 'Rename'. PowerPoint files have the 'Rename' command directly under 'Files'.

Demo:

https://kalmstrom.com/Tips/SharePoint-Online-Course/Create-Content-in-SharePoint.htm

To have documents created and named automatically based on specified templates; *refer to* 25.9, The Document Set Content Type.

9.6   OPEN BEHAVIOR FOR OFFICE FILES

By default, Office documents are opened in the browser – Word documents are for example opened in Word Online. Administrators can change that setting in the Library settings >Advanced settings.

In the image below, documents are instead set to open in the client application.

Default open behavior for browser-enabled documents:

- ⦿ Open in the client application
- ○ Open in the browser
- ○ Use the server default (Open in the browser)

If the client application is unavailable, the document will open in the browser even if you have set documents to open in the client application.

9.   FIND A FILE LINK

When you have the link to a file in a library, you can use it to share the file or embed it in a page. You can of course open the file and take the URL from the browser's address bar, but both library experiences have a link command under the item ellipsis.

⋮ ➡ Copy link

With this link, you don't have to open the file, and you will have a possibility to set permissions on the file before you share it.

The **modern** interface also shows a Copy link button in the command bar when you select an item.

Refer to 14.6, Share a File, for more information on file sharing and permissions.

9.8   EDIT A FILE OR AN ITEM

When you select an item in a library app Standard view mode, you either want to edit the file or the metadata.

9.8.1   *Edit Properties*

In the Grid view mode, you can edit the metadata of all items by simply changing the values in the cells.

In the Standard view mode, click on 'Properties' in the command bar or in the ribbon to edit the metadata of the selected item.

In the **modern** interface, you can also open the Information pane for the selected item and click on 'Edit all' to change the properties, as described in the Rename section above.

The 'Edit' option is still visible when you select multiple library items. This means that you can edit multiple items at the same time, which is convenient when you want to give multiple items the same value in one or more columns. The values you enter in the right pane will be applied to all selected items.

9.8.2   *Edit Office Files*

When you want to edit an Office file, you can just click on the file name to open the file in edit mode. By default, it will open in the browser edition.

If you use the 'Open' button in the **modern** command bar, you will have a choice where to open the file.

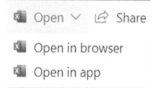

In the **classic** interface, left-click on the ellipsis at the file name and select 'Open', as described in 9.2.3, Other Unique Features, if you want to open the file in the desktop edition.

The Online editions of the Office apps run in the browser, and they automatically save your files to the document library where they were created or opened. These online editions are similar to the desktop/client editions, but some features are missing.

On the other hand, an online document can be edited by multiple people at the same time, which in some scenarios is a fantastic benefit, and the browser editions have some features that facilitates cooperation: different kinds of editing and a possibility to have a Comments thread in a right pane.

The PowerPoint browser edition also has options for presenting the slideshow.

9.8.2.1   Editing by Multiple Users

Several people can work on the same Word Online, Excel Online or PowerPoint Online file at the same time in a SharePoint library, where all participants have access to the file. You can also use a shared OneDrive for Business folder, *refer to* 12.2.4, Sharing from OneDrive.

If you select to edit a Word, Excel or PowerPoint file in the Online edition, and another person is editing the same document, you will have a message about it:

Antonio Moreno is editing this document.

You can also see where in the document the other user is working.

Antonio Moreno
Lorem ipsum dolor

You may continue with your editing, because all changes, no matter which one of the users who made them, will be visible in the document.

You can be more than two users on the same document. I have seen around 15 people collaborating on a document in Word Online!

Demo:

https://www.kalmstrom.com/Tips/SharePoint-Online-Course/Word-Offline-Overview.htm

9.9   THE TITLE COLUMN

When you create a new item in a list app, you cannot save it until the "Title" field is filled out. Therefore, most users learn to add values that give relevant information in the title field.

When you create a new file in a SharePoint library, on the other hand, there is no such compulsion. On the contrary, the "Title" field is rather hidden, because by default it is not visible in the "All documents" view. To enter something in the "Title" field, users must therefore edit the file properties. This means that the 'Title' field is often left empty in library items, which is a pity as it is important for the SharePoint search engine.

In SharePoint searches, the "Title" field has the highest rank of all, so the title is where SharePoint begins the search after you have written a search word or phrase.

Hits in the title also comes first in the results. For the search to work well, it is therefore important that "Title" columns are filled out with words that give relevant information.

When the "Title" column in a SharePoint library is empty, the file name becomes prominent. Imagine how the search will work if users leave the title field empty and don't change the default file name, 'Document', 'Book' or 'Presentation'!

On the other hand, if people don't use the "Title" field, why have it there at all? It is possible to hide it, but before we come to that, I will give a few suggestions on how to get data into the field.

9.9.1 Add to View and Change the Display Name

If you add the "Title" column to the default view, users will hopefully consider it more than if it is hidden. It is a good idea to combine this with changing "Title" into something that is more explanatory. Renaming the "Title" column can also be an alternative to adding a new column.

Sometimes people avoid filling out "Title" fields, or fill them out badly, because they don't understand the meaning of the field.

For example, if the documents in a library have IDs, changing the display name of the "Title" column to "DocumentID", would make it very easy for users to understand the meaning of the column and also to search and sort

When you change the column name in this way, only the name displayed to the users will be changed. The internal column name, which is used in queries and some other contexts, will still be "Title".

This method works well in SharePoint list apps, where something must be entered anyway, and a relevant name gives relevant input.

In libraries, users might be more inclined to actually fill out a visible field called "Keywords" or something else that they understand, but showing and renaming the "Title" field does not force them to do it.

9.9.2 Auto-fill the Title Field

If we assume that users change the default file names when they create new files in SharePoint libraries, it is possible to let a flow or workflow add the same value as in the file name to the "Title" field.

This solution is not optimal, but it is better to have the file name in the title field than having it blank. This flow/workflow is also useful if you want to add titles to a lot of files where the field is empty. At the end of chapter 24, SharePoint Automation, I have suggested a flow and a workflow that gives the "Title" field the same value as the "Name" field.

9.9.3 Hide the Title Field

As a last resort, you can hide the "Title" field in a library. I would only do this when it is not used or repeatedly is filled out in the wrong way. The best way to hide the "Title" field, is to create a dedicated content type, *refer to 25.5, Create a Content Type for a Site*.

9.10 LIBRARY FOLDERS

The old and tried folder is the most popular but least recommended way of categorization in SharePoint. It has some benefits, though, especially when used with OneDrive for Business, *refer to* chapter 12.

The main argument for folders is that users will feel at home, and you will not have to change the way information is stored compared to the file server. However, you will quickly experience that folders have some major drawbacks. SharePoint is not built for handling folders in a good way, and it has some serious folder-related annoyances.

If you don't want to allow user to create new library folders, you can hide that option from the '+New' dropdown, *refer to* 9.10.3, Hide the Folder Option, below.

9.10.1 Create a New Folder

To create a new folder in a SharePoint library, click on '+New' and select the folder option.

Give the folder a name that tells what kind of items it contains and click on 'Create'.

In the **classic** experience, you can also select 'New Folder' under the 'FILES' tab.

9.10.2   *Move Files Into and Out of Folders*

To move a document **into** a folder in a SharePoint library, click on the file and drag and drop it on the folder. This works in the same way in both experiences.

To move a document **out of** a folder in the **modern** experience, select the file and drag and drop it on the upper level heading.

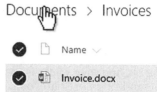

In the **classic** experience, you should instead drag the file to the document library link in the Site navigation to move it out of the folder.

The drag and drop method does not always work well, but in the **modern** experience, you can instead use the 'Move to' command in the command bar and under the item ellipsis, to move files into and out of a folder.

The best method is probably to move the files in the File Explorer by synchronizing, *refer to* 12.3, Synchronize with a Local Folder. When you use that method the drag and drop works better, and you can also cut and paste.

Demo:

https://www.kalmstrom.com//Tips/SharePoint-Online-Course/Categorization-Folders.htm

9.10.3   *Hide the Folder Option*

When you click on '+New' in a SharePoint library, you may by default also create a folder. As mentioned above, I generally don't recommend the use of library folders.

If you agree and don't want users to be able to create folders, you can hide that option in the Library settings >Advanced settings.

Make "New Folder" command available?

◯ Yes   ◉ No

Note that this only hides the button to create new folders from the library interface. It is still possible to create folders in other ways.

9.11   CHECK OUT / CHECK IN

When you work with an Office file that is stored in a SharePoint document library and don't want other users to see your changes, or you don't want them to be visible in the version history quite yet, you can check out the file.

A check out also prevents that several people edit the same file simultaneously. When a file is checked out, you can edit it online or offline and save it as many times as you wish. No other user will be able to see your changes until you check in the file again.

When a file is checked out, it has a red icon to the right of the file name in the **modern** interface.

In the **classic** experience, the file type icon has a green arrow on checked out files.

9.11.1   *Check Out / Check In Commands*

Both library experiences have a 'Check out' option under the ellipsis at the file name.

Modern document libraries also have a 'Check out' command under the ellipsis in the command bar when a file is selected.

When you have checked out a file, the 'Check out' command is replaced with two other commands: 'Check in' and 'Discard check out'.

Check in the file when you want other users to see your changes.

Discard the check out if you don't want to keep your changes. When you do that, the Version history of the file will not be affected.

The **classic** interface, instead has 'Check Out', 'Check in' and 'Discard Check Out' buttons under the FILES tab in the ribbon.

9.11.2 *Require Check Out*

Check out can be set to be mandatory, in the Library settings >Versioning settings. The default setting is No.

Require documents to be checked out before
they can be edited?

○ Yes ◉ No

If you set check out to be required before editing, you will overcome the issue with several people editing the same document. On the other hand, you will probably have issues because people forget to check in the edited file again!

Demo:

https://www.kalmstrom.com/Tips/SharePoint-Online-Course/Check-Out.htm

9.12 COPY ITEMS

It is possible to copy one or more items from one document library in the tenant to another, by selecting or entering the destination library in the source library.

The item in the destination document library will always contain the file, but metadata is only added to the new library when there are columns for it. When the source library and the destination library have columns of the same type with the same name, the copied item's values in these fields will be copied too.

9.12.1 *Modern*

Libraries with the modern interface have a 'Copy to' link in the command bar and under the item ellipsis.

Select one or multiple items, click on 'Copy to' and a right panel will open. Here you can select first site and then library (and folder) to copy to.

Copy 2 items ✕

Places

Choose a destination

⬚ Current Library

☁ Your OneDrive

Contoso

🅿 Production

Cs Communication site

☐ Contoso Team

Browse sites

9.12.2 *Classic*

You will find a 'Copy' link if you right-click on the ellipsis at a selected file in the classic experience. Here you can only copy one file at a time, and you must enter the path to the destination library yourself.

On the other hand, the dialog that opens in the classic interface gives a possibility to rename the file and to have alerts when the original file is changed.

Copy ✕

Destination

Specify a destination and file name for the copy - the destination must be a URL to a SharePoint document library.

Note that you are copying the published version of this document.

Destination document library or folder (Click here to test):

[   ]

File name for the copy:

[BookSales   ] .xlsx

Update

The system can request that your copy be updated whenever the document is checked in. You can also request to receive notifications when the document changes by creating an alert on the source document.

Prompt the author to send out updates when the document is checked in?

◯ Yes

◉ No

☐ Create an alert for me on the source document

[OK]   [Cancel]

9.13 MODERN '+NEW' MENU OPTIONS

The modern library interface makes it easy to upload a template to use with the +New command and to edit the '+New' menu.

[+ New ⌄]   ⤒ Upload ⌄   ▤

✎ Edit New menu

+ Add template

Note that the template option is only suitable for simple templates that should be used with the modern library interface, because the template cannot be selected in the classic interface. If users switch to the classic interface, the template you want them to use will not be displayed!

In the same way, changes in the '+New' menu made from this command will *not* reflect to the classic interface.

In general, I would recommend that you instead use content types for more advanced template options, *refer to* chapter 25. A custom content type is the only option for the classic interface. When you use content types, you can also add and remove them from the '+New' menu as you like.

9.13.1   *Upload an Office Template*

In the modern library interface, you can upload any Office document and use it as a template. Create the template in your desktop application and save it with a suitable name. You don't have to use a specific template format, .docx. .pptx and .xlsx will do fine.

1. Click on the '+New' button in the command bar and select '+ Add template', OR click on the 'Upload' button and select 'Template'.

2. Select the template you have created. It will now be uploaded and added to the templates in the '+New' dropdown.

9.13.2   *Edit the '+New' Menu*

When you want users to only use custom templates when they create new documents in a modern SharePoint library, or when you want to limit their choices, you can edit the menu to only show the template(s) that should be used.

The image to the right shows an example.

1. Click on the '+New' button and select 'Edit New menu'.

2. A right pane with all templates will open, and you can uncheck the templates you want to hide.

3. To reorder the templates, select any template in the right pane, open its ellipsis and move it up or down.

   You can also just drag the templates to your preferred order.

4. Save your changes.

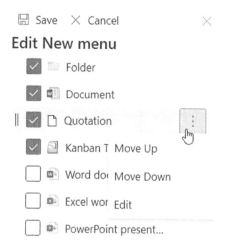

9.14   SUMMARY

This chapter about SharePoint libraries has shown how to create content in libraries and how to upload files and folders. I have also explained how you can check out documents to keep your changes to yourself and how several people can work with the same Excel, PowerPoint or Word Online file.

Discussions about using folders and about the "Title" field in library items have also been included in this chapter, and I have described how to edit, copy and move files and properties in the modern as well as in the classic experience.

Finally, I have pointed out some new features in the modern library interface that makes it easier to manage the templates used in a document library.

In chapter 25, Content Types, I describe how an administrator can make it easy for users to fill out metadata right in a document, instead of going into the item properties.

In the next chapter, I will introduce a tool that is helpful when you work with SharePoint: SharePoint Designer.

10   SHAREPOINT DESIGNER

If you want to be a SharePoint power user, it is a good idea to have SharePoint Designer 2013 installed on your computer. SharePoint Designer is mostly known as a workflow creation tool, but it is also useful for managing SharePoint sites and apps.

In this chapter, you will learn how to find and install SharePoint Designer and how to open a SharePoint Online site in SharePoint Designer. I will also explain how to create a list and how to import files to a library with SharePoint Designer.

All kinds of SharePoint sites can be managed in SharePoint Designer, but Microsoft is regretfully not continuing to develop this useful tool. There will be no "SharePoint Designer 2016" or later, and each time you install a later Office version on a computer that has SharePoint Designer 2013 installed, it will be removed. You can continue using SharePoint Designer 2013, but you will have to download it and install it again.

10.1   INSTALL SHAREPOINT DESIGNER 2013

SharePoint Designer 2013 is a free Office application, but it is not included in any Office package installation. You will have to install it separately.

1. Click on your profile picture in the right part of the 365 navigation bar and then on 'View account' to open your 365 account page.

2. Click on 'Office apps' in the left menu and then on 'Tools & add-ins'.

::: **My account**	⚙ ?

Tools & add-ins

⌂ My account

♀ Personal info

▭ Subscriptions

✎ Security & privacy

🔒 App permissions

↓ Apps & devices

🔧 Tools & add-ins

Microsoft Support and Recovery Assistant for Microsoft Office

Get help troubleshooting and fixing problems you might run into using Outlook or Microsoft Office.

InfoPath 2013

Use InfoPath 2013 to design sophisticated electronic forms that help you quickly and cost-effectively gather information.

SharePoint Designer 2013

Use SharePoint Designer 2013 to create workflows and modify the look and feel of your SharePoint sites.

Language Accessory Pack for Office

Language packs add additional display, help or proofing tools. You can install additional language accessory packs after installing Microsoft Office.

3. Click on SharePoint Designer 2013. You will now be directed to a Microsoft download page.

4. Select language if you want another language than the default one.

5. Click on the 'Download' button.

6. Select the 32- or 64-bit version. It should be the same as your installed Office version.

7. Click on 'Next' and save the file to your computer.

8. Run the file.

10.2 OPEN A SITE IN SHAREPOINT DESIGNER

You should always open the *site* in SharePoint Designer, even if you want to work with an app. Then you can select the app you want to work with.

Open Site

1. In SharePoint Designer, click on the 'Open Site' button.

2. Paste or type in the URL of the site you want to open.
   Note that only the first part of the URL you see when you open the site should be entered, like this:
   https://kalmstromdemo.sharepoint.com/sites/Example/.

3. Click on Open.

When a SharePoint site is open in SharePoint Designer, you can see the site contents in the menu to the left. To the right, there is a summary page with information about the item you have selected in the left menu. This is what you work with in SharePoint Designer: one site and its contents, design and settings.

Above the site contents and summary page there is a ribbon with various controls. Which controls are displayed, depends on what has been selected.

Demo:

https://kalmstrom.com/Tips/SharePoint-Online-Course/SharePoint-Designer.htm

10.3   CREATE A LIST IN SHAREPOINT DESIGNER

Instead of creating a new app in the web browser interface, you can use SharePoint Designer 2013. It is quicker and saves you some clicks and loading of new pages.

1. Open the site in SharePoint Designer.

2. Click on either the 'SharePoint List' or the 'Document Library' button in the ribbon.

3. Select the list or library type you want to use.

4. Give the app a name (and a description) and click OK.

Now the list or library options are shown on the SharePoint Designer summary page, and you can customize your app more quickly than in the browser. You can select settings options and add, remove and edit columns, views and forms.

When you have the app open in SharePoint Designer, you can preview it in the browser with the preview button above the ribbon.

Demo:

https://kalmstrom.com/Tips/SharePoint-Online-Course/SharePoint-Designer-2013-Create-List.htm

10.4   IMPORT FILES OR FOLDERS WITH SHAREPOINT DESIGNER

This is the process to add files and folders to a SharePoint library with SharePoint Designer 2013.

1. Open the site in SharePoint Designer.

2. In SharePoint Designer, open the 'All Files' folder in the left menu.

3. In the main area, select the document library that you want to add files or folders to.

4. The 'Forms' folder will be selected automatically when the library opens. Make sure that you de-select that folder, because you probably do not want to add files in that hidden folder.

5. Click on the 'Import Files' button in the ribbon.

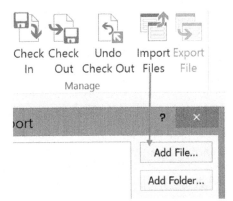

6. Click on the 'Add File...'" or "'Add Folder...' button in the dialog that opens.

7. Select the files or folder from your computer that you want to add to the document library.

8. Click on Open and then OK, and the upload begins.

Demo:

https://www.kalmstrom.com/Tips/SharePoint-Online-Course/Import-Files-SPD.htm

10.5   SUMMARY

This chapter has introduced SharePoint Designer. You have learned how to find and install SharePoint Designer 2013 and how to open a site in SharePoint Designer.

Now you also know how to create a SharePoint list or library in SharePoint Designer, but you can do much more, for example automate SharePoint processes. We will come back to that in chapter 24, SharePoint Automation.

11 SharePoint Navigation

SharePoint administrators need to understand how the SharePoint navigation is built and can be manipulated, so that users can easily find content they are looking for not only by search but also by using the navigation.

11.1 Site Navigation / Quick Launch

Home

Conversations

Documents

Notebook

Pages

Site contents

Recycle bin

Edit

All SharePoint Team sites by default have a navigation panel to the left on the page. It is called Site navigation, as it usually shows links to content within the current site. Other names are Quick launch and Current navigation. Quick launch is the classic name that is often used in settings pages.

By default, the Site navigation has links to content in the same site that a team might need for collaboration, like a Notebook and a document library.

When new apps are created in the site, links to them are usually added here. The Site navigation also has links to the "Site Pages" library and the Site contents.

The left panel Site navigation can be hidden via the Site settings >Navigation Elements. This can be suitable in certain contexts when you don't want users to be able to easily reach other content on the site.

Communication sites have the Site navigation on top of the page, not to the left, and the default navigation includes Documents, Pages, and Site contents. These links are helpful when you are building the site, but they might not be the best for people who visit the Communication site to get information. Therefore, you should plan to replace these links with more relevant links when you are ready to launch the Communication site.

The links in the Site navigation are the same on every page in the site, so when you change anything in the Site navigation on one page, it will be changed for the whole site.

11.1.1 Add an App to the Site navigation

Often, and especially in Team sites, you want to make it easy for users to find apps that are commonly used in the site. When that is the case, you should add links to the apps to the Site navigation.

A link in the Site navigation is added by default when you create an app from a **modern** homepage or a modern Site Show in site navigation contents interface. Select 'List' or Document library in the '+New' button dropdown and keep the box checked in the dialog or pane where you give the new app a name.

For other app creation methods, you can add the app to the Site navigation at List settings >List name, description and navigation.

Select the radio button 'Yes' for 'Display this list/library on the Quick launch'.

Settings ▸ General Settings

Name and Description

Type a new name as you want it to appear in headings and links throughout the site. Type descriptive text that will help site visitors use this document library.

Name:

Documents

Description:

Navigation

Specify whether a link to this document library appears in the Quick Launch. Note: it only appears if Quick Launch is used for navigation on your site.

Display this document library on the Quick Launch?

● Yes   ○ No

| Save | Cancel |

11.1.2   *Add a Subsite to the Site Navigation*

When you create a subsite, you can decide to show a subsite link in the parent site Site navigation. The default option is No.

Navigation

Display this site on the Quick Launch of the parent site?

○ Yes   ● No

There are also top link options when you create a subsite, but they are only valid for classic sites, *see* below.

In Communication sites, where the Site navigation is placed on top of the page, the link to the subsite will be placed under a 'Subsites' heading, if you select 'Yes' to display the site on the Quick launch of the parent site.

The "Development" site in the image below has two subsites: Current and Future.

Development

Home   kalmstrom.com   Documents   Pages   Subsites ⌄   Site contents   Edit

+ New ⌄   ⚙ Page details   Current   Future

11.2 CLASSIC TOP LINK BAR

The navigation bar on top of SharePoint pages in classic Team sites is called the Top link bar or Global navigation. The Site navigation – or Quick launch – is to the left, as in all Team sites.

You can add any links to both navigations, but I would recommend that you use them differently. It is easier for users to learn that content of the same site is found to the left, while other links, that they might use more seldom, are found at the top of the page.

11.2.1 *Inherit links*

When you create a subsite, you can decide if the subsite should inherit the top link bar from the parent site. I often find it useful to change the default setting into 'Yes' for classic Team sites, to have a connection to the root site. (Remember, other sites, do not have a Top link bar.)

Navigation Inheritance

Use the top link bar from the parent site?

○ Yes   ◉ No

You can stop inheriting the navigation under the Site settings >Top Link Bar.

Future   Current

Site Settings ▸ Top Link Bar ⓘ

✕ Stop Inheriting Links

11.3 HUB NAVIGATION

When a site is registered as a Hub site, it gets an extra hub navigation bar on top of the page. This hub navigation will be inherited by any other site that is associated with the Hub site, and it can only be edited in the Hub site. In classic sites, the hub navigation will only appear on modern pages.

The image below shows the Hub navigation on the Development hub site. As you see, this is a Communication site with its Site navigation just below the site name.

Development   Future   Current   Edit   ⬅

D   **Development**

Home   kalmstrom.com   Documents

Hub site owners should customize the Hub navigation to include resources that might be of interest to users in all the associated sites. Often, you want to add links to the associated sites in the Hub navigation, so that users can easily reach the other sites in the hub family.

The hub site navigation can have up to three levels, so site owners don't need to add all links in a long row on top of the page. Instead, the links can be organized in a way that helps users discover and find relevant content.

11.4   EDIT NAVIGATION

The navigation can be edited in several ways, and I recommend that you consider which navigation options are the best for each site. Bad or lacking navigation can be very frustrating to users, while good navigation will make work smoother and more efficient.

11.4.1   *Navigation Settings*

The navigation for all sites can be edited from the Site settings, via links under the Look and Feel heading. Only classic Team sites and modern Team sites without a group have all the links shown in the image to the right.

Communication sites have no 'Top link bar' or 'Navigation Elements' links and Group Team sites have no 'Top link bar' or 'Title, description and logo'. These two site types have no Top link bar.

Look and Feel
Title, description, and logo
Quick launch
Top link bar
Navigation Elements
Change the look

Modern Team sites without a group have the 'Top link bar' control, even if they don't have a Top link bar, so by adding links there you can get a Top link bar in these sites. It will however be placed in the same space as the Hub navigation.

The Hub navigation cannot be edited at all under the Look and Feel heading.

The 'Quick launch' control gives most options. On the Quick launch page, you can create new links in the Site navigation and change their order. You can also create headings, to group the navigation links, and change the order of links and headings.

New Navigation Link | New Heading | Change Order

Notebook

Team Calendar

Team Documents

You can edit or delete each link by clicking on the edit icon to the left of the link display text.

The 'Top link bar' page, only has the 'New Navigation Link' option.

The 'Navigation Elements' page gives two options: to hide the Site navigation and to show a tree view. Unfortunately, the tree view only works in the classic experience.

11.4.2   Modern Experience

When you use the modern interface, the navigation can be easily edited via the 'Edit' link. You can find this link at the bottom of the Site navigation in Team sites and to the right in the Site navigation in Communication sites.

Edit

The 'Edit' command opens a left pane where you can see the Site navigation in edit mode.

When the navigation is in edit mode, each link will have an ellipsis with various options, see the image below.

To add a new link, move the cursor to where you want to place the link and click on the plus sign that appears when it is possible to insert a new link (above 'Documents' in the image below).

Documents

KTM Tasks   Edit   ]

Pages   Move up
                                                           !
                             Move down
Site Contents

                             Make sub link

                             Remove
    Save   **Cancel**

When you add a new link, the Hub navigation and Site navigation in Communication sites give an extra option: a choice between Link and Label. When Label is selected, the Address field is greyed out.

Add

Choose an option

| Link   ∨ |

Address

| https://m365x446726.sharepoint.com
/sites/ContosoWorks |

Display name

| Contoso Works |

| OK | | Cancel |

The Group Team site navigation pane instead have suggestions on links to shared group resources above the 'Address' and 'Display name' fields.

When you select one of the resources instead of the Link option, the link and the display name will be added automatically. Conversations give a link to the group's shared e-mail inbox.

Modern Team sites without a group, only have the option to add a link and a display text.

Add

Choose an option

| Link   ∨ |

Link

Conversations

Calendar

Notebook

Planner

Teams

11.4.3   *Classic Experience*

Click on 'EDIT LINKS' to open the navigation in edit mode when the page has the classic experience interface. The image below shows the Top link bar, but the Site navigation can be edited in a similar way.

kalmstrom.com demos   ✕   Sales   ✕   Development   ✕   Drag and drop link here   ⊕ link   Save   Cancel

- Use the X icon to delete a link.

- Use the eye icon to hide a link.

- Change the order of links by drag and drop.

- Add new links by clicking on the '+link' icon. Give the new link a display text and paste or type in the path in the dialog that opens.

11.4.4   *Site Navigation Hierarchy*

When you have many navigation links, it is useful to arrange them in groups with headings and sub links.

11.4.4.1   Modern Experience

As mentioned above, you can arrange the links in a hierarchy by using the 'Make sub link' command in the modern Site navigation.

Edit

The command moves the selected link a little bit to the right, and the command changes into 'Promote sub link' – which moves the link back again.

Promote sub link

Remove

By combining links and sub links with labels, *see* above, you can create a three level mega menu.

Global Marketing	Who we are ∨	What we do ∨	Happenings ∨	Edit

+ New ∨   ⚙ Page details

Our Vision   **Leadership**

FY20 Planning   Leadership team

Strategy   Customer Success

Our culture   Employee advocacy

Investment Framework

Operating Framework

11.4.4.2   Classic Experience

In the classic experience, you can drag the links in the Site navigation, but that is more difficult. If you have a possibility to use the modern experience just when you arrange the links, for example by switching interface in an app, that is a quicker method.

In classic Team sites, you can also use the Site settings >Quick launch.

New Navigation Link | New Heading | Change Order

'New Heading' puts a heading to the far left in the Site navigation. You must link this heading – it cannot remain unlinked, like labels in the Hub and Communication site navigation.

When you click on 'New Navigation Link' you can enter a URL and its description and select under which heading the link new link should be placed.

URL

Type the Web address:

| http:// |

Type the description:

| |

Heading

| Home ▼ |

In the classic interface, it is possible to create a hierarchy in the top link bar. When you need a heading, create a link without a path and drag other links under it. In the image to the right, the 'Departments' caption is not linked.

Departments ▾

If you want to test this, be prepared that you might need to try several times before you get the dropped link to stay under the heading.

Development

Sale

It is easier to create headings in the top navigation when you use the Navigation Settings page. This page is available when the SharePoint Server Publishing Infrastructure has been activated for the site collection; *refer to* 27.2, Navigation Changes with Publishing Infrastructure.

Demo:

https://www.kalmstrom.com/Tips/SharePoint-Online-Course/SharePoint-Navigation.htm

11.5   HIDE THE NAVIGATION

In the classic experience and in apps with the modern interface, each user can temporarily hide the navigation to see more of the content on the screen.

Modern apps have an 'Expand content' icon to the right in the command bar.

All **classic** pages have a 'Focus on content' icon to the right under the 365 navigation bar.

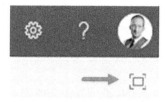

In both experiences, click on the icon again to show the navigation.

All sites but Communication sites have a 'Navigation Elements' control in the Site settings, *see* 11.4.1 above. Here, site owners can permanently hide the Site navigation from the users by unchecking the 'Enable Quick Launch' box.

11.6   SUMMARY

In this chapter, you have learned how to edit the different kinds of navigation found in SharePoint sites. You have now seen the extra possibilities given by Hub and Communication site navigation, and you also know the specifics of the navigation in other sites.

As the navigation is the same for the whole site, you also understand that you sometimes can switch between app interfaces to have the best possibilities for your navigation.

In the next chapter, I will introduce SharePoint content that is personal to each user. You have already met Microsoft Lists, that can be used for personal lists and not only for shared data. Now it is time to look at the options on the SharePoint Online start page and to learn to take advantage of OneDrive for Business.

12 PERSONAL CONTENT

SharePoint has a few parts that are not primarily intended for collaboration but instead for personal use. On the SharePoint Online start page, users can find important content and create sites and news, and in OneDrive for Business each user has a personal site for content storage.

12.1 THE SHAREPOINT ONLINE START PAGE

When a user clicks on the SharePoint tile in the 365 App Launcher, or on 'SharePoint' in the left part of the 365 navigation bar, he/she is directed to the SharePoint Online start page..

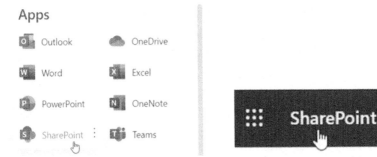

The SharePoint Online start page is a kind of SharePoint Favorites page. Here each SharePoint user can find links to SharePoint sites he or she has decided to follow, to recent or frequently used sites, to news and to sites promoted by the organization.

In this section I will explain how to follow and unfollow sites and how to save items for later. For site creation, *refer to* chapter 6, SharePoint Sites, and for News creation *refer to* section 13.4.11, The News Web Part.

12.1.1   *Follow Sites*

To follow an open site, each user can click on 'Not following' (modern) or 'FOLLOW' (classic) in the top right corner of the screen:

☆ Not following   ☆ FOLLOW

To follow a site from the SharePoint Online start page, click on the star to the right of the site icon. (Click again to stop follow the site.)

Team Site

12.1.1.1   Stop Following

When you follow a site in the **modern** experience, the text will be changed into 'Following'. Click on 'Following' to stop following the site, and the text will be changed into 'Not following' again.

In the **classic** interface, the text will not change. Instead, you must go to the SharePoint Online start page and click on the star to the right of the site icon to stop following.

12.1.2   *Save for Later*

The "Save for later" feature gives users a way to bookmark news and documents that are displayed on the SharePoint Online start page.

Save this item for later

When you click on the icon, the notation will change to "Saved for later", and the item will be visible under its own heading in the left menu. If you click on the icon again, the entry will be removed from the left menu.

Saved for later

Latest on the election   🔖

12.2   ONEDRIVE FOR BUSINESS

OneDrive for Business contains a personal site that gives each SharePoint Online user a 1 TB storage space. In the E3 and E5 Office 365 subscriptions, the storage space is even unlimited. The files stored in that site are private, unless the owner decides to share them.

In this section, I will describe the OneDrive for Business document library and explain how sharing files in that library works. I will also show how you can use OneDrive for Business to synchronize the OneDrive for Business library and any other SharePoint library that you have access to, with your computer.

Finally, I will explain how users can create a site that has many more of the useful SharePoint features than the default OneDrive for Business site, providing that the default Admin settings are kept.

The path to the OneDrive site collection looks like this:

https://TENANTNAME-my.sharepoint.com/personal/LOGINNAME/

(Note that there is also a "OneDrive" included in Windows 8.1 and 10. It is connected to a Microsoft account – not to an organizational 365 account. It has less storage space and does not build on SharePoint, and that "OneDrive" is *not* what we are talking about here.)

Demo:

https://www.kalmstrom.com/Tips/SharePoint-Online-Course/OneDrive-Intro.htm

12.2.1   *The "My Files" Library*

When you click on the OneDrive for Business icon under the 365 App Launcher or at office.com, you will reach your OneDrive for Business document library, "My files".

As you see from the image below, the 'My files" library resembles other SharePoint document libraries, but some of the features you can find in other document libraries are missing.

You can share files and folders in the "My files" library, and you can add new content to it in the same way as with all SharePoint libraries. But the "My files" library lacks many of the other library features.

For example, you cannot create more columns for metadata or edit the existing columns, and there is no possibility to create different views.

Moreover, you cannot create new apps, pages or subsites from the "My files" library.

	Name ∨	Modified ∨	Modified ... ∨	File size ∨	Sharing
	Microsoft Teams Chat Files	August 8	MOD Administratc	1 item	Private
	Notebooks	August 12	MOD Administratc	1 item	Private
	Microsoft Teams Data	August 15	MOD Administratc	2 items	Private
	Documents	September 22	MOD Administratc	5 items	⊖ Owner: Future
	Apps	October 25	MOD Administratc	1 item	Private
	Consumer Website traffic.pbix	July 31	MOD Administratc	568 KB	Private
	NC460 Sales Team.pbix	July 31	MOD Administratc	584 KB	Private
	Contoso Q2 Division Sales.pbix	July 31	MOD Administratc	305 KB	Private
	Finance.pbix	July 31	MOD Administratc	3.18 MB	Private
	HR.pbix	July 31	MOD Administratc	1.42 M	Private
	X1050 Launch Team.pbix	July 31	MOD Administratc	1.79 MB	Private
	Employee Engagement Plan.do...	July 31	MOD Administratc	731 KB	⁀ Shared

The left menu cannot be edited. It has the following tabs below 'My files':

- Recently used files

- Shared files

- Recycle bin for OneDrive, where deleted content can be restored or permanently deleted

- Shared libraries: SharePoint document libraries that you have access to. Libraries that you have added a shortcut to are prominent here.

- More libraries: libraries you have access too, grouped by Frequent and Followed in the main area

- Create shared library: create a modern Group Team site, for collaboration or for your own use, *see* Create a Site below

- Get the OneDrive apps: get a download link to the Android or iOS OneDrive for Business mobile app

- Return to classic OneDrive: to show the library in the classic interface

12.2.2   *User Settings*

Each user can reach his or her personal OneDrive settings from the 365 Settings icon of the "My files" library.

Settings   ✕

OneDrive

OneDrive settings

Restore your OneDrive

Here, each user can turn off notifications and make some other settings that are available under the Site settings in standard SharePoint sites.

Adele Vance

🔔 Notifications

⚙️ **More Settings**

More Settings

Manage access

Site collection administrators

Run sharing report

Region and Language

Regional settings

Language settings

Features and storage

Site collection features

Storage Metrics

Can't find what you are looking for?

Return to the old Site settings page

12.2.3   *Restore OneDrive*

Each user can restore his/her OneDrive to an earlier time 30 days back, to undo unwanted changes:

1. In the OneDrive "My files" library, open the 365 Settings icon and select 'Restore your OneDrive'.

2. Select 'Custom date and time'.

221

3. Move the slider to the left and study the changes. The activity chart shows the volume of activities each day, so that you can see when an unusual activity, like when your OneDrive was infected by malware, has happened.

4. Select an activity. All activities that occurred after that will be selected automatically.

5. Click on the Restore button, and your OneDrive will be restored to the selected activity. All activities after that will be undone.

Restore your OneDrive

If something went wrong, you can restore your OneDrive to a previous time. Select a date preset or use the slider to find a date with unusual activity in the chart. Then select the changes that you want to undo.

Select a date

| Custom date and time | ⌄ |

All changes after 9/26/2020, 1:03:46 PM will be rolled back

| Restore | Cancel |

Move the slider to quickly scroll the list to a day.

29 28 27 26 25 24 23 22 21 20 19 18 17 16 15 14 13 12 11 10 9 8 7 6 5 4 3 2 1 0
Days ago

Select a change in the list below to highlight it and all the changes before it. Then select the Restore button to undo all the highlighted changes.

		Change		File name
	⌄	Change		File name
	⌄	17 days ago - 9/27/2020 (2)		
◉	✎	Updated by Kate Kalmström 1:13:24 PM	☐	IMG_0565.JPG
◉	+	Added by Kate Kalmström 1:13:21 PM	☐	IMG_0565.JPG
	⌄	18 days ago - 9/26/2020 (5)		
◉	+	Added by Kate Kalmström 1:03:46 PM	☐	Garden-19-20-14de0c66-a744-4aea-84bb-d4431a29cb...
	⁄	Updated by Kate Kalmström 12:50:42 PM	⊟	...

12.2.4   *Sharing from OneDrive*

All files and folders that you store in OneDrive for Business are private until you decide to share them. To easily share files with different groups of people in your organization, you can place files that should be shared with the same people in folders and then share each folder.

The sharing is done with the 'Share' button or by sending a link, and it works in the same way as sharing a file from a SharePoint document library, *refer to* 14.6, Share a File.

You can manage the access in the same way as in a SharePoint document library too, but the "My files" library also has an automatically filled out "Sharing" column in the library interface. It has the value 'Private' or 'Shared', and when you click on a 'Shared' value you can see and change access to the file.

If you hover over the file name, you will see a card that shows information about the file and who has viewed it.

DetailedDescriptionShareTask.do...   :

w   DetailedDescriptionShareTask.d

👥 5 Views

↪   See details

↗ This item is popular with your colleagues

3 Viewers · 5 Views ⓘ

Rituka Rimza viewed this
Just now

You viewed this
Yesterday at 9:33 PM

Kate Kalmström viewed this
Yesterday at 9:32 PM

In your OneDrive settings, you can download a CSV file with sharing data. You can open this file in Excel.

12.2.5   *Create a Site*

You cannot create new apps, pages or subsites from the "My files" library, but you can still get much better SharePoint functionality from OneDrive than what you have in the default library. Here, I will describe how you can create a Group Team site from OneDrive and either use it for yourself or invite other people.

When you click on "Create shared library" in the OneDrive left menu, you will get a simplified experience for creating a Group Team site. (This experience respects all existing admin settings and behaviors around Team site creation.)

In the image below, I have invited a few people and opened the advanced settings. If you want to use the site for yourself, you only need to enter a name and then click on 'Create'.

Create a shared library

A shared library lets your group store and access files from anywhere on any device. The group automatically gets access to the files that members put in the shared library.

Name

Team Outing

Members

Adele Vance ×   Nestor Wilke ×

Alex Wilber ×

Hide advanced settings ⌄

Site and email address ⓘ

TeamOuting

The site and email addresses are available
Site address: https://m365x446726.sharepoint.com/sites/TeamOuting
Email address: TeamOuting@m365x446726.onmicrosoft.com

Privacy

Private - only members have access ⌄

[Create] [Cancel]

When the site has been created, the new document library will be displayed as a folder in the OneDrive for Business main area. Click on the folder to open the document library. This library is also limited compared to SharePoint document libraries, even if it has some more features than the 'My files' library.

The important thing here is the link to the SharePoint site in the top right corner of the page. Except for the limited "Documents" library, what you have created is a full Group Team site.

If you create a new document library from the site's homepage, it will have all the features of other SharePoint document libraries. You can of course also create other apps and pages.

OneDrive

Go to site ↗

Document Libraries

Documents

When you have clicked on 'Go to site' and the site opens, be sure to click on 'Not following' to follow the new site. Now, the new site will show up in the left menu of your SharePoint start page, and the document library can be found under 'Shared libraries' in the OneDrive for Business left menu.

The new Group Team site that you have created, has the same kind of link as other sites (https://TENANT.sharepoint.com/sites/SITE), and it is not stored under my.sharepoint.com. The site will be displayed in the SharePoint Admin center.

12.2.5.1   Multiple Libraries Benefits

One way of taking advantage of your Group Team site is to create multiple libraries. This gives important advantages and lets you share and synchronize in a more controlled way than if you use only the default OneDrive for Business library:

- SharePoint does not work well when you have more than 5000 files in a library. If you create more libraries in your site, you will overcome that problem.

- You can share different libraries with different groups of people.

- When you create several libraries, you can choose to not synchronize all of them to your device. The libraries you don't synchronize, can be used for storage of files that you don't need to access very often. You can also sync different libraries with different devices.

12.3   SYNCHRONIZE WITH A LOCAL FOLDER

OneDrive for Business manages synchronization between files in SharePoint and a local File Explorer, so that you can add SharePoint and OneDrive document libraries (or library folders) as folders in your personal computer or smart device and edit them there.

You can also add new files to these library folders, and they will be uploaded to the SharePoint or OneDrive library when you are signed in to SharePoint.

You can access the files even if you are offline, and they are synchronized automatically when you sign in to SharePoint again.

There is also a manual synchronization via the Sync button in the modern command bar and under the LIBRARY tab in classic libraries. Sync

In this section I will describe how the synchronization between libraries and the File Explorer folders should be set up.

12.3.1   *First Sync between a SharePoint Library and a Folder*

Once you have set up the synchronization between a library and your device, OneDrive for Business will keep track of changes and synchronize this library and folder automatically.

However, the first time you must do it manually. You can also perform the steps below anytime, if you need to make a manual sync.

1. Open any SharePoint document library.

2. Click on the 'Sync' button in the command bar or under the ribbon LIBRARY tab.

3. A 'Getting ready to sync' dialog will open. It has a link to download OneDrive for Business, but as it is included in the Office 365 subscription, you should not have to use that link.

4. You might be asked to open OneDrive for Business and/or to log in with your Office 365 account. Then you will see the location and name of the library folder that will be created on your computer. You now have a possibility to change the location.

5. When you click on 'Next', you will get a presentation of OneDrive for Business in 6 screens. You will also have a possibility to download the OneDrive for Business mobile app.

To add items, drag them into the OneDrive folder.

6. Then you are finished.

Open my OneDrive folder

Now you have a new folder in your File Explorer. From now on, OneDrive for Business will keep track of changes and synchronize the library and folder automatically.

If you add the new library folder to your Favorites/Quick access, it will be smooth to move files between that folder and your other folders. When you drag or copy/cut and paste items to the synchronized library folder, they will be automatically uploaded to the library when you are online and logged in to Microsoft/Office 365.

When you synchronize the OneDrive for Business "My files" library, the folder name will be OneDrive - COMPANY.

☁ OneDrive - Kalmstrom Enterprises AB

When you synchronize other SharePoint document libraries, they will be gathered as subfolders under a COMPANY folder. The subfolders have the names SITE - LIBRARY

🏢 Kalmstrom Enterprises AB 📌   Sales - Sales Documents

Demo:

https://www.kalmstrom.com/Tips/SharePoint-Online-Course/OneDrive-Sync.htm

12.3.2   Sync Issues

If the synchronization does not work, you can consider if one of these points can be the problem.

- The file is open.
- The file or folder name has a character that is not supported: \, /, :, *, ?, ", <, >, | , # , %,~.

12.3.3   Sync Settings

Click on the OneDrive icon in the task bar on your computer to reach the synchronization settings. (You might need to click on the 'Show hidden icons' arrow to see the OneDrive icon.)

12.3.3.1   Files On-Demand

OneDrive Files On-Demand is a feature that saves storage space on the computer, as it helps users to access synchronized files without downloading all of them. The Files On-Demand setting is found under the Settings tab in the synchronization settings.

Settings Account Network Office About

General

☑ Start OneDrive automatically when I sign in to Windows

☑ Automatically pause sync when this device is in battery saver mode

☑ Automatically pause sync when this device is on a metered network

Notifications

☑ Notify me when sync is auto-paused

Files On-Demand

☑ Save space and download files as you use them
More info

OK	Cancel

When the Settings box for 'Save space and download files as you use them' is checked, you can access your files without having to download them and take up storage space on your device:

Right-click on folders or files on your device and select either 'Always keep on this device' or 'Free up space'.

☁ › OneDrive - Kalmstrom Enterprises AB

^   Name   ^

itation   Attachments
                  Böcke   **Open**
sts   Files   Open in new window
ïce   Micro   Pin to Quick access
e   Micro
         MS Fl ☁ Share
skMan   Noteb   View online
:   ⊖ Quote   Always keep on this device
ESKTOF   websi   Free up space

230

New files created online or on another device appear as online-only files, so they don't take up space on your device. When you are connected to the internet, you can use the online files like every other file on your device.

In your File Explorer, each synchronized file has a status icon that shows how the file is available. These are the icons, from top to bottom in the image to the right:

Status

- Online-only: These files don't download to your device until you open them. You can only open these files when the device is connected to the internet.

- Locally available: When you open an online-only file, it downloads to your device and becomes a locally available file. Now you can open it anytime, even if you don't have internet access.

  These local files are cached, and if the drive gets low on space, some of the oldest files that have not been accessed in a while may be moved back to a cloud state to free up space. You can set this in Windows 10 under Storage >Change how we free up space automatically.

- Always keep: Files marked "Always Keep On Device" will always stay on the device and will not be moved back to cloud state automatically, even if drive space is low.

- Sync: synchronization is pending for the file.

12.3.4   *OneDrive Admin Center*

There is a link to the OneDrive Admin center in the SharePoint Admin center left menu.

In the OneDrive Admin center, Global and SharePoint administrators can control OneDrive users' sharing, synchronizing, storage, devices and more. The Compliance tab give links to the Security and Compliance center in Microsoft 365 Admin center.

The OneDrive settings are synchronized with the corresponding settings in the SharePoint Admin center. The OneDrive settings can be more restrictive than the SharePoint settings, but never more allowing.

The default settings for sharing and syncronization are generous. For example, 'Anyone with the link' is default for sharing, just like in SharePoint, and synchronization can be made to folders belonging to other organizations.

These generous permissions can of course be beneficial for business cooperation, but I strongly recommend that you study the default OneDrive admin settings and restrict them if necessary.

OneDrive admin center

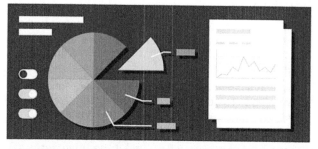

Home
Sharing
Sync
Storage
Device access
Compliance
Notifications
Data migration

Welcome to the OneDrive admin center

This is the new place to manage all your organization's OneDrive settings. We'll be adding reports and many other features soon, and would love to hear your suggestions on what to add or change.

Send feedback

12.3.5   *Control OneDrive Usage for Specific Users*

Administrators can control each user's OneDrive for Business usage from the Microsoft 365 Admin center >Active users. Click on the account name you want to check or manage to open the right panel. Then select the OneDrive tab. Now you can for example get a link to access the user's "My files" library (but not to any sites created from that library) and manage external sharing and OneDrive storage.

Nestor Wilke

🔍 Reset password   ⊘ Block sign-in   👤 Delete user

Change photo

Account   Devices   Licenses and Apps   Mail   **OneDrive**

Get access to files

Create a link to view and edit Nestor
Wilke's OneDrive files.
Create link to files

Storage used

0% (0 MB of 1024 GB)

Edit

Sharing

Control the external sharing of Nestor
Wilke's files and folders.
Manage external sharing

OneDrive settings for your organization

Data retention ⓘ

30 days
Manage data retention

Storage space

1024 GB per user
Manage default storage

12.4   SUMMARY

In this chapter, you have learned how to reach your personal SharePoint
Online start page and how you can use it to find content that you access
often.

I have also introduced OneDrive for Business. I have explained the
limitations of the "My files" library and described how to create a site that
can give many more options.

After reading this chapter, you should also know how OneDrive for Business
manages synchronization with folders on your computer of both the 'My files'
library and any other SharePoint document library.

As an admin, it is important that you now understand how you can control
OneDrive for Business via the OneDrive Admin center.

Security and permissions are important all over Microsoft 365, and we will
come back to that. But before we do that, we will have a look at the
SharePoint building block that we have not gone into yet: the page.

In the next chapter you will learn about the different kinds of SharePoint site
pages, and I will explain how you can create and customize them.

13 SHAREPOINT SITE PAGES

As we have seen earlier, SharePoint sites can store a lot of various content, and all content that should be visible to users is displayed on pages inside a site.

Each page is an ASPX file, which you can see on the URL. We have already talked about the homepage of a site. Its URL ends with Home.aspx, and each page that you create yourself ends with the page name + .aspx.

Some pages, like settings pages, are created by SharePoint and cannot be customized. They usually have a classic interface.

Apps are also contained in automatically created pages, and even if you can customize the app, you cannot customize the page it is contained in.

This chapter is about so called site pages – pages that users can create and customize. The automatically created homepages are also site pages and can be customized. By default, all users with Edit or Contribute permission level or higher can create and customize the pages described here.

The most common reason for creating a new page is probably that users need to have an additional space for some specific content. Instead of adding the content to an existing page, it is often better to create a new page for it. If you give a good name to the page, the content will be easier to find than if you add it to a page that already has other content.

By default, pages inherit the permissions from the site.

SharePoint Online offers three types of pages that can be customized: the modern page and the classic wiki and web part pages.

Today, the **modern** page is the most used site page in SharePoint Online. Even if modern pages give less customization possibilities than the wiki pages, the options are easy to understand and use. In some contexts, the term "site page" only refers to the modern page.

Modern pages are customized with specific web parts that are added to the page and modified. These web parts cannot be used in classic pages.

Classic pages use another kind of web parts. They give more options but are often a more complex to use. In wiki pages, you can also add text or links or insert images, videos etc. directly in the content area of the page.

I hope this chapter will explain the differences between the three types of site pages clearly. You will learn how to:

• Open pages in edit mode.

• Add and edit modern and classic web parts.

• Edit modern pages.

• Edit wiki pages and use the commands in the ribbon.

• Edit web part pages.

• Save and publish page modifications.

If you want to have more layout options than given by the default three page types, *refer to* chapter 27. There, I describe how to make a site use Publishing pages instead.

Demo:

https://kalmstrom.com/Tips/SharePoint-Online-Course/Site-Pages-and-Application-Pages.htm

13.1 THE SITE PAGES LIBRARY

SharePoint pages are files, and all modern pages and the classic wiki pages are stored in the site's "Site Pages" library. You can reach this library from the Site contents, and often also via a 'Pages' link in the Site navigation. (The classic web part pages are by default stored in the "Site Assets" library.)

The "Site Pages" library is created automatically by SharePoint when a new site is created. Generally, it works in the same way as a document library, but there are no buttons for upload or download.

You can add extra columns to the "Site Pages" library, to categorize the pages with metadata, and you can make columns mandatory to fill out. If a mandatory property is missing at publishing, the page author will have a message about it, and the page cannot be published until the mandatory property has been filled out.

The page properties can be managed in the "Site Pages" library in the same way as file properties in a document library. They can also be seen and edited directly on the page, via the 'Page details' button in the command bar.

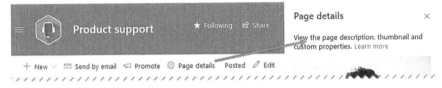

13.1.1 *Site Type Differences*

Team sites have more features in the "Site Pages" library than Communication sites.

Experience:

- In modern and classic Team sites, you can use both experiences in the "Site Pages" library, and you can switch interface with a link under the Site navigation, just like in other libraries.
- In Communication sites, the "Site Pages" library can only have the modern interface.

New pages:

- In Team sites, you can create both modern and classic pages from the "Site pages" library.

* In Communication sites, you can only create modern pages.

13.1.2   *Experience Differences*

The classic "Site Pages" interface gives less features than the modern, so I recommend that you use the modern interface in all "Site Pages" libraries, also in classic sites.

* When you use the modern interface in a "Site Pages" library, you can create approval flows and other flows for new pages, *refer to* chapter 24, SharePoint Automation.

* When you use the modern interface, you can schedule the publication of modern pages.

* The modern interface lets you make a page, modern as well as classic, homepage of the site.

* The modern interface has icons that show if the page is unpublished or checked out.

New-ergonomics-program.aspx	⊘ 📖	Santiago Earnest
6-ways-to-collaborate-with-your-team.aspx		Adele Vance
New-benefits-options-for-your-family1.a... 📖		Santiago Earnest

13.1.3   *Check Out*

Conflicting situations, where several people edit the same page, cannot occur in modern pages. For classic pages a setting is available to avoid such conflicts.

13.1.3.1   Modern Check Out

Modern pages are checked out automatically when someone opens the page in edit mode, whether check out is set to be required or not. Therefore, conflicting situations can never occur in modern pages.

Users who start editing a modern page, can see if someone else is already editing the same page, who that person is and how to contact him/her.

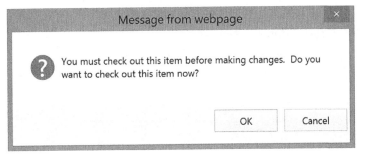

Peter Kalmström is editing this page 🔒 Edit ∨

Peter Kalmström

✉ Send email 💬 in

· · ·

Contact >

✉ peterk@kalmstrom.com

Show more

The page cannot be edited, but the site owner can discard the other person's changes.

13.1.3.2   Classic Check Out

If you are concerned about editing conflicts in classic pages, you can set the "Site Pages" library to always require check out of pages that go into edit mode. That is done under Library settings >Versioning Settings and applies to all pages in the "Site Pages" library.

1. In the Library settings, open the Versioning settings under the General Settings heading.

2. Select Yes at "Require documents to be checked out before they can be edited". (Pages are documents too, remember?)

Require documents to be checked out before they can be edited?
⦿ Yes   ○ No

When a user tries to edit a classic page after the mandatory check out setting has been activated in the "Site Pages" library, a warning message is displayed, and the user must click OK to check out the page.

Message from webpage   ×

? You must check out this item before making changes. Do you
   want to check out this item now?

                                        OK   Cancel

Even if check out is not set to mandatory in the "Site Pages" library, users can check out a classic page while editing it. Click on the 'Check Out' button under the ribbon PAGE tab to check out.

The 'Check Out' button will now be replaced with a 'Check In' button, which you can use when you are finished editing. The page will also have a status message.

BROWSE   PAGE

Edit   Check Out   Prc

Edit

⚠ **Status:** Checked out and editable.

If you save the page without checking in, it will remain checked out. You must check in the page to give other users access to the edited version and to let other users edit the page.

If you check in the page without saving first, it will be saved automatically.

13.1.4 *Version History*

Just as document libraries, the "Site Pages" library has version history enabled by default. It gives a possibility to restore earlier page versions and works just as described in section 7.12.

Modern pages have a link to the page's Version history in the 'Page details' pane.

Version history   ✕

⬤─ Highlight changes on the page

Current published v51.0   ···

Kate Kalmström published this page October 23

Changes made between v51.0 and v50.0

✎ Edited **List properties**

Published v50.0   ···

Kate Kalmström Compare with selected version

Delete

Published v49

Kate Kalmström Restore

13.1.5 *Scheduled Page Publishing*

The command bar in the "Site Pages" library **modern** interface has a 'Scheduling' button. It opens a right pane where you can enable scheduling for the site.

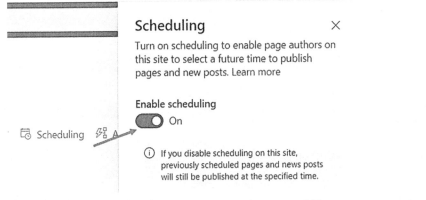

Scheduling   ✕

Turn on scheduling to enable page authors on this site to select a future time to publish pages and new posts. Learn more

Enable scheduling

🔘 On

🛈 If you disable scheduling on this site, previously scheduled pages and news posts will still be published at the specified time.

When scheduling has been enabled in the "Site Pages" library, page creators can schedule the publishing of new or modified pages if needed. This is done in the page's "Page details" pane, *refer to* 13.4.9. below.

This also applies to modern news posts, as each news post is a page, *see* 13.4.11, The News Web Part, below.

13.1.6   *Copy a Page*

In the "Site Pages" **modern** interface, you can use the 'Copy to' command that I earlier described for libraries to copy a page with all its content and layout. (That is not possible with the classic 'Copy' command.)

The page will be copied to the same "Site Pages" library, so that you can use the page as a template for another page in the site.

1. Select the page file you want to copy.

2. Click on 'Copy to' in the command bar or under the item ellipsis.

3. Click on 'Copy here' in the right pane (it is not possible to change the destination location).

4. The page will be copied and named with the suffix "1" after the original page name.

5. Select the new page, click on the ellipsis and rename the page.

Copy 1 item   ✕

📄 IT-Tickets.aspx

Places **Site Pages**

Copy here

13.1.7   *Set a Page as Homepage*

From the "Site Pages" library, you can easily replace a site's homepage with another page from the same site.

When you use the **modern** "Site Pages" interface, select the page you want to set as the site's homepage and click on the ellipsis in the command bar or at the page file. Select 'Make homepage'.

This command can make a homepage from both modern and classic pages, even if the command itself is only available in the modern interface.

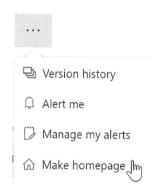

In the **classic** "Site Pages" interface, you can only make a classic page homepage. Open the page and click on the 'Make Homepage' button under the PAGE tab in the ribbon. There is no command to make a modern page homepage from the classic interface.

13.2   WEB PARTS INTRODUCTION

All three types of pages can be customized with web parts. A SharePoint web part is a building block that you can add to a SharePoint page. Most often, you also need to fill the web part with content, and there are different web parts for different kinds of content.

Modern pages have their own web parts that cannot be used with other page types. The modern web parts are very easy to use, but they have limited customization possibilities compared to classic web parts.

As the modern page is prioritized by Microsoft, new useful web parts are published continuously, and modern pages now have many web parts that don't have a corresponding web part in classic pages.

The **classic** web parts are used in wiki and web part pages. They cannot be used in modern pages, but I would recommend that you explore the classic web parts too. They give some possibilities that are not present in the modern web parts, as you will see later in this book.

13.2.1   *App Parts*

App parts are **classic** SharePoint web parts connected to apps that exist within the current site. When app data is displayed in app parts, they can be added to wiki and web part pages in that site in the same way as the other web parts.

From a user perspective app parts and web parts are the same, and some parts are found under both Web Parts and App Parts when the classic page is in edit mode. Therefore, I don't go into the differences here. You can use app parts in the same way as web parts.

Modern pages also have web parts that display app content, but here they are called web parts.

13.3 CREATE A PAGE

Modern pages can be created in several ways, but Classic pages can only be created from the "Site Pages" library in Team sites.

13.3.1 *Create a Page from Site Pages*

In Team sites, all kinds of pages can be created from the "Site Pages" library with the **modern** interface. When you click on '+ New' to create a new page, you can create all three types of site pages. Here, the modern page is called Site Page.

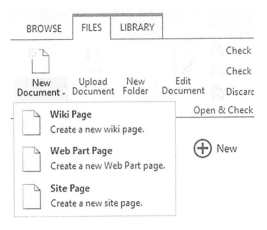

In Communication sites, only the 'Site Page' and 'Link' options are given under '+ New' in the "Site Pages" library. This means that you only can create modern pages in Communication sites.

If the "Site Pages" library has the **classic** interface, you can only create a wiki page from the '+new' button, but under the FILES tab you can create all three page types.

13.3.2 Create a Modern Page from +New or Add a Page

You can create modern pages outside the "Site Pages" library in three ways:

- Click on the 365 Settings icon and select 'Add a page'.

  This will give you a modern page even if you create the page in a classic site or from a page with the classic interface.

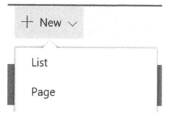

- In a modern homepage or in the modern 'Site contents' interface, click on '+ New' and select 'Page'.

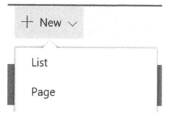

- In an existing modern page, click on '+ New' and select 'Page' or 'Copy of this page'.

13.4 MODERN PAGES

Modern pages have their own web parts that cannot be used in other types of pages. These web parts can be combined on the page to make it interesting and useful.

By default, all users with Edit permission are allowed to create modern pages, also called site pages, in modern as well as classic sites. This possibility can be disabled in two places:

- In the SharePoint Admin center >Settings >Pages, the possibility to create modern pages can be turned off for the whole organization.

- Site owners can deactivate the possibility to create modern pages for the site, under Site settings >Manage site features >Site pages.

When the possibility to create modern pages is disabled, you can still create classic pages in all Team sites, but no pages can be created in Communication sites.

Microsoft is planning to offer a tour the first time a user creates a new page or news post, to show how to pick a template, add and edit sections and web parts, title the page, and choose a title image.

13.4.1 *Page Templates*

When you have begun creating a modern page in one of the ways described above, a right pane will open where you will have a choice of templates. Select the template you want to use and click on 'Create page'.

By default, a blank page is pre-selected, but site owners can make another template pre-selected via the ellipsis on the template card.

From the template card ellipsis, you can also open the template, and custom templates can be edited or deleted from the site.

The custom templates are only displayed on the site where the page was saved as a template, and they can only be used there.

The Built-in templates are displayed in all sites. They cannot be edited or removed, so the ellipsis dropdown only shows the option 'Set default selection'.

Page templates are draft copies of pages. The custom templates are stored in an automatically created "Templates" folder in the "Site Pages" library, and you can reach the templates there or from the link at the bottom of the Template pane.

When you have selected your template, the new page will open in edit mode.

13.4.1.1   Save a Page as a Template

When you have created a page, you can let other people who have access to the site use your page as a template.

When you do that, the template will show up among the other templates when users create new modern pages.

To save a page as a temple, click on the 'Promote' button in the command bar when the page is in view mode and select the template option.

The 'Promote' right pane also opens automatically when you publish a page.

13.4.2   *Edit and Publish a Modern Page*

To open an existing modern page in edit mode, click on
the Edit button to the right in the command bar.

 🖉 Edit

When the page is open in edit mode, there will instead be
a 'Publish' button to the right in the command bar. Use it to publish your
modifications, so that other users can see them.

 📖 Publish

After the first publication, the button text is 'Republish' when you edit the
page again.

The page in edit mode has a title area on top, a canvas for the web parts
below the title area and panes for web part editing that open to the right.

When you are working with the page, the command bar has an option to
undo or redo recent modifications.

 🖫 Save as draft ∨   ⟲ Undo ∨   🖾 Discard changes

When the page has been published before, you can also select to discard all
changes and go back to the earlier version of the page.

Use the 'Save as draft' button to see how the page looks for users or to
continue working with the page on another occasion.

13.4.3 Title Area

There is no name giving when you create a modern page. Instead, you should change the text "Name your page" in the title area of the new page. That text will be used for automatic naming.

You can rename the page later, but the original name will be kept in the page URL. Therefore, you should think twice before you give the page a name, so that you don't need to change it!

No styles can be applied in the title area, but there are some limited customization options. The toolbar with these options appears when you hover the mouse cursor over the top left corner of the title area. Here, you can change the background image and reset the default image.

When you click on the edit icon in the title area toolbar, a right pane will open where you can make some modifications to the area. Use the 'Plain' option if you don't want to use a background image at all.

Title area   ✕

Customize the title area of your page including layout, publish date, and topic header.

Layout

| ◉ Image and title | Plain | Color block |

Overlap

Alignment

◉ Left

○ Center

Text above title

Enter text

40 character limit - 40 characters left

Show text block above title

(◯) No

Show published date

(◯) No

13.4.4   *Comments*

By default, the modern page has a Comments section at the bottom. You can removed it with the toggle to the right of the text 'Comments' when the page is in edit mode.

Comments ●━○ On

13.4.4.1   Disable Comments

When a modern page is made into a homepage, the comments section will be disabled automatically on that page.

Administrators can disable the comments section for all modern pages. This is done in the SharePoint Admin center >Settings >Pages.

13.4.5   *Sections*

To organize the content on a modern page, you should use the sections feature to compose a nice-looking page.

To show the layout options, click on the plus sign to the left under the title area or under an existing section. The one column section is default.

A section can have one, two or three columns. The web parts are placed inside the columns. When you put one

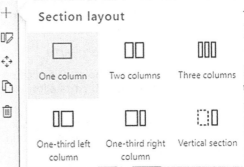

web part in each column, a section can have one, two or three web parts. It is also possible to stack multiple web parts inside one column.

With the option 'Vertical section', you can add a new column to the right that will run along all the other sections.

The image above comes from a Group Team site. Communication sites have an additional option: a full-width column, where the layout expands to the full width of the page.

A page often has several sections, and each section can have its own color and layout. Just click on the left plus sign again to select a new section.

SharePoint automatically adds a text web part to each column when you add a new section to a modern page, but if no text is entered, the text web part will not be visible on the published page.

13.4.5.1   Edit Sections and Web Parts

When you have added a section, some icons will appear under the section plus sign to the left.

The Edit icon in the Section command bar opens a right pane with options for layout and background color. There are currently four colors to choose from.

With the Move icon, you can drag the whole section up and down on the page.

The Duplicate icon adds a section of the same kind below the original section.

The waste basked icon deletes the section.

When you add web parts to the section columns, the same kind of icons will appear to the left of the web part when you select it. Here, the commands apply to the web part and not to the section. The content in the right Edit pane is different for each web part.

13.4.6 *Add Web Parts*

The modern page gives a choice of dedicated web parts that can be added to the page. Some modern web parts allow extensive customization, but many of them only have a few options.

When you have added a section to the page, it is time to start adding web parts to the section. Click on the plus sign in the middle of a column to show the web part selection.

Start typing in the Search box to easily find the web part you are looking for.

You can also search for web parts by category, and there is a toggle to switch between grid view and a list view with web part descriptions. Your most frequently used web parts will be shown on top.

Add the web part you prefer to the page by clicking on its icon.

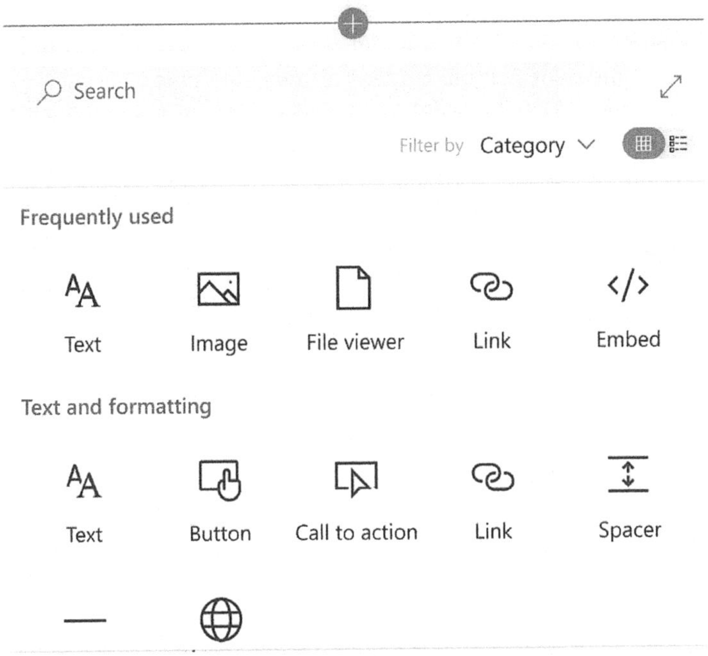
Search
Filter by
Category
Frequently used
Text
Image
File viewer
Link
Embed
Text and formatting
Text
Button
Call to action
Link
Spacer

When you have added and edited the web part, you can add more web parts in the same section or add a new section to add more web parts below or above the first section.

You can also anytime add new sections and web parts between existing sections and web parts.

13.4.7 *Add Content to Web Parts*

Most web parts are empty until you fill them with a specified kind of content. This content is linked to the web part, not added directly on the page. All content is governed by permissions, so users will only see what they have access to.

When you upload content from your computer to a web part, everyone who has access to the page will also get access to the content from your computer.

Uploaded content will be added to a "SitePages" folder in the site's "Site Assets" library. Each page will have its own folder inside the "SitePages" folder.

Most often, your changes to the web part will be saved automatically, but if you see an 'Apply' button at the bottom of the right Edit pane you should click on it!

In many web parts, the content is added in one these ways:

- The web part opens with a field where the content, for example text or a link, can be added directly into the web part.

- The web part and the right Edit pane opens at the same time.

- When you have clicked on the web part to add it to the page, a wide, right pane for location selection opens. Here you can find a menu to the left and content options to the right.

🕒 Recent

🖼 Stock images

🔍 Web search

☁ OneDrive

🌐 Site

🖥 Upload

🔗 From a link

The left location menu is the same in most web parts. Select a link in the left hand menu and then select the content you want to add from the main area to the right (except for the Upload option, which opens your File Explorer).

- The web part opens on the page, and you can add content by clicking on a button in the web part. When you do that, either the location selection pane or the right Edit pane opens, so that you can make your choices.

You can also always select the web part to display the left command bar, *see* above in 13.4.5.1, Edit Sections and Web Parts. Click on the pen icon to edit the web part or replace the content.

13.4.7.1   Add an Image or File

When you want to add just one image to a page, you should use the Image web part, and for just one file you should use the File Viewer web part.

When you use these web parts, you don't have to add the web part to the page first. You can just drag the image or file to the canvas area when the page is in edit mode.

Drop the file when you see a line on the page. Now the Image or File viewer web part will be added automatically, filled with the image or file that you dragged to the page.

13.4.8   *Web Part Examples*

When this is written, Microsoft supplies 44 web parts to use with modern pages, and new web parts are published continuously. In addition to that, each tenant can have third party apps/add-ins that have been added to the organization's App Catalog and are available for the whole tenant.

Most web parts have names that tell what they can display, and they are not difficult to figure out. Therefore, I will not go into each of them here but just give a few examples on how you can use modern web parts. I will also mention and describe several modern web parts in other chapters of this book.

Should you need assistance, Microsoft has a good online guide where most modern web parts are described in detail: https://support.office.com/en-us/article/Using-web-parts-on-SharePoint-Online-pages-336e8e92-3e2d-4298-ae01-d404bbe751e0

The web part setting options I describe in the sections below are set in the right pane that opens when you edit the web part.

13.4.8.1   Button and Call to action

The Button and Call to action web parts let you create a button that loads the content you specify with a link.

13.4.8.2   Divider

The Divider web part is simply a vertical line that divides web parts. Its color follows the theme of the site, but you can control the length and to some extent also the thickness.

13.4.8.3   Document Library and List

The Document library and List web parts show the library or list you select (only from within the site). These web parts don't have all the features that are present in the apps, but for many purposes the existing features are enough to work with the app.

When you have added the web part to the page, the libraries or lists in the site will be displayed in the web part, so that you can select one of them to display.

In the Document library web part, all libraries in the site will show up for selection, not only document libraries. Therefore, you can add other kinds of libraries to this web part too, for example a Picture library, *refer to* 17.1, Picture Library.

List

- Bugs
- Calculation
- Computers
- Content and Structure Reports

With list apps, it is the other way around. When this is written, you can only add custom list apps and lists built on the Announcements, Contacts and Issue tracking templates to the Lists web part.

When you add a Document library or List web part to a page, files and items can be opened directly from the page. You can also do much other work without leaving the page. You can switch view and open the grid, and when you select an item and click on the Information icon, the right pane will open in edit mode so that you can edit the metadata.

New items can be created, and in the library web part, files can be uploaded or downloaded.

13.4.8.4   Hero

The Hero web part is by default added to the homepage of a new Topic and Showcase Communication site, but you can add it to other modern pages too.

In the Hero web part, you can add up to five items in tiles or layers and use images and text to draw attention to each of them.

Videos can also be added, but they are not played on the page. Instead, users are taken to the video player or link source when they click on the video tile.

In the right Edit pane for the Hero web part, you can select several layout options.

When you have chosen layout, add the items by clicking on the 'Select link' buttons. Then you can edit each item with the icons you see when you hover over a tile.

From left to right, the icons on the tiles let you:

• Open the right pane to edit the tile.

- Move the item. Select with the icon and then use Ctrl + left or right arrow to move.

- Set the focal point of the tile.

- Enlarge or decrease what is shown in the tile.

The right Edit pane for each item gives options for text and settings. It is also here you can change the item in the tile or layer.

13.4.8.5   Highlighted Content

The Highlighted content web part uses the search engine to get content. By default, it searches for and displays your most recently used content in the site, but you can customize what the web part should search for and display.

As the web part uses the search engine, all content will be security trimmed and users will only be shown content that they have access to.

The Highlighted content web part can also filter and sort the items, and you can select layout and decide how many items should be displayed.

With the Highlighted Content web part you are invited to specify source, content type (*refer to* chapter 25) and metadata, and the web part will show items according to that.

This means that you must in some way narrow the search to display exactly the content you want to show. You can, for example:

- keep the content you wish to display in a specific document library

- select to show a certain kind of content type, for example videos or documents

- give a specific keyword to each item you want to include

- filter by a managed metadata.

Source

All sites ⌄

Type

All ⌄

＋ Add content type

Document type

Any ⌄

＋ Add document type

Filter and sort ⌃

Filter

Managed property ⌄

Enter a word to narrow down the list of property names, and select a property from the dropdown.

Find a managed property

Enter a word to find properties

Managed property name

🗑 Remove

Filter

Title includes the words ⌄

Enter search words

🗑 Remove
＋ Add filter

Sort by

Most recent ⌄

13.4.8.6   Organization Chart

With the Organization chart web part, you can generate an organization chart centered on an individual.

When you have added the web part, enter any user and then select in the Edit pane how many levels to display.

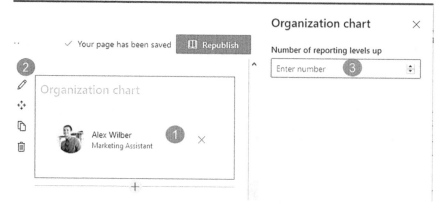

When you have entered a figure in the field, more people will show up in the web part, but it does not become interesting until you publish it.

After publication, you can select any person in the chart and see the people who report to them. Here I have created a chart with three levels, starting from Alex Wiber.

No people report to Alex Wiber. Therefore, I instead show an image of how the chart looks when I select Miriam Graham. Multiple people report to her, and one of them is Alex Wiber. You can select any of the people in the chart, to see the people who report to that person.

13.4.8.7   Spacer

The Spacer web part gives a horizontal space that divides sections or web parts. It is possible to change the size by dragging the bottom line up and down. You can also use the arrow keys.

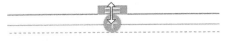

Drag or use up and down arrow keys to resize

13.4.8.8   365 Apps

Several 365 apps and services have their own modern web parts, where you can display content that has been created with the apps. Such web parts are Bing maps, Group calendar, Microsoft Forms, Microsoft Stream, Power BI and Yammer conversations and highlights.

My book *Office 365 from Scratch* gives information about these apps and services.

Demos:

https://www.kalmstrom.com/Tips/SharePoint-Online-Course/New-Page-Model-Intro.htm

https://www.kalmstrom.com/Tips/SharePoint-Online-Course/New-Page-Model-Text.htm

https://www.kalmstrom.com/Tips/SharePoint-Online-Course/New-Page-Model-Highlighted.htm

13.4.9   *Page Details*

When you click on the Page details button in the modern page command bar when the page is in Edit   ⚙ Page details
mode, you can add a description and a custom thumbnail for the page. These will be shown in the SharePoint search results and news.

You can also add an audience if that feature is enabled in the "Site Pages" library, *refer to* 14.12, Audience Targeting, and see when the page was last modified.

Page details   ✕

View and edit the page description, thumbnail,
and custom properties. Learn more

| Change thumbnail | ⓘ |

Description ⓘ

Enter description here

255 character limit - 255 characters left

Properties   ∧

    𝔸 **Audience**

Enter a name or email address

More details   ∧

Modified

10/16/20, 11:34 AM

When the page has been published, the Page details shows the same
information, but now you can also find a link to the Version history for the
page, below the Modified
information.

The Version history link opens
another right pane, where you can
compare versions and restore or
delete earlier versions.

Version history   ✕

   ◉▬   Highlight changes on the page

Current published v2.0   ···

MOD Administrator published this page about a
minute ago

Draft v1.1   ···
                ↓

MOD Administra Compare with selected version
ago

                Delete

Published v1.0 Restore

MOD Administrator published this page 6 hours

When scheduling has been enabled in the "Site Pages" library, *refer to* 13.1.5, Schedule Page Publishing, the Site details pane has a scheduling option.

Scheduling ∧

On

Publish Start Date

Enter a date 📅

12:00 AM ∨

With the page in edit mode, open the page details and set the Scheduling toggle to On. Now you can select a date and a time for the publishing.

13.4.10   *Promote a Page*

The Promote right pane, gives several options for sharing information about the page.

This pane opens when you publish a page and when you click on the 'Promote' button in the modern page command bar.

You can also promote the page via the e-mail button in the command bar.

Also *refer to* 14.7, Share a Page.

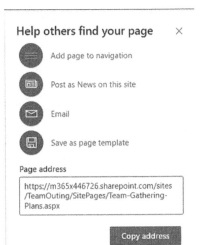

Help others find your page ✕

Add page to navigation

Post as News on this site

Email

Save as page template

Page address

https://m365x446726.sharepoint.com/sites /TeamOuting/SitePages/Team-Gathering-Plans.aspx

Copy address

13.4.11   *The News Web Part*

When you add a News web part to a page, you only select the source(s) for the news and decide the layout. The actual content in the News web part comes when you and other users start creating news posts.

News posts can come from the site, from all sites in the hub or from one or more individual sites.

News Source ∧

Select a news source

◯ This site

◉ All sites in the hub

◯ Select sites

◯ Recommended for current user

You can also choose the option 'Recommended for current user', which displays different posts for each user: from people the user works with, managers and connections and followed and frequently visited sites.

You can select from multiple layouts for the News web part. The default layout depends on what kind of modern site the page is created in.

By default, the News web part shows the news posts in the order they are published, with the most recent on the prominent place, but you can reorder them by drag and drop under 'News Order' in the right Edit pane. The News web part also has many other settings in the right pane.

A News web part is added to the site's homepage when you create a modern Group Team site and a Topic Communication site.

13.4.11.1   Create a News Post

News posts are modern SharePoint pages. They are shown and can be managed in the "Site Pages" library, and they are created in the same way as other modern pages. The only difference is how you start creating them.

News posts can be created from the SharePoint Online start page.

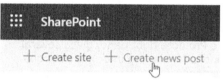

A right pane will open, where you must select site where the news post should be posted. Then a blank modern page will open, and you can start creating the page with any web parts you wish to use.

When you are done with creating your new post, click on 'Post news' to the right in the command bar to publish it.

The news post will now be published to the site you selected and to other pages with a News web part that fetches news posts from that site.

News posts can also be created from the '+ New' button in modern homepages and from the 'Add' dropdown in News web parts.

News

+ Add ⌄

News post 🖑

News link

+ New ⌄   ⚙ Page deta

List

Document library

Page

News post

      🖑

News link

In this case, you will have a possibility to select template before you start editing the page, but there is no site selection. The post will be published in the News web part on the current site and in other pages with a News web part that fetches news posts from that site.

Demo:

https://www.kalmstrom.com/Tips/SharePoint-Online-Course/New-Page-Model-News.htm

13.4.11.2   Create a News Link

As you see from the images above, it is also possible to add a news post via a link to content inside or outside the tenant. The content you link to will be displayed as a news post.

When you select 'News link' option from the '+ New' button in a modern homepage or from the 'Add' dropdown in a News web part, a right pane will open where you can paste the link.

In this case, you don't have to create a new page. All the editing is performed in the right pane, which also has a 'Post' button.

When the link is added, a preview of the content is loaded, and a title and a description are suggested. You can of course change the preview image and edit the title and description before you post the news.

13.4.12   *Space*

Microsoft has very recently introduced a new kind of modern page called Space. Standard release is from mid-February to mid-April 2021.

A Space page is very graphic, with a possibility to add 2D and 3D web parts and to rotate the page 360°.

$+$ New $\vee$ ⚙ ı

When this is written, spaces can only be created in Communication sites. These sites have a Space command under the '+New' button in the homepage and the "Site Pages" library.

List

Document library

Page

Click on the 'Space design' button in the command bar to open a right pane and give the space a name and description. Here, you can also select a structure, a background image and an ambient sound, and you can add an audio file with a recorded welcoming message.

Space

The web parts are few, so far, and they remind of the other modern web parts – but when you add them to the page, you will see a difference.

You can add the web parts anywhere around the 360° area, and they are minimized until a user clicks on one of them to bring it to the front – as I have done with a document in the image below.

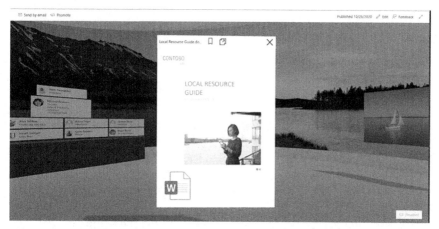

When you understand how to create modern pages, the space pages are not difficult to figure out. Therefore, I will not go into spaces more deeply here.

13.4.12.1   Disable Space

Space pages are enabled by default, but site owners can deactivate the feature for a site under Site settings >Site Actions >Manage site features.

If you don't want 'Space' to be displayed in the '+New' menu across the tenant, you'll need to enable tenant-level control by executing the following PowerShell command with the latest version of the SPO module: Set-SPODisableSpacesActivation -scope tenant -Disable $true

When that script has been run, space creation must be activated for each site, under Site Actions >Manage site features.

To learn more about Space pages, please refer to Microsoft: https://support.microsoft.com/en-us/office/sharepoint-spaces-7b65edfb-7cc9-42e3-af37-178d79364a5e?ui=en-US&rs=en-US&ad=US

13.5   CLASSIC PAGES

Classic pages can only be created from the "Site Pages" library in Team sites, but they can be created in classic as well as modern Team sites.

13.5.1   *Edit a Wiki Page*

The wiki page is the site page that gives you most customization possibilities. Here you can add text or links or insert images, videos etc. directly into the page or insert various kinds of web parts and customize them.

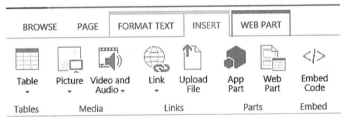

New wiki pages will open in edit mode. There are three ways to open an existing wiki page in edit mode:

- Click on the 'EDIT' button in the top right corner of the page.

- Click on the 'Edit' button under the ribbon 'PAGE' tab.

- Click on the 365 Settings icon and select 'Edit page'.

When the page opens in edit mode, the 'EDIT' button will be replaced with a 'SAVE' button. There is also a 'SAVE' button to the left under the 'PAGE' tab.

Wiki pages are coded in HTML, but various tools in the SharePoint ribbon make it easy to modify the pages and insert items. It is also easy to undo changes.

If you want to use HTML code, you should be aware that there are some restrictions in the use of CSS and JavaScript. Here I will only show how to reach the HTML code and instead focus on no-code customization with the SharePoint tools.

BROWSE	PAGE	FORMAT TEXT	INSERT	WEB PART
Table	Picture	Video and Audio	Link	Upload File	App Part	Web Part	Embed Code
Tables	Media		Links		Parts		Embed

Besides customizing the wiki page directly, you can add web parts to the page and customize them.

13.5.1.1   Enter and Format Text

You can enter and format text in a wiki page just like you do in Word and other Office apps. Place the mouse cursor where you want to start typing or where you want to paste test. Under the ribbon FORMAT TEXT tab, there are many options for text formatting.

BROWSE	PAGE	FORMAT TEXT	INSERT	WEB PART
Save	Check In	Paste	Undo	Body	13px	B I U abc x, x² A	
Edit		Clipboard		Font			Paragraph

You can easily undo changes with the Undo button or with the Ctrl key + the Z key. Use Ctrl + Y to repeat.

Instead of using the controls in the 'Font' ribbon group, I would recommend that you use styles. The 'Styles' ribbon group is found further to the right under the FORMAT TEXT tab.

The styles are stored in a "Styles" library that is common for a site and all its subsites. It is a bit of work to edit the styles so that they become as you want them, but when the work is done the styles are there and can be used in other pages too.

The styles will give your SharePoint site a consistent look, and if you want to change something, you can just change the style. Then the change will be applied on all pages where that style is used.

Demo:

https://www.kalmstrom.com/Tips/SharePoint-Online-Course/Start-Edit-Webpart.htm

13.5.1.2   Add a Table

It is not as easy as in Word, and there are not as many features, but it is quite possible and not very difficult to add a table to a SharePoint wiki page.

1. Under the INSERT tab, click on the Table button.

2. Select Insert Table to open a dialog OR use the grid below the button.

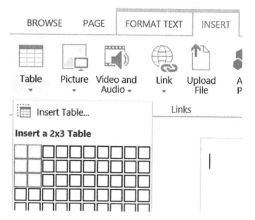

3. In the Insert Table dialog, enter the number of columns and rows you want the table to include, OR drag the mouse over the preferred number of columns and rows in the grid.

4. When you click OK in the dialog OR let go of the mouse, the table will be inserted into the page.

When you place the mouse cursor inside the table, two table tool tabs will be displayed: TABLE LAYOUT and DESIGN. Here you can edit the table.

BROWSE	PAGE	FORMAT TEXT	INSERT	TABLE LAYOUT	DESIGN				
					Table Width	100%	Column Width	17%	Summary:
					Table Height	95 px	Row Height	31 px	
Merge Cells ▾	Split Cells ▾	Insert Above	Insert Below	Insert Left	Insert Right	Delete			
Merge			Rows & Columns				Width & Height		Properties

If you prefer to create the table in Word or another Office application, you can copy that table and paste it into the SharePoint wiki page.

Demo:

https://www.kalmstrom.com/Tips/SharePoint-Online-Course/Table.htm

13.5.1.3   Edit Source

Far to the right in the ribbon, under the FORMAT TEXT tab, you can find the Edit Source button. This control opens the web part in HTML so that you can edit the code or paste code from another editor.

Note that only the code of the body is displayed, and there are some limitations when it comes to JavaScript and CSS. Also *refer to* chapter 26, Add CSS. JavaScript or RSS to a Classic Page.

Edit
Source

13.5.1.4   Insert a Web Part

These are general step for adding a web part to a wiki page:

1. Open the page in edit mode.

2. Place the mouse cursor where you want to add the web part.

3. Open the INSERT tab and click on the Web Part button.

4. Select a category.

5. Select a web part and click on the Add button.

6. Edit the web part; *refer to* 13.5.3, Edit Classic Web Parts, below.

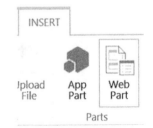

13.5.1.5   Save

When you have finished editing the page, you must save it to keep the changes.

Click on the SAVE link on the top right of the page. You can also click on the Save button under the ribbon PAGE and FORMAT TEXT tabs.

The Save button has more options. Use the Stop Editing option when you want to discard your changes.

Save   Check Out   Paste

Edit

Save

Save and Keep Editing

Stop Editing

Edit in SharePoint Designer

13.5.1.6 The Get Started Web Part

When you create a classic team site, the start page is a wiki page. It has a "Get started with your site" web part with five links displayed as tiles, so called promoted links.

The "Get started with your site" web part is the only web part you can delete without first opening the page in edit mode, and that is because Microsoft has given a "REMOVE THIS" link for removal of the Get Started web part.

If you want to have the Get Started web part back again, you need to add it like you add other web parts to a wiki page.

Demo:

https://kalmstrom.com/Tips/SharePoint-Online-Course/Get-Started-Web-Part.htm

13.5.2 *Edit a Web Part Page*

In web part pages the customization is not done freely, as in the wiki pages, because it is not possible to simply type directly into a web part page. Instead, the customization is structured with web part zones.

When you create a web part page, you will have a choice of layouts, with different options for header, footer, columns and body.

Choose a Layout Template:

Header, Footer, 3 Columns
Full Page, Vertical
Header, Left Column, Body
Header, Right Column, Body
Header, Footer, 2 Columns, 4 Rows
Header, Footer, 4 Columns, Top Row
Left Column, Header, Footer, Top Row, 3 Columns
Right Column, Header, Footer, Top Row, 3 Columns

To open a web part page in edit mode, click on the 365 Settings icon and select 'Edit page'. This is the same as the third option for opening wiki pages in edit mode, see above.

The page will open in edit mode. It will now have a 'Stop Editing' button under the ribbon 'PAGE' tab, and the page will be saved automatically when you click on that button.

13.5.2.1 Add a Web Part to a Web Part Page

Web part pages have an 'Add a Web Part' link on top of each web part zone, and the web part page is often published instead of saved. Otherwise, the steps to add web parts in a web part page are like the steps for the wiki page, and the same web parts can be used.

Header

Add a Web Part

Left Column

Add a Web Part

Middle Column

Add a Web Part

Right Column

Add a Web Part

Footer

Add a Web Part

1. Open the page in edit mode.

2. Click on an 'Add a Web Part' link.

3. Select a category.

4. Select a web part and click on the Add button.

5. Edit the web part, *refer to* 13.5.3, Edit Classisc Web Parts below.

6. (Repeat step 2-6 to add more web parts in the same or another zone.)

7. Save the changes by clicking on the 'Save' button or link.

8. Stop editing the page.

13.5.3   *Edit Classic Web Parts*

Wiki and web part pages use the same kind of web parts, and those can be edited and highly customized.

Modify the classic web part properties by clicking on the arrow in the top right corner of the web part and selecting 'Edit Web Part'.

Here you can also delete and minimize the web part, and some web parts can be exported to your computer.

Minimize

✕ Delete

Edit Web Part

Export...

Another way to reach the Edit Web Part command is to open the WEB PART tab in the ribbon and click on the 'Web Part Properties' button.

The 'Edit Web Part' panel is shown to the right of the web part and has the name of the web part in the top banner. These panels look different for each web part, but all of them have multiple options. The image below shows the panel for a "Documents" web part.

Documents   ✕

List Views   ⌃

You can edit the current view or select another view.

Selected View

| <Current view> | ☑ |

Edit the current view

Toolbar Type

| Full Toolbar | ☑ |

⊞ Appearance

⊞ Layout

⊞ Advanced

⊞ AJAX Options

⊞ Miscellaneous

| OK | Cancel | Apply |

Most web parts require that you press OK or Apply to save the web part property modifications. Otherwise, the changes will not be saved when you save the page.

Below, I will give one example of an app part and one example of a web part, but later in this book you will find many more examples.

13.5.3.1   The Content Editor Web Part

In SharePoint 2007 and earlier, the Content Editor web part was the only way to insert text, images and so on in a web page, and it still works in the same way.

The most common reason for using the Content Editor web part in a web part page, is to give a web part page the same features as a wiki page. That is because the Content Editor ribbon gives the same options as you get in wiki pages without adding a web part.

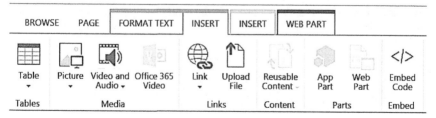

Therefore, if nothing else is mentioned, when I just say classic pages in this book, I refer to wiki pages as well as web part pages where the Content Editor web part has been added.

There are however reasons to use the Content Editor web part in wiki pages too. You can for example add JavaScript and CSS to a page with the Content Editor, something that cannot be done directly in a wiki page.

You will find the Content Editor web part in the Media and Content category. Edit the web part and set the Chrome Type to None to avoid having the Content Editor caption on the web part.

Demo:

https://kalmstrom.com/Tips/SharePoint-Online-Course/Content-Editor-Intro.htm

13.5.3.2   Add a Web Part to a Form

Maybe you want to add something on the new item form page that is not part of the form itself, for example information on how the form should be filled out? That can be done by adding a web part to the list form page. This method is only possible with the **classic** app interface, and only with list apps. (Libraries do not open a form page when you click on 'new'.)

The classic SharePoint list forms are contained in web part pages, and the existing web parts cannot be customized without extensive coding. You can however add another web part which can be customized, and I would recommend the Content Editor web part.

In the Content Editor web part, you can embed code and add tables, links, pictures, videos or even another web part, so this is the only no-code way to show for example an instruction or a video above the new item form.

The classic experience has three item forms: New, Display and Edit. In the steps below, I will describe how to add a web part to the New form. That web part will only be visible in the new item form, not in the Display or Edit forms.

You can either select the form under the LIST tab in the ribbon or just open the form you want to edit.

1. Click on 'new' in the list or select 'Default New Form' in the ribbon.

2. Open the 365 Settings icon and select 'Edit page'.

3. Add the Content Editor web part from the Media & Content category.

4. Add the content you wish to add from the options under the ribbon tabs.

5. Edit the web part and set the Chrome Type to None to avoid having the Content Editor caption on the web part.

6. Click on the 'Stop Editing' button.

To add a web part to the Edit or Design forms, open these pages and edit them in the same way as described above.

The modern experience uses a right pane for data entry, display and modification, not a web part page, and it is not possible to modify this pane without coding. If you use the classic interface to edit the form and then switch to the modern interface, your modification will not be visible.

Demo:

https://kalmstrom.com/Tips/SharePoint-Online-Course/SharePoint-Forms-Browser.htm

13.5.3.3 The Calendar App Part

When you have created a team calendar, you probably want to display it on a page, maybe on the homepage the Team site, instead of having it as a separate list. To do that, you can insert a calendar app part in a classic page.

1. Open a page in edit mode.

2. Add the calendar web part. (You can also find it under 'App Part').

3. Edit the web part as you prefer and save the page.

(Modern pages have a Group Calendar web part, but it can only be used for calendars belonging to a Microsoft 365 group. There is currently no possibility to add other calendars to a modern page.)

Demo:

https://www.kalmstrom.com/Tips/SharePoint-Online-Course/Calendar-App.htm

13.6 ADD FILES TO PAGES

Shared documents should be kept in one place, so that you don't have to change in several libraries when the documents must be edited.

Therefore, it is a bad idea to upload the same document to multiple libraries. It is better to add the file to pages in those sites, because then they will be updated automatically when the file is updated in the library.

I would recommend that you add an Enterprise Keywords column, *refer to* 15.4.2, to SharePoint libraries that contain files you want to share between sites. This makes the files easy to find in filtering and search.

13.6.1 *The No Access Issue*

When you add files to SharePoint pages to share them, you need to consider how a file is displayed to users who don't have access to it.

SharePoint only shows content to those who have permissions to see it. Normally, all site members have access to all files in the site, but if the file is stored in another site, there might be a problem. Therefore, you should always consider how the page will look for people who have access to the page but not to all the shared files.

Below, I will describe methods to add files in a page and also comment on the no access issue.

Of the methods I describe below, the classic Content Search method is the best for users without access, because it only shows links – or a small empty space from missing links for people without access.

13.6.2   Add One File to a Page

Modern pages have two web parts that are suitable for showing one specific file embedding: File viewer and Embed.

- The File viewer web part can only show content from inside the tenant.
- The Embed web part can show content from a range of common sites. Site administrators can however control this embedding under Site settings >HTML Field Security.

In **classic** pages, a file can be embedded with its embed code.

All these methods to show one file, will show the web part even to users who don't have access to that file. Instead of the file, users without permission to view it will have an Access Denied message and a possibility to request access. Imagine how a page with several such messages would look!

Sorry, you don't have access.

I'd like access, please.

Request Access

13.6.2.1   File Viewer

The **modern** File viewer web part lets you add files from sources within the tenant that you have access to without an embed code. You can select files from your recently used files, from your OneDrive, from the current site or from your computer.

Excel, Word, PowerPoint, Visio, PDFs, 3D models are among the supported files. Images embedded in other files, like in a slideshow, are displayed, but image files are currently not supported. Therefore, it is a bug that Microsoft's stock images are active in the File viewer file picker dialog.

Use the link option when you want to display a file from another site. When you have the link to the file, you can add any file that you have access to from the SharePoint tenant, and as we have seen in 9.4, Find a File Link, you can easily get these links in the library where the file is stored.

The File viewer web part can only display a file that is stored in SharePoint Online or OneDrive for Business. When you select to upload a file to the File viewer web part, it will be saved in the site's default document library.

Office files that are displayed in the File viewer web part are updated on the modern page automatically when they have been edited, and they can be downloaded and printed directly from the page.

When the Office file has been published, there is a small toolbar when you hover the mouse over the bottom right corner of the web part. Click on the menu icon to see the options.

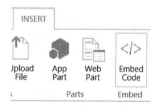

Download a Copy

Print to PDF

Accessibility Mode

Embed Information

Terms of Use

Privacy and Cookies

100%

PFD files have another toolbar, and here the open in new window icon to the right is important. You need to use it to be able to print the file.

13.6.2.2   Modern Embed

Sometimes the modern Embed web part accepts a link, but I have found that an embed code that starts with <iframe>works best. Many sites give such code snippets, so look for "Embed code" or the "</>" icon if you want to embed content from a website.

13.6.2.3   Classic Embed

To embed a file in a wiki page you need the embed code. Open the page in edit mode and click on the 'Embed Code' button under the INSERT tab. Paste the embed code into the form (and modify it if needed) and click on 'Insert'.

Refer to section 9.2.3. for information on how to get the embed code for Word and PowerPoint files.

INSERT

Jpload File   App Part   Web Part   Embed Code

Parts   Embed

13.6.3   *Add Multiple Files to a Page*

You can add a library in a web part in both modern and classic pages, and that is a good solution if you have relevant files there and want users to be able to work with them on the page.

When you want to add selected files to a page, some additional planning is necessary, because the files need to have some common categorization to be able to search.

An advantage with showing multiple files in a web part, is that there are no "access denied" messages. Users will only see the files they have access to, and the web part adapts better in size than the one file web parts.

13.6.3.1   Modern Highlighted Content Method

We have already met the Highlighted content web part in section 13.4.8.5, and if you combine it with an Enterprise Keywords column in the library, you can make this web part display the shared documents.

13.6.3.2   Classic Content Search Method

With the Content Search web part, you can quickly gather files from several sites to one classic page. In this example, the web part gives links to all files that are tagged with a certain keyword. Note that this is a classic web part that only can be used in classic sites.

1. Add the Content Search web part to a classic page.

2. Edit the web part.

3. In the Query Builder, set the query to show only documents that are tagged in a certain way.

   a. Select the query 'Items matching a tag (System)'.

   b. Select to not restrict the results by app if you want to have files from the whole tenant.

   c. Restrict the results by tag and enter the tag you wish to use.

   d. Click OK.

4. Define the other settings for the web part and click on Apply.

5. Publish or Save the page.

Demo:

https://kalmstrom.com/Tips/SharePoint-Online-Course/Share-Docs-Between-Collections.htm

13.7   PAGES INSTEAD OF DOCUMENTS

The easiest way to share documents is of course to just upload them to a document library, but there is a more elegant way: pages. I will give an example of how pages can be used instead of documents. Pages are easier to read than documents, and pages load much quicker than documents and can be more interactive, containing videos etc.

To use this method, add the content of each document on a separate page and link to those pages from the Site navigation. This can be done with modern pages as well as with wiki pages.

Most organizations have documents for company guidelines that should be shared among users. Therefore, I have used company guidelines as document examples here, but the method can be used for all kinds of content.

1. Create a new site for the guidelines.

2. Create a new page and give it the same name as one of the guideline documents.

3. Add the content of the document to the page.

4. (Add additional content if needed.)

5. Repeat step 2-4 for all documents.

6. Remove all links from the Site navigation.

7. Add links to the guideline pages in the Site navigation instead.

   a. Open the Site contents and then the "Site Pages" library.

   b. Click on 'Edit' at the bottom of the Site navigation and then on 'Edit Links'.

   o When the "Site Pages" library has the **modern** interface, select one of the pages and click on 'Add to navigation' in the command bar. That page will now get a link in the Site navigation.

   Add to navigation

   o In the **classic** experience, click on 'Edit links' at the bottom of the Site navigation and drag and drop the page files to the navigation.

   c. Repeat the addition to the navigation for each page.

The site should have a suitable homepage, and for that you can either customize the default homepage or make one of the guidelines pages the homepage, *refer to* 13.1.7, Set a Page as Homepage.

Demo:

https://www.kalmstrom.com/Tips/SharePoint-Online-Course/Company-Guidelines.htm

13.8   VIEWS LANDING PAGE

SharePoint apps have the limitation of displaying only one (modern) or three (classic) views right on the page. To reach the other views, you must open a dropdown.

If you want to give users an overview of all views, you can create a landing page that is displayed when users open the app. To this page you can of course also add more data than just the view links.

The image below shows a modern page where the Quick Links web part has been used with the Tile layout.

![Communications page showing IT Tickets landing page with navigation menu on left (Notebook, Team Calendar, Team Documents, Shared with us, Teams Channel, Comms OneNote, Strategy Reviews, Press Releases, Legal, Pages, Recycle bin) and tile links: My Tickets, Active Tickets, All Tickets, Permission Issues, Printer Issues, Upgrade Issues]

The landing page is created in two steps:

1. Create the page with links to the views. The view URLs are copied from the app address field and pasted into the landing page, so keep the list open in another tab so that you quickly can move between the app and the landing page you are creating.

2. Replace the links to the app, so that they point to the new landing page.

13.8.1   *Modern Views Landing Page*

For a modern page, I recommend the Quick links web part, but a Text web part can also work. The description below is for a Quick links web part.

1. In a modern page in edit mode, click on the plus sign to the left and select the layout that is most suitable for the views you want to add.

2. Click on the plus sign in the middle of the top border and select the Quick Links web part.

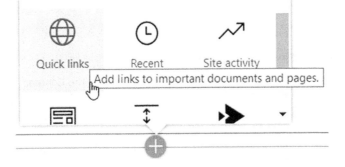

3. Click on the Edit web part pen icon and select layout.

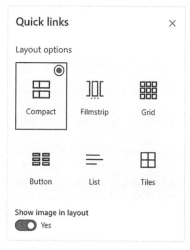

4. Click on '+Add links' in the web part and then on 'From a link'.

5. Copy a URL for one of the views from the list's address field and paste it into the dialog that opens.

6. The right Edit pane opens with various options for the link. As you see, you can have a custom image for each link. (In the image above, all tiles have the same background.)

7. Repeat step 5 for each link and Publish the page.

Link

/sites/demosite/Lists/Phone%20Messages/AllIte ms.aspx?viewid=c4c9e0fc-d397-4f36-9cd3-0db611af38d58&web=1

Change

Title

| All items |

110 characters limit - 101 characters left

Thumbnail

⦿ Auto-selected

○ Custom image

○ Icon

13.8.2   *Classic Views Landing Page*

This description is for a wiki page. For a web part page, first add the Content Editor web part and then add the links in the same way as for the wiki page.

1. Open the page in edit mode.

2. Copy the URL for one of the views from the list.

3. Click on Insert and select the 'From Address' link option.

4. Write a display text in the dialog and paste the URL. Click OK.

5. Repeat step 2-4 for each view.

13.8.3   *Replace the Site navigation Link.*

The app link in the Site navigation should of course point to the Views landing page and not directly to the app. Edit the navigation as described in chapter 11 to replace the link.

Demos:

https://kalmstrom.com/Tips/SharePoint-Online-Course/View-Combining.htm

https://www.kalmstrom.com//Tips/SharePoint-Online-Course/View-Landing.htm

Also *refer to* 23.6, Landing Page with Tasks, where we expand the landing page with a list and then add a dynamic Excel chart to the page.

13.9   SUMMARY

This chapter has explained the difference between the three types of site pages, and now you should be able to recognize and start customizing all three of them. You should also be able to judge which kind of page will be best in each case, when you need to create a new page.

You have also learned where to find the "Site Pages" library, where you can manage the settings for all pages in a site.

We have looked at both classic and modern web parts, and I have described how to set a page as homepage. Finally, I have given examples on how files can be shared via pages, how pages can be used instead of documents and how you can create a views landing page.

For more information about web parts, *refer to* chapter 18, Connect Web Parts. I will also give examples on page customization in other chapters later in this book.

Now it is high time to look at the SharePoint permissions. When you share content, it is important to consider the permissions you give, so I have included the sharing in the same chapter as the general permission information.

14 PERMISSIONS AND SHARING

All SharePoint content is governed by permissions. If the permissions are set correctly, users will never see anything that they don't have access to, and they can never do anything they should not be allowed to do.

For this ideal situation to come true, it is important that SharePoint administrators understand how permissions are set and inherited.

SharePoint permissions are very easy to use when you accept the default settings. That can work for a small team, but if you want to have more control over what users can see and do, SharePoint permissions get more complex.

However, when you understand how the SharePoint permissions work, you can also take advantage of the benefits they give. That is what we will study in this chapter.

In all site types, site owners can manage the permissions in the Site settings, *refer to* section 14.9, Advanced Permission Settings, below. We will however start with the basic permission settings. These are more easily accessed and used, especially in the modern experience, than if you go via the Site settings. For many organizations, these basic permissions are quite enough.

14.1 INHERITANCE

SharePoint pages, apps, subsites and items, by default inherit the same permissions as the higher level. This means that subsites inherit the same permissions as the root site, apps inherit the site permissions – and pages and other items inherit the app permissions.

- Site collections
  - Sites
    - Lists and Libraries
      - Items

Therefore, users who have Edit permission on a site, by default also have Edit permission on all apps in that site, and they even have Edit permission on all items in each app – if you don't break the inheritance, *refer to* 14.10.

14.2 PERMISSION LEVEL CONSIDERATIONS

As we saw in chapter 3, administrator roles are defined in the Microsoft 365 Admin center.

Permissions for other users are set in the sites, and there you can by default select between Full control, Edit and Read. In some site types, the default permission is Edit, *refer to* 14.4.1, Default Site Permissions.

The Edit permission allows users to do a lot in SharePoint even if they don't have access to admin centers. They can view, add, update and delete items, and they can also add, edit and delete whole apps, as well as create, edit and delete columns and public views. It is important that you are aware of this, so that you can decide if you should keep the default permission or change it.

In my opinion, Edit is a high default permission level. It gives users the ability to do a lot of damage to the site. They can for example delete an entire app, maliciously or by accident.

I recommend that you always consider permission levels and give users the lowest permission required for them to do their jobs.

In contradiction to the above I would also urge that you consider what users will do if they do *not* have enough permissions in SharePoint. Instead of creating a new document library, they will create a new file folder, instead of creating a new view they will export the data to Excel to make summaries, instead of using external sharing they will e-mail a copy of a file etc. To do the right thing, users must have both the right knowledge and the right permissions.

14.3   SHAREPOINT GROUPS

The permission levels in SharePoint are packages of connected permissions. Users who have the same permission on a site belong to the same permission group, also called SharePoint group.

Note that a SharePoint group is not the same as a Microsoft 365 group. In a Microsoft 365 group, colleagues share several resources and work together on them. In a SharePoint group, the only thing that is common for everyone is the permission level.

- Site Owners have Full control over the site content and can do anything with it – except perform actions that have been forbidden in the SharePoint or Microsoft Admin centers.

  By default, Site admins and Site owners are the same people, but that can be changed in the SharePoint Admin center. If a separate Site admin is appointed, the Site owner still has full control over all content in the site, but there are some technical limitations. *Refer to* 6.5, Site Permission Levels.

- Site Members have Edit permission, which means that they can view, add, update and delete apps, items and folders in a site.

- Site Visitors have Read permission. They can only view pages and items, but they can download files.

You can set site permission for people directly on a site or in an app, and when you do that, you normally use one of the pre-defined SharePoint groups.

When you create a site, SharePoint automatically creates a set of SharePoint groups for that site.

People or groups who have access to a **modern** site can have either Full control, Edit or Read permission. Classic sites can have some more levels.

In the modern experience, you can see the SharePoint groups and their members under the Settings icon >Site permissions.

When you expand a SharePoint group, you can see all members of that group in Communication sites and Team sites without a group.

Permissions ✕

Manage site permissions or invite others to collaborate

Share site

∨ Site owners

∨ Site members

∧ Site visitors

 Adele Vance
Read ∨

Diego Siciliani
Read ∨

Joni Sherman
Read ∨

In Group Team sites, you will at first only see the SharePoint group, not the individual members. This way, you can change the permission level for the whole group. When you hover over the group, a dialog with member information will open.

∨ Site owners

∧ Site members

 Office 365 Adoption Members
Edit ∨

∨ Site visitors

In the classic interface, you need to use the Site settings, *refer to* 14.9, Advanced Permission Settings.

14.4   SHARE A SITE

The settings for how much sharing should be allowed are made in the SharePoint Admin center for the whole tenant, and administrators can also limit sharing options for individual sites.

You can share a site in different ways, but in all cases, you start by typing a name or an e-mail address. Then you will get suggestions to select from. You can either keep the default permission level for the invited person or group or change it.

Note that the people you invite also will get access to other content that have shared permissions with this site. For example, if subsites have inherited the parent permissions, you will share all the subsites by sharing the parent site.

14.4.1 Default Site Permissions

When you share a site from the modern experience, you can select Read, Edit or Full Control permission for each user or group that you share the site with. When you share from the classic experience, you can select among more levels.

The default permission is different depending on site type:

- For Communication sites and modern Team sites without a group, the default permission option is Read.

- For classic Team sites and modern Group Team sites, the default option is Edit. The default Home site also has Edit permission for all users.

As you see, the default permissions are extensive for Team sites, but site owners can restrict the options, and Global and SharePoint administrators can also restrict the options for the tenant. Site settings can never allow more than what is set in the tenant settings.

14.4.2 Share a Site with the Share Button

Sites without a group have a 'Share' button in the top right corner of all pages. When you use that button, you share the whole site with the people you invite.

🔗 Share

14.4.2.1 Modern Share Button

In the modern experience, the 'Share' command will open a right pane where you can add people and groups and select permission level.

Start writing a name or e-mail address to get suggestions. Select one of the suggestions, and the person or group will be added below the field.

The default permission for the site type is assigned automatically, but you can change it before you share the site. This is done with the little arrow at the permission information below the name of the added person or group.

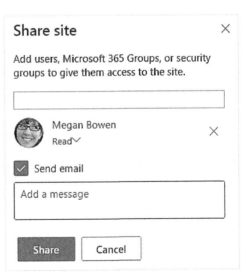

An e-mail invitation will be sent by default, and you can also add a message.

14.4.2.2   Classic Share Button

In the classic interface, a dialog will open when you click on the 'Share' button. Here, you have the option to enter 'Everyone' if you want to include all people in the organization.

🔔 **Share**

Share 'Support Cases'   ✕

Shared with ☐ Nestor Wilke

Invite people   ┌───┐
                           │ Enter names or email addresses...   │
Shared with   │   │
                           └───┘

                           ┌───┐
                           │ Include a personal message with this   │
                           │ invitation (Optional).   │
                           │   │
                           └───┘

                           SHOW OPTIONS

                                              [Share]   [Cancel]

Under 'SHOW OPTIONS' you can send an e-mail invitation (default) and set another permission level than the default 'Edit'.

HIDE OPTIONS

☑ Send an email invitation

Select a permission level

┌──┬───┐
│ Support Cases Members [Edit]   │ ⌄ │
└──┴───┘

                          [Share]   [Cancel]

Under the Shared with tab in this dialog, you can also see who is already sharing the site. You can e-mail everyone, and via the 'ADVANCED' link you can reach the site's permissions page in the Site settings, *see* below.

Share 'Support Cases'   ✕

Shared with ☐ Nestor Wilke

Invite people   [photo]   MOD Administrator

Shared with

                       [photo]   Nestor Wilke
                                 Director, Operations

        EMAIL EVERYONE   ADVANCED

                                            [Close]

14.4.3   *Share a Site from the Modern Permissions Pane*

The modern experience has a 'Site permissions' link under the 365 Settings icon. It opens a right pane where you can invite users and manage permissions and sharing settings. All modern sites can be shared from the Site permissions pane.

14.4.3.1   Share from Sites without a Group

In Communication sites and modern Team sites without a group, the Permissions right pane has a 'Share site' button on top. When you click on the 'Share site' button, the same invitation pane opens as when you use the modern 'Share' button, *see* above.

14.4.3.2   Share from Group Team Sites

Group Team sites have a button with the text 'Invite people' in the Permissions pane. You can select to add the new people to the Microsoft 365 group or just to the site.

Permissions

Manage site permissions or invite others to collaborate

Add members to group

Share site only

When you select to only share the site, the same right pane as with the modern 'Share' button will open.

If you select to add new members to the group, a new pane will open with an 'Add members' button. Here. you can see all the current members in the Microsoft 365 group.

The 'Add members button opens the same right pane as the modern 'Share' button.

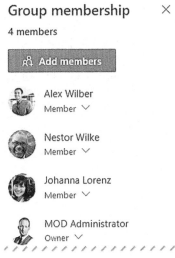

Group membership   ✕

4 members

Alex Wilber
Member ∨

Nestor Wilke
Member ∨

Johanna Lorenz
Member ∨

MOD Administrator
Owner ∨

14.4.4   *Share a Group Team Site with an External Guest*

When external guest access is allowed for the Group Team site, the guests are invited from Outlook, not from SharePoint. (*Refer to* 14.11.2, External Guest Access to Group Team Site, for information on how guest access is allowed.)

1. Under Groups in Outlook, click on the group to which you want to invite guests.

2. Open the group contact card and click on the Members link.

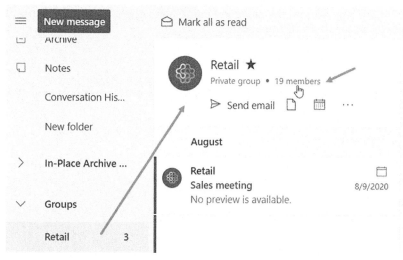

3. Click on 'Add members' in the dialog that opens.

4. Type the guest's e-mail address and then click on 'Add'.

5. Click on Close when you have finished adding guests.

14.4.5   *Manage Site Members in the Modern Experience*

As you know by now, the modern experience has a 'Site permissions' pane, where you can invite users and manage permissions and sharing settings.

Only Site owners can add and remove site members from sites and change the SharePoint group for another group member.

In sites that are not connected to a Microsoft 365 group, the site memberships are managed directly in the Permissions right pane. When the site belongs to a Microsoft 365 group, the site membership can be managed in the Permissions pane or in Outlook.

14.4.5.1 Manage Members in Sites without a Group

In Communication sites and Team sites without a group, the Permissions right pane shows the three SharePoint groups below the share button. Here, Site owners can change member permissions and remove people from the site.

When you select another permission level, the person will automatically be moved to that SharePoint group.

If you, for example, change Allan Deyoung's permission (*see* the image to the right) from Edit to Full control, he will be moved to the Site owners SharePoint group.

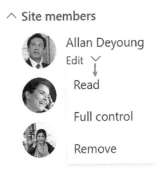

14.4.5.2 Manage Members in Group Team Sites

In Group Team sites and classic Team sites where a Microsoft 365 group has been added, only the group name is displayed under the SharePoint groups in the Permissions pane. Here, only the permissions for the whole SharePoint group can be edited but not the permission level for an individual member.

If you want to manage individual members, you can click on 'Invite people' in the Permissions pane and then select to add members to the Microsoft 365 group, as described in 14.4.3.2 Share from Group Team Sites above.

Now all members are displayed, and you can change their status with the little arrow to the right of the current status.

Group membership   ✕

2 members

  Add members

 MOD Administrator
Owner ∨

Adele Vance
Member ∨

✓ Member

Owner

Remove from group

You can also manage the Microsoft 365 group in Outlook, in the same way as when you invite guests, *see* above.

1. Under Groups in the Outlook left menu, select the Microsoft 365 group you want to manage.

2. Click on the Members link in the group's contact card.

3. A dialog will open, where you can change permission level or remove users from the Microsoft 365 group – and thereby also from the site – with the x icon.

Adele Vance	Retail Manager	Member		×
Alex Wilber	Marketing Assistant	Owner Member ∨		×
Christie Cline	Buyer	Member ∨		×

14.4.6   Manage Site Members in the Classic Experience

In the classic experience, you can see the people and groups who have access to the site in the 'Share' dialog, *see* above, but you cannot change a permission level or remove a user there. If you want to do that, you must go into the Site settings, *refer to* 14.9, Advanced Permission Settings.

14.4.7   Site Sharing Settings

In the **modern** experience, site owners can click on the "Change how members can share" link in the 'Permissions' pane, to modify who can share the site and its files and folders. You can, for example, decide that only owners can share files, folders and the site.

← **Site sharing settings**   ×

Control how things in this site can be shared
and how request access works.

Sharing permissions

◉ Site owners and members can share files,
  folders, and the site. People with Edit
  permissions can share files and folders.

○ Site owners and members, and people
  with Edit permissions can share files and
  folders, but only site owners can share the
  site.

○ Only site owners can share files, folders,
  and the site.

To manage the sharing from the **classic** experience, open the Site settings and select 'Site permissions' under the Users and Permissions heading.

This page can also be reached from the ADVANCED link in the classic 'Share' dialog. We will come back to the settings here in section 14.9, Advanced Permission Settings.

14.4.7.1   Access Request

If someone who is not a site owner uses the 'Share' command to invite other people to a site, an access request for the site will be sent to site owners or to a specified e-mail address. If the invitation is accepted, the approver can specify the permission level for the user.

The access request also allows people to request access to content that they do not have permission to see.

When 'Allow access requests' is enabled, an e-mail with an access request will be sent to the specified e-mail address. Requests can also be seen and acted on under Site settings >Users and Groups >Access requests and invitations.

From the **modern** experience, you can reach the Access request settings from the Permissions right pane >Site sharing settings. Access requests are enabled by default.

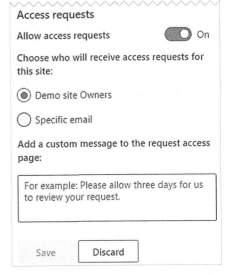

From the **classic** interface, you need to go into Site settings >Site permissions >the ribbon 'Access Request Settings' control.

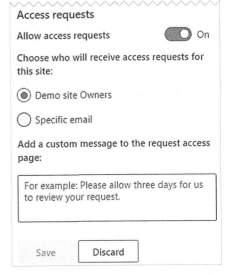

The first two boxes, that allow sharing, are checked by default.

☑ Allow members to share the site and individual files and folders.

☑ Allow members to invite others to the site members group, c

If you uncheck these two boxes, the sharing will be blocked for all users but the site owner.

Note that the 'Share' buttons will be displayed to the users even if sharing is disabled. If "access requests" has not been activated, the user will receive an error message when trying to use a 'Share' button.

If you instead uncheck the two sharing boxes in the 'Access Request Settings' dialog and instead activate the third box, 'Allow access requests', all users can share the site or site contents, but the site owner has the ultimate authority over who gets access to the site and what level of permission users are assigned.

If a subsite has inherited permissions from an upper level, the Access Request settings link will not be visible in the ribbon. You must first stop inheriting or change the sharing in the parent site instead.

14.5   SECURITY GROUPS

For easier permission management, I would recommend that you create Security groups of people who should have the same permission level.

As we saw above, a SharePoint group is a group of people who have the same permissions on a specific site- A security group, on the other hand, can be used in several sites and can have different permission levels in different sites – but everyone in the group has the same permission.

Security groups are created in the Microsoft 365 Admin center and can be used in the whole tenant. This simplifies the management, for example when you want to give people access to several sites.

Security groups show up among the user accounts when you start typing a name and when you give permissions, so it is much quicker to add a security group to a SharePoint group in a site than to add each user separately.

14.5.1   *Create a New Security Group*

Security groups are created in the Microsoft 365 Admin center >Groups.

1. Expand the 'Groups' accordion in the left menu and click on 'Active Groups'.

2. Click on the '+ Add a group' button.

3. Select the Security group and click on 'Next'.

4. Give the group a name and a description and click on 'Next'.

5. Review the details and click on 'Greate group' when everything is good.

6. To add group members, select the new security group in the list of active groups. A right pane will open, and here you can add owners and members to the group.

7. At first the group has no owners, so there is a 'Add group owners' button under the General tab.

8. When you have added at least one group owner, you can add members of the security group under the Members tab. It is also here you manage both owners and members.

↺ ✕

SA Sales Agents

🗑

Security group • 2 owners • 4 members

General   **Members**

Owners (2)

Allan Deyoung
AllanD@M365x446726.OnMicrosoft.co
m

Christie Cline
ChristieC@M365x446726.OnMicrosoft.c
om

View all and manage owners

Members (4)

Allan Deyoung
AllanD@M365x446726.OnMicrosoft.co
m

Cameron White
CameronW@M365x446726.OnMicrosof
t.com

Chris Green
chris@M365x446726.onmicrosoft.com

Ben Andrews
ben@M365x446726.onmicrosoft.com

View all and manage members

The new security group will show up among other groups when you add members to a site.

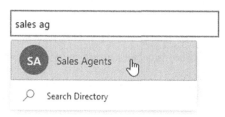

← **Share site**   ✕

Add users, Microsoft 365 Groups, or security
groups to give them access to the site.

sales ag

SA Sales Agents 🖑

🔍 Search Directory

Select a SharePoint group and set the permission level for the security group, just as you do with single users. That will give all owners and members of the security group the selected permission level on that site.

SA Sales Agents
Read∨   ✕

ⓘ 1 g   Full control

        Edit
✓ Senᴅ ᴇᴍᴀɪʟ

You can add new users to a security group anytime. They will then have all permissions given to that group on different sites.

Accordingly, when you remove a user from a security group, that user will lose all permissions connected to the group.

Demo:

https://kalmstrom.com/Tips/SharePoint-Online-Course/SharePoint-Permissions.htm

14.6   SHARE A FILE

Users with Edit permission can by default share files with people who don't have access to the document library where the files are stored. Here I will describe file sharing, because that is most common, but folders and list items can be shared in the same way.

Note that only the file will be shared even if you select the whole item when sharing. If you select a folder or a list item, all columns will be included.

When you share a file, the link in the e-mail will become a so-called short link, showing the document name and the file type icon.

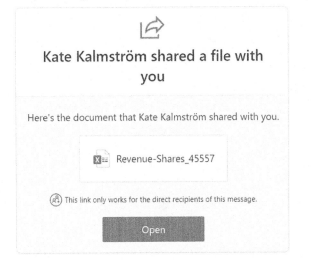

Kate Kalmström shared a file with you

Here's the document that Kate Kalmström shared with you.

Revenue-Shares_45557

This link only works for the direct recipients of this message.

Open

14.6.1 *The 'Share' Command*

To share a file, you can open the ellipsis at the item you want to share and click on the 'Share' link.

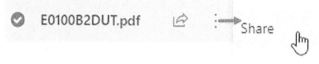

Start typing the name of a person or group who should have access. Then you will have suggestions to select from.

By default, an invitation is sent by e-mail to the people who are given access, but in the classic interface you can uncheck that box if you want to inform about the sharing in another way. You can also get a link to the shared item.

Another option is to select the item and click on the 'Share' button. I describe in the sections below where you can find it in the modern and classic interfaces.

14.6.1.1 Modern Sharing with the 'Share' Command

In the **modern** interface, you can find the 'Share' button in the command bar when you select an item. You can also hover over the item to see the button, *see* the image above.

The modern interface opens a dialog where you can give names or e-mail addresses to specific people or groups with whom you want to share the file. Above that field, there is a Permission selector.

You can – and should! – decide which people should be able to use the sharing link and if the link should give edit permission or not.

You must however click on the permission selector above the field where you fill out the person/group you want to share with, before you can see and change the permission you are giving.

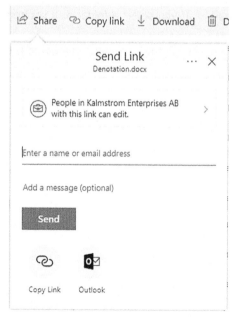

In my opinion, the link settings are more difficult to discover in the modern interface than in the classic experience, and this is a problem as the default permission when sharing is 'Edit'.

The permission options are: Anyone with the link, People in the organization with the link, People with existing access and Specific people. The number of options can be limited in the SharePoint Admin center, so 'Anyone with the link' might not be active.

I recommend that you think twice before you use the option 'Anyone with the link', even if it is available, because this option allows even people outside the organization to access the file. They don't have to log in, so their access cannot be audited, and you cannot see who has used the file.

The option 'Open in review mode only' is only present when you share Word files. It lets a receiver without edit permission comment on the file but not edit it.

Link settings   ✕

Who would you like this link to work for? Learn more

⊕ Anyone with the link

✉ People in Contoso with the link

🗛 People with existing access

🗛 Specific people   ✓

Other settings

☑ Allow editing

🗗 Open in review mode only ⓘ   ⚫○

⊖ Block download   ⚫○ ⓘ

[Apply]   [Cancel]

When you uncheck the 'Allow editing' box, the 'Block download' option will be active, so that you can enable it if you want the recipient to be able to view the shared file but not download it.

Currently, users can create SharePoint and OneDrive read-only sharing links that block download for Office files, PDF files, images, audio files and video files.

If you have selected the 'Anyone with the link' option, you will get the option to set an expiration date and a password for the link. (If you set a password, you must distribute it yourself.)

In the SharePoint Admin center >Policies >Sharing, administrators can set such links to always expire after a certain time, and in that case, users can only make the time before expiration shorter, not longer.

Link settings   ✕

Who would you like this link to work for?
Learn more

⊕ Anyone with the link   ✓

✉ People in K-lmstrom Enterprises

📅 Set expiration date   ✕

🔒 Set password

⊖ Block download   ○○ ⓘ

[Apply]   [Cancel]

14.6.1.2   Classic Sharing with the 'Share' Command

In the classic interface, libraries have a 'Share' button above the files, and there is a 'Share' button under the FILES tab in the ribbon.

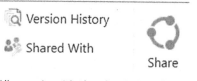

All apps in with the classic interface also have a 'Shared With' button in the ribbon. It opens the same dialog as the 'Share' button, *see* the image below, but with the 'Shared with' tab selected.

The classic interface 'Share' dialog for files resembles the dialog for site sharing, *see* 14.4.2.2, Classic Share Button, but also gives a link to the file that should be shared.

Share 'VAT-rapport-31-dec-2020'	✕

Shared with ☐ Nestor Wilke

Invite people	Enter names or email addresses...	Can edit ⌄
Get a link		Can edit
Shared with	Include a personal message with this invitation (Optional).	Can view

HIDE OPTIONS

☑ Send an email invitation

| Share | Cancel |

In the classic sharing dialog, you can set the permission on the file directly after adding the people or group you want to share with. The options are 'Can edit' and 'Can view'. To have options corresponding to the modern usage options, you need to share a link instead, *see* below.

14.6.2   *Share with a Link*

Instead of sharing with the 'Share' command, you can send a link to the SharePoint content that you want to share. By default, only the people you have specified can use the link.

To have the correct link, use the command 'Copy link', which you can find in the command bar and under the item ellipsis in **modern** apps.

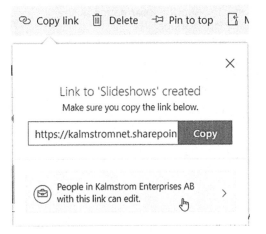

You must click on the people or group selection to see and be able to uncheck the 'Allow editing' box and block download, just like when you use the 'Share' command.

In the **classic** experience, you can only find the 'Get a link' command in libraries, and there only under the ellipsis at the selected file or folder. In lists, you must go via the 'Shared with' button in the ribbon or 'Share' under the item ellipsis to get a link.

The classic 'Get a link' dialog is similar to the 'Share' dialog shown above, but it has options for the link instead of a permission selection. How many options you see, depends on how much sharing is allowed in the SharePoint Admin center.

Share 'Maps'
×

Shared with Kate

Invite people	Edit link - no sign-in required ∨
Get a link	Restricted link - Only specific people can open this link (created)
Shared with	View link - Kalmstrom Enterprises AB account required
	Edit link - Kalmstrom Enterprises AB account required
	View link - no sign-in required
	Edit link - no sign-in required

Close

14.6.3   *Manage Access*

In both app interfaces, you can see whom the file has been shared with.

In the **modern** interface, you can see the sharing information in the selected item's Information pane. Click on 'Manage access' to have details on the sharing and permissions.

Has access

In the 'Manage Access' right pane that opens, you can easily edit the permissions from the dropdown at each user or group. Here, you can also stop sharing the file.

Manage access

To grant access to more people, you can click on the icon with a plus above 'Manage access' in the Information pane. Now, you will have a simpler sharing dialog with just two permission options: Can edit and Can view. Use the 'Share' command to have more options, as described above.

Grant access   ··· ✕

Kanban-Task-M...-Manual.docx

Enter a name or email address
_____

✎   Can edit   ⌄

Add a message (optional)

☑ Notify people

Grant access

A link to the 'Manage access' pane is also available under the ellipsis at the item and from the ellipsis in the Sharing dialog.

🡅 Share   ☍ Copy link   ↓ Download   🗑 Delete   ⌁ Flow ⌄

Send Link   en 27 januari, 2018
Denotation.docx   ··· ✕

                        Manage Access

People in Kalmstrom Enterprises AB

In the **classic** interface, you can see the sharing under the item ellipsis and under the 'Shared with' tab in the sharing dialog, but it is more complicated to edit the permissions. I suggest that you switch to the modern experience if you want to edit item permissions.

14.6.4   *E-mail Attachments*

When you click on the 'Attach' button in an e-mail that is open in Outlook on the web, you will have several options, and they give different possibilities to set permissions on the file:

- Browse the computer and upload a file.

- Browse libraries in OneDrive and SharePoint Online.

- Upload a file from the computer to OneDrive and share it from there.

- Attach a recently used OneDrive or SharePoint file.

📎 Attach ⌄   🔏 Encrypt   🗑 Discard   ⋯

🖳   Browse this computer

☁   Browse cloud locations

☁   Upload and share

Suggested attachments

KTMSP-Reseller-N...-2020-10-14.docx
Opened 3 minutes ago

When you share an attachment from OneDrive or SharePoint, you are sharing a link to the file.

To share a link instead of the actual file saves mailbox space, and it also gives you a possibility to modify the permissions on the file. Another important benefit is that you are not creating a duplicate of the file. When users access the file, they will always see the latest version.

By default, the receiver will get edit permission on the file if it is an Office file, but in all options where the file is stored in the cloud, you will have a possibility to change the permission.

Event reminder manuscri... ✕
Recipients can edit   ↓ ⌄

Preview	
Manage access >	Recipients can edit
Download	Recipients can view
Attach as a copy	Anyone in my organization can edit
Open in new tab	Anyone in my organization can view
Copy link	Anyone can edit
	Anyone can view

When you upload the file from your computer, there is no possibility to modify the permission. But when the file has been attached, you can upload it to OneDrive and then you will have the same options as in the image above. (It is of course quicker to use the 'Upload and share' option directly.)

| Progress Bars.docx | ✕ |
| 1 MB | ↓ ∨ |

Preview

Download

Upload to OneDrive - Kalmstrom Enterprises AB

Sometimes it is necessary to give the receiver(s) permission to edit the file, so that several people can edit the same copy of a file, *refer to* 9.8.3, Editing by Multiple Users. In other cases, it is more secure to limit the permission.

When users share Word files, the sharing e-mail will include information about the estimated time it will take a user to read the document as well as a list of the key points in the document. Files that have been marked as sensitive by Data Loss Prevention will not include that information.

14.7   SHARE A PAGE

SharePoint pages are files, so in the "Site Pages" library, pages can be shared in the same way as other files. Open the ellipsis at the page you want to share and click on 'Share'.

Modern pages also have a 'Promote' button in the command bar. It opens a right pane with four options for sharing.

Help others find your page   ✕

Add page to navigation

Post as News on this site

Email

Save as page template

Promote   Page details

Page address

https://kalmstromnet.sharepoint.com/sites/
demosite/SitePages/Welcome!.aspx

Sync   Export to Excel

Copy address

When you click on 'Add page to navigation' and 'Post as News on this site', the action is taken immediately, and you don't need to do anything more.

The 'Email' link opens a dialog where you can enter an e-mail address and a message to send a link to the page.

When you save the page as a template, it will show up among the templates when users create another page on the same site.

14.8   STOP SHARING AN ITEM

To stop sharing a file, page or list item, open 'Manage Access' (modern) or 'Shared with' (classic) in the app where the item is stored.

14.8.1.1   Stop sharing with everyone

In both interfaces, click on 'Stop sharing' to remove all sharing of the file or item.

14.8.1.2   Stop sharing with one person or group

To stop only one person or group from sharing in the **modern** interface, open the dropdown for that person/group in the 'Manage Access' pane.

(Here, you can also change the permission level for that person/group.)

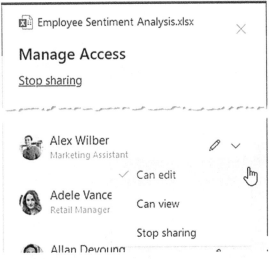

In the **classic** interface, click on ADVANCED in the 'Shared with' dialog. This will take you to the Permissions page in the Site settings, where you can select the user you want to stop sharing with. Then click on 'Remove User Permissions' in the ribbon.

14.9   ADVANCED PERMISSIONS SETTINGS

Advanced permissions management for a site, app, page or item is performed in the Site settings. You can reach these settings in several ways:

- For a site, open the Site settings and select 'Site permissions' under the Users and Permissions heading.

This page can also be reached from the ADVANCED link in the classic Share dialog and from the link 'Advanced permission settings' in the right Permissions pane in modern sites. (This link is the only option for modern Group Team sites, as these sites do not have the link in the Site settings page.)

- For an app, open the List settings and select 'Permissions for this list' or 'Permissions for this document library' under the Permissions and Management heading.

- For a file, folder or item in an app with the **modern** interface, open the ellipsis at the item and select 'Manage access'. In the right pane that opens, click on the 'Advanced' link at the bottom.

- For a file, folder or item in an app with the **classic** interface, open the ellipsis at the item and select 'Share'. Then click on the 'ADVANCED' link or under 'Shared with' in the dialog that opens.

The image below shows the Permissions page for a site. The permissions pages for other content looks the same, but they don't have as many commands in the ribbon.

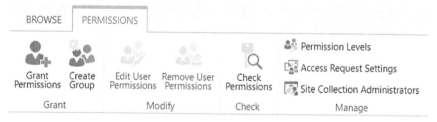

In all permissions pages, you can check the permission for each team member or group by clicking on the 'Check Permission' button in the ribbon and enter the name of the person or group.

Instead of adding and removing members from the site interface, you can manage SharePoint group memberships from the Site settings >People and Groups in all sites except Group Team sites. The Microsoft 365 Group is instead managed from Outlook, as described above.

Modern sites are designed to work with the three default SharePoint groups and their default permission levels, so if you modify the permission level for a SharePoint group or create your own SharePoint group, the modern site permissions panel and Share buttons do not work well.

Therefore, what I suggest below is primarily intended for **classic sites and the classic interface**.

14.9.1 *Permissions Levels*

When you click on the 'Permission Levels' button under the 'PERMISSIONS' tab in the Permissions page for a site, you can see what the different levels give users permission to do.

It is possible to edit the Permission Levels, but I would recommend that you don't do that even for classic sites. It is safer to create your own custom permission levels, *see* below.

You can also remove levels on this page, but think twice before you do that, and test three times in a non-production site!

Permissions › Permission Levels ⓘ

◻️Add a Permission Level | ✕ Delete Selected Permission Levels

	Permission Level	Description
☐	Full Control	Has full control.
☐	Design	Can view, add, update, delete, approve, and customize.
☐	Edit	Can add, edit and delete lists; can view, add, update and delete list items and documents.
☐	Contribute	Can view, add, update, and delete list items and documents.
☐	Read	Can view pages and list items and download documents.
☐	Limited Access	Can view specific lists, document libraries, list items, folders, or documents when given permissions.
☐	View Only	Can view pages, list items, and documents. Document types with server-side file handlers can be viewed in the browser but not downloaded.
☐	Approve	Can edit and approve pages, list items, and documents.
☐	Manage Hierarchy	Can create sites and edit pages, list items, and documents.
☐	Restricted Read	Can view pages and documents, but cannot view historical versions or user permissions.
☐	Restricted Interfaces for Translation	Can open lists and folders, and use remote interfaces.

14.9.1.1   Modify Permissions

In classic sites, it is not difficult to change the default permission. When you modify the permission level for a group, the new level will be reflected in the sharing dialog.

You can for example set the default permission level for the Members group to be Contribute instead of Edit, to restrict users from creating and deleting apps:

1. In Site settings >Site permissions, select the Members group.

2. Click on 'Edit User Permissions' in the ribbon.

3. In the new page that opens, uncheck the Edit box and check the box for Contribute.

4. Click OK.

Unfortunately, the modern pages are not yet adapted to such modifications.

In Communication sites and Team sites without a group, the 'Edit User Permissions' button is active, and the modification can be made, but the result does not affect the Permissions right pane and the Share button in a good way. In Group Team sites, the button is greyed out.

14.9.1.2   Remove Users

To stop sharing a site with a user, go into the Site settings >People and Groups. Here you can see everyone that is sharing the site and take actions. External sharers will show up here after they have accepted the sharing invitation.

Actions ▾	Settings ▾

E-Mail Users
Send an e-mail to selected users.

Call/Message Selected Users
Call the selected users.

Remove Users from Group
Remove selected users from this SharePoint group

14.9.2   *Custom Permission Level*

If none of the pre-defined levels fit, you can easily create your own permission level, but once again this does not work well with modern sites.

In a classic site, click on 'Add a Permission Level' in the Permission Levels page, and a new page will open where you can select what the new permission level should allow. One such commonly requested permission level is "Add but not delete".

List Permissions

☐ Manage Lists - Create and delete lists, add or remove columns in a list, and add or remove public views of a list.

☐ Override List Behaviors - Discard or check in a document which is checked out to another user, and change or override settings which allow users to read/edit only their own items

☐ Add Items - Add items to lists and add documents to document libraries.

☐ Edit Items - Edit items in lists, edit documents in document libraries, and customize Web Part Pages in document libraries.

☐ Delete Items - Delete items from a list and documents from a document library.

When you have created the new permission level, you should assign that permission level to a SharePoint group.

If you add a person to a custom SharePoint group on a modern site without a Microsoft 365 group, via Site settings >People and Groups, that person will be invited and get access to the site. The person will however not show up in the Permissions right pane among the other users.

14.9.3 *Create Custom SharePoint Group*

Administrators can create a custom SharePoint group by pressing the 'Create Group' button in the ribbon of the Site Permissions page.

At the bottom of the creation page, you can specify what permission level should be used for this group. Any custom permission levels you have created will also show up here.

Choose the permission level group members get on this site:
https://m365x446726.sharepoint.com/sites/SupportCases

- ☐ Full Control - Has full control.
- ☐ Design - Can view, add, update, delete, approve, and customize.
- ☐ Edit - Can add, edit and delete lists; can view, add, update and delete list items and documents.
- ☐ Contribute - Can view, add, update, and delete list items and documents.
- ☐ Read - Can view pages and list items and download documents.
- ☐ View Only - Can view pages, list items, and documents. Document types with server-side file handlers can be viewed in the browser but not downloaded.

When you have created the SharePoint group, the group page opens so that you can add users.

Under 'Actions', you can e-mail and remove users.

New ▾   Actions ▾   Settings ▾

Add Users
Add users to this group.

☐   ☐ Peter Kalmström

Under 'Settings', you can see the permissions that this group has in the site and make the group default.

14.10   BREAK THE INHERITANCE

By default, permissions are inherited from the upper level, *see* 14.1, Inheritance, but you can break this inheritance. Breaking the inheritance can be done for all levels down to item level, but not on column level.

Note that an alternative to breaking the inheritance is to create more sites, with different permissions. This is especially interesting for modern sites, that can be connected to a hub site.

For classic sites, subsites with broken inheritance might be a better option in some cases, but breaking inheritance should be an exception on all levels. It complicates management and might be confusing for users.

301

Also, consider if the goal achieved by breaking inheritance is convenience or security. I often encounter a confusion between these two in requirement documents.

- Convenience: "Users should be shown their own assigned items". Can very easily be achieved by a filtered view.

- Security: "Users should never be allowed to see the tasks assigned to others". Requires breaking the inheritance.

14.10.1   *Break Inheritance at Subsite Creation*

When you create a new subsite, you can just select another radio button than the default one.

User Permissions:

○ Use same permissions as parent site

◉ Use unique permissions

When you check the radio button for unique permissions, a permissions page will be displayed where you can define the SharePoint groups for the site and add people to them if needed.

People and Groups › Set Up Groups for this Site

Visitors to this Site

Visitors can **read** content in the Web site. Create a group of visitors or re-use an existing SharePoint group.

◉ Create a new group   ○ Use an existing group

Permission Visitors

Members of this Site

Members can **contribute** content to the Web site. Create a group of site members or re-use an existing SharePoint group.

◉ Create a new group   ○ Use an existing group

Permission Members

Kate Kalmström

Owners of this Site

Owners have **full control** over the Web site. Create a group of owners or re-use an existing SharePoint group.

◉ Create a new group   ○ Use an existing group

Permission Owners

Kate Kalmström

OK

14.10.2   *Break Inheritance After Creation*

Permission inheritance for pages and other items can be broken directly in the app, but you must go into the advanced permissions to break inheritance for apps and already created subsites.

14.10.2.1   Break Item Inheritance

As we saw in 14.6.3, Manage Access, you can set unique permissions on files, folders and list items in the modern 'Manage access' right pane or via the classic 'Share' dialog. You can even stop sharing an item with everyone and then only give access to a one person or a few people.

In the "Site Pages" library, you can do the same with page files. For example, you might not want users to be able to change the homepage of a site, after you have spent a lot of time on making it appealing. Then you can just open the page's Information pane and click on 'Manage Access'. There, you can easily change the permission level for the Members SharePoint group to View, instead of the default Edit.

(In the classic "Site pages" interface, you need to use the Advanced permissions, see the section below.)

14.10.2.2   Break App and Subsite Inheritance

To break the permission inheritance for apps and subsites that have already been created, open the app or subsite permissions page as described in section 14.9, Advanced Permission Settings, above. Do the same if your "Site Pages" library only can show the classic interface and you want to stop inheritance for a page.

Click on 'Stop Inheriting Permissions' in the ribbon to stop the inheritance.

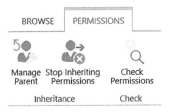

Now the ribbon will change, so that you can grant new permissions and/or remove users or groups.

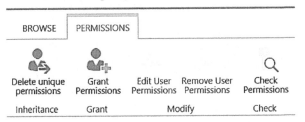

Click on 'Delete unique permissions' if you want to go back to the inherited permission levels.

14.11 EXTERNAL USERS

If allowed in the SharePoint admin settings and in the site, it is possible to share sites, files and folders with people outside the tenant and not only with internal users. The external users will have an e-mail invitation with a link when something is shared with them.

As we have seen earlier, external sharing is allowed by default for the tenant. This setting in the SharePoint Admin center can of course be changed, but external sharing can also be restricted for single sites by SharePoint admins, under 'Active sites' in the SharePoint Admin center.

On top of the direct content sharing, Microsoft 365 Group owners can invite guests to Group Team sites. These guests can be from inside the organization but if allowed, but also people from outside can be invited to the Group Team site.

In all cases, you must be aware that all kinds of external users are not the same.

14.11.1 *Authenticated and Anonymous Users*

There are two kinds of external users:

- **Authenticated** users have a Microsoft account or a work or school account in Azure AD from another organization, and they are asked to log in when they click on the link. You can share sites and files with these users, and permissions and groups work as they do for internal users.

  When authenticated users log in for the first time, they are added to the tenant's as well as the site's users lists. They can do many of the things internal users can do, but they don't have access to more advanced features.

  Authenticated external users cannot create Power Automate flows for the content they have access to, and they have no OneDrive for Business storage. For those things, they will need a license in the tenant.

- **Anonymous** users can view or edit without having to log in. Only files and folders can be shared with anonymous users, and you can set an expiration date for the sharing link.

This is important to consider if you use the 'Share' or 'Link' command:

- By default, all users get Edit permission, even if they are external.
- When you share with authenticated users, you can see which user has made any modifications.
- When a file has been changed by an anonymous user, you can only see that it is modified by a 'Guest Contributor', so you have no control over who is changing your files when you give the default Edit permission!

Demo:

https://www.kalmstrom.com/Tips//SharePoint-Online-Course/External-Sharing.htm

14.11.2 *External Guest Access to Group Team Site*

A Microsoft 365 group might need to share their Group Team site with people outside the organization. Therefore, it is possible to share Group Team sites with external guests, but access must be granted on several levels.

Guest access must always be authenticated, and it must be allowed on the higher level to be possible to enable on a lower level.

1. Guest sharing must be allowed in in the Azure Active Directory >All services >External Identities > External collaboration settings. The image below shows the default settings.

   Here, you can change settings for which permissions guests should have, who should be allowed to invite guests and to which domains these invitations can be sent.

   External collaboration settings   ×

   🖫 Save   ✕ Discard

   Guest user access

   Guest user access restrictions (Preview) ⓘ
   Learn more
   ◯ Guest users have the same access as members (most inclusive)
   ◉ Guest users have limited access to properties and memberships of directory objects
   ◯ Guest user access is restricted to properties and memberships of their own directory objects (most restrictive)

   Guest invite settings

   Admins and users in the guest inviter role can invite ⓘ
   [Yes   No]

   Members can invite ⓘ
   [Yes   No]

   Guests can invite ⓘ
   [Yes   No]

   Enable Email One-Time Passcode for guests (Preview) ⓘ
   Learn more
   [Yes   No]

   Enable guest self-service sign up via user flows (Preview) ⓘ
   Learn more
   [Yes   No]

   Collaboration restrictions

   ◉ Allow invitations to be sent to any domain (most inclusive)
   ◯ Deny invitations to the specified domains
   ◯ Allow invitations only to the specified domains (most restrictive)

2. Guest invitation must be allowed in the Microsoft 365 Admin center >Settings >Org settings >Microsoft 365 Groups.

Make sure that the 'Let group owners add people outside your organization to Microsoft 365 Groups as guests' and 'Let guest group members access group content' are enabled. These are the default settings.

Microsoft 365 Groups

Choose how guests from outside your organization can collaborate with your users in Microsoft 365 Groups. Learn more about guest access to Microsoft 365 Groups

☑ Let group owners add people outside your organization to Microsoft 365 Groups as guests

☑ Let guest group members access group content
If you don't select this, guests will still be listed as members of the group, but they won't receive group emails or be able to access any group content. They'll only be able to access files that were directly shared with them.

3. The sharing options must be at least 'New and existing guests'in the SharePoint Admin center >Sharing. *Refer to* 5.2.3.1, Sharing.

4. In the SharePoint Admin center >Sites >Active sites, the sharing level must be set to at least 'New and existing guests' under the 'Policies' tab, *refer to* 6.6.2.1, Edit an Active Site.

    Here you can also set several other options for the external site sharing.

5. The necessary sharing options for the site should be set under Site settings >Site permissions, *refer to* 14.4.7, Site Sharing Permissions.

Now, people who are allowed to invite guests can do so. The guest will have an e-mail invitation with links to the group's e-mail inbox, SharePoint site and Notebook.

14.12   AUDIENCE TARGETING

In **modern** sites, you can promote content to specific audiences. This feature is off by default, but when audience targeting is enabled, certain content is shown only to the specified audience.

Audience targeting can be enabled for navigation links, pages and other items and for the modern News and High-lighted content web parts. Audience targeting can also be used in classic pages.

It is possible to add single people in the audience, but I recommend that you use Microsoft 365 or Security groups. It is often more convenient to have people who need the same kind of information in a group.

Note that audience targeting is a way to *direct* relevant content to users. It is not a way to hide content from users. For that, you should use permissions, as described above.

When a user lacks permission to see content, that content is hidden from the user, and the user cannot reach it. Audience targeted content can still be reached by other users than the audience, for example if they search for it or have a link to it.

14.12.1   *Target Links*

Open the Site navigation in edit mode to enable audience targeting of links in the menu. At the bottom of the menu, you can find the toggle for audience targeting.

Enable site navigation audience targeting ⓘ

On

Once the audience targeting has been enabled in the Site navigation, it applies to links in all menus in the site, including hub and footer menus.

Save | Cancel

When you open the ellipsis at a link in the navigation and select 'Edit', you can add groups that this link should be displayed to.

Audiences to target

Start typing to select groups to target.

10 audiences limit - 10 audiences left

Audience targeting for navigation must be enabled by a Site owner, but when that is done, all users with Edit permission can target menu links to specific audiences.

14.12.2   *Target Files and Pages*

To direct certain files or pages to certain audiences, you must first enable the audience targeting in the Library settings or "Site Pages" library that has the content you want to target.

1. In the settings click on click on 'Audience targeting settings' under the General settings heading.

2. Enable audience targeting.

3. A new "Audience" column will be added to the library.

Now, you can select an item and open its Information pane to specify an audience.

There may be a delay before the audience targeting take effect.

14.12.3 *Target Modern Web Parts*

When you have enabled targeting in the "Site Pages" library, you can enable targeting for the modern web parts News and High-lighted content in pages in that site. That will direct the content in the web part to users who are members of the audience you specified.

1. Open the page in edit mode.

2. Add the web part, or use an existing web part.

3. Edit the web part and enable targeting in the right pane.

Enable audience targeting ⓘ

 Off

14.12.4 *Target Classic Web Parts*

SharePoint lists and document libraries give a possibility to enable audience targeting for classic web parts like the Content Query web part. *Refer to* section 27.3 for more information about this web part. The image below comes from a library, which gives both the modern and the classic option.

Enable Audience Targeting

Promote content to specific audiences. An audience can include Office 365 groups and Azure Active Directory groups.

Select Enable audience targeting for use with modern web parts such as News, Highlighted content, and others.

Select Enable classic audience targeting for use with classic web parts such as the Content Query web part.

☑ Enable audience targeting

☑ Enable classic audience targeting

When classic audience targeting is enabled, you should specify the audience in the item properties in the same way as described above. Then you can specify under 'Query' in the web part that content should be fetched from the list or document library.

Under 'Query', you also need to check the box for audience targeting.

Audience Targeting:

☑ Apply audience filtering

Note: All classic web parts also have a 'Target Audiences' in the Edit web part pane. This setting determines whether the web part is visible to the current user or not.

14.13 SUMMARY

SharePoint Online is a place in the cloud where teams and organizations can share content, but the sharing can get out of hand if administrators don't understand how the permission and sharing processes work.

In this chapter, we have looked at sharing via the 'Share' command, sharing by link and sharing to people outside the organization, and we have seen how both administrators and site owners can restrict the default permissions when sharing.

You now understand how the SharePoint permission inheritance works, and you know the difference between Microsoft 365 groups, SharePoint groups and Security groups.

I have also described the two kinds of external users and explained what must be in place before you can share content to people outside the tenant. To control external sharing is of course an important security measure. I will come back to data security in SharePoint in chapter 20, Security.

At the end of the chapter, I introduced Audience targeting, which is not permission setting but a way to help users find relevant content.

After this chapter, we will go back to the more hands-on work with the SharePoint content. I will first give some tips on how you can categorize the content, and after that we will have a closer look at how you can use links and pictures in SharePoint.

15 CATEGORIZATION

When you add more and more documents and list items to SharePoint, it becomes increasingly important to have them categorized in a good way, so that users quickly can find the data they need.

In this chapter, we will look at various ways to categorize items in SharePoint apps. I will point out how you, as a content creator or administrator, can make it easier for users to categorize content, and I will discuss benefits and drawbacks of each method.

I will also describe how to manage keywords centrally for the whole organization. It means that users are given suggestions when they start writing a keyword, so that the categorization becomes more consistent.

These are the categorization methods I discuss in this chapter:

- Create columns. Items can be sorted and filtered based on the values in the columns, so columns are very useful for categorization.

- Required Column Values. Make it mandatory to enter a column value.

- Default column value. Use a static or calculated value that is added by default.

- Tag items with Enterprise Keywords. Such keywords can be used by the whole organization, and they are synchronized between all apps and managed centrally in the Term Store.

- Use dedicated term sets. These can be shared across the organization or within specific site collections.

- Create multiple apps. You should for example use different document libraries for different content instead of adding new folders to the default library. Adding content to a specific app is a type of categorization that most users are familiar with.

- Let users rate app items.

15.1 COLUMNS

Imagine if a hotel booking site was organized into folders. Folders rely on information being categorized in one dimension only, and it would start out rather well. I could click my way into the Europe folder and then into the London folder – but then I would quickly realize that once I get into deeper categories it gets complex. Where will I find the hotels that have both "Free breakfast" and "Free Wi-Fi"? In one of those folders or both?

As you see, at a certain level of complexity the folder way of storing information breaks down. Most likely your information is that complex too. A good way of categorization is to create columns and combine them with views.

If we continue using the hotels example from above, I would create a country column based on the Choice, Managed meta data or Lookup column type, and then I would create two Yes/No Choice columns for the breakfast and the Wi-Fi.

If I fill out the column values for my hotel descriptions correctly, it would be very easy for anyone to find hotels with free Wi-Fi and breakfast in London by filtering the list for those three values.

Title		Town ▼	Rating	Price level	Free Wifi in room ▼	Breakfast included ▼	Pets	Room Service
Elite ✻	...	London	5 stars	High	Yes	Yes	No	Yes
Star ✻	...	London	3 stars	Low	Yes	Yes	No	No
Johnson's ✻	...	London	4 stars	Middle	Yes	Yes	No	Yes
More ✻	...	London	3 stars	Middle	Yes	Yes	Yes	No

15.1.1   *Mandatory Column Values*

With mandatory, or required, column values you can be sure that all new files and list items will be categorized.

To make a column value mandatory, click on the 'Yes' radio button under "Require that this column contains information" in the Edit Column dialog.

Require that this column contains information:

◉ Yes   ○ No

15.1.1.1   Mandatory List Columns

In list apps, some columns may very well be set to required, because when you do that, a new list item cannot be saved until a value is entered in the mandatory field.

% Complete *

| |%

You can't leave this blank.

Users will have more work, but you can feel sure the categorization will be done.

15.1.1.2   Mandatory Library Columns

With libraries there is more to consider before you set a column to be mandatory. When there is a required column in a library, a file can still be uploaded or created.

In the **modern** interface, there is a message in the column where a value is missing.

Importance ∨

① Required info

Properties   Edit all

① This file is missing required information

The **classic** interface instead checks out the file and shows a Check in dialog. The file cannot be accessed by other users until the required field has been filled out and the file has been checked in.

When a new file is created in the library, or when a file is added to a library that is opened in the File Explorer, no dialog will be shown. Instead, both experiences mark the file will with the checked out icon, *refer to* 9.11, Check Out / Check In. The modern file also has the message in the column.

Demo:

15.1.2   *Default Column Values*

If you want to avoid mandatory columns and still want to have items categorized, you can use a static or calculated value that is added by default to each new item. Default values increase the risk of wrong categorization, but on the other hand, default values can help users get started with categorization.

The default value is set at item creation and is not changed when the item is updated.

15.1.2.1   Set Static Default Value

The default value for a column can be set in the Edit Column dialog. Enter or select the value that should be default. The default setting looks a bit different in different column types.

Default value:

◉ Choice ○ Calculated Value

(2) Normal

When a default value has been added, it can be seen and changed in the List Settings, 'Column default value settings' under the General Settings heading.

▸ Change Default Column Values ⓘ

Column (click to edit default value)	Type	Default Value	Source of Default Value
Importance	Choice	Choice 1	Document Library

Importance : Edit Default Value   ✕

Default Value

Specify whether you want to apply a default value for this column to items added in this location.

◉ Do not specify a default value for this location
○ Use this default value:

Default value:

OK   Cancel

15.1.2.2   Set Calculated Default Value

When a column has a default value, it is nice if you can calculate that value for each item instead of setting a static value.

If you, for example, want to register the year when an order was placed, you can use a single line of text column with the calculated default value of the current year (when the item was added to the app).

1. Create a Single line of text column and call it "Year". (It will not work with a Date & Time column.)

2. Under default value, in the right pane or in the Create column page, check the box for 'Use calculated value'.

3. Add the formula =Text([TODAY],"YYYY") in the formula box.

Default value

> =TEXT(Today;"YYYY")

☑ Use calculated value ⓘ

Demo:

https://www.kalmstrom.com/Tips/SharePoint-Online-Course/Categorization-Default-Values.htm

15.2   RATING

SharePoint apps have two options for rating: stars and likes. When this is written, rating is only available in Group Team sites and classic Team sites.

Rating has several benefits:

- You can filter the column by rating.

- You can create views based on the rating.

- Search results are shown in rating order. By default, the highest rated/most liked hits are shown first.

- SharePoint shows how many users have rated the item.

Rating columns can be used for other than strict rating also. You can for example use rating to indicate urgency or importance.

15.2.1   Enable Rating

To allow rating in an app, go into the List settings and click on the 'Rating settings' link under General Settings.

Now you can allow rating and decide which kind of rating, likes or stars, should be used.

Rating Settings

◉ Yes   ○ No

Which voting/rating experience you would like to enable for this list?

○ Likes   ◉ Star Ratings

A new rating column will be created and displayed in the default view. You may of course also include the column in any other view.

15.2.2   Rate with Stars

The star rating column has five empty stars, and you can rate each item by clicking on a star. When you do that, all stars to the left of the star you clicked on will

★ ★ ★ ☆ ☆ | 1

be filled, so if you want to rate an item with three stars you should click on the third star.

15.2.3   Rate with Likes

The **modern** interface shows the likes with hearts. Click on the heart again to unlike.

♥ 1 Likes

In the **classic** interface, the like rating has a 'Like' link, and when you click on it, a smiley emoticon is shown at the item. It is possible to remove the linking by clicking on 'Unlike'.

☺ 1   Unlike

Demo:

https://www.kalmstrom.com//Tips/SharePoint-Online-Course/Categorization-Ratings.htm

15.3   MULTIPLE APPS

The categorization methods mentioned in the sections above work well for all apps, and what I say in this section also applies to all kinds of apps – it is better to have more! In my discussion below, though, I focus on libraries.

When you share documents in SharePoint, it is possible to put all your files directly into a big document library with lots of folders within folders. Most things will work as they do in a file server, and you will have the additional features of version history, full text search, flows and workflows, views and alerts. But there are better ways!

Once you start building a library with views and columns, it quickly becomes apparent which files fit into your document library and which don't. To continue with the hotels example I started above, it would be silly to fill out the "Swimming Pool" value on an excursion and the "Mode of transportation" value for an hotel building.

Instead of trying to fit both excursions and hotels in one document library, it makes sense to create one document library for each of those information types. Using multiple libraries for different kinds of files is generally a good idea. These four features work better if you use multiple libraries, instead of one library with folders:

- Permissions
- Search
- Navigation
- Scaling. A SharePoint app cannot display more than 5000 items, so if you put all your documents in one library you will sooner or later have to move files to new libraries anyway.

Demo:

https://www.kalmstrom.com//Tips/SharePoint-Online-Course/Categorization-Create-Libraries.htm

15.4 TAGGING

The concept of tagging is well-known from social media, and it usually works well in SharePoint too. SharePoint has a special column type for tags, or keywords, called Managed Metadata.

When values are added to a Managed Metadata column in any app, they are synchronized between all the tenant's apps, and they can be managed centrally in the Term store.

The Managed Metadata column type can be used in two ways, one free and one more controlled. In both cases, the values added to Managed Metadata columns in the whole tenant can be seen and managed in the SharePoint Admin center >Term store.

15.4.1   Term Store

You can find the tenant's Term store under 'Content services' in the SharePoint Admin center left menu. Here, you can manage the terms added to Managed Metadata columns.

In the Term store, you can find all terms added in Managed Metadata columns by users, but you can also create a taxonomy for the organization.

A taxonomy is a collection of terms that should be used in tagging. In SharePoint, the terms are organized based on similarities in a hierarchy with

315

three levels: Term group >Term set >Term. The 'Term' level can however have multiple sublevels, so in practice you can have more levels than three.

15.4.1.1   Add Terms in the Term Store

Here, I will describe how you can add a new term group and term set in the Term store, but you can of course also add terms to existing term sets and term sets to existing groups in the same way as described below.

1. In the Term Store, click on the top level, Taxonomy, and select 'Add term group'.

2. Enter a name for the new group.

3. Click on the new Term group to add a new Term set, or click on 'Import term set' to import data from a CSV file.

4. Enter a name for the new Term set.

5. In the same way, click on the Term set to add a Term.

6. Enter the term.

7. (Click on the term and add another term if you want to add a sublevel of terms).

8. Click on the Term set again to add another term.

As you see, there is first a click on the Term set each time you want to add a new term, so even if you don't already have the terms in a CSV file, it might be quicker to enter the keywords in an Excel file, save it as .cvs and import it to the Term store.

15.4.1.2   Term Store Settings

In the main area to the right of the left menu and taxonomy hierarchy, there are settings for Term groups, Term sets and Terms. The commands on top are the same as under the ellipses, and below you can find various other settings.

The Term sets have most settings. Under the 'General' tab you can manage the people who are responsible for the Term set.

Term store

🔍 Search terms	⊡ Add term ✐ Rename term set ⋯
⌂ Taxonomy	**Department** Edit
∨ ▢ People	Add a description to help users understand the purpose of this term set.
〉 ⊘ Department ⋮	General Usage settings Navigation Advanced
〉 ⊘ Job Title	

The 'Usage settings' tab lets you decide how the terms should be sorted, and if the Term set should be open or closed. By default, Term sets are open – that is, users can add terms by tagging with terms that do not exist in the Term set. When the Term set is closed, only terms from the Term set can be selected for tagging.

General	**Usage settings**	Navigation	Advanced

Submission policy   Edit

🔘 Open policy: Users can add terms from a tagging application.

Available for tagging   Edit

This term set will be available to end users and content editors of sites consuming this term set.

🔘 Enabled

Sort order   Edit

Terms can be sorted alphabetically or in a custom order.

🔘 Alphabetical

Each term can be managed with translation and synonyms. Select the term and click on '+ Add' under the term's General tab.

Term store

Search terms   Add te

□ Taxonomy

> □ Contoso

∨ □ kalmstrom.com Solutions

   ∨ ⊘ Templates Manager

     ⊘ Publisher

     ⊘ Template

     ⊘ Templates Manager

     ⊘ Test method

   > ⊘ Testing

     ⊘ Trial period

> □ People

Templa

General

Translation

+ Add

Add translation and synonyms

Language *

Swedish

Translation *

Mall

Description

Synonyms

Add synonyms for this term.

Mönster   Add

Save   Cancel

15.4.2   *Enterprise Keywords*

An "Enterprise Keywords" column is a column of the type Managed Metadata that is connected to a single, non-hierarchical Term set called "Keywords" under the 'System' group in the tenant's Term store. It is added to apps in a specific way, *see* below.

The "Keywords" Term set is a folksonomy – a collection of terms that have been added to Enterprise Keywords columns in the whole tenant.

Any user with Edit permission on a SharePoint app that has an "Enterprise Keywords" column can add keywords to the column, and they will then be added to the folksonomy and available across the organization.

If you need to edit the keywords, for example to remove inappropriate or wrongly spelled words, like in the image to the right, you can edit term in the "Keywords" Term set in the Term store.

318

15.4.2.1   Add an Enterprise Keywords Column

When you want to add an "Enterprise Keywords" column to a SharePoint app, open the List settings and click on 'Enterprise Metadata and Keywords Settings' under Permissions and Management. When the page opens, check the box for Enterprise Keywords.

Enterprise Keywords

☑ Add an Enterprise Keywords column to this list and enable Keyword
   synchronization

Click OK, and an "Enterprise Keywords" column of the type Managed Metadata will be added to the app.

The "Enterprise Keywords" column is not automatically added to the default view, so it can only be seen when you open the properties of a document. I would recommend that you edit the view, so that the column becomes visible in at least the default view.

When the "Enterprise Keywords" column is added to the view, you can also open the app in grid view mode and enter keywords there.

15.4.2.2   Tag with Enterprise Keywords

When users create or edit an item, they will have keyword suggestions from the whole Term store as soon as they start writing.

Users can also see in which Term set the term is stored, which will make it easier to select the right term. If no suggestion is good enough, users can add their own keyword.

Demo:

https://www.kalmstrom.com/Tips/SharePoint-Online-Course/Categorization-Enterprise-Keywords.htm

15.4.2.3   Remove the Enterprise Keywords column.

To add the "Enterprise Keywords" column, you just check a box in the app settings, as described above, but you cannot remove the column by unchecking the same box. Of course, you can remove the column from any view, but the column will still be visible in the properties.

To remove the "Enterprise Keywords" column from a SharePoint app, you must do like with other columns; *refer to* 7.11.2, Delete a List Column.

When the column has been deleted, the "Keywords" Term set is still left in the Term store and can be used in other apps. If you want to remove them totally, you must delete the Term set.

Demo:

https://www.kalmstrom.com/Tips/SharePoint-Online-Course/Categorization-Remove-Keywords.htm

15.4.3   *Managed Metadata*

If you want a more controlled tagging, or if you create a column where a limited number of options should be possible, you can create a Choice column. That works well for few options, but if the options are many, or if you want to control them centrally for the whole tenant, a custom Managed Metadata column is a better alternative.

When you use a custom Managed Metadata column, you add the choices users should select from to a term set in the Term store, and then you connect the column to that term set.

The column you use for the keywords can be called anything, but it must be of the Managed Metadata type. I recommend that you create it as a site column, so that you can reuse it.

15.4.3.1   Connect a Column to a Term Set

To connect a column to a term set and use the keywords stored there for tagging, create a column, give it any name and check the radio button for the Managed Metadata column type.

⦿ Managed Metadata

In the Create Column dialog you can then connect the column to one of your term sets.

⦿ Use a managed term set:
Find term sets that include the following terms.

| Department | 🔍 🗐 |

```
⏴  🔾 Taxonomy_hcRL3VioiV2xubyCk0o+0A==

    ⏴  📇 People

        ▷  🗐 Department

        ▤  . . ⎯ .
```

Now all keywords that are added to this Term set will be displayed as suggestions to users, *see* below. By default, users can add their own keywords, but that is only possible if the Term set is open in the Term store settings, *see* above.

You can always open an existing Managed Metadata column from the List settings to change the Term set the column should be connected to. If you do that, you probably want to change the name of the column also.

15.4.3.2   Tag Custom Managed Metadata Field

When users create or edit an item with a custom Managed Metadata column, they will see a Term store icon in the right part of the column field. The image to the right is from the modern experience. The classic interface has a double icon.

        :≡ Department

        Type term to tag

When users click on the icon in the **modern** interface, a right pane will open where they can select among all the terms in the connected term set. When terms have sub terms, these are also displayed and possible to select.

Department   ✕

| Type term to tag |

Select a tag

   Department

      ◯ Engineering

      ◯ Executive Management

      ◯ Sales

      ◯ Sales & Marketing

   Apply   Cancel

Return to classic

The **classic** experience work in a similar way, but it opens a dialog instead of a right pane.

Demo:

https://www.kalmstrom.com/Tips/SharePoint-Online-Course/Categorization-Term-Store-Start.htm

15.5   PAGE CATEGORIZATION

SharePoint site pages are stored in the "Site Pages" library, as described in chapter 13, and there you can add new columns to categorize the pages. Users will benefit from these columns in searches.

15.5.1   *Add Property Column*

To add a column that stores page properties, open the "Site Pages" library and create a new column. This is done with the '+Add column' command, in the same way as when you create a list column in a list or document library.

The properties column can be of any type. A choice column is often suitable to categorize site pages, but you can also create a Managed Metadata column as described in the section above – or any other column that suits your pages.

In the image below, I have created a "Category" choice column and a "Metadata" Managed Metadata column.

Site Pages

	Name ∨		Metadata ∨	Category ∨
∨				
∨ Created By : Kate Kalms				
	Demo.aspx		Templates Manager	Development

You can filter the columns and create views for the "Site Pages" library, just as you can do in other SharePoint libraries.

Additionally, the **modern** web parts Highlighted content and News give a possibility to display pages with specified properties, if you select to show content from the "Site Pages" library in the current site.

The image to the right shows how a Highlighted content web part is edited to show only pages that are categorized with "Templates Manager".

You can combine multiple filters to narrow down the options.

Source

The page library on this site	∨

Type

Pages	∨

Filter and sort   ∧

Filter

Page properties	∨

Property name

Metadata	∨

Equals	∨

Templates Manager	∨

15.5.2   Edit Page Properties

Once the property column has been added to the "Site Pages" library, the property can of course be edited for all pages in the library. All pages also give users a possibility to view and edit the page properties in the page itself.

15.5.2.1 Modern Page Details

The properties of modern pages are reach via the 'Page details' control in the modern page command bar, which opens a right pane. When the page is in Edit mode, the properties can be changed.

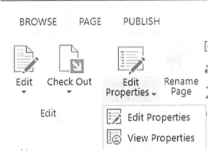

15.5.2.2 Classic Page Details

To see or edit the page properties of a classic page, open the PAGE tab in the ribbon and click on 'Edit Properties'.

A dialog will open in read or edit mode, depending on choice. Filter by Page Properties.

15.6 MANAGED PROPERTIES

When you want SharePoint to search only among content with specific properties, you can use Managed Properties. These are written before the search term, with a colon as separator.

Example: to find files with the word "consumer" in the file name, you should write Filename:consumer in the search box. Note that there must not be any space between the property and the term!

When you enter the search term like this, you are telling the search engine to give you all files with the word "consumer" in the filename. (By default, if you do not supply a managed property, you are searching all content.)

When you want to search for a name or another term that has two parts, use quotation marks around that term to indicate that it should be considered as one term: author:"Lisa Morrison".

You can even use the operators AND and OR. The operators must be written in capitals.

author:"Lisa Morrison" OR author:"Robert Smith"

author:"Lisa Morrison" AND author:"Robert Smith"

Which managed properties are the most relevant ones depends on how you are using SharePoint, but the Body, Title, Author and FileType managed properties are often very useful.

15.6.1   *Automatic Managed Properties Creation*

When you create **site columns**, SharePoint will create managed properties from the column names if you use columns of the type:

- Single line of text
- Choice
- Managed Metadata
- Date and Time
- Number
- Currency
- Yes/No

For example, if you create a single line column named Street, you can use "street" as a managed property and search for street:avenue. That will give you all the street names that include the word "avenue".

15.6.2   *Find Managed Properties*

You can find and learn new managed properties from the Site settings of any site. Click on 'Schema' under the Search heading to see all the tenant's managed properties.

All managed properties are not searchable, but you can use those who are marked with Search, like AccountName and AnchorText in the image below.

Filter									
Managed property									

Property Name	Type	Multi	Query	Search	Retrieve	Refine	Sort	Safe	Mapped Crawled Properties
AADObjectID	Text	-	Query	-	Retrieve	-	Sort	Safe	People:msOnline-ObjectId
AboutMe	Text	-	Query	-	Retrieve	-	-	Safe	People:AboutMe, ows_Notes
Account	Text	-	Query	-	Retrieve	-	-	Safe	ows_Name
AccountName	Text	-	Query	Search	Retrieve	-	-	Safe	People:AccountName
AnalyticsPath	Text	-	Query	-	Retrieve	-	-	Safe	
AnchorText	Text	-	-	Search	-	-	-	Safe	Basic:28

The search schema determines how content is collected and retrieved from the search index. Click on a managed property to modify it.

Demos:

https://kalmstrom.com/Tips/SharePoint-Online-Course/SharePoint-Search-Managed-Properties.htm

15.7 Summary

In this chapter, I have given some tips on how you can categorize content in SharePoint apps, to make it easier to find. You have learned categorization methods like rating and required and default column values.

A bit more complicated, but very rewarding in the long run, is to use the column type Manage Metadata. I have shown some different ways to take advantage of this column, and I have explained how to reach the Term Store and manage keywords centrally there.

We have also seen how pages can be categorized in the "Site Pages" library and how you can edit page properties directly in classic and modern pages.

Finally, you have learned some about how managed properties can be used in searches.

Now we will go over to something else: links. Ever since we started using the internet, everyone knows what a link is, and in next chapter you will learn how links can enhance your SharePoint system.

16 LINKS

Links are the foundation of everything on the web. A link, also called hyperlink or shortcut, is usually a reference to another specific web page, section, document, image or sound.

To create a link, you often need to know the web address, or URL, to the content you want to link to.

In SharePoint, the mouse cursor transforms into a hand when you hover over text or an image. When you hover over text, the link will often be highlighted or underlined.

In this chapter you will learn:

- Where to find the URL to a SharePoint item
- How links can be added, edited and used in SharePoint Online
- Different ways to add links that point to pages, apps and images
- How to write and use wiki links
- How to add captions and make a link open in a new window
- How to create promoted links
- How to create a Links app and add links to it

16.1   GET THE URL

To copy a URL, you can select it in the browser's address field, right-click and select Copy. You can do this for any URL, and for SharePoint apps and pages it works well.

For apps, you will have the link to the current view (and filter).

When you need a link to a SharePoint site or item there are better options.

16.1.1   Site Link

The easiest way to get the correct link to a site, is to right-click on the SharePoint banner or site icon in the top left corner of any page in the site you want to open.

Then select 'Copy link address' or 'Copy Link Location'. That will give you the correct URL for the site. It is often shorter than the URL in the address field, which also might include the specific page.

The kalmstrom.com

Open link in new tab

Open link in new window

Open link in incognito window

Bugs

Calendar

Save link as...

Customers

Copy link address

16.1.2   *Item Link*

When you copy the URL to a list item or library file as described in chapter 14, Permissions and Sharing, you will also have permission choices for the shared link. *Refer to* 14.6.2, Share with a Link.

16.2   ADD LINKS TO A PAGE

Links can be added to pages in many ways. The classic pages give a few more options than the modern pages, especially when it comes to linking images. Pages must always be in edit mode when links are added.

16.2.1   *Add Links to a Modern Page*

Modern pages have two web parts dedicated to links, Links and Quick Links. It is also possible to add links in some other web parts, like the Hero, Button, Call to action and Sites web parts, and to link text in the Text web part.

16.2.1.1   The Link Web Part

In the Link web part, you can paste any link directly into the web part. If available, a preview of the item will be displayed. You can only add one link to each Link web part.

16.2.1.2   The Quick Links Web Part

The Quick Links web part is more of a "pin" tool where you can add multiple links. There are several layout options, but some of them are only for links from SharePoint. This web part is described in 13.8.1 Modern Views Landing Page.

16.2.1.3   The Highlighted Content Web Part

In the Highlighted content web part, there is a possibility to show only links.

Type

Links

16.2.1.4   The Sites Web Part

In the Sites web part, links are shown as tiles in a modern SharePoint page. This web part can only show links to sites within the tenant.

The image below shows the web part Edit pane in a hub site, which gives some more options than other sites.

There are two automatic options: to show all sites in the hub or do show frequent sites for the current user.

You can also enter URLs to sites. Add the links one by one in the field below 'Select sites' or search for them. The site name will be added below the field with a checkbox, and when you check it, the site will be added to the page. Then you can add another site in the same way.

You can also select sites among associated, frequent and recent sites.

16.2.2 Add Links to a Classic Page

When you want to add links to classic pages in classic sites, you have two options: 'From SharePoint' and 'From Address'. Both are found under the ribbon INSERT tab.

When you create a wiki page in a modern Team site, you will only have the 'From Address' option, but you can of course use it for links from SharePoint too.

Place the mouse cursor where you want to add a link, or select the text or image you want to add a link to. The click on the 'Link' button in the ribbon and select the link option you want to use.

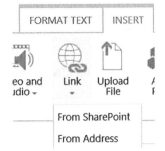

16.2.2.1 From Address

Use the 'From Address' link option, when you want to add a link to a page that is outside the site or even outside your tenant. When you select 'From Address', a dialog will open where you can enter a URL.

If you have selected a text, it will be filled out under Text to display. Otherwise, you can enter an anchor text to be displayed. You can also try the link before you click OK.

Insert Hyperlink ✕

Text to display:
kalmstrom.com

Address:
http://www.kalmstrom.com ✕

Try link

OK   Cancel

16.2.2.2 From SharePoint

Use the 'From SharePoint' link option, when you want to select a page, document or item in the same site. When you select 'From SharePoint', a new page will open where you can select the location to link to.

16.2.2.3 Link Options

When you place the mouse cursor next to the new link, the LINK tab will open.

BROWSE   PAGE   PUBLISH   FORMAT TEXT   INSERT   LINK

URL: https://www.kalmstrom.c⟨   ☐ Open in new tab

Description: ☐ Display Icon

Remove Link

Link   Properties   Behavior

Here you can add a description that will be shown in a pop-up window when users hover the mouse cursor over the link.

Check the box for 'Display icon' if you have linked to an Office file and want the file type to be indicated with an icon. In other cases, you will just have a white icon of no interest.

Under the LINK tab you can also set the link location to open in a new tab and remove the link. When you remove the link this way, the display text or image that you have linked will still be visible on the page.

16.3   ADD LINKS IN APPS

SharePoint Online apps have a specific column type for links, but if rich text is allowed, users can also add links in Multiple lines of text fields.

16.3.1   *The Hyperlink Column*

To make it possible to add links to app items, you can create a hyperlink column. When you do that from a modern app, select the type Hyperlink. In classic apps, or if you create the column from the List settings, the same column type is called 'Hyperlink or Picture'.

⦿Hyperlink or Picture

When you add a link to a Hyperlink column, the link source will open in a new tab in the browser when someone clicks on it.

In standard view mode, you can enter the URL and display text in the right pane (modern) or in the properties dialog (classic).

In grid view mode, you can add the URL and display text in a dialog. This dialog opens when you select the cell and then click in the cell in the modern interface.

Link ∨   +
_____

The kalmstrom.com website

┌─────────────────────────┐
│   │
│   │
└─────────────────────────┘

Link

┌─────────────────────────┐
│   │
└─────────────────────────┘

Display text

┌─────────────────────────┐
│   │
└─────────────────────────┘

✓ ✕

In the classic interface, you should instead click on a link icon to open the dialog.

16.3.2   *The Multi-Line Column*

You can add links in list columns of the type Multiple lines of text, if enhanced rich text is enabled in the column settings. Note that only list apps have this option in the Multiple lines of text column.

More options ∨

Use enhanced rich text (Rich text with pictures, tables, and hyperlinks)

 Yes

When you add a link to a Multiple lines of text field in the **modern** experience, you must open the ellipsis to the right in the tool bar to open a dialog where you can add a display text. There are currently no other options, and the link does *not* open in a new tab. In this case, it is therefore better to switch to the classic experience.

Edit Instructions   ✕

| Calibri ∨ | 11 ∨ | ■ A ∨ ☐ ▽ ∨ | **B** | *I* | U̲ | ⋯ |

≣ Alignment   >

≣ List or edit hyperlink >

🔗 Add or edit hyperlink

→≣ Increase indent

←≣ Decrease indent

✎ Clear format

🖼 Insert image

[**Save**] [Cancel]

Return to classic experience

When you add a link to a 'Multiple lines of text' field in the **classic** experience, you should not paste the link directly in the field.

Instead, you will have the same options in the ribbon as when you add links to a classic page, *see* above, when you click in the field. Add the link from Address or SharePoint, and you will have the same link options as in the classic page.

16.4   LINK AN IMAGE

In **modern** pages, you can add a link to an image that is added to the Image web part. When you have added the image, edit the web part and enter the link in the right pane.

Image   ✕

Change your image and image options. Turn on or off the display of text over your image, add a link, and add or modify alternative text.

> Change

Link

> https://

Add text over image

⬤) Off

A text overlay is similar to a caption, but it appears on top of the image. Turn on text overlay and then enter the web part to edit the text.

Alternative text

If you add a picture to a **classic** SharePoint page, you can link the image just like you link text. Select the image instead of text, add from Address or from SharePoint and you will have all the link options.

Demo:

https://kalmstrom.com/Tips/SharePoint-Online-Course/Links-From-Images.htm

16.5   WIKI LINKING

Wiki links can be added to wiki pages in edit mode and help you achieve things that are difficult to manage in other ways. With wiki links, you can for example link from one page to another page that has not been created yet.

Wiki links only work within one site. This means that you can link to pages, apps and even to a certain view or item, but you cannot use a wiki link to link to content in another site or outside SharePoint.

The wiki link syntax has to be typed in, and the links must start and end with double square brackets, [[...]]. When you type the first two brackets on a SharePoint wiki page, you will be shown a list of the site's pages, apps and views. Select one of the options, and the closing brackets will be added automatically.

You can also type in the syntax instead of selecting, for example if you want to link to a non-existing page. Then you must add the closing brackets manually too.

16.5.1   *Wiki Link and Create a Wiki Page*

When using wiki links, you can first create the link and then create the page you have linked to:

1. Write the name of the new page surrounded by double square brackets, for example [[Sales]].

2. Save the page you are working on, and the link will be displayed with a dotted underline, to show that the page does not exist yet.

Sales

3. Click on the link, and you will be asked to create the page.

Add a page   ✕

The page 'Sales' does not exist. Do you want to create it?

Find it at https://m365x446726.sharepoint.com/sites/ci/SitePages/Sales.aspx

Create	Cancel

4. Click on 'Create', and the new page will open in edit mode, so that you can customize it. It will be another wiki page.

5. When you return to the page where you created the link, it will no longer be underlined, and the link will take you to the page you just created.

16.5.2   *Wiki Link to an App*

When you link to an existing app, you can use the select option instead of typing the syntax within the double brackets.

1. Write the two brackets and click on List:

[[

Home
How To Use This Library
Sales
    List:
    View:

2. Now all apps will be displayed, and you can click on the list/library you want to link to.

```
[[List:|

        Documents/
        KTM Lanes/
        KTM Phases/
        KTM Projects/
        KTM Responsibles/
        KTM Tasks/
        KTM Weight/
        MicroFeed/
        Site Assets/
        Site Pages/
```

3. The two end brackets are added automatically.

[[List:KTM Tasks/]]|

4. Save the page, and the link will be shown with the list
   name as display text.

KTM Tasks

16.5.3   *Wiki Link to a View*

To create a wiki link that points directly to a view, you must perform some more
steps when you have selected the app.

1. Write the two brackets and click on View.

2. All apps are displayed. Click on the app that has the view you want to link to.
   Now the link is completed – but it still only points to the app.

3. Remove the two end brackets.

[[View:Documents/|

4. Press the Ctrl key + the space
   key. Now the views of that list will
   be displayed, and you can select
   the view you want to link to.

   All Documents
   Manuals
   Slideshows

5. When you save the page, the link
   will be shown with the view name
   as display text.

Demo:

https://kalmstrom.com/Tips/SharePoint-Online-Course/HelpDesk-Landing-
Page.htm

16.5.4   *Wiki Link to an Item*

When you want to link to a specific item in a list or library, the process is nearly
the same as when you link to a view.

1. Write the two brackets and click on List.

2. All apps are displayed. Click on the app that has the item you want to link to.
   Now the link is completed – but it still only points to the app.

3. Remove the two end brackets.

4. Press the Ctrl key + the space key. Now the items of that list will be displayed, and you can select the item you want to link to.

5. If there are many items in the list, you will first be asked to start typing to have choice. In the image below I have written an s, and then all items that begin with an s are displayed so that I can select one of them.

[[List:KTM Tasks/s]]

Send notices
Select samples before the meeting
Send receipts

6. When SharePoint creates the link, the ID number of the item is added as the actual location for the link. After that comes a pipe (vertical bar) and then the display text, which is the title of the item.

[[List:KTM Tasks/6|Send notices]]

7. When you save the link, the item title or file name will be shown as display text for the link.

16.5.5   *Manipulate Display Text*

As we have seen in the section above, the wiki link to an item uses the item ID and then adds the item name after a pipe (|) to get the link to show the item name as display text.

Pipe + display name can be used in all wiki links:

1. Create the wiki link as described in one of the sections above.

2. Type a pipe + the word(s) you want to use as display text before the two square brackets at the end.

3. Save the page, and the text after the pipe will be shown as display text.

Demo:

https://kalmstrom.com/Tips/SharePoint-Online-Course/Wiki-Pages.htm

16.6   CREATE A LINKS APP

A nice way of adding links to SharePoint is to add them to an app that is designed to display links. The Links app is such an app, and it can have both the classic and the modern interface. A Links app can also be added to a page.

Sales Links

URL ∨	Notes ∨
The kalmstrom.com website	SharePoint solutions and tips

Create the links app by opening the 365 Settings icon and selecting 'Add an app'. Then search for the Links app.

Links

To add links to the links app, click on '+New' and 'Item' in the command bar (modern) or 'new link' (classic).

Enter the address in the URL field and write a description that gives a suitable display text. The Notes text will be shown in a separate column, *see* the image above.

New item

🔗 URL *

https://www.kalmstrom.com/

The kalmstrom.com website

☰ Notes

SharePoint solutions and tips

Demo:

https://kalmstrom.com/Tips/SharePoint-Online-Course/Links-List-App.htm

16.6.1   Add a Links App to a Page

The Links app can be added to the List web part in a **modern** page in the same site. Add the List web part to the page, and the available lists will be displayed in the web part so that you can select one of them.

When you edit the List web part, you will have various options on what to show.

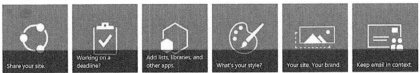

When you edit a **classic** page, you will find the Links app among the app parts or among the web parts in the App category. Select it and click on 'Add' and you will have the same information as in the Links app displayed on the page.

Sales Links

⊕ **new link** or edit this list

✓	☐	Edit	URL		Notes
	☐	📝	The kalmstrom.com website	•••	SharePoint solutions and tips

16.7   PROMOTED LINKS

When you create a classic Team site, the homepage has links in the shape of moving tiles. These links are called promoted links. You can create such tile links yourself by using the Promoted links app template.

Get started with your site   REMOVE THIS

The image below shows two tiles in an embedded Promoted links app. One has a background image, and one is without an image. The title is always visible, but the description is only displayed when you move the mouse cursor over the tile.

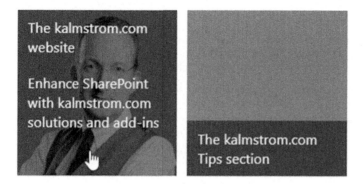

The kalmstrom.com website

Enhance SharePoint with kalmstrom.com solutions and add-ins

The kalmstrom.com Tips section

16.7.1 Create a Promoted Links App

Use the command 'Add an app' to create a Promoted Links app.

1. Open the Promoted Links app.
2. Click on '+New' in the command bar (modern) or 'new item' (classic). (In the classic interface you must first go to the 'All Promoted Links' view.)
3. Enter a link to a background image, a target link and a description.
4. You should also set the sequence order of the tile and select if the link location should open in the same page, in a new tab or in a dialog.
5. Click on Save when the form is filled out.

New item

Title *

The kalmstrom.com website
_____

Background Image Location

https://www.kalmstrom.com/images/People/peter_banner.png
_____

The kalmstrom.com website
_____

Description

Enhance SharePoint with kalmstrom.com solutions and add-ins
_____ ⁄⁄

Link Location *

https://kalmstrom.com/
_____

The kalmstrom.com website
_____

Launch Behavior *

In page navigation   ⌄
_____

Order

1
_____

[**Save**]   Cancel

6. Repeat step 2-5 for each tile.

16.7.1.1   Promoted Links Images

You don't need to add images to the promoted links, but if you want to do
that, any image can be used. The size will be 150x150px, so if you use a
bigger image it will be compressed. Avoid using a smaller image, as it will
give bad quality. (It is only possible to change the size of the promoted link
tiles by using code.)

16.7.2 *Add Promoted Links to a Page*

When you have created a promoted links app, you can add it in a **modern** List web part or a **classic** app part on a SharePoint page. This is done in the same way as with the Links app, *see* above.

Demo:

https://kalmstrom.com/Tips/SharePoint-Online-Course/Promoted-Links.htm

16.8 Summary

As the SharePoint site grows, it becomes increasingly important to have a good navigation. In this Links chapter, I have introduced promoted links, wiki links and links apps in addition to the more well-known kinds of hyperlinks. I have also shown how to add captions and how to make a link open in a new window.

In the next chapter, we will look at different ways to add images to SharePoint.

17   PICTURES

Images can be added to SharePoint from different sources. They can be
edited in various ways, and they can also be linked, as we saw in the
previous chapter.

In this chapter I will introduce picture libraries and explain how you can add
pictures to pages. I will also show two ways to create and add images that
have different links in different areas of the image, so called hotspot images.

17.1   PICTURE LIBRARY

Instead of using the default Site Assets library to store images
that should be used in a SharePoint site, you can create a
picture library. You may very well create several picture
libraries, to categorize the images.

Picture Library

The benefit of using a picture library is that it by default will
have two extra views, in additional to the standard library
views:

- The Thumbnails view, which shows thumbnails of all pictures.
- The Slides view, where you can move between different pictures like in a
  slideshow.

To create a Picture Library, use the command 'Add an app' under the 365
Settings icon and search for the Picture Library template.

An important picture library benefit is that you can add the library to a web
part in a page and show pictures in a slideshow on that page, *see* below.

17.2   ADD IMAGES TO PAGES

Images make SharePoint pages more interesting, and sometimes an image
can be more explanatory than text. The images can be fetched to the page
from multiple sources, but you should consider how to do with updates.

When you add an image that you have no control over, for example from an
external website, it will no longer be shown on your SharePoint page when it
is removed from the original site. If the image is updated on the original site,
it will be updated on your site too.

To have full control over the image, download it and add it to the page from
your computer. Then it will be saved to SharePoint, and you don't risk losing
it on the page. But this of course means that your picture will not be updated
when the original picture is updated!

Be careful to only use creative commons or images that are free to share
and use, when you take images from a website that you don't control. You
can filter by license in the browser.

17.2.1   *Modern Page Picture Options*

The modern Hero and Highlighted content web parts can have both images and other content, but Microsoft also offers two modern web parts that are solely intended for images: Image and Image gallery. When images are added to one of these web parts, users can see the images, but they cannot do anything with them.

If you want to give users a possibility to work with the images, you can instead use the Document library web part.

17.2.1.1   The Image Web Part

The Image web part is intended for one picture. When you add the web part to a page, the right pane will open so that you can select the image source.

Another option is to just drag an image to a modern page that is open in edit mode. The image will automatically be added to an Image web part.

When you have added the image, a toolbox will be displayed above it so that you can work with the image. From left to right, you can:

- Resize the image by dragging in the handles that appear when you click on the icon.
- Crop the image.
- Crop with aspect ratios.
- Align the image.
- Reset the image to the state it was when you last saved it.
- Save the change to the image.

When you click on the edit icon to the left of the web part, you can add a text overlay to the image. You can also add a link and an alternative text.

17.2.1.2   The Image Gallery Web Part

If you want to add multiple images in the same web part, you can use the Image gallery web part. Here you can display selected images or show images dynamically from a document library.

Image gallery   ✕

Image options   ⌃

◉ Select images

◯ Dynamically display images from a document library

Layout   ⌃

Brick   Grid   Carousel

Switch to grid layout to reorder images

In the Image gallery web part, you cannot resize or crop images, but you can choose between Brick, Carousel and Grid layout. The Carousel layout shows the images in a slideshow.

When you add images to an Image gallery web part, you can either click on the 'Add' button to open the right pane with the source options or drag the images to the web part. In this case, you need to add the web part first.

If you just drag multiple images to a page without an Image gallery web part, they will be placed in one Image web part each.

I suggest that you first add the images to the web part and then try different layouts with them. Generally, the Image gallery works best if the images are of similar size.

When you have added images to the Image gallery web part, click on the edit icon on each image to add text. Links are currently not possible here.

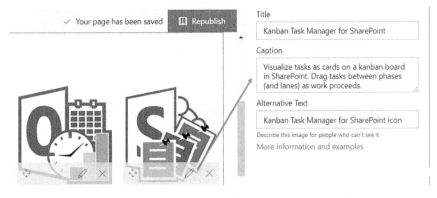

✓ Your page has been saved   🕮 Republish

Title

Kanban Task Manager for SharePoint

Caption

Visualize tasks as cards on a kanban board in SharePoint. Drag tasks between phases (and lanes) as work proceeds.

Alternative Text

Kanban Task Manager for SharePoint icon

Describe this image for people who can't see it
More information and examples

17.2.1.3   Picture Library in Document Library Web Part

It is not (yet) possible to dynamically display images from a Picture library in the Image gallery web part. You can however add a picture library to the Document library web part, because the picture library will show up among the options you can select when you have added the web part.

When a Picture library has been added to a Document library web part, the images can only be displayed in the document library specific layouts List, Compact list and Tiles. The app specific layout options, Thumbnail and Slides, are visible in the View selector but they don't work.

Adding the Picture library to a Document library web is still a good option, when you want to give users a possibility to work with the images, like downloading them and seeing their properties.

17.2.2   Classic Page Picture Options

In classic sites, images can be added directly to SharePoint wiki pages from three different kinds of sources: Computer, Address and SharePoint

Modern sites with a wiki page only have the options Computer and Address.

Follow these steps when you want to add an image to a page, no matter which source you wish to use.

1. Open the page in edit mode.

2. Place the mouse cursor where you want the image to be placed.

3. Open the INSERT tab and click on Picture to see the options.

4. Select one of the options.

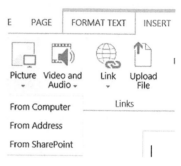

17.2.2.1   Add a Picture 'From Computer'

When you select the 'From Computer' option to add a picture, a copy will be uploaded to a SharePoint library in the site. In the Upload Image dialog, you can select a destination library where you want to place your picture.

The default option is the 'Site Assets' library, but if you have created a picture library you may choose it instead.

17.2.2.2   Add a Picture 'From Address' or 'From SharePoint'

When you select 'From Address' you can enter the URL any picture.

When you add an image 'From SharePoint', it means "from this SharePoint site" and you can pick the image without needing a URL.

17.2.2.3   Picture Display

When you select a picture on a wiki page in edit mode, the IMAGE tab will be displayed. Here, you can modify how the image is displayed in several ways.

BROWSE	PAGE	FORMAT TEXT	INSERT	IMAGE

	Address: /sites/kalmstrom.comdemos,				Horizontal Size:	380 px
Change Picture ▾	Alt Text: SharePoint Hiearchy		Image Styles ▾	Position ▾	Vertical Size:	193 px
						☑ Lock Aspect Ratio
Select	Properties		Styles	Arrange	Size	

From left to right you can:

- Change Picture. This button gives the same options as the Picture button under the INSERT tab.

- See the path to the image.

- See and change the Alt text, which is a text that is shown instead of the image if the image cannot be shown.

- Set image borders in various styles.

- Set the relative position of the image. (If you want to give the image an absolute position, I would recommend that you first insert a table, *refer to* 13.5.1.2, Add a Table, and then insert the image in a cell.)

- Change the size and lock the aspect ratio while doing so.

Demos:

https://kalmstrom.com/Tips/SharePoint-Online-Course/Add-an-Image-from-the-Computer.htm

https://kalmstrom.com/Tips/SharePoint-Online-Course/Adding-an-Image-from-Address.htm

https://kalmstrom.com/Tips/SharePoint-Online-Course/Adding-an-Image-from-SharePoint.htm

17.2.3   *Classic Picture Web Parts*

When you insert a picture web part on a classic page and add your images there, you will have additional options.

17.2.3.1   The Picture Library Slideshow Web Part

If you want to show all the images in a picture library, you can add it in the Picture Library Slideshow web part. It shows the images one by one, either with controls for manual selection or with a timer that switches images automatically.

Consultants

A limitation of the Picture Library Slideshow web part is that the picture library must be stored in the same site as the page where you insert the web part.

1. Add the Picture Library Slideshow web part from the Media and Content category to the page.

2. Edit the web part.

◄◄ ▶ ▶▶

3. Select which picture library should be used and how the images should be displayed.

4. Click OK and save the page.

Demo:

https://kalmstrom.com/Tips/SharePoint-Online-Course/Picture-Library-Slideshow-Web-Part.htm

17.2.3.2 The Image Viewer Web Part

In SharePoint versions before 2010, the Image Viewer Web Part was the only way to add a picture to a SharePoint page. Nowadays this web part is not so commonly used, but it is still there and possible to use for single images.

1. Add the Image Viewer web part from the Media and Content category to a classic page.

2. Edit the web part and type or paste the image URL in the 'Image Link' field. The picture will be displayed on the page.

3. Make other changes you prefer and then click OK and save the page.

Demo:

https://kalmstrom.com/Tips/SharePoint-Online-Course/Image-Viewer-Web-Part.htm

17.3 HOTSPOT IMAGE

Images with clickable regions are often called HTML maps, image maps or hotspot images. Such pictures with areas linked to different destinations can be created in Excel or PowerPoint. The creation is out of scope for this book, but you can see the process in the demos I refer to in this section.

The PowerPoint option is the easiest one, and the file can be added to modern as well as classic SharePoint pages with the file's embed code.

The Excel option gives a cleaner picture, but it can only be added to classic pages.

In both options you must first save or upload the file to the SharePoint site where you want to add the picture.

The Excel image can be updated automatically from the computer to SharePoint. For the PowerPoint file you must save a new image to SharePoint.

17.3.1   *Add a PowerPoint File to a Page*

When you have saved a .pptx file to a SharePoint library, you can add it to a page. The links will work, but unfortunately you cannot get rid of the slideshow banner at the bottom when you use a PowerPoint file.

In a **modern** page, add the file to the modern File Viewer web part, or copy the Embed Information of the file, *refer to* 9.2.2, One Item Selected, and paste it in the Embed web part.

In a **classic** page, copy the Embed Information of the file and paste it in the page by INSERT >Embed Code.

Demo:

https://kalmstrom.com/Tips/SharePoint-Online-Course/Clickable-Links-PowerPoint.htm

17.3.2   *Add an Excel image to a Classic Page*

When you have created an Excel image, it should be added to the classic Content Editor web part in the Media and Content category.

1. Save the image sheet as a web page to the site where you want to show it. Click on Save as >More options and select the Web Page file type. At 'Save' select the option 'Selection Sheet'.

   File name: Sales-per-country.htm

   Save as type: Web Page (*.htm;*.html)

   Authors: kalmstrom.com Busin...

2. Click on 'Publish...' and check the box to allow 'AutoRepublish every time this workbook is saved'.

   Save: ○ Entire Workbook
   ● Selection: Sheet

   Publish...

3. Save the file as an .xlsx file to your computer, so that you can continue working with it, and select the radio button for 'Enable the AutoRepublish feature'.

4. Open the SharePoint page in edit mode and insert the Content Editor web part from the Media and Content category.

5. Edit the web part and set the URL to the .htm file you saved from Excel to SharePoint

6. Make any other changes you prefer before you apply and save the page.

Now, each time you change something in the file on your computer and save it, the SharePoint image will be updated automatically.

‹ Content Editor	✕
Content Editor	
Content Link	
To link to a text file, type a URL.	
tePages/Sales-per-country.htm	...
Test Link	
⊞ Appearance	
⊞ Layout	
⊞ Advanced	
OK Cancel Apply	

Demo:

https://www.kalmstrom.com/Tips/SharePoint-Online-Course/Clickable-Links-Excel.htm

17.4 SUMMARY

In the Pictures chapter you have learned about the Picture library and how to add pictures to SharePoint modern and classic pages. I have also shown some ways to add hotspot images to SharePoint pages.

We have already talked a lot about web parts and page customization, but in next chapter I will introduce something new. I will explain how you can connect web parts to each other, so that the content in one of them depends on a selection in the other web part.

18 Connect Web Parts

SharePoint web parts are very useful, and you have already learned how to take advantage of different kinds of web parts in modern and classic site pages. In this chapter, we will go into more advanced use of web parts.

We will look at how web parts can be connected on a page. By connecting web parts, you can give users an interactive and dynamic experience. This can be done in both modern and classic site pages, but the classic pages give most options so far.

It is most often suitable to use the two columns layout for connected web parts, so that users don't have to scroll to see the result of their selection.

If you get problems with the connections described below, check if one of the apps has the datasheet/grid view as the default view. That can create problems, so try with a standard view instead.

18.1 Web Part Connection in Modern pages

When you connect two web parts in a modern page, you must add both web parts to the page first. Then you can make the connection by selecting the appropriate values.

When users select an item to show content in a connected web part, they must select by clicking in the ring to the left of the item. If they click on the first column, the document or list item will open in a new tab.

18.1.1 Connect to Source

The modern List properties and File viewer web parts can connect to another web part and display content depending on what has been selected in that web part.

Connect via the 'Connect to source' command under the ellipsis in the top right corner of the web part's Edit pane.

List properties   ×

                                              ···

Connect to a list or li   🔌 Connect to source
to dynamically displა
list. Select your list source, the list you want to
connect to, and then choose your display and
editing options.

In the image below I have used a Library web part with a Picture library in a File viewer web part. A .png file is selected in the Document library web part to the left, and the image is shown in the File viewer to the right.

Picture library   See all

⮦ Share ℗ Copy link ↓ Download ·· ✕ 1 selected ≡ Thumbnails ∨

	Name ∨	Picture Size ∨	File
	Azure.png		5.38
	flow-icon-small.png		2.21
✓	KE256x256.png ⮦ ⋮		14.1
	SharePoint-Designer.png		115

You can only connect the web part to an app in the same site. When you do that, users can select any item added to the Document library, and it will be displayed in the File viewer web part.

1. Add the Document library web part to the page and select the library you want to display.

2. Add the File viewer web part and cancel the file selection.

3. Edit the File viewer web part.

4. Open the ellipsis in the top right corner of the right pane and select 'Connect to source'.

5. Select the library you added to the Document library web part.

In the same way, you can connect a List properties web part to a List web part and display items based on what the user selects in the List web part.

18.1.2   *Dynamic Filtering*

The modern List and Library web parts can filter one app based on a selection made in another app. For this, you should apply Dynamic filtering in the web part you want to filter.

In the image below, the Employees list has been filtered to only show staff in the West department – that is, the department of the item that is selected in the Departments list.

Departments   See all   Employees > West   See all

Department ... ↓ ∨	Manager ∨	Staff ∨
⊘ West ↩ ⋮	Kate Kalmström	4
South	Peter Kalmström	3
North	Peter Kalmström	200
East	Kate Kalmström	50

First Name ∨	Last Name ∨	Department ▽ ∨
Kalie	Kula	West
John	Smith	West
Violet	Johnson	West
John	Green	West

For this scenario, use two List web parts, and enable Dynamic filtering in the web part where you have added the list you want to filter. Select the list in the other List web part and also select the corresponding columns in both web parts.

Dynamic filtering can be used with multiple items too. You can for example select two items in the Departments list, so that staff belonging to these two departments will be displayed in the Employees list.

Dynamic filtering
Filter by items selected in another list or library Learn More

⬤ On

Column in Employees to filter

Department	∨

List or library containing the filter value

Departments	∨

Column containing the filter value

Department Name	∨

Apply

18.2 WEB PART CONNECTION IN CLASSIC PAGES

In classic pages it is possible to connect two web parts, so that specified content from one web part is displayed in another web part on the same page.

To connect a web part to another web part, you must have the Edit pane open in the first web part. Otherwise. you will not get the connect option when you click on the edit arrow in the top right corner of the web part.

In this section, I will use country information from a "Customers" list app as an example of how connected web parts can be useful. The list has a "Country" column, and I will show three different ways to let users select or click on a country and see all customers in the list that are tagged with that country.

18.2.1   *Choice Filter Web Part*

When you edit the Choice Filter web part, it has a field similar to a list choice field, where you can enter the options you want to filter by. If you already have these data in a list column, it is easy to copy them and paste them into the Choice Filter web part.

The Choice Filter web part is not available when you create the classic page in a modern site. If you are on a modern site, use a modern page instead, *see* above.

When you add a Customers web part on a page where you also add a Choice Filter web part, users can click on the icon to the right of the search box in the Choice Filter web part to see the choices.

Select Filter Value(s)

Choice Filter

In this case, the choices are countries, and when users click in the radio button to the left of a country name, they will see the customers in the selected country in the Customers web part.

- ○ Argentina
- ○ Austria
- ○ Belgium
- ○ Brazil
- ○ Canada
- ○ Denmark
- ○ Finland
- ○ France

1. Add the Customers web part to the page.

2. Place the mouse cursor outside the Customers web part on the page and add the Choice Filter web part from the Filters category.

3. Edit the Customers web part and enter your choice alternatives in the right pane, in this case all the countries. You can very well copy and paste them into the web part.

4. Click on 'Apply' at the bottom of the Edit pane.

5. Expand the edit accordion in the top right corner of the Choice Filter web part and select Connections >Send Filter Values To >Customers.

6. In the pop-up window, select 'Get Filter Values From'. (Allow pop-ups if the pop-up window does not open).

7. Click on 'Configure' and select the 'Country' Choice Filter.

8. Click on 'Finish' and save the page.

Demo:

https://kalmstrom.com/Tips/SharePoint-Online-Course/Connect-Web-Parts-Choice.htm

18.2.2 *Click to Filter with Connected List Web Parts*

Instead of using the Choice Filter web part, as described above, you can connect the "Customers" list to a "Countries" list by adding them as two separate web parts on the same page.

This method reminds very much of the dynamic filtering in modern pages, and it can be used on classic pages in modern as well as classic Team sites. The result lets users click on an icon to the left of a country to see all customers from that country.

To use this method, you must first create a separate list that contains all the country names from the "Customers" list. You must also allow pop-up windows.

1. Add the "Countries" and the "Customers" lists as web parts on the page.

2. Edit the Countries web part (but don't do anything in the right pane).

3. Expand the edit accordion in the top right corner of the Countries web part and select Connections >Send Row of Data To >Customers.

4. In the pop-up dialog, select 'Get Filter Values From'.

5. Click on 'Configure Connection'.

6. Connect the 'Country' field in the Provider to the 'Country' field in the Consumer.

1. Choose Connection	2. Configure Connection

Connection Settings

Provider Field Name: | Country | ∨ |
Consumer Field Name: | Country | ∨ |

| Finish | Cancel |

7. Click on 'Finish' and save the page.

This method is quicker to use than the "Choice Filter", at least for the alternatives on top of the list, because no extra dialog must be opened. But if the list is long, users will have to scroll – first down to find their country and then up again to see the customers. The solution in the next section might work better if you have customers in many countries.

Demo:

https://www.kalmstrom.com/Tips/SharePoint-Online-Course/Connect-Web-Parts-Click-To-Filter.htm

18.3 SHOW CONNECTED LIST DATA IN DISPLAY FORM

In this connection example we will use the same two lists as in the section above, but we will create a new kind of connection. We will not connect the lists on a page.

Instead, we will enhance the display form of the "Countries" list, so that all customers from that country in the "Customers" list are shown when you open a country list item.

This method can be used with classic pages in a classic as well as a modern Team site. The 'Form Web Parts' control is inactive in the modern Team site, but you can open one of the items in the "Countries" list instead to get the Display Form.

The "Countries" list must use the classic interface for the customers to show, and pop-ups must be allowed in the browser for the connection creation.

Countries - Sweden   ✕

VIEW

Version History   ⚐ Alert Me
Shared With   ⚙ Workflows
Edit
Item   ✕ Delete Item
   Manage   Actions

⊕ **new item** or edit this list

✓	Edit		CustomerID		CustomerName	Contact first name	Contact last name	E-mail	Contact Title
	🗇	🗋	DRACD	⋯	Drachenblut Delikatessen	Sven	Ottlieb	sven.ottlieb@adventureworks.com	Order Administrator
	🗇	🗋	FOLKO	⋯	Folk och fä HB	Maria	Larsson	maria.larsson@adventureworks.com	Owner

Country   Sweden

Created at 7/28/2015 1:05 PM by   Peter Kalmström
Last modified at 7/28/2015 1:05 PM by   Peter Kalmström   [Close]

The list item Display form is a web part page, so you can very well enhance it to show data from another list by connecting web parts.

1. In the "Countries" list, using the classic interface, open the ribbon LIST tab and click on 'Form Web Parts'. Select 'Default Display Form' and its web part page will open in edit mode.

   OR

   Open one of the items in the "Countries" list. Click on the 365 Settings icon and select 'Edit page' to open the web part page in edit mode.

2. Click on the link 'Add a Web Part' and select the Customers web part. Click on Add.

3. Open the accordion in the top right corner of the Countries web part and select Connections.

4. Select 'Provide Row To' and then "Customers".

5. In then pop-up dialog, select 'Get Filter Values From' and click on 'Configure'.

6. Connect the "Country" field in the Provider to the "Country" field in the Consumer.

7. Click on 'Finish' and 'Stop Editing'.

Now users can click on a country in the "Countries" list, and when the item opens, they will see all customers from that country.

Demo:

https://www.kalmstrom.com/Tips/SharePoint-Online-Course/Connect-Web-Parts-Display-Form.htm

18.4 SUMMARY

In this chapter, we have seen how you can connect two web parts to one another on a page, so that specified content from one web part is displayed in another web part on the same page.

We have seen what possibilities the Connect to source and Dynamic filtering features in modern web parts can give.

I have also shown three different examples on connecting classic web parts. You have learned how to connect the Choice Filter web part to a list web part and how to connect two list web parts to each other.

In the next chapter, I will introduce three different surveys that can be used in SharePoint. A survey can be used for all kinds of questions, from simple lunch meeting setups to advanced questionnaires about work processes.

19   SURVEYS

SharePoint offers three different options when you want to create survey questions that colleagues or even people outside the organization can answer.

Use a survey when you want to know people's opinion about things. You can also use a survey when you want to measure knowledge but not show the correct answers or give points for them.

Among the three kinds of questionnaires that can be reached from SharePoint Online, the Survey app has been there for a long time. The Excel survey and the Excel form are newer additions.

In this chapter, we will have look at all three survey options. They can be used in different types of sites:

	Survey app	Excel form	Excel survey
Group Team	Yes	Yes	
Modern Team, no group	Yes		Yes
Communication			Yes
Classic Team	Yes		Yes
Classic Team with group	Yes	Yes	
OneDrive		Yes	

19.1   SURVEY APP

The Survey app has its own interface, which is neither modern nor classic but rather a "before classic". Thus, it cannot be used in Communication sites.

New logo suggestions

 Respond to this Survey   Actions ▾   Settings ▾

Survey Name:	New logo suggestions
Survey Description:	
Time Created:	1/25/2017 5:00 PM
Number of Responses:	0

▣ Show a graphical summary of responses

▣ Show all responses

19.1.1   *Create a Survey App*

A Survey app is created like other apps, and when it has been created you can add your questions to it. There are several options to choose from depending on what type of response you want to collect. Among the most common response types are Rating Scale, Number and Choice with a dropdown menu or radio buttons.

1. When you have added the Survey app to a site and opened it, expand the Settings accordion and select 'Add Questions'.

Settings ▾

> Add Questions
> Add an additional question to this survey.

2. A new page will open that resembles the Create a Column page. Select question type and enter choices if necessary.

Settings › New Question ⓘ

Question and Type

Type your question and select the type of answer.

Question:

Type your question here...

The type of answer to this question is:

○ Single line of text
○ Multiple lines of text
◉ Choice (menu to choose from)
○ Rating Scale (a matrix of choices or a Likert scale)
○ Number (1, 1.0, 100)
○ Currency ($, ¥, €)
○ Date and Time

3. When you have added the first question, click on 'Next Question' to add more questions and repeat the process. Click on 'Finish' when all questions are added.

19.1.1.1   Survey Branching Logic

Some answers need a follow up question while other answers don't, and for that you can use the Branching Logic. Each question has a Branching Logic option, where you can decide which should be the next question depending on the answer.

After you have entered your questions, open the question(s) that should have a Branching Logic. Under Jump To you can select the correct question to come next for those answers that should not have all questions.

Possible Choices	Jump To
Every day	No Branching ☑
Now and then	No Branching ☑
Never	What should be the name of our next bicycle ☑

19.1.2   Respond to a Survey App

When the Survey app has been setup, users can click on the 'Respond to this Survey' link in the app and answer the questions.

 Respond to this Survey

19.1.3   See Survey Results

Once answers to a Survey app have been submitted, you will see a graphical summary of the responses via the View dropdown in the top right corner of the Survey dashboard.

You can also export the survey results to a spreadsheet, like Excel. This is done' under 'Actions'.

View: Overview ▾

Overview

All Responses

Graphical Summary

Actions ▾   Settings ▾

Export to Spreadsheet
Analyze items with a spreadsheet application.

View RSS Feed   o   o
Syndicate items with an RSS reader.

Alert Me
Receive notifications when items change.

By default, all users who can respond to the survey also can see the results of it. However, under Survey Settings >Advanced Settings, you can set the Read access, so that each user only sees their own responses.

Item-level Permissions

Specify which responses users can read and edit.

Note: Users with the Cancel Checkout permission can read and edit all responses. Learn about managing permission settings.

Read access: Specify which responses users are allowed to read

○ Read all responses
◉ Read responses that were created by the user
Create and Edit access: Specify which responses users are allowed to create and edit

○ Create and edit all responses
◉ Create responses and edit responses that were created by the user
○ None

When you have exported the results to an Excel spreadsheet, you can just refresh the sheet to have new responses included. From the Excel sheet you can create graphical representations of the survey answers.

Demo:

https://www.kalmstrom.com//Tips/SharePoint-Online-Course/Survey-setting-responding-and-using.htm

19.2 EXCEL SURVEY

The Excel survey can be used in Team sites without a group, as well as in Communication sites. A drawback is that external sharing with anyone must enabled in the site, and of course also in the tenant.

19.2.1 *Create an Excel Survey*

When that most allowing sharing option is enabled, the Excel survey option is shown when you create a new item in a document library.

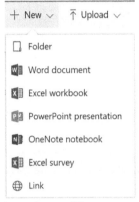

When you have given the survey a name and clicked on 'Create', an 'Edit Survey' dialog will open in Excel Online. Enter a title and a description for the survey and start adding your questions.

Each question is edited in a pane where you can enter your question (and subtitle if needed) and select a response type. You can also set a default answer and decide that an answer is required.

The various response types remind of SharePoint column types. The Paragraph Text option corresponds to a Multiple lines of text column and gives a bigger field to enter the response.

In the image below, you can see an example on a simple prompt to sign up for a newsletter. The 'Type of products' field will be answered by selection. The other fields will be filled out by the responder.

19.2.2 *Share an Excel Survey*

To share the survey, click on 'Share Survey' at the bottom of the Edit Survey dialog.

You can also click on the 'Survey' button under the Insert tab in the Excel ribbon and select 'Share Survey'.

Now you will have a link to the survey. Share the link by pasting it on a website or in an e-mail or chat.

This dialog is also where you can stop sharing the survey.

Share Survey ✕

Give the link below to anyone you'd like to share this survey with:

https://m365x446726.sharepoint.com/sites/Commun

Stop sharing this survey

Close

People who click on the link you have shared, will be directed to the survey and can fill out or select their answers.

Below is the simple newsletter survey created in the image above as it looks when shared.

Sign up for newsletter

Hear the latest news first from us!

First Name

Last Name

Email address

Type of products
Which type of product are you most likely to be interested in?

Submit   **Never give out your password.** Don't give your personal information to someone you don't trust.

Powered by Microsoft Excel

19.2.3   *See Excel Survey Results*

As soon as a respondent has submitted an answer, it will be visible in Excel Online.

To edit the spreadsheet in Excel, and for example create a pivot table or chart from it, you must stop sharing the survey.

FILE   HOME   INSERT   DATA   REVIEW   VIEW   Q Tell me

Paste   ✂ Cut   📋 Copy   ✎ Format Painter   Calibri   ▾ 11   ▾ A A   **B** *I* U̲ D̲   ▦ ▾ ◇ ▾ A ▾

Undo   Clipboard   Font

  stina@stensson.com

	A	B	C	D
1	First Name ▾	Last Name ▾	Email address ▾	Type of products ▾
2	Peter	Kalmström	peter@kalmstrom.com	Economy
3	Stina	Stensson	stina@stensson.com	Luxury
4	Kalle	Kula	kalle@kula.se	Luxury

Demo:

https://www.kalmstrom.com/Tips/SharePoint-Online-Course/Excel-Survey.htm

19.3   FORMS FOR EXCEL

Document libraries in modern Group Team sites, and in the default OneDrive for Business library, have a link to a simplified edition of the 365 service Forms under the '+ New' command.

When you click on the 'Forms for Excel' link, the Forms site at https://forms.office.com/ opens in a new tab.

Here, you can add questions under the 'Questions' tab and see the answers under 'Responses' tab.

+ New ∨   ⬆

▦ Folder

◨ Word document

◨ Forms for Excel

Questions   Responses

Newsletter

19.3.1   *Create a Form*

When you click on the 'Add new' button on the Forms site, you will have several options on how people should answer your questions.

| + | ⊙ Choice | Abc Text | 👍 Rating | 📅 Date | ⌄ |

	↑↓	Ranking
	▦	Likert ⓘ
	↑	File upload
	⊘	Net Promoter Score®
	▯	Section

- For the 'Text' option, the answers must be typed in, but you can restrict them to be a number and even limit the number span.

- The 'Likert' option is easy to answer, because here the respondents just need to rate how much they think a statement is right or wrong.

- The 'Rating' option, just as the default 'Choice' and the 'Net Promoter Score' options, are also easy for respondents to fill out. They only need to select an option.

- When you select 'File upload', respondents can upload files to a new folder that will be created in SharePoint. The uploading person's name and file details will be recorded in SharePoint.

- With the 'Section' control, you can categorize the questions in a long survey, so that they will be easier for respondents to overview. Sections are especially useful when you want to branch the questions, *see below*.

When the first question has been finished, click on 'Add question' again to continue with the next one. The form is saved automatically.

19.3.1.1   Edit

Click on a question to edit it. In the top right corner of each question in edit mode, you can find icons for copying and deleting the question and for moving the question up and down in the form.

19.3.1.2   Branching

When the form is in edit mode, you can find an ellipsis in the bottom right corner of each question. One of the options is to add branching. (Some question types have more options under the ellipsis than subtitle and branching.)

With branching, questions will have an option to continue in a specific way: to the next question, to another question or to the end of the form.

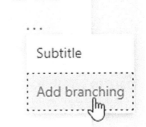

That way, you can follow up with questions that only apply to certain answers and/or let respondents skip questions that are not relevant to them.

6. Vegan?

○ Yes   Go to   7. Why?   ∨

○ No   Go to   8. Why not?   ∨

19.3.2   *Share the Form*

Click on the 'Share' button in the right part of the top command bar to share the form. Select one of the four options and copy the link/embed code if needed. These are the options:

- Copy a link and paste it in a shared area, for example a chat.
- Download a QR-code and paste it where your intended audience can scan it, for example with a mobile device.
- Copy the embed code and embed the form into a blog, a SharePoint page or other web page.
- Send a link in an e-mail by selecting the fourth option. This opens an e-mail with the link and some explaining, editable text. The first time you use this option, you must specify from what e-mail account the e-mail should be sent.

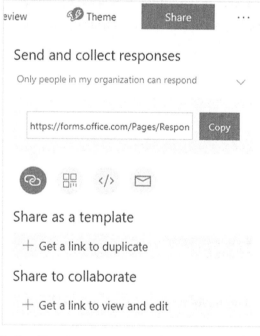

In the Share pane, you can also share the form to people who are not supposed to answer it:

- Get a template link. All receivers of this link can use the form as a template. Responses are not included.

- Get a collaboration link. Receivers of this link can work with the form, for example add or remove questions, see the responses and share the form with others.

By default, all users with a 365 work or school account can view and edit using this colloaboration link, but you can restrict the permission to people within the tenant or even specific people.

19.3.3   Check Form Results

To see the answers as they come in, open the 'Responses' tab on the Forms site and see statistics.

For more elaborate analysis you can open the results in Excel directly from the 'Responses' tab.

Questions		Responses ❶
1	**00:13**	**Active**
Responses	Average time to complete	Status

••••

View results   X‖ Open in Excel

1. How do you feel about our intranet?
   More Details

▣ Bad   ⬝ Meh   ▣ Fantastic

Look and feel

Discoverability

Usability

100%   0%   100%

19.3.4   Form Options

The Form settings are found under the ellipsis in the top right corner of the Form page. Here, you can also find some more commands.

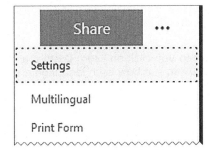

Share   •••

Settings

Multilingual

Print Form

19.3.4.1 Settings

The image to the below shows the default settings. The non-default options include a start and end date for the form and an e-mail notification of each response.

You can also set the questions to be shown in random order for each respondent (shuffle questions).

For multi-page forms, you can show the respondents a progress bar that indicates how much of the form has been answered.

Settings

Who can fill out this form

O Anyone can respond

◉ Only people in my organization can respond

   ☑ Record name

   ☐ One response per person

O Specific people in my organization can respond

Options for responses

☑ Accept responses

☐ Start date

☐ End date

☐ Shuffle questions

☐ Show progress bar ⓘ

☐ Customize thank you message

Response receipts

☐ Allow receipt of responses after submission

☐ Get email notification of each response

19.3.4.2 Multilingual

The Multilingual link lets you translate the questions. Each user will see the questions in his/her default language. This option is currently only available for forms, not for quizzes.

When you click on 'More Details' at each question under the Responses tab, you can see how each language group has responded.

19.3.4.3 Print

Under the ellipsis, form owners can print the form for respondents who is unable to complete the form online.

19.3.5   Forms Admin Settings

In the Microsoft 365 Admin center >Settings >Org settings >Microsoft Forms, administrators can turn off the default permission to share forms and results with users outside the organization.

When an external setting option is turned off, only people within organization will have access to that option, and only when they are signed in.

The image below shows the default settings, where everything is allowed. Phishing protection is also enabled by default.

Microsoft Forms

Create surveys, quizzes, and polls, and easily see results as they come in. Learn how to create a form.

External sharing

Control how people in your org can collaborate on forms with people outside your org.

☑ Send a link to the form and collect responses

☑ Share to collaborate on the form layout and structure

☑ Share the form as a template that can be duplicated

☑ Share form result summary

Record names of people in your org

By default, your forms will capture the names of people in your org who fill them out. This setting can be changed on individual forms.

☑ Record names by default

Allow YouTube and Bing

 Include Bing search, YouTube videos

Allow users in your organization to add images from Bing and YouTube videos to Forms. Note: If unchecked, previously added images from Bing will remain, but any previously added YouTube videos will be converted into a YouTube link that will launch outside of Forms.

Demo:

https://www.kalmstrom.com/Tips/Office-365-Course/Forms.htm

(This demo shows the full Forms edition, which you can reach from the 365 App Launcher.)

19.4   SUMMARY

Microsoft/Office 365 offers three survey options, and in this chapter, we have seen how they can be used and shared. You now also know how to analyze the results when the answers come in and how to add branching to a survey when that is possible.

In the next chapter, we will look at two totally different security measures that you can apply and combine to protect your SharePoint data: declaring record and IRM.

20 SECURITY

As we saw in chapter 14, you can use permissions and sharing settings to keep your SharePoint content safe. SharePoint also has some additional security measures that limit what users can do with items, files and e-mails.

20.1 DECLARE RECORD

When you want to protect an item in a SharePoint app, you can declare it as a "record", if that feature is activated for the site. *See* below how to do that.

Declare record means that you put certain restrictions on an item, restrictions that are not tied to permissions. Most often you want to protect items from being edited or deleted when you declare them record. When people try to edit or delete metadata or file content in such items, the changes to column values or file content cannot be saved.

In both interfaces, you can declare record via the item ellipsis >More/Advanced >Compliance details.

A dialog will open, where you can declare the item as an in place record. (If the feature has not been activated in the site, there is a message that the item cannot be declared record.)

Compliance details

Use this dialog to determine what retention stage an item is in. You can also take action to keep this item in compliance with c

Retention Stages		
Event	Action	Recurrence
This item is not subject to a retention policy		
Name	Kanban-Task-Manager-Multiboard-Manual-2.docx	

In Place Records Management Status	Not an in place record
	Declare as an in place record
Label Status	None

When you have declared the item as an in place record, the link text will be changed into 'Undeclare in place record', and the text above the link will give the date when the item was declared as a record.

In the **classic** interface, you can also click on the 'Declare Record' button under the FILES tab in the ribbon. This button is only visible when the Declare Record feature has been activated in the site.

Declare Record

20.1.1 *Declare Record Indication*

In library apps, you can see in the app interface if an item has been declared record:

- In the **modern** interface, an item that has been declared record will have an icon to the right of the file name.

TaskManagerSPUserManual.pdf

- In the **classic** interface, the file type icon will have a lock.

List items that have been declared record are not marked in any way, but when you try to edit or delete it you will have a message:

This item cannot be updated because it is locked as read-only.

20.1.2   *Activate the In Place Records Management*

In Place Records Management can only be activated by Site admins, as it is done under the Site collection Administration heading.

When 'In Place Records Management' has been activated, you can define which restrictions should be set on files that are declared record. If you don't do this, the default settings will be applied.

1. Open the Site settings.

2. Under Site Collection Administration, click on 'Site collection features'.

3. Activate 'In Place Records Management'.

 In Place Records Management

Enable the definition and declaration of records in place.

Activate

4. When an 'Active' button appears to the right and the 'Activate' button text is changed into 'Deactivate', go back to the Site settings.

5. Click on the new link 'Record declaration settings' under the Site Collection Administration heading.

6. Make the settings you prefer. The image below shows the default settings.

○ No Additional Restrictions
   Records are no more restricted than non-records.
○ Block Delete
   Records can be edited but not deleted.
◉ Block Edit and Delete
   Records cannot be edited or deleted. Any changes will
   declaration to be revoked.

Manual record declaration in lists and libraries should be:

○ Available in all locations by default
◉ Not available in all locations by default

The declaration of records can be performed by:

◉ All list contributors and administrators

○ Only list administrators

○ Only policy actions

Undeclaring a record can be performed by:

○ All list contributors and administrators
◉ Only list administrators
○ Only policy actions

20.1.2.1   Allow Record Declaration for a Single App

As you see in the image from the 'Record declaration settings' above, you can decide whether manual records declaration should be available for all apps. The default option is 'Not available in all locations by default', and I would recommend that you keep it that way.

Instead of giving a general possibility to declare record, you can allow record declaration for each app where you want to use the feature. This way, you will have more control over how record declaration is used.

Here I will give the necessary settings for a document library that should have the possibility to declare record. The principle is the same for other SharePoint apps

1. Open the Library settings.

2. Click on the link 'Record declaration settings' under the Permissions and Management heading. A new page will open, which is called 'Library Record Declaration Settings' even if you open it from a list.

3. The default record declaration setting is to use the same setting as for the site. If you have kept 'Not available in all locations by default' checked, you must change the setting in the Library settings to "Always allow" for this library.

Library Record Declaration Settings ⓘ

Manual Record Declaration Availability

Specify whether this list should allow the manual declaration of records. When manual record declaration is unavailable, records can only be declared through a policy or workflow.

◉ Use the site collection default setting:
   Allow the manual declaration of records
○ Always allow the manual declaration of records
○ Never allow the manual declaration of records

Automatic Declaration

Specify whether all items should become records when added to this list.

☐ Automatically declare items as records when they are added to this list.

OK	Cancel

Another option in the 'Library Record Declaration Settings' is to automatically declare files as records when they are added to this app. If you check that box, you don't have to manually declare items as records. Instead, you can place items that should be declared records in this app.

Demo:

https://kalmstrom.com/Tips/SharePoint-Online-Course/Declare-Record.htm

20.2 INFORMATION RIGHTS MANAGEMENT

Files and e-mails are often the weakest points in an organization's security system. When documents without any inside protection are sent as e-mail attachments or shared on memory sticks, they are accessible to aggressors.

In the same way, e-mails without protection can be forwarded outside the organization and constitute a risk, from both attacks and mistakes. That is why you need Information Rights Management, or IRM.

If you enable IRM, you can limit what users can do with e-mails and files that have been downloaded from SharePoint libraries. The IRM settings can for example allow users to read files but not print or copy them.

The actual protection settings are made in each app, but before that can be done, IRM must be enabled both for the tenant and for SharePoint.

IRM is an important 365 selling point, because it is much easier to implement IRM on a 365 tenant than it is for on-premises installations. Here I will explain how to enable basic IRM for the whole tenant and how to enable IRM in a SharePoint document library.

IRM is currently only included in the 365 Business Premium and Enterprise E3 and E5 subscriptions.

20.2.1 *Enable Basic IRM for the Tenant*

Before you can enable IRM in SharePoint, a Global administrator must enable IRM in the Microsoft 365 Admin center.

1. In the Microsoft 365 Admin center, open the Settings tab in the left menu and select 'Org settings' and then 'Microsoft Azure Information Protection'.

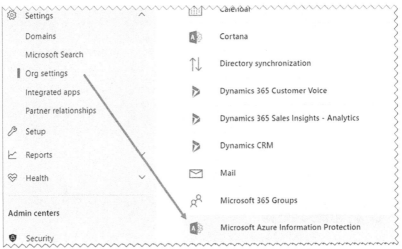

2. In the right pane that opens, click on the link 'Manage Microsoft Azure Information Protection settings'.

Microsoft Azure Information Protection

Keep your information safe, online or offline

With Microsoft Azure Information Protection you can add another layer of protection to the data you store in Office 365. The rules you set protect your files whether they're viewed using Office on the web or downloaded to a user's device. Policies and encryption let you safely share files in email or OneDrive and safeguard confidential information.

Manage Microsoft Azure Information Protection settings

3. Now you will be directed to the Azure management site, where you can find links to more information about IRM. Click on the 'Activate' button to activate Basic IRM.

rights management

 Rights Management is not activated

Rights Management safeguards your email and documents, and helps you securely share this data with your colleagues.

To enable Rights Management, click activate.

activate

additional configuration

You can configure advanced features for Rights Management using Microsoft Azure.

advanced features

4. Confirm the activation.

20.2.2   *Enable Basic IRM for SharePoint*

When IRM has been activated for the tenant, you can enable IRM for SharePoint.

1. Open the SharePoint Admin center.

2. Click on 'Settings' in the left menu.

3. Click on the link to the classic settings page.

4. Scroll down to Information Rights Management (IRM) and make sure that the radio button for 'Use the IRM service specified in your configuration' is enabled.

Information Rights Management (IRM)	⦿ Use the IRM service specified in your configuration
Set IRM capabilities to SharePoint for your organization (requires Office 365 IRM service)	○ Do not use IRM for this tenant
	Refresh IRM Settings

5. Click on the 'Refresh IRM Settings' button.

6. Click OK at the bottom of the page.

20.2.3   *Enable and Configure IRM for an App*

When you have enabled IRM for the tenant and for SharePoint, site owners can IRM-protect their SharePoint apps, and users can IRM-protect their personal OneDrive library.

When an app is IRM protected, shared documents are automatically protected by the Azure Rights Management service, according to the IRM settings for the app.

1. Open an app where you want to use IRM.

2. Open the List settings and click on the 'Information Rights Management' link under the Permissions and Management heading.

3. Check the box for permission restriction on download.

Settings › Information Rights Management Settings

Information Rights Management (IRM)
IRM helps protect sensitive files from being misused or distributed without permission once they have been downloaded from this library.

☑ Restrict permissions on this library on download
Create a permission policy title

Add a permission policy description:

SHOW OPTIONS

OK Cancel

4. Enter a Permission policy title and a description.

5. Click on SHOW OPTIONS.

6. Check the boxes for the restrictions you want to set for the app and for the items in it.

Set additional IRM library settings
This section provides additional settings that control the library behavior.

☐ Do not allow users to upload documents that do not support IRM
☐ Stop restricting access to the library at
   2/4/2021
☐ Prevent opening documents in the browser for this Document Library

Configure document access rights
This section control the document access rights (for viewers) after the document is downloaded from the library; read only viewing right is the default. Granting the rights below is reducing the bar for accessing the content by unauthorized users.

☐ Allow viewers to print
☐ Allow viewers to run script and screen reader to function on downloaded documents
☐ Allow viewers to write on a copy of the downloaded document
☐ After download, document access rights will expire after these number of days (1-365)   90

Set group protection and credentials interval
Use the settings in this section to control the caching policy of the license the application that opens the document will use and to allow sharing the downloaded document with users that belong to a specified group

☐ Users must verify their credentials using this interval (days)   30

☐ Allow group protection. Default group:
   Enter a name or email address...

Demo:

https://www.kalmstrom.com/Tips/SharePoint-Online-Course/Information-Rights-Management.htm

20.3 SUMMARY

In this chapter, you have learned how to use various features that help making your SharePoint environment secure. You understand how the Declare record feature can be used to protect items, and you know to enable IRM in several steps and how to configure IRM for an app.

Now we will go over to something different: When you have been trying apps with the modern interface, you have probably already seen that there is a Power Apps button in the command bar. In the next chapter, we will see what you can do with it.

21 POWER APPS

Power Apps is an Office 365 app that is often used with SharePoint list apps, as the service makes it possible to create user friendly list and form interfaces that work for computers as well as for mobile devices.

With Power Apps, IT professionals can create apps for both mobile and desktop devices and distribute them to users within their organization. Users with Edit permission and a Power Apps license can even create their own apps, because it is not very difficult.

Powerapps can be created from other data sources than SharePoint, for example from Excel files and data bases, but here we will focus on what you can do when you start from SharePoint.

Power Apps are owned by the user who created them, so I recommend that you create a special user account for powerapps that should be available to a group of people or to the whole organization.

From a user perspective, a powerapp can be regarded as a touch screen adapted view, where users can see and edit the data in the SharePoint list that the powerapp is connected to. Such a powerapp can be created directly from the list it should display.

You must use the modern interface at the powerapp creation. Once created, the powerapp can be used with the classic interface too, because a new view will be added automatically among the other views. That view will have the same name as the app, and it will open in the Power Apps homepage.

All SharePoint apps with the modern interface have a Power Apps button in the command bar. From here, you can customize the form used in the list or library, and you can reach your powerapps.

In list apps, you can also create a powerapp directly from the list. That is not possible in library apps.

Here I will give an overview of Power Apps and show how a form can be customized and how you can create a powerapp from a SharePoint list.

Most of the features I show in the form customization section are applicable to the powerapp creation too, so start with the form even if you are only interested in the powerapp!

21.1   THE POWER APPS STUDIO

Powerapps and forms are edited in the Power Apps Studio. You can either work in the Power Apps Studio web application at https://create.powerapps.com/studio/ or use the Power Apps Studio desktop application. Both have similar interfaces.

When you open a powerapp in the Power Apps Studio, you will see panes to the left and right and a workspace with the form or app in the middle. The values of the first item in the app are filled out when you create a powerapp or form from SharePoint.

The form or app can be resized with Ctrl + the plus or minus key.

Above the panes and the workspace, there is a command bar, for changes in look and behavior, and a formula bar that shows the value for the selected property. The value can be a number, a string of text or a formula, just like in Excel.

Each field in the powerapp or form is represented by a card in Power Apps, and all the cards are listed to the left of the workspace.

An ellipsis at each card gives options on what to do with the card. The options depend on what kind of field the card represents.

- Unlock
- Cut
- Copy
- Rename
- Reorder >
- Align >

The pane to the right in PowerApps Studio has different content depending on which card is selected in the workspace or in the left menu. Here you can change which fields will be displayed, in which order they should come, how they should look and much more.

21.1.1   *Preview, Save and Publish*

When you have made changes to the app or form, you can try it by clicking on the Play button to the right in the command bar on top.

Click on File >Save, to save the app or form when you have previewed it and are satisfied with it, or when you want to stop working with it temporarily. Click on File >Publish, to publish the form for all users.

From this area, you can also reach and work with all versions of the form app.

Customers on Demo site forms

New

Open

Account

Connections ⊏⁺

Flows ⊏⁺

Settings

Save

SharePoint list
https://kalmstromnet.sharepoint.com/sites/demosite/Lists/Customers/AllItems.aspx

Saved: 10/25/2020, 6:31:11 PM

✓ All changes are saved.

Make your changes visible to end users by publishing to SharePoint.

Publish to SharePoint   See all versions

21.2   CUSTOMIZE A LIST FORM IN POWER APPS

SharePoint forms can be customized in different ways. In this section, I will explain how to customize a SharePoint list form in the Power Apps Studio.

The option 'Customize forms' under the Power Apps button in the modern command bar, creates a special kind of powerapp that is only used with SharePoint. It does not show up among the apps you can reach via 'See all apps'.

When the modified form has been published, it will automatically replace the default list form in new as well as existing items. The custom form will be displayed in both app experiences.

You can switch back to the original form in the List settings >Form settings, under General settings. When you have set the list to use the default form again, a delete link will be displayed below the Power Apps form option.

Form Options

Use Microsoft PowerApps to customize the forms for this list. You can modify the form layout, add pictures and formatted text, add custom data validation, create additional views, and add rules.

◉ Use the default SharePoint form

○ Use a custom form created in PowerApps (requires new list experience)
   Modify form in PowerApps
   See versions and usage
   Delete custom form

Note that text "requires new list experience" in the custom form setting only applies to the creation of the custom form. Once the form is published, it will be displayed in the classic interface too.

The customize form feature is rather new, and unfortunately there is not yet an easy way to import a custom form to another app. Exporting the form works well, but not the import!

21.2.1   Customize Form Commands

We have already seen that the Power Apps button in the modern command bar has a command for forms customization.

$\varnothing$ Edit form $\vee$

You can also open the Information pane for an item and click on Edit all. The new right pane that opens, has an 'Edit form' button on top. It opens a dropdown with an option to customize the form in Power Apps.

Edit columns

Customize with Power Apps

Microsoft is planning to give a third option in this dropdown: a possibility to configure the layout of the app form directly from the user interface. That feature is not yet implemented when this book is published.

21.2.2   Why Customize a Form?

Why customize list forms at all, in the first place? Isn't it enough that you can add and remove or hide columns and put them in any order you want? Yes, those features are certainly useful, and we should absolutely take advantage of them, but they don't solve all form issues.

One of the reasons for form customization is to avoid unnecessary scrolling. In most SharePoint forms the fields are just put below each other, even if the value should be something short and maybe only requires a number or a choice of yes and no. Such fields can very well be put side by side instead. Or, you might want to have more space in the description field, to avoid scrolling there.

21.2.3   Example Form

I use a "Customers" list in this example, and the default form is very long and requires scrolling.

To make the form quicker to fill out, and to give a better overview, I first used the Power Apps command 'Customize forms' in the "Customers" list. That gave me an automatically created form that I needed to modify to make it work well. These are the changes I made:

- Added the fields that were missing in the automatically created app.

- Shortened the column names in the form, so that there is more space.

- Edited the fields so that they are shown in rows with two fields.

- Hid the State field from the view.

- Removed the field boxes for the fields that are filled out automatically.

The image below shows how the form looks after these modifications.

21.2.4 Modifications

The command 'Customize forms' opens the current list form in the Power Apps Studio, where Power Apps generates a single-screen form app. This app can be modified in several ways.

21.2.4.1 Edit the Form

When the new app opens, the level SharePointForm1, is selected to the left, so that the properties of the whole form are displayed and can be modified.

The right Edit pane gives multiple customization possibilities.

When you click on some of the properties in the right Edit pane, the formula bar opens with the current data so that you can make changes. Other changes can be made directly in the Edit pane.

The Fields pane is also shown when the app form first opens in Power Apps. Here, you can modify the control type for each field and see additional information. Open the Fields pane anytime by clicking on 'Edit fields'.

Under the ellipsis at each field, you can remove the field or move it up or down. It is also here I will add the fields that were not included in the auto-created app.

Turn off 'Snap to columns' if you want to size the fields manually according to the space needed, instead of having them equally distributed.

The cards can have the display name and the field displayed vertically (like two rows) or horizontally (display name + field), and they can be shown under each other or in two or more columns. I will keep the vertical layout but change into two columns.

Snap to columns		On ⬤
Columns	2	∨
Layout	Vertical	∨

The setting in the image to the right above, gives a form that is easy to overview, as there are two columns instead of the default one. When the vertical card layout is selected, the column names are displayed above the fields. (A horizontal layout would not be practical together with two columns, as there would be very little space for each title and field!)

21.2.4.2   Edit Fields

When you select a card in the left pane or in the form in the workspace, you can make changes to that card in the right pane. You can change its color and size, add a border and more.

Maybe you don't want to display all the fields in the form? In that case you can easily hide a field by toggle the Visible control in the right pane to Off.

Some cards might be locked for editing, but you can unlock each locked card under the Advanced tab in the card's Edit pane. Then open the Properties tab again make your modifications.

Sometimes you want to make a field read only, so that users cannot edit it. This is suitable for example if the field data is fetched from outside the SharePoint list. Select the 'View' option to make the field read only.

To change the display name for a field, select the card and open the Advanced tab in the Edit pane. Click in the DisplayName field to edit the text.

Demo:

https://www.kalmstrom.com/Tips/Office-365-Course/Customize-Form-Power Apps.htm

21.3 CREATE A POWERAPP FROM A SHAREPOINT LIST

When you select 'Create an app' in the Power Apps dropdown, a panel will open to the right. Here you should enter a name for the new app.

Click on 'Create', and the powerapp will be created from the data in the list where you clicked on the button. It will open in the Power Apps Studio.

The Power Apps Studio Design page that opens when a new powerapp has been created reminds of the form page, but the controls are listed to the left under the headings BrowseScreen, DesignScreen and EditScreen.

For a simple app with just a few columns, the powerapp works reasonably well without modification.

For a more complex list, the design of the automatically created powerapp might be less optimal. You can however make the app more useful and appealing by customizing it.

You can for example change which fields are displayed and in which order they are shown in the same way as when you customize a form.

21.3.1 Change the General Layout

Select 'BrowseGallery' in the left menu tree view to change the general layout of the app.

Click on the 'Layout' dropdown under the 'Properties' tab to select layout.

21.3.1.1   Hide a Field

As the app is meant to be used in mobile devices, you don't want to have too many fields to scroll among. I recommend that you hide the cards and not delete them, in case you want to use them later.

To hide a field, so that it is not displayed in the app, select the card and set the 'Visible' control under the 'Properties' tab in the right panel to 'Off', as explained in the list form section.

To show the field again, select the card in the left menu tree view, so that the right panel opens, and you can set the control to 'On'.

21.3.1.2   Change what is Displayed

The Browse screen in a mobile app only shows a little bit of each item, so the most informative fields should be displayed first. Maybe the auto-created powerapp does not show the data that is most important to show in an app? In that case, you can change that manually.

Select a control, which might be empty, and change the text in the function field. In the image below, the first field card is empty because it shows a non-existing ComplianceAssetId.

Normally you want the title there, and if you write Title after the dot instead, the card will show the title.

When you start typing, you will have suggestions on parameters to add to ThisItem

The function can also be edited under the 'Advanced' tab in the right pane.

Another way to change what is displayed is to first select the Browse gallery in the left pane, to open its right pane and click on 'Edit' at 'Fields' to open the Data pane.

Select first the field you want to change on the dashboard and then another field than the current one from the dropdown in the Data pane.

In the image below the Approved Budget will replace the Project Description in the second field, because the description is too long to show in the Browse screen.

Projects ↻ ⇅ +	Data ✕
🔍 Search items	Body1
	Legal Approval ⌄
7 Habits feature in KTM	Subtitle1
450 ❯	Approved Budget ⌄
Approved	

21.3.2   Add a Field

If you want to add an extra field on the Browse screen, select the first card in the Browse screen and click on 'Label' under the Insert tab. Change what 'ThisItem' should display, in the way that is described above, and drag the new field to the place where you want it to be displayed in the cards on the Browse screen.

Home	**Insert**	View	Action	Label

New screen ⌄ | ✎ Label | 🔲 Button | [Abc] Text ⌄ | Controls ⌄ | Gallery ⌄

t   ⌄ = *fx* ThisItem.Called.

≡ 🔠

owseScreen1

Claims

Department

DisplayName

You can also edit the display text in the field under the Advanced tab in the right Edit pane.

21.3.3   Change the Search Parameter

Select the BrowseGallery to see how the auto-generated powerapp searches among data. Most often you want the Title column to be searched, so make sure that the search parameter shown in the Functions field has "Title".

Example: SortByColumns(Filter([@Projects], StartsWith(Title, TextSearchBox1.Text)), **"Title"**, If(SortDescending1, Descending, Ascending))

21.3.4   *Change Text Color*

To change the text color in a specific field, select the text where you want to add another color. Then select the property you want to change in the top left dropdown, in this case 'Color'.

The default color is shown as RGBA, but if you don't have the code you can start typing a color and get suggestions on nuances.

| Color | ✓ | = | *fx* ✓ | RGBA(0, 0, 0, 1) |

21.3.4.1   Conditional Formatting

To take the color modification a step further, you can add conditional formatting, so that the text only changes color when a specific column has a specific value.

In the image below, I have entered a condition instead of the default color. It says that the color should be green when the value of the Legal Approval column is 'Approved'.

If(ThisItem.'Legal Approval'="Approved",Green)

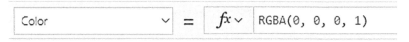

Build the function like this:

1. Enter If and select If from the dropdown. Now a start parenthesis will be added.

2. Start typing This and select ThisItem.

3. Add a dot after ThisItem.

4. Start typing the column name and select the correct option.

5. Add an equal sign and a quotation mark.

6. Start typing the value and select the correct option.

7. End the quotation.

8. Add a comma.

9. Start typing the color and select the correct option.

10. Finish the parenthesis.

With the options mentioned above, the title texts are now green for approved projects.

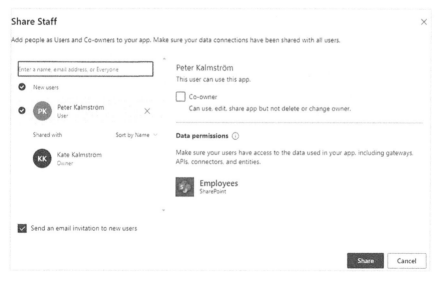

21.3.5   Share a PowerApp

To share a powerapp, you need to first save and publish it. When the powerapp has been published, it is available for sharing, and instead of the 'Publish' button under 'Files' there is a 'Share' button.

You can also select 'Share' in the left menu and from the ellipsis at each powerapp in the list under 'Apps'.

The 'Share' command will open a right pane, where you can add the names or e-mail addresses of the people or groups that you want to share your app with and select among the suggestions that will come up.

Make sure that the people you share the app with have access to the data you have used.

For some data sources, read permissions are given automatically when an app is shared. In other cases, the app creator must share the data source, or the user must take steps to connect to the data source.

The creator of the powerapp is the owner, but you can give the people or groups you share it with co-owner permission. This means that the users can run and customize the app and share it, but they cannot delete the powerapp or change its owner.

By default, an e-mail with a link to the new app is sent to people with whom you have shared the PowerApp.

21.3.5.1 Publish Changes

When you want to propagate your changes to a shared app, you must first publish it again with the 'Publish this version' button under the 'Files' tab.

Be aware that any changes you make to a shared app will flow through to the people you shared it with as soon as you have published your changes. This is good when you improve the app, but if you remove or significantly change features, it may have a negative impact on other users.

21.3.6 *Use a PowerApp*

Power Apps has a web player, a mobile player and a Windows desktop player. When you use a powerapp, all changes will be saved back to the list you created the app from, and vice versa.

21.3.6.1 Power Apps Mobile

When you have Power Apps installed on a smartphone or tablet, you will have the new powerapp among the other apps in your device. You can download Power Apps Mobile from the App Store or Google Play.

Power Apps running on a mobile can take advantage of the location and camera of the device, but you must give your consent to that before you use the app.

21.3.6.2 Add to a Page

A powerapp can be added to a modern page with the Microsoft Power Apps web part. For that, you need a link or an ID, which you can find on the Power Apps site.

1. Open the Power Apps button in a SharePoint app and select 'See all apps'.

2. Click on the ellipsis at the powerapp you want to add to the page and select 'Details'.

3. Now you can see both the URL and the ID on the page that opens.

Demo:

https://www.kalmstrom.com/Tips/Office-365-Course/First-Powerapp.htm

21.4   POWER APPS ADMIN CENTER

You can reach the Power Apps Admin center via the Microsoft 365 Admin center >All admin centers >Power Apps.

A new "Power Platform admin center" will open in a new tab, and here, administrators can study Power Apps statistics, create environments and set security policies.

21.5   SUMMARY

In this chapter we have looked at Power Apps, a service that makes it possible to customize list forms and create apps that show list data in a mobile and touch friendly interface.

I have shown some examples on what you can do, and I hope my descriptions will act as a starting point for your own powerapps creation.

I have also explained how to share a powerapp and what to think about when you share such apps.

SharePoint may be used with more Microsoft services than Power Apps. In the next chapter, we will have a look at more options. Power Apps can only be reached from the modern experience, but some of the options we will look at next is the other way around: you need to switch to the classic interface to use them.

SharePoint list apps with the **classic** interface, can be opened in other platforms, where you can take advantage of features that make it easier to work with the data. You can find the Connect & Export ribbon group under the LIST/LIBRARY/CALENDAR tab.

Export to Excel

Open with Access

Connect to
Outlook

Connect & Export

SharePoint lists that build on the Tasks template, also has another button, for synchronization with Project; *refer to* 22.3 below.

The **modern** experience currently only has the Export to Excel feature.

Export to Excel

However, modern apps can also be opened in Access if you select to do it from within Access and not via a SharePoint button, refer to 22.4.2 below.

In this chapter, I will show several different ways to connect and synchronize SharePoint with Outlook, Excel, Project and Access. I will explain how the result of the connection is different for connections to Excel compared to Outlook, Project and Access, and I will make a comparison between Excel and SharePoint.

I will also give some examples on how Access can be used with SharePoint, and I will describe how to show content from Excel in a web part.

22.1 CONNECT SHAREPOINT AND OUTLOOK

The Calendar, Tasks and Contacts list types have a lot of semi-hidden functionality that allows them to synchronize with the personal desktop edition of Outlook. You can also synchronize SharePoint libraries with your desktop Outlook. You need to use the classic interface to make this connection.

Connect to
Outlook

1. In the list or library that you want to connect to Outlook, click on the 'Connect to Outlook' button under the LIST/LIBRARY/CALENDAR tab.

2. Click on the 'Open link' button.

https://m365x446726.sharepoint.com wants to open a **stssync** link.

This link needs to be opened with an application.

Send to:

Outlook	
Choose other Application	Choose...

☐ Remember my choice for stssync links.

Open link   Cancel

3. Click 'Yes' to the warning message.

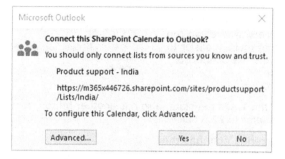

4. Enter your password if you are asked to do that.

Usually, the Outlook desktop app stores its data in the Exchange Server mailbox, but the connected SharePoint data (appointments, contacts, tasks and files) is *not* stored in Exchange. Instead, the connected data is stored in SharePoint.

You can work with the SharePoint apps and files in Outlook even if you are off-line. As soon as you are connected to SharePoint again, the items will be synchronized with SharePoint.

22.1.1   The Outlook Folders view

When apps are synchronized with Outlook, they are displayed under the heading SharePoint Lists in the Outlook Folders view.

To open the Folders view, click on the ellipses at the bottom right corner of any Outlook view.

Contacts and Calendar lists are also displayed in the Outlook Contacts/Calendar view.

◢ SharePoint Lists

    Documentation - D

    Sales - Consultants

    Sales - calendar

    HR-Consultants

22.1.2   Sync a SharePoint Library with Outlook

When you connect a SharePoint library to Outlook, you can work offline with the library files. Note that metadata is not synchronized, only the files. Also note that you need to use the classic library interface to synchronize with Outlook. For the modern interface, you can instead use the OneDrive method I described in section 12.3, Synchronize with a Local Folder.

When you open a file in Outlook, you must first enable editing to be able to work with it. Then you can edit and save the files as usual, and the changes will be synchronized to SharePoint next time you are connected to SharePoint Online.

As you have the files in Outlook, you can also use other Outlook settings, like send and receive settings, on the folder that is synchronized with SharePoint.

Demo:

https://www.kalmstrom.com/Tips/SharePoint-Online-Course/Sync-SharePoint-Files-with-Local-Outlook.htm

22.1.3 *Synch Calendar, Contacts and Tasks with Outlook*

When you add a SharePoint list built on the Calendar, Contacts or Tasks template to your local Outlook, these lists will be shown as separate folders in Outlook. Here, I will show the calendar. Contacts and Tasks lists work in the same way, but they are added to your personal Contacts and Tasks.

In the image to the right, from the Outlook calendar view, the calendar named "Calendar" is a personal calendar. The calendar called 'HR – HR Events' is the SharePoint calendar. The two parts of the name are the name of the site (HR) and the name of the calendar within that site (HR Events).

▲ ✓ My Calendars

    ✓ Calendar

    ✓ HR - HR Events

When the boxes for both lists are checked, they will be displayed side by side. Uncheck one of the boxes if you want to see only one calendar.

When you show the calendars side by side, you can drag and drop or copy and paste items from one app to the other.

22.1.3.1 Calendar Benefits in Outlook

Outlook has more calendar features than SharePoint has, so it is often useful to connect the SharePoint team calendar to your personal Outlook..

In Outlook, you can categorize the SharePoint calendar events with colors, just as you do with your personal calendar, but these colors are not displayed in SharePoint.

Demos:

https://www.kalmstrom.com//Tips/SharePoint-Online-Course/Outlook-Sync-Calendars.htm

https://www.kalmstrom.com//Tips/SharePoint-Online-Course/Outlook-Sync-Contacts.htm

https://www.kalmstrom.com/Tips/SharePoint-Online-Course/Sync-SharePoint-Tasks-List-with-Outlook.htm

22.1.4 *Import an Outlook Calendar to SharePoint*

You can import calendar info from an Outlook calendar to a new SharePoint calendar by using the Connect to Outlook feature.

1. Create a SharePoint calendar app.

2. Connect the new calendar to Outlook, as described above.

3. In Outlook, change the view for the Outlook calendar you want to import from into List view, *see* the image to the right.

4. Select all the items in the original Outlook calendar

with Ctrl+A and copy them with Crtl+C.

5. Open the SharePoint calendar, still in Outlook, and change the view into List.

6. Paste all the items into the SharePoint calendar with Ctrl+V.

You can even use this method to get a calendar ICS file from another place, for example a website, into SharePoint. Use Outlook as an intermediate step, so that you first import the external calendar to Outlook and then copy the items to the synchronized SharePoint calendar in Outlook, as described above.

Demo:

https://www.kalmstrom.com/Tips/SharePoint-Online-Course/Copy-Events-from-Calendar-or-ics-File.htm

22.1.5   *Remove a Synchronized App from Outlook*

If you no longer have a 365 license, or you don't want to have a synchronized SharePoint list or library in your Outlook for some other reason, it is very easy to remove the app. You just need to right-click on the app and select 'Delete Folder'.

The data will not be deleted in SharePoint. You are only removing the connecting link between SharePoint and Outlook.

Demo:

https://www.kalmstrom.com/Tips/SharePoint-Online-Course/Remove-Synched-SharePoint-List-from-Outlook.htm

22.2   CONNECT SHAREPOINT AND EXCEL

SharePoint lists and Excel tables have many similarities – but also important differences. Even if Microsoft Excel was not originally created for data sharing, it is often used that way.

SharePoint, on the other hand, was designed for collaboration from the beginning, and therefore, SharePoint has advantages that make it more suitable for data sharing than Excel:

- Editing. A SharePoint list app does not get locked when someone is editing it. An Excel file on a file server is locked, so that no one else can access it until the editing is finished and the new version of the file has been saved.

- Version history. SharePoint can show and restore earlier versions of each row in a list. Excel does not have a versioning feature, so to have several versions of a file you must give them different names – and even if you do that, you have to manually find out the differences between the two files.

- Alerts. SharePoint lists have an Alert feature, so that you can have an automatic e-mail each time a list item has been changed. There are different options for when this alert should be sent.

  You can also create more advanced notifications with SharePoint using a flow or workflow, *refer to* chapter 24, SharePoint Automation. Excel does not have this possibility without extensive coding.

- Independence. In a SharePoint list, each item is independent from the others, so that you can edit and lock each row (=item) and set independent row Permissions. That is not possible in Excel.

SharePoint also has some problems that you should be aware of:

- Portability. A SharePoint list cannot be transferred as easily as an Excel file. (This might also be a benefit! It is not always an advantage that you easily can share an Excel file.)
- Re-training and moving costs. If you already have your data in Excel, it will take some time to move it to SharePoint. It is always easier to let people work as they have always done!
- The 5000 items list limit. Currently SharePoint Online has a list limitation of 5000 items in a view. Therefore, you should split up the data if it will give more than 5000 list items. (Another option is to upload the Excel files to SharePoint and share them that way.)

The conclusion is that SharePoint is much better when it comes to sharing, so data that should be shared should be kept in SharePoint.

On the other hand, Excel has excellent calculation, analysis and visualization features. The good thing is that you can use these Excel features on your SharePoint list data too. In this section I will explain how it is done.

In all methods described in this section, except the add to page option, you need to make any changes in the SharePoint list, to have them reflected in the Excel file. It does not work the other way around.

Excel does not give you an error message if you try to edit the data in Excel, but your input will not be visible in SharePoint, and when you refresh the table it will be overwritten with any changes in SharePoint.

Note: I have already described how a new SharePoint list can be created from an Excel file in the Microsoft Lists app, *refer to* 8.2.1.2, From Excel. That method gives a totally separate list with no connection to Excel, so it is not included here.

Demo:

https://www.kalmstrom.com/Tips/SharePoint-Online-Course/Excel-vs-SP.htm

22.2.1   *Export a SharePoint List to Excel*

The SharePoint export feature saves the app's current view to Excel, so that you can take advantage of the analysis, calculation and visualization features where Excel shines.

Different browsers give different options, so I have put parentheses around steps that are not available in all browsers.

1. In the SharePoint list, click on the Export to Excel button in the command bar (modern) or under the ribbon LIST tab (classic).
2. Download the file to your computer or open it directly.

3. Click on 'Enable' on the warning message.

4. (Log in to 365 again.)

5. (Select how you want to view the data in Excel. The default option, Table, is often the most useful. If there is no choice, the list opens as a table.)

All the columns of the SharePoint view that you export will be included and visible in Excel. You will also have two extra columns, Item Type and Path, which you will probably want to hide.

Demo:

https://www.kalmstrom.com/Tips/SharePoint-Online-Course/HelpDesk-Totals-ExcelExport.htm

22.2.1.1   Analyze SharePoint List Data in Excel

When you have worked with a SharePoint list for a while, you probably want to study the data in it. By exporting the list to Excel, you can both analyze the data and visualize it in charts.

1. Click anywhere in the Excel table and then on 'PivotTable' under the Insert tab.

2. Select what data you want to view in the Pivot table. The default option is the table you clicked in.

3. Drag and drop the fields you want to work with to some of the Pivot areas.

4. To create a chart, click in the Pivot table to open the PivotTable Analyze tab.

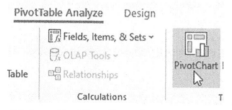

5. Click on the PivotChart button.

6. Select the chart type and design you prefer, to visualize the data from the SharePoint list.

Demo:

https://kalmstrom.com/Tips/SharePoint-Online-Course/HelpDesk-PivotTable-Chart.htm

In my book *Excel 2016 from Scratch*, you can learn much more about Excel. My focus is on calculation and visualization, from basics to advanced, and I give links to more than 60 online articles with video demonstrations and downloadable exercises.

22.2.2   *Direct Export/Import from Excel to SharePoint*

Exporting or importing Excel data to SharePoint gives many sharing advantages. The transfer can be done in several ways, and the major question is how much functionality and control you need.

Should you take the extra trouble and use Access, or can you do with the simpler methods of direct export or import that I will describe below? For the Access option, *refer to* 22.4.3, Export an Excel Table to a SharePoint List via Access.

Here I will first show two other methods that are quick, but they have some serious drawbacks.

- A new SharePoint list will be created for your data. Excel cannot push data into an existing list.
- The columns created in the new list are list columns, not site columns.
- When you have exported the Excel data to SharePoint, it can only be updated in SharePoint. Changes in SharePoint can be pulled down to Excel with the Excel Refresh button, but not vice versa.
- You cannot change the order of columns or exclude columns from the export/import. The range or table will be transferred just as it is.

There are also other problems with this method of transferring Excel data to SharePoint, but they can be helped by a "clean up" of the SharePoint list, *refer to* 22.2.2.3, Enhance a SharePoint List Created from Excel Export/Import.

Demo:

https://www.kalmstrom.com/Tips/SharePoint-Online-Course/Problems.htm

22.2.2.1   Export from Excel with the Export button

The easiest way to move items from Excel to SharePoint is to export an Excel table to a SharePoint list by using the 'Export Table to SharePoint List' button in Excel. The data will be exported to a new list app in the site you specify.

1. Copy the URL to the SharePoint site where you want the new list to be created. Note that you should only copy the site URL, *refer to* 16.1.1, Site Link.

2. In Excel, format the data as a table if it is not already done.

3. Click on the 'Export' button under the Table Design tab and choose 'Export Table to SharePoint List'.

4. Paste the URL you copied in the 'Address' field in the dialog that opens.

5. Check the box for read-only connection.

6. Write the name you wish to use for the SharePoint list that will be created. You may also add a description for it. Click on 'Next.'

7. In the new dialog that opens, you can see the different list columns that will be created. It is not possible to change anything here, so if the list looks wrong you must go back and make changes in the Excel table. Click on 'Finish'.

Now a new SharePoint list app will be created in the site you gave the URL to, and the data from the Excel table will be added to the list.

When the process is finished, you will get a message dialog with a link to the new list.

You can also open the list from Excel by clicking on the new 'Open in Browser' button.

Demo:

https://kalmstrom.com/Tips/SharePoint-Online-Course/Export-Excel.htm

22.2.2.2 Import Excel to SharePoint

Above I showed how to export an Excel table to a SharePoint list. You can also do it the other way around and import the Excel table to SharePoint with the Import Spreadsheet app.

This method only works in Internet Explorer, and you might have to add https://*.sharepoint.com to the local intranet under Internet options >Security.

I have still chosen to include this option in the book, because it allows you to import a range of cells without formatting them as a table. The data will be imported to a new list.

1. Select the 'Add an app' option under the 365 Settings icon.

2. Search for Excel and click on the icon for the Import Spreadsheet app.

3. Give the app a name and browse to the Excel file you want to import.

Import Spreadsheet

4. Click on 'Import'.

5. Select the table or range that you want to import and click on Import.

Now the Excel data you selected will be imported to a new SharePoint list app.

Demo:

https://kalmstrom.com/Tips/SharePoint-Online-Course/Import-Excel-Spreadsheet.htm

22.2.2.3 Enhance a SharePoint List Created from Excel Export/Import

Unfortunately, the SharePoint list that is created when an Excel table is exported or imported to a SharePoint list does not take advantage of all SharePoint features. Here are some tips on how you can make the new list better adapted to SharePoint:

• Enable version history, so that you can see different versions of the list. This possibility is one of the major benefits with having the data in SharePoint, instead of in Excel.

• At export, the default view of the new list is grid view, but having the grid as default view creates problems if you want to display the list in a web part or automate a process with the list. Therefore, you might want to create a new standard list view and make that the default view.

• Make the view cleaner by not showing all columns.

• Create more views to show the data from different perspectives.

• Add the list to the Site navigation.

Demo:

https://www.kalmstrom.com/Tips/SharePoint-Online-Course/Clean.htm

22.2.3   *Display Excel Data in a Web Part*

When you store an Excel file in a SharePoint library, you can display all or just a part of the workbook in a web part. This is possible in modern as well as classic pages, but the classic web part gives more options for the user interaction with the Excel content.

When you use a web part, the Excel data is not exported or imported to SharePoint, so you can edit the Excel file in either Excel Online or the client edition. The web part will be updated each time you save your changes.

The Excel file can be placed in a page anywhere in the tenant, but make sure that users have permission to access the file.

22.2.3.1   Show Excel Data in a Modern Page

In a modern page, you can use the File Viewer Web Part to display Excel data.

When you have added the web part to the page, the right pane for location selection opens. Select one of the options and add the file.

Edit the web part, if you want to show something else than the whole workbook or change the default settings for grid lines, headers, sorting and filtering.

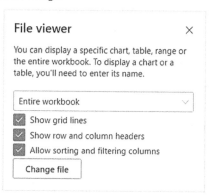

22.2.3.2   Show Excel Data in a Classic Page

The Excel Web Access web part can only be used in classic pages, but it gives a lot of options for the user interaction with the Excel data.

Unfortunately, the Excel Web Access web part is only available in the SharePoint Enterprise Plans E3 and E5. If you have that and still cannot find the web part, make sure that 'Enterprise Site Collection Features' is activated under Site settings >Site collection features and in Site settings >Manage site features in the root site.

Here I will just go through the most basic: how to define what workbook and what part of that workbook should be displayed in SharePoint.

1. Open the page where you want to add content from Excel in edit mode and add the Excel Web Access web part from the Business Data category.

2. Edit the web part: enter
   the URL to the Excel file
   in the 'Workbook' field
   or click on the 'Browse'
   button to the right of
   the field and find the
   Excel file.

3. If you want to show the
   whole workbook, click
   on 'Apply' and then
   save the page.

4. If you want to show
   only part of the
   workbook, select that

◂ Excel Web Access	✕
Workbook Display	
Workbook:	
	···
Named Item:	
	···
Toolbars and Title Bar	

part in Excel and give it a name. Then add the name in the 'Named Item' field
in the web part panel before you apply and save.

Demo:

https://www.kalmstrom.com/Tips/SharePoint-Online-Course/Excel-Web-
Access.htm

22.3 CONNECT SHAREPOINT AND PROJECT

Microsoft Project is a project management software with powerful features that
help managers develop plans, assign tasks, track progress, manage budgets and
analyze workloads. Project can be used with SharePoint, and once connected, the
synchronization between SharePoint and Project is simple

When you synchronize Project tasks to a SharePoint list, they can be shared with
users who don't have a Project license. All users don't need all the project
management features, but by connecting Project to SharePoint, they can still
have an overview over their tasks and update the progress.

Another advantage is that you can create a project from a SharePoint Tasks list, if
you find that you need more powerful project management features.

This section will describe the integration between SharePoint Online and the
Project client app. There is also a Microsoft product called Project Online which
also integrates with and uses SharePoint in many ways. Project Online is however
out of scope for this book.

22.3.1 *Sync a Project*

If you want to sync a project file with SharePoint, go to File >Save as in the
Project desktop app and click on 'Sync with SharePoint'. Now you can select to
either use an existing site or create a new subsite to the site you have selected or
pasted a link to.

• Select the new site option when you want to share a project created in
  Microsoft Project with SharePoint users. A new subsite with a SharePoint Tasks
  list will be created automatically.

Save As

Recent

Kalmstrom Enterprises AB

OneDrive - Kalmstrom Enterpri...
kate@kalmstrom.com

Sites - Kalmstrom Enterprises AB
kate@kalmstrom.com

Other locations

This PC

Add a Place

Browse

Sync with SharePoint

Sync with SharePoint Tasks List

Sync with:

New SharePoint Site

Project name:

Demo site-Tasks

Site address:

https://kalmstromnet.sharepoint.com/   /   Demo site-Tasks

A new SharePoint Site with a Tasks List will be created at the address
above. The project file will also be saved to the SharePoint site.

Save

- Select the existing option when you have a blank project open in Project, but the tasks you want to use are in a SharePoint list.

  When you use an existing site, there is a 'Verify site' button that loads all Tasks lists on the site. Select the one you want to connect to Project. Under File >Info, you can map Project fields to SharePoint columns.

  Click on 'Save' to create items in the Tasks list from all the Project tasks and establish links between the Project and SharePoint fields.

  The Project file itself will be saved in the site's "Site Assets" library.

22.3.2   Sync a Task List

When you open a SharePoint Tasks list in Project Online, you use Project to view the data. However, everything (like views and permissions) is stored in SharePoint, and you can manage the Project web app from the SharePoint Admin center >Active sites in the same way as you manage other sites.

There are two methods to open a SharePoint Tasks list in Project:

- In the Project desktop app, open File >New and click on 'New from SharePoint Task...'. Then paste or select the URL to the site and click on 'Check Address'. Now all the site's Tasks lists will be displayed, so that you can select the one you want to use with Project.

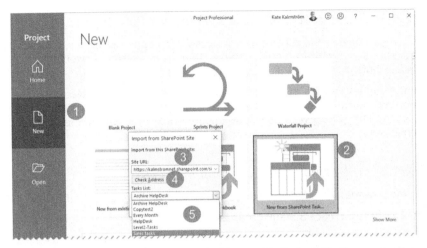

- In the SharePoint Tasks list, click on the 'Open with Projects' button under the ribbon LIST tab. (This requires that you have the Project desktop edition installed.)

Open with Project · Connect to Outlook · Export to Excel

Connect & Export

In both cases, a new Project file will be created, connected to the SharePoint list and added to the SharePoint site's "Site Assets" library.

Demo:

https://www.kalmstrom.com/Tips/SharePoint-Online-Course/Project.htm

22.4 CONNECT SHAREPOINT AND ACCESS

When you open a SharePoint app in Access, you can take advantage of Access features like 'Find' and 'Replace', and you can copy and paste more easily in Access than in the SharePoint grid/datasheet view mode.

Access is also a good to use as an intermediary to connect SharePoint to data from a platform that cannot be directly connected. You can, for example, work with SharePoint lists from different tenants or connect an SQL Server database with SharePoint.

You can also export an Excel table to SharePoint via Access. This will give you more influence over the connection than if you make a Direct Export/Import from Excel to SharePoint.

In this section, I will first explain how the synchronization between SharePoint and Access works and how you can open a SharePoint app in Access. Then I will give a few examples on what you can achieve when you use Access as an intermediary to get data in to or out of SharePoint.

22.4.1 *SharePoint-Access Synchronization*

When you open a SharePoint app in Access, the app and the resulting Access table are synchronized. You can make changes in Access, as well as in SharePoint.

When you enter data in the Access table, it is saved to the SharePoint app as soon as you move to another row. When you enter data in the SharePoint app, the linked Access table will be updated next time it is opened or refreshed.

22.4.2 *Open a SharePoint App in Access*

In most cases, it is best to connect SharePoint to Access from within Access:

1. In Access, create a blank database.

2. A table will be created automatically. Now you can choose between two methods:

   o Click on 'New Data Source' under the 'External Data' tab and select 'From Online Services' >SharePoint List.

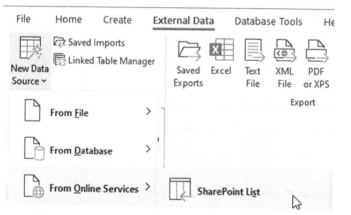

   o Right-click on the automatically created table and select 'Import' and then 'SharePoint List'.

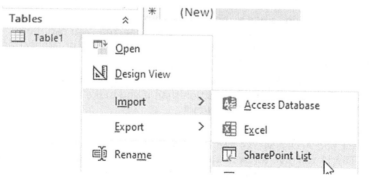

3. In both cases, a dialog opens where you can select, paste or type the path to the site that has the list you want to open in Access.

4. Select the linked table option and click Next.

This selection controls where the data is going to be stored. When you import, the data will be stored in in the Access file and no connection to SharePoint will be maintained. When you link, only the connection is stored in the Access file and every data update is immediately saved to the SharePoint list.

5. Now all apps in the site will be displayed. Check the box for the app you want to use and click OK. Now a new table with the same name as the app will be created.

You can also select multiple apps. Each of them will be connected as a separate linked table.

22.4.2.1   Open from SharePoint

When you use Internet Explorer and the classic app interface, and if Access is installed on the computer, the 'Open with Access' button under the LIST tab in SharePoint will be active. In that case, you can just click on it and select the default option, 'Link to data on the SharePoint site'.

22.4.2.2   User Info

The "UserInfo" list is a hidden SharePoint list that becomes visible when you link Access to SharePoint. When you connect an app that has People or Group type column, Access creates a linked UserInfo table from the "UserInfo" list as well, even if you don't check the box for it.

22.4.3   Export an Excel Table to a SharePoint List via Access

Above I have described how to send Excel data to SharePoint with export or import. This is a quick method, but as I mentioned it has some drawbacks.

The Access method is more complicated than the direct method, but it gives you better control over how data is added to the SharePoint list:

- You can decide which Excel columns you want to include in the SharePoint list.

- You can decide how data should be distributed.

- You can use an existing app with site columns for the import of Excel data.

- Changes can be made in both Access and SharePoint.

With the Access method, you do import both a SharePoint list and an Excel datasheet to Access, where they are shown as database tables. Then you can create a query that copies the data you want to use from the Excel table to the SharePoint table.

1. In Access, create a blank database and import the SharePoint list, as described above.

2. Import the Excel file in the same way and select the option 'Link to the data source by creating a linked table'.

3. Check the box for headings if your Excel table has headings.

4. Give a name to the new, linked table with your Excel data.

5. Now you can hide the automatically created "Table1" and "User info", as they are not needed in this exercise.

6. In Access, click on the 'Query Design' button under the Create tab.

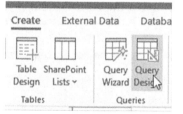

7. Drag the Excel table from the left menu into the Query field.

8. Under the Design tab, click on the 'Append' button.

9. Select to append to the SharePoint list you have opened in Access, and click OK.

10. In the Excel table in the 'Query' field, double click on the names of the columns you want to include in the SharePoint list. They will then be displayed in the grid below, so that you can append them. You may also drag and drop the column names to the grid.

11. Append the Excel columns to the corresponding columns in the SharePoint list.

12. Save the query and give it a more suitable name than the default one.

13. Run the query by clicking on the 'Run' button under the Design tab.

When you go back to the SharePoint app and refresh it, you can see the Excel data distributed in the columns in the way you mapped it in Access.

This method of using Access to get data into SharePoint works very well with other data sources too, not only Excel data sources. *Refer to* 22.4.5, Import Data from SQL to SharePoint Online to see an example.

Demo:

https://www.kalmstrom.com/Tips/SharePoint-Online-Course/Import-Access.htm

22.4.4   *Recurring Tasks*

In this section, I will give another example of how you can use an Access query to update a SharePoint app. The starting point is a table in Excel. This table shows tasks that must be done repeatedly each month, and it has info about tasks, assigned people and due dates in columns called "What", "Who" and "Day of Month".

SharePoint has no simple way to handle recurring tasks, but you can still make it easy to both remember recurring tasks and to verify that the tasks have been done.

The trick is to let an Access query update a "To Do" Tasks list in SharePoint. Then you can let SharePoint Alerts remind the responsible people about the tasks, and when the task is done the responsible can set the task to completed.

22.4.4.1   Export to SharePoint

The first step is to make a direct export of Excel data to SharePoint, so that you get the recurring tasks data into a SharePoint list app. Here I will call that list "Every Month".

22.4.4.2   Create a To Do List

When you have the Excel data in SharePoint, create a new app on the Tasks list template. Here I will call this list "To-Do". Now, you could copy and paste the "What" and "Who" data from the "Every Month" list into the "To Do" list by using the grid views.

However, the Due date column cannot be copied as easily as the other columns – you must copy and paste recurring tasks for every month.

A better solution is to let Microsoft Access handle the update with a query. Then you will just have to run the query for each month to have everything in the SharePoint "To Do" list – including the due dates.

22.4.4.3   Update the To Do list with an Access Query

Here I will give the steps to create a query that takes data from the SharePoint lists "Every Month", (imported from Excel) and "UserInfo" and appends it to a new SharePoint "To Do" list.

The "What" field in the "Every Month" list can be directly appended to the Task name field in the "To Do" list, but the "Who" field cannot be directly appended to the "Assigned To" field. Instead, you need to use the "UserInfo" table.

1. In Access, create a blank database and import the "Every Month" and "To Do" lists from SharePoint in the way that is described in the section above. Now two new tables with the same names and content as the lists will be created in the database. A "UserInfo" table will also be created, and this time we will use that table.

2. Under the Create tab, click on the 'Query Design' button.

3. Drag the "Every Month" table from the left menu into the Query field.

4. Drag the "What" field to the Design grid at the bottom.

5. Click on the 'Append' button under the Design tab and select to append to the "To Do" list.

6. In the Design grid, append the "What" field in the "Every Month" table to "Task Name" in the "To Do" table.

7. Click on the 'Add Tables' button under the Design tab to open a right pane.

8. Select the "UserInfo" table in the right pane and click on the 'Add Selected Tables' button at the bottom of the pane.

9. Append the "ID" field in the "UserInfo" table to the "Assigned To" field.

Field:	What	ID
Table:	Every month	UserInfo
Sort:		
Append To:	Task Name	Assigned To
Criteria:		

10. To have the Due Date info into the To Do table, select the Every Month table in the left pane and click on the 'Parameters' button under the Design tab.

11. Enter the two parameters Year and Month. Both should be Integers.

12. Put the mouse cursor in the cell to the right of the ID cell in the Design grid.

13. Click on the 'Builder' button under the Design tab to create an expression for the selected cell.

14. Select Functions >Built-in Functions >Date/Time >Date Serial.

15. Double-click on 'Date Serial' to display the expression.

16. Still in the Builder, select the query. Select 'year' in the expression and then double-click on the parameter 'Year'. Select 'month' in the

411

expresseion and double-click on the 'Month' parameter to get the parameters into in the expression.

17. Select 'day' in the expression. Then, select the "Every Month" table and the "Day of Month" field. Double-click on 'Value' and then OK.

18. Click Ok, and the expression you have built will be filled out in the third Design grid column, where you put the mouse cursor.

19. Change the text "Expr1" into "Due" and append to the Due Date field.

Field:	What	ID	Due: DateSerial([Year],
Table:	Every month	UserInfo	
Sort:			
Append To:	Task Name	Assigned To	Due Date

20. Save the query and give it a more suitable name than the default one.

21. Click on the 'Run' button under the Design tab to run the query. You will now be asked to enter values for the parameters Year and Month. Use numbers for both.

22. Run the query for every month and year, to have the SharePoint "To Do" list updated with all the recurring tasks.

Demo:

https://kalmstrom.com/Tips/SharePoint-Online-Course/Recurring-Tasks.htm

22.4.5   Import Data from SQL to SharePoint

When you want to input data from an SQL Server database to a SharePoint list, you cannot do it directly. Instead, you can open both the SQL Server database table and the SharePoint list in Access and create a query that copies data from the SQL Server to SharePoint.

Here I will describe how to add data from a "Contacts" SQL database table to a SharePoint Online "Contacts" list.

1. In SharePoint, create a list app on the Contacts template. Here, I will call it "Contacts'.

2. Add and remove columns as you prefer.

3. Import the "Contacts" list to Access.

4. Under the External tab in the ribbon, select New data Source >From Other Sources >ODBC Database.

5. In the window that opens, check the radio button 'Link to the data source by creating a linked table' and click OK.

6. In the Select Data Source dialog, click on 'New' to create a new data source, and select SQL Server.

Select Data Source / Create New Data Source dialogs

7. Click on 'Next' and type in or browse to the data source.

8. Click 'Next' and 'Finish'.

9. In the wizard, fill out or select your data and change the default database to pick up the new data source.

10. When you are back in the Select Data Source dialog again, select the new data source and link it to the Access table.

11. Select the appropriate id SQL column as the Unique Record. Usually, it is the first column.

Now we have two connections in Access, with SQL and with SharePoint, and we can connect the SQL contacts database to the SharePoint contacts list. It is time to create a query that selects data from the SQL database table and appends it to the SharePoint list. This is done in the same way as in the examples above.

1. Click on the 'Query Design' button under the Create tab and select the SQL database table.

2. Click on the 'Append' button under the Design tab to append data from the SQL Server daabase to the SharePoint list.

3. Select how the data from the SQL database table should be added to the SharePoint list.

Query1

Sales_vStoreWithCo...

*
🔑 BusinessEntityID
Name
ContactType
Title
FirstName
MiddleName
LastName
Suffix
PhoneNumber
PhoneNumberType
EmailAddress
EmailPromotion

	Stores with Conta ^
	ID
	Content Type
	Last Name
	App Created By
	App Modified By
	First Name
	Full Name
	Email Address
	Company
	Job Title
	Business Phone
	Home Pho
	Mobile Number
	Fax Number
	Address ∨

Field:	Name	FirstName	LastName	PhoneNumber	
Table:	Sales_vStoreWithCon	Sales_vStoreWithCon	Sales_vStoreWithCon	Sales_vStoreWithCon	
Sort:					
Append To:	Company	First Name	Last Name	Business Phone	

4. Click on the 'View' button under the Design tab to view the result.

5. If everything looks good, click on the 'Save' icon and give the query a more suitable name.

6. Run the query. Now the SQL Server data will be imported to the SharePoint list.

Demo:

https://kalmstrom.com/Tips/SharePoint-Online-Course/Import-data-from-SQL-to-SharePoint-online.htm

22.4.5.1   Update Imported SQL Data

If you continue to update the information on the SQL Server, you need a way to keep imported data up to date in the SharePoint list too. You can do this by creating an additional query that deletes the old data from the SharePoint list.

If you do that, you will have two queries: the add query, which adds the SQL Server data to Access and appends it to the SharePoint list, and the delete query. If you run first the delete query and then the add query, you the data will be updated in SharePoint.

If you create a macro that runs the two queries in sequence and a 'Run' button in Access, you can update the SharePoint list even more quickly when data has been changed in the SQL Server database table.

Create a delete query:

1. Click on the 'Query Design' button and drag the Contacts table into the query design area. Make sure that the * sign is selected, to remove all data from the list.

2. Click on the 'Delete' button under the 'Design' tab to create a delete query.

3. Save and name the query.

4. Run the query to test that it removes the SQL Server data from the SharePoint list and click OK to the warnings.

A macro is a way to automate a task that you perform repeatedly or on a regular basis. It consists of a series of commands and actions that can be stored and run when you need to perform the task.

Here is how you create a macro that runs the two queries mentioned above in sequence, first the delete query and then the add query.

1. Click on the 'Macro' button to the right under the Design tab.

2. In the 'Add New Action' dropdow, select the action 'Open Query' and the query that deletes data.

3. Select the action 'Open Query' again and now select the query that adds the updated contacts to SharePoint.

4. Select the action 'Close the database' from the dropdown.

5. Save and name the macro.

To further simplify the update, you can add a 'Run' button that runs the macro. The image to the right shows such a button with the default Access macro image.

(Remove the macro from the design area before you start creating the button, to make the 'Blank Form' button active.)

6. Click on the 'Blank Form' button under the Create tab.

7. Click on the button icon under the Design tab and then in the form design area. A button and a wizard dialog will open in the design area.

8. Select the action Miscellaneous >Run Macro.

9. Select the new macro you just created.

10. Give the button a text or a picture and click on Next.

11. Give the button a name before you finish.

12. Save and name the form.

13. Click on 'Options 'under the File tab, and select the new form as Display Form for the Current Database.

14. To test, close Access and open it again. Then click on the button to run the query.

Demo:

https://www.kalmstrom.com/Tips/SharePoint-Online-Course/Update-Imported-SQL-Data.htm

22.5 SUMMARY

In this chapter we have seen how SharePoint app data can be used with Outlook, Excel, Access and Project. In Outlook and Access the content is synchronized in both directions.

I have shown how to make the connections and given examples on more advanced use of Access as an intermediary when exporting data from Excel and from an SQL Server database table to a SharePoint list.

23 ISSUE TRACKING TIPS

SharePoint Tasks or Issue Tracking list templates are useful for helpdesk and support groups, but these templates are also suitable for incident management, issue tracking and other shared tasks. In this section I will give some tips on how you can handle and enhance such list templates.

My intention is not to give a recipe on the perfect helpdesk list. Instead, I want to point to these various options, so that you can make the modifications that best suit each team:

- Comparison of the two templates
- Suggestions for a helpdesk list
- Data entry and edit button
- Edit multiple list items
- Landing page with views, issues list and Excel chart

23.1 TASKS AND ISSUE TRACKING LIST TEMPLATES

SharePoint provides two list templates that can be used as helpdesk lists and often can replace each other: Tasks and Issue Tracking. Both have their benefits and drawbacks, and there are some differences you should be aware of when you decide which list template to use.

- When this is written, Tasks lists only have the classic user interface, so there is no way to switch to the modern experience. This also means that the Tasks list cannot be embedded in a modern page with the List web part.

  Lists that build on the Issue Tracking template can have the modern interface and be used with all modern web parts that interact with lists.

- Only the Tasks list has a timeline.
- The Tasks list has more built-in views than the Issue tracking list.
- Only Tasks list items have a 'Show more' link in the open form, but there is no way to decide what should be hidden when you open the list form.

  The Issue tracking list item shows all fields as soon as you open it.

- Only the Tasks list has a 'Start Date' column.
- Only the Issue Tracking list has a "Category" column.
- Only the Issue Tracking list item has a "Comments" column.
- The "Predecessors" column in the Tasks list has a corresponding "Related Issues" column in the Issue Tracking list.
- If you use the Issues Tracking list template, you cannot synchronize the list with Outlook and Project.
- The Issue Tracking list uses an "Issue Status" column with the choice options 'Active', 'Resolved' and 'Closed'. The Tasks list has a "Task Status"

column with choices: 'Not Started', 'In Progress', 'Deferred', 'Waiting on someone else' and 'Completed'.

- The Tasks list has a "Completed" column with the options 'Yes' and 'No'.

The Tasks list "Completed" column is calculated, so that the "Completed" column is automatically set to 'Yes' when the "% Complete" value is '100' and vice versa.

Tasks	Issue Tracking
classic	classic and modern
timeline	-
6 views	3 views
Show more	-
Start Date	-
-	Category
-	Comments
Sync with Outlook/Project	-

It is easy to add and delete columns and views, so I would recommend that you disregard those differences when you choose which of the list templates to use. Instead, consider which you will need most: the timeline, the compatibility with the modern experience or the synchronization with Outlook or Project.

In the following articles I will give you some tips on how to enhance the Issue Tracking and Tasks list templates.

Note that both the Issue Tracking and Tasks list templates are missing by default when you add an app from a modern Communication site. If you want to use a Communication site to cooperate around issues or support cases, instead of one of the Team sites, you can activate the Team Collaboration Lists Feature in the Site settings to show them, *refer to* 7.4.1.1, Apps in Communication Sites.

Demo:

https://www.kalmstrom.com/Tips/SharePoint-Online-Course/Tasks-Issues.htm

23.2 CREATE A HELPDESK LIST

Here are some suggestions on how you can modify the default SharePoint Issue Tracking or Tasks list to make it suitable for a support team.

Create a new list based on the Issue Tracking or Tasks template. Then make the following changes:

- When the list has been created, open its settings >General Settings >List name, description and navigation, and select to display the list in the Site navigation.

- Make sure that version history is enabled, *refer to* 7.12, so that you can see different versions of the list items.

- Make sure that multiple selection is not allowed for the "Assigned To" column. To allow multiple selections can create problems in several scenarios, for example when you want to group the "Assigned To" column by assigned in a view. If several people need to be responsible for a task, create a Security group for them instead, *refer to* 14.5, Security Groups.

  Allow multiple selections:

  ○ Yes ◉ No

- If necessary, add a new column for stakeholders or other additional people you want to assign a task to (instead of allowing multiple selections).

- Delete any columns you will not need, for example the "Predecessors" or "Related Issues column".

- Add new columns for additional important metadata, for example "Minutes Worked" if you want to keep track of time spent on each task.

- In an Issue Tracking list, change the "Category" options names into something that suits your team better than 1, 2, 3.

- Click Yes to 'Send e-mail when ownership is assigned' under List settings >Advanced, if you don't intend to create an alert workflow.

- Create a grid "Data Entry" view. Remove columns from this view, so that you only keep those that are important when users create a new item.

- The modern experience has an 'Edit' button in the command bar, but for a **classic** experience you can save users a few clicks if you add an 'Edit' button to the standard view mode. Go into the List settings and open the view to edit it. Check the Display checkbox for 'Edit (link to edit item)'.

  ☑ Edit (link to edit item) 1 ∨

Demo:

https://www.kalmstrom.com/Tips/SharePoint-Online-Course/HelpDesk-Creation.htm

23.3   EDIT MULTIPLE LIST ITEMS

When you want to edit several list items, it is convenient to edit them all in one step, instead of changing them manually one by one – especially if they should be changed in the same way.

If you open the list in grid view, you can change values more quickly. When you want multiple items to be changed in the same way, you can do like in Excel and drag the little handle in the bottom right corner of a cell.

Yes ▼

In the **modern** interface, you can also select multiple items and then click on the 'Edit' button in the command bar to bulk edit the items in the right pane that opens. The values you enter in the right pane fields will be applied to all selected items.

When you open the list in Access; refer to 22.4.2, and drag the table into the main area, you can copy and paste more quickly than in SharePoint. In Access, you can also:

- Use the Access Replace feature (under the Home tab) to edit multiple items that should be changed in the same way.

- Run an Access Query. When you have a SharePoint list open in Access and want to change multiple items in the same way, the quickest method is to run a query. With this method, you can even replace two different values with one other value.

    a. Click on the 'Query Design' button under the Create tab in the ribbon.

    b. Drag the list table to the query area.

    c. Click on the 'Update' button under the Design tab.

d. In the grid area, select the field you want to update.

e. Fill out the update value (= the new value).

f. Fill out the criteria (= the current value(s)).

g. Click on the 'Run' button under the Design tab in the ribbon and click OK to the warning messages. Now the values will be replaced quickly.

Demo:

https://www.kalmstrom.com/Tips/SharePoint-Online-Course/HelpDesk-Edit-Multiple-Items.htm

23.4   DATA ENTRY VIEW

In some situations, there are many users who create new items, for example to report an issue, but fewer people who handle them. In such cases, it is suitable to give a simpler entry form to the people who report and leave the more complicated form to the people who actually work with the issue.

When you create a Data Entry view, users are directed to a datasheet view when they select that view. Of course, you might as well click on 'edit this list' or 'Quick Edit', but in a Data Entry view you can also remove columns and only keep those that are important when a user creates a new item.

You can for example remove the ID and the status columns. The ID is not important when the item is first added to the list, and at that time the issue or task is always Active/Not started – the default value.

If you don't want to show any previously created items in the Data Entry view, you can filter the view to only show items where the ID is 0. There are no such items, so you will not see any of the other items. The view will only show an empty grid row to fill out.

1. Open the list where you want to create a new view.

2. Create a new view from the List settings and select the Datasheet View.

3. Give the new view a name and uncheck the boxes for columns that should be hidden in this view.

4. At 'Filter', set the view to show only items where the ID column is equal to zero.

⊟ Filter

Show all of the items in this view, or display a subset of the items by using filters. To filter on a column based on the current date or the current user of the site, type **[Today]** or **[Me]** as the column value. Use indexed columns in the first clause in order to speed up your view. Filters are particularly important for lists containing 5,000 or more items because they allow you to work with large lists more efficiently. Learn about filtering items.

○ ⊞ Show all items in this view

◉ ⊞ Show items only when the following is true:

Show the items when column

ID	∨

is equal to	∨

0

In chapter 25, Content Types, I explain how you can create a content type form and a workflow that switches to the full form the second time the item opens.

Demo:

https://www.kalmstrom.com/Tips/SharePoint-Online-Course/HelpDesk-Data-Entry-View.htm

23.5 MY TASKS VIEW

It is often convenient to let each user only see his/her own open issues or tasks. When you create a new Tasks or Issue Tracking list, a "My Tasks" or "My Issues" view will be created automatically. In this view, the "Assigned To" column is hidden, as it will always show the name of the current user.

By default, the "My" views show *all* tasks/issues assigned to the current user, even if completed tasks are crossed over in the Tasks list, but most often users only want to see the items they need to work with. Therefore, it is preferable to add another filter to the view.

This description uses the default column names and options.

1. Open the List settings and click on the "My Tasks"/"My Issues" view to open it.

2. Scroll down to 'Filter' and add a second filter after the "Assigned To" filter.

   a. For the **Tasks** list, select the column 'Completed' and set it to 'is not equal to' 'Yes'. (This is a more secure option than "is equal to' 'No'.)

   b. For the **Issue Tracking** list, select the column 'Issue Status' and set it to 'is equal to' 'Active'. (You must type Active).

   Even more secure, is to set two filters for 'Issue Status': 'is not equal to' 'Resolved' and 'is not equal to 'Closed'.

   ⊙ ▦ Show items only when the following is true:

   Show the items when column

   | Assigned To ▼ |

   | is equal to ▼ |

   | [Me] |

   ⊙ And ○ Or

   When column

   | Completed ▼ |

   | is not equal to ▼ |

   | Yes |

23.5.1   *Embed My Tasks/My Issues*

You can add a web part that shows each user his/her tasks to a page that is often visited, for example a site's homepage.

This can be done by adding the tasks or issue tracking list to a web part and select to show the My Tasks view when you edit the web part. For a single list, it is easy and works well. I describe how to do that below.

When a user has tasks/issues in multiple lists it becomes more complicated, but we can use the modern Highlighted content web part or the classic Content Search web part.

As we have seen earlier, both these web parts can display items with a specific content type from all sites, and they can show the current user's tasks independently of which site the tasks were created in.

For just viewing My tasks/issues, the Highlighted content and Content Search web parts work well, but they are not as good as the List web part/app part when it comes to editing. There is no command bar, so you need to open the task/issue to do something with it.

Another problem with the Highlighted content and the Content Search web part is that they do not open the task/issue in a new tab, which the List web part does. When you have edited the item and close it again, the original list will open. The user must go back in the browser a couple of steps to reach the page again.

Unfortunately, there is currently no other no-code solution to show tasks/issues from multiple sources on a SharePoint page.

23.5.1.1   Add My Tasks/Issues to a Modern Page

When tasks are created in just one site, you can use the List web part to add an **Issue tracking** list to a modern page. When you have added the web part, it will show a selection of list apps from the site, and you can just click on the Issue tracking list to add it to the page.

List   ✕

List

| Issues   ∨ |

View

| My Issues   ∨ |

When the list has been added, edit the web part and select the 'My Issues' view in the right pane.

Tasks lists are not displayed in the List web part, so for tasks lists you need to use the Highlighted content web part instead, but then you will get the problems mentioned above.

1. Edit the web part and keep the default 'Filter' radio button selected.

2. At 'Source', select if you want to get lists from all sites or specific sites.

3. At 'Type', select Issues or Tasks.

4. In the 'Filter 'dropdown, select Managed property.

5. Start writing Assigned To in the 'Find a managed property' field. When 'Managed property name' becomes active, select AssignedTo.

6. Keep 'Equals' and set the search value to [Me].

Highlighted content   ✕

Source

| All sites   ∨ |

Type

| Tasks   ∨ |

+ Add content type

Filter and sort   ∧

Filter

| Managed property   ∨ |

Enter a word to narrow down the list of property names, and select a property from the dropdown.

Find a managed property

| Assig |

Managed property name

| AssignedTo   ∨ |

| Equals   ∨ |

| [Me] |

23.5.1.2　Add My Tasks/Issues to a Classic Page

Both tasks and issue tracking lists can be added as app parts in a classic page. Edit the web part and select the view as for the modern page.

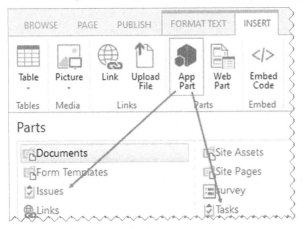

When tasks/issues are created in multiple lists or sites, you should use the Content Search web part from the Content Rollup category. By default, this web part shows the latest changed items in a site, but the search query can be modified.

1. Edit the web part and click on the 'Change query' button.

2. In the Query Builder, select 'Items matching a content type'. Do not restrict by app. Restrict the content type to the Task or Issue type.

Build Your Query

BASICS　REFINERS　SETTINGS　TEST

Switch to Advanced Mode

Select a query
Choose what content you want to search by selecting a result source.

Items matching a content type (System) ▼

Restrict by app
You can scope the search results to a specific site, library, list or URL.

Don't restrict results by app ▼

Restrict by tag
You can limit results to content tagged with specific terms, including site navigation terms.

◉ Don't restrict by any tag
◯ Restrict by navigation term of current page
◯ Restrict by current and child navigation terms
◯ Restrict on this tag: ⬚

Restrict by content type
You can limit results to a particular content type and all those that inherit from it.

Task ▼

3. Switch to Advanced Mode.

4. At Property Filter, select 'AssignedTo'.

5. At Contains, select 'The name of the user who runs the query'.

Keyword filter		Property filter	
Query from the search box	⌄	AssignedTo	⌄
	Add keyword filter	Contains ⌄	Name of the user who runs ⌄
			Add property filter

6. Click on 'Add property filter'.

7. At Property Filter, select 'Status'.

8. For the Task content type, select 'Not equals' and type the manual value 'Completed'.

9. For the Issue content type, select Equals' and type the manual value 'Active'.

10. Click on 'Add property filter' again and then OK.

11. Click OK to the web part right pane and save the page.

12. Make any other web part settings you prefer, apply and save the page

Demo:

https://www.kalmstrom.com/Tips/SPSearch-My-Open-Tasks.htm

Another way to collect tasks from several sites in a collection on a classic page, is to use the Content Query Web Part, refer to 27.3.

23.6   LANDING PAGE WITH TASKS

In section 13.8, we created a simple views landing page for a list app. Such a page can be enhanced with a web part that shows the list items in the default view, for example "My Tasks", on the same page as the links to other views in the original app.

A landing page with the default view is especially useful for classic pages, because when you add an app as an app part to a classic page, there is no possibility to change view from the app part.

IT Tickets

⊕ **new item** or edit this list

- All Issues
- My Issues
- Active Issues
- Data Entry

✓	Edit	Title		Issue Status	Priority	Due Date
✓		Yuku-Baja-Muliku Coastal Area Protection Phase 2 ✻	⋯	Active	(3) Low	
		Restoring the Natural Burnett ✻	⋯	Active	(3) Low	

1. With the page in Edit mode, click on the 'Text Layout' button under the ribbon FORMAT TEXT tab and select a layout. One column with sidebar is a good layout for this kind of page.

2. Move the view links to the sidebar by copy and paste.

3. Add your Tasks or Issue Tracking list web part.

4. Edit the web part. Under 'Selected View', select the list view you want to show by default and click on 'Apply'. Save the page.

5. Now the default view is displayed in the web part, and you can work with the list items as usual. The only limitation is that you must select an item to see the LIST and ITEM tabs in the ribbon.

Demo:

https://kalmstrom.com/Tips/SharePoint-Online-Course/HelpDesk-Landing-Page-Webpart.htm

23.6.1   *Landing Page with Chart*

We can further enhance the Views landing page described above with a chart that visualizes the data in the list. (If the chart size does not fit the SharePoint page, you can change it in Excel. Save and refresh the SharePoint page, to check if it looks better.)

In Excel, save the Excel chart to SharePoint. Select a view option under 'Browser View Options...' Most common is to show the entire workbook. After that, the steps depend on if you want to use a modern or classic page.

23.6.1.1   Excel Chart in a Modern Page

Use the File viewer web part to insert an Excel chart in a modern page. Upload the Excel file with the chart that you want to display and then select the chart when you edit the web part.

Demo:

https://kalmstrom.com/Tips/SharePoint-Online-Course/Excel-Modern-Page.htm

23.6.1.2   Excel Chart in a Classic Page

To insert an Excel chart in a classic page, you need to use the Excel Web Access web part in the Business Data category, which is available in the Enterprise Plans of SharePoint Online. You also need to use a Team site without a group, modern or classic.

If you have an Enterprise plan and still cannot see the Business Data category and the Excel Web Access web part, check that the SharePoint Server Enterprise Site Collection features are activated under Site settings >Site collection features. It is activated by default in the classic but not in the modern Team site.

1. Copy the path to the workbook.

2. Open the SharePoint page in edit mode and place the mouse cursor in the column where you want to add the chart.

3. Add the Excel Web Access web part.

4. Edit the web part and click on the ellipsis to select the workbook.

5. Type the name of the item you want to show in the web part.

6. Uncheck the box for All Workbook interactivity and make other settings to customize the web part before you click OK.

7. Save the page.

Workbook Display

Workbook:

| /sites/IT/Shared Documents/IT | ... |

Named Item:

| Chart 1 | ✕ | ... |

Demos:

https://kalmstrom.com/Tips/SharePoint-Online-Course/HelpDesk-Landing-Page-Chart.htm

23.6.1.3   Refresh an Excel Chart on a SharePoint Page

When an Excel chart is added to a SharePoint page in the way described above, it will *not* be updated automatically when the SharePoint list data is changed. Instead, you must open Excel and refresh the chart. This can be done in two ways:

- Click on the 'Refresh' button under the 'PivotChart Analyze' tab and select Refresh All.

- Click on the 'Refresh All' button under the Data tab.

The chart will be updated automatically if you edit the Excel file in Excel Online, or if you open the file in the Excel desktop app and save the changes to SharePoint.

Demo:

https://kalmstrom.com/Tips/SharePoint-Online-Course/HelpDesk-Chart-Update-Overview.htm

23.6.1.4   VBS Script that Updates an Excel Chart on a SharePoint Page

If you don't want to update Excel manually, by refresh, you can add a scheduled task with a script that updates the Excel chart automatically. This is the script when the URL to the Excel file that has the chart is https://kalmstromdemo2.sharepoint.com/sites/IT/SharedDocuments/ITTicketsSummary.xlsx:

Set xl = CreateObject("Excel.Application")

set wb = xl.WorkBooks.open("https://kalmstromdemo2.sharepoint.com/sites/IT/SharedDocuments/ITTicketsSummary.xlsx")

xl.DisplayAlerts = False

WScript.Sleep 1000

wb.RefreshAll

wb.Save

wb.Close

xl.Quit

Save the log in information in your browser, so that the script can work automatically.

To run the script, use the Windows Task Scheduler.

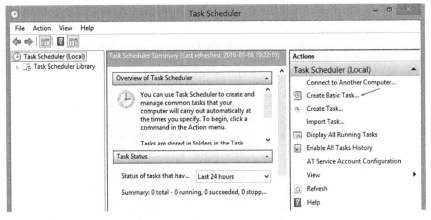

1. Open the Task Scheduler.

2. Create a basic task, give it a name and click on Next.

3. Set how often the task should be run and click on Next.

4. Set when the task should start running and click on Next.

5. Select the option 'Start a program' and click on Next.

6. Browse to the VBS file and click on Next.

7. Check the box for 'Open the Properties Dialog for this task when I click Finish' and click on Finish.

8. Under the Triggers tab, select the Daily task and click on the Edit... button. Set the task to be repeated with the interval you prefer and click OK.

9. Click OK to the Properties Dialog.

10. Select the new task and enable the All Tasks history if you want to have a log over what is happening.

11. Right-click on the new task and select Run.

When you have updated the Excel file, refresh the page that have the chart to see your changes.

Demo:

https://kalmstrom.com/Tips/SharePoint-Online-Course/HelpDesk-Update-Excel-Chart-Script.htm

Note that if you have Excel as part of Microsoft 365 Apps license, you must log in to Excel once a month to make sure the subscription is updated. This is not necessary with a regular Office license.

23.7   SUMMARY

Most organizations use SharePoint lists for different kinds of issue tracking, and in this chapter. I have explained the differences between the two most common list apps used for cooperation around tasks and given suggestions on various ways to enhance such lists.

I have also described how to create a My Tasks view and embed it in a classic or modern page and how to build a landing page with view links, list items and an Excel chart that visualizes the list data.

In the next chapter, I will introduce flows and workflows. These are important for making SharePoint processes more exact and efficient. I have written separate books about both flows and workflows, and they of course contain much more information than we have room for in this book.

24   SHAREPOINT AUTOMATION

SharePoint flows and workflows can be used in all kinds of SharePoint apps to automate time consuming processes. They are often used for notification sending, but they can also calculate time, archive items and perform many other tasks that would have been tedious and time consuming – or not performed at all – without a flow/workflow.

The principle of all flows and workflows is that you select conditions to be met and actions to be taken when these conditions are met. A predefined trigger decides when the flow or workflow should run.

Here I will first give an overview over how flows and workflows are created in general and then show a few examples. I hope this chapter will make you understand the flow/workflow possibilities and encourage you to explore them and create your own. For more information about flows and workflows, and how they can be used with SharePoint, *refer to* my books *SharePoint Flows from Scratch* and *SharePoint Workflows from Scratch*.

This chapter will cover:

- The general principle behind flows and workflows
- Some differences between a flow and a workflow
- How built-in flows can be used for approvals and alerts in modern apps and pages

At the end of the chapter, I will give two exercises with flows and workflows that you can create yourself, to compare and try the two automation methods. These are simple automation examples, and both the flow and the workflow achieve the same thing.

24.1   WHY AUTOMATE?

Most organizations have processes that need to be performed in a specific way and order, but when processes are performed manually, you can never be sure that everything is done 100% correctly. Therefore, the best way to make sure that such processes are correct and quick, is to automate them.

Another benefit of automation is that flows and workflows make it easy to track processes. They can log and document what has been done, something that is often requested by the management and sometimes even by law. Such tasks are often tedious and boring to perform manually, and they sometimes tend to be performed insufficiently or not at all.

Demo: https://www.kalmstrom.com/Tips/SharePoint-Flows/Flow-Why-Automate.htm

24.2   COMPONENTS

A flow/workflow is built with three components: trigger, condition(s) and action(s). You create the flow/workflow by combining these components in a way that gives the result you require. A trigger and action must always be present, but the condition is optional.

- The trigger decides in general when the flow/workflow should be run.

- Actions make things happen. You are creating a flow/workflow because you want actions to be performed, for example an e-mail to be sent.

- A condition controls under which condition an action should be performed within a flow/workflow. For example, an e-mail about a new task should only be sent if the task priority is high.

24.3   FLOW VERSUS WORKFLOW

Workflows are the traditional way of automating processes, and they are most often created in and limited to one SharePoint site.

Microsoft Power Automate is a more modern 365 service, and the workflows created with Power Automate are often called flows.

While workflows are mostly limited to SharePoint, flows can be used extensively for many cloud-based services, and several such services are often combined in one flow. The ability to communicate with the services is defined in a "connector".

Microsoft wants Power Automate to be a no-code, rapid application development environment, and as such it has certain limitations. However, given that you have a possibility to call a REST service from a flow, Power Automate has a high potential.

There are however still things that can only be done with a workflow, and to have the best flexibility, I recommend that you learn to create both flows and workflows. The examples I give below, will hopefully show the differences but also the similarities.

24.3.1   *Storage*

While workflows are stored in SharePoint and accessible for all with enough permission, flows are owned by the users who created them. This might be good for personal flows, but it creates issues if a user who has created flows for the organization leaves his/her position.

Therefore, any organization that decides to automate things with flows, should make sure that flows are not limited to one person's user account.

The most secure method is to create a dedicated account that is used for all flows that automate business processes within the organization. However, the number of flow runs that are allowed each month is counted per account, not per tenant. If the organization uses many flows that run often, a better solution might be to make sure that all business flows have multiple owners.

24.3.2   *Changes in SharePoint*

If you change a name in a SharePoint app, it affects any automation tied to the app in different ways depending on if a workflow or a flow is used.

SharePoint workflows will continue to run even if you change the name of an app or a column that is used in the workflow.

In Power Automate it is more complicated, because when you change an app or column name that is included in a flow, you must change the name in the flow also. Otherwise, the flow will stop working. The more mission-critical a flow is, the more serious this issue becomes.

24.4 POWER AUTOMATE BUILT-IN FLOWS

Power Automate has its own 'Automate' button in the command bar of apps with the **modern** interface. It gives some options to use built-in SharePoint flows that are very easy to create.

The 'Automate' button lets users:

- Create a new custom flow from a template

- Reach the Power Automate site to manage the flows they have already created and create new flows from scratch; *see* below.

- Configure built-in approval flows for the app.

Apps with a custom Date and Time column also give another option: a built-in reminder flow.

⚡ Automate ∨ · · ·

⟩ Power Automate   〉 Create a flow

                         See your flows

                         Configure flows

24.4.1 *Reminder*

When an app has the modern interface and a custom Date and Time column, it also gets a built-in flow to send an e-mail reminder any number of days in advance of a specific date. It is possible to set multiple reminders for the same app and column, but users can only set reminders for themselves.

Enable the reminder under Automate >Set a reminder >the Date and Time column you want to use.

⚡ Automate ∨ · · ·   ≡

  Set a reminder   〉 Quote Date

  ⟩ Power Automate   〉 Decision Date

(If you cannot see the 'Set a reminder' option, the app does not have a *custom* Date and Time column.)

A right pane with flow information will open. Here, you can sign in if needed, but in most cases, you are already signed in to the services used in the flow.

A green check means that you are signed in. A plus sign indicates that you need to sign in.

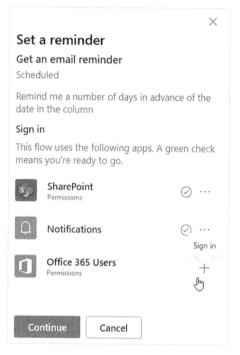

When you have clicked on 'Continue', you can give the flow a name and decide how many days before the date in each item that you want to receive a reminder by e-mail.

This reminder flow can be seen and edited in the Power Automate site, under 'My flows'.

It is also on the 'My flows' page that users can remove the reminder. When this is written, the reminder cannot be removed from within the app.

Set a reminder

Get an email reminder

By Microsoft

Remind me a number of days in advance of the date in the column

Flow name *

| Get an email reminder |

Remind me this many days in advance *

| 1 |

Create   Cancel

24.4.2   *Approve/Reject App Items*

New or changed business documents must often be approved by someone else than the author, and that process can be managed in many ways. The easiest way is to use one of SharePoint's built-in flows for requesting and giving approval on new app items.

In libraries, it is the document that gets approved. In list apps, it is the whole item.

Click on Automate >Power Automate >Configure flows to open a right pane, where you can set approvals on and off.

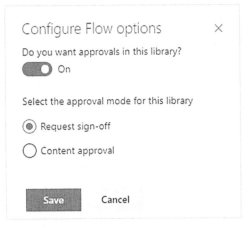

By default, the approvals feature is set to On, and the option Request sign-off is selected.

The Request sign-off option can only be set this way, and it can only be used with the modern app interface.

The other option, Content approval, can be set via the List settings also, and it can be used with the classic interface as well.

These two flows are hidden and cannot be edited in the Power Automate site >My flows.

24.4.2.1   Request Sign-off

When approvals with request sign-off is enabled in an app, there is no mandatory approval process. Instead, it is up to each author to ask for feedback on a new or updated list item or library file, by running an approval flow.

The request sign-off option is displayed under 'Automate' when an item has been selected and if the feature has not be turned off.

Request sign-off 🖱

⟫ Power Automate   >

When a user requests sign-off, a right pane will open. Here, the user can see information about connectors and permissions, and connect if necessary. Normally the user just needs to click on 'Create flow'.

When the user clicks on the 'Create flow' button, another right pane will open with fields for approver and a message. If more than one approver is added, anyone of them can approve the request.

When the flow is run, it sends an e-mail to the approver(s). When Microsoft Teams is used, there might also be a message under the Activity button.

All messages have a link to the file or item and buttons for approval and rejection, and there is also room for a comment that is sent to the requester.

The first time someone requests sign-off, a 'Sign-off status' column is added to the app. This is a standard SharePoint text column. It works like any other text column and can be reached and edited from the list/library settings.

×

Run flow

Request sign-off

This flow lets you send an item to others to get their approval. Any one of the approvers can approve. You can track the status for this request using the Sign-off status column.

Approver *

| PK Peter Kalmström × |

Message *

| Please comment! |

This flow uses SharePoint, Approvals, and Notifications.
Review connections and actions

| Run flow | Cancel |

The value of the 'Sign-off status' column is blank for items where no request sign-off flow has been used. The value is Pending when an item is sent for approval, and then either Approved or Rejected. The item can be seen by all users, whichever status it has.

To turn off the possibility to send Request Sign-off messages, select 'Configure flows' again and disable approvals.

24.4.2.2   Content Approval

The Content approval option can be enabled in the modern Configure flows right pane and in the List settings >Versioning settings. The List settings is the only option for the classic interface.

Specify whether new items or changes to existing items should remain in a draft state
until they have been approved. Learn about requiring approval.

Require content approval for submitted items?

◉ Yes   ○ No

When the Content approval option is selected, *all* new items must be approved, and the approver marks the approval or rejection in the app. No e-mail is sent.

The modern interface has the 'Approve/Reject' dialog under the item ellipsis >More >Approve/Reject.

The classic interface has the 'Approve/Reject' option in the ribbon, when the pending item is selected, and under the item ellipsis >next ellipsis >Advanced >Approve/Reject.

An advantage with this type of approval is that you can easily set the app to hide the new item from everyone but the creator and the approver before it has been approved. This is done in the List settings >Versioning settings.

Who should see draft items in this document library?

◉ Any user who can read items

○ Only users who can edit items

○ Only users who can approve items (and the author of the item)

Note that when you use the built-in Content approval functionality, the approval is not registered as a modification of the item. This means that the approval is not shown in the document's version history, so there is no easy way to see who made the approval. For some business scenarios that information is required or very important.

24.4.3   *Approve/Reject Pages*

The "Site Pages" library has its own built-in approval flow. In many respects, the Page approval flow reminds of the Sign-off request flow. There are however important differences:

- The Page approval flow will apply to *all* pages in the library, also classic pages.

- The Page approval flow can be seen and edited on the Power Automate site >My flows.

- The new or modified page can be hidden from other users than the approver and creator until it has been approved.

New and modified **modern** pages can be approved or rejected in the library, on the page, on the Power Automate site and in e-mails sent by the flow.

Classic pages can only be approved/rejected in the "Site Pages" library.

24.4.3.1 Configure the Flow

The **modern** "Site Pages" library interface in SharePoint Online has an 'Automate' button in the command bar, where site owners can configure the page approval flow.

Automate ∨   · · ·

Power Automate   >   Create a flow

See your flows

Configure page approval flow

When you click on 'Configure page approval flow', a right pane for the flow configuration will open. Click on 'Create flow'.

When you have clicked on "Create flow", you will have connectors information, just as when you create an approval request for an app.

When you click on 'Continue', you will be asked to give the flow a name and add approvers. These must have at least edit permission over the site. By default, anyone of these approvers can approve.

When you click on 'Create', the approval flow will be created automatically, and a new 'Approval Status' column will be added to the "Site Pages" library.

×

Create a page approval flow

Submit SharePoint page for approval

By Microsoft

When a new page is submitted for approval everyone on the approvers list will receive an email. Any one on the approvers list can approve the page. When approved, the page will be published for all readers and the approval status of the page will be Approved.

See less ∧

Flow name *

Submit SharePoint page for approval

Approvers *

Add one or more people

Create   Cancel

It is possible to add multiple flows, for different approvers. If another flow is created, no additional status column will be added. All flows in the "Site Pages" library will use the same column.

When there is more than one flow, the person who submits the page for approval will have a selection in the upper left corner of the **modern** page.

Approval by Kate

Approval by Peter

440

24.4.3.2   Process

Even if the page approval flow works on all new or modified pages in the library, the process is different for modern and classic pages.

The 'Publish' button on the page is replaced by a 'Submit for approval' button in **modern** pages, and the page author must enter a message in the right pane before submitting the page for approval.

✓ Your page has been saved   **⌂ Submit for approval**

The page will be published automatically once it has been approved.

When the page approval flow has been configured in the modern interface of the "Site Pages" library, it works for **classic** wiki pages too, and for web part pages if you select to save them in the "Site Pages" library.

However, no e-mail is sent, so the approver must open the "Site Pages" library in the classic interface and approve or reject the page under the FILES tab. Pages can also be approved or rejected under the file ellipsis >Advanced >Approve/Reject.

24.4.3.3   Turn Off Page Approval

In the "Site Pages" Library settings >Versioning settings, you can set the approval to No to stop requesting approvals at page creation. You can also turn off or delete the page approval flow on the 'My Flows' page on the Power Automate site.

24.4.3.4   Edit a Page Approval Flow

The page approval can be edited in two ways.

• In the library settings >Versioning settings you can decide who should be allowed to see the page before it has been approved. Any user is default, but it might not be the best option for you.

• The flow will show up under 'My flows' on the Power Automate site, *see* below, and it can be modified there. You can for example, edit the approvers or change the Approval type.

24.5 POWER AUTOMATE CUSTOM FLOWS

Flows are built and managed in the Power Automate site at
https://flow.microsoft.com. If you select the 'See my flows' from the modern
command bar in a SharePoint app, you will be directed to the 'My flows' page
in that site. Here, you can see a list of all your flows and manage them in
various ways, like edit, delete and turn flows on or off.

When you click on the Power Automate tile in the 365 App Launcher, you will
be directed to the homepage of the same site.

When you create a flow, you can either start with a template or start from scratch (called "blank" in Power Automate).

There are many predefined templates to choose from, and you can reach all of them from the Power Automate homepage. When you select the template for the flow, you also select the trigger. Therefore, what you do in the creation is to define parameters for the trigger and set condition(s) and action(s).

The templates that include SharePoint can also be reached from all SharePoint apps with the modern interface, but as soon as you have selected a template you will be directed to the Power Automate site.

When this is written, you cannot start from blank from the SharePoint command bar in modern apps. Instead, you must go to the Power Automate site >My flows. The first step in a blank flow creation is to set the flow trigger.

24.5.1   Flow Editor

Flows are built in a Flow Editor with boxes where you select the right triggers, actions and conditions. The image above, in the section "Edit a Page Approval Flow", shows such boxes in the Flow Editor.

The steps in the Flow Editor vary with each flow. When you use a template, actions and conditions are often pre-defined, but they can of course be changed. If you start from blank, you can add actions and conditions as you prefer.

443

24.5.2   Create a Flow from SharePoint

Click on the 'Automate' button in the command bar, to create a flow directly from a SharePoint app with the modern interface.

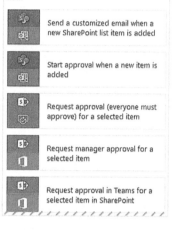

When you select Power Automate >Create a flow, a right pane where you can select a template for the flow will open.

Here, the choice of templates is of course limited to templates where SharePoint is one of the services.

Select a template, and you will be directed to the Power Automate site to continue building your flow there.

If you cannot find a suitable template, click on 'Show more' and then 'See more templates'. That will take you to the Power Automate site.

24.5.3   Create a Flow from Blank

I often create my flows from blank instead of from a template, as I find that it gives better control over the flow.

When you use a template, the connector(s) and trigger are always chosen for you, but with a blank flow you must start with selecting a suitable connector and trigger.

Start building your blank flow by selecting 'New' and then one of the "from blank" options under 'My flows' on the Power Automate site.

The Automated options give flows that run automatically when triggered, while the Instant options give flows that are run manually. The Scheduled option is intended for flows that should be run with specific intervals.

≡		+ New ⋎ ↩ Import
⌂	Home	🗐 Create from template
🗂	Action items ⌄	🗐 Create from Visio template
𝑜ᵃ	My flows	+ Automated cloud flows—from blank
+	Create	+ Instant cloud flows—from blank
		+ Scheduled cloud flows—from blank
🗂	Templates	+ Desktop flow—from blank
𝜎ᵍ	Connectors	+ Business process—from blank

444

When you have selected one of the "from blank" options under 'New' in the 'My flows' page, a dialog will open. Here you can give the flow a name, and for the automated and instant flows you can select a trigger. If you cannot find the trigger you want to use, click on 'Skip'.

Build an automated flow   ×

Flow name

Add a name or we'll generate one

Choose your flow's trigger * ⓘ

🔍 Search all triggers

	When a file is created Dropbox	ⓘ
	When a file is created (properties only) Dropbox	ⓘ
	When a file is modified (properties o... Dropbox	ⓘ
	When a record is created Dynamics 365	ⓘ
	When a record is deleted Dynamics 365	ⓘ
	When a record is updated Dynamics 365	ⓘ

Free yourself from repetitive work just by connecting the apps you already use—automate alerts, reports, and other tasks.

Examples:
• Automatically collect and store data in business solutions
• Generate reports via custom queries on your SQL database

Skip   Create   Cancel

The scheduled flow gives another dialog, where you can set the start date and frequency for the flow.

When you click on 'Create', the Flow Editor will open so that you can continue building your flow.

If you instead click on 'Skip', you must first select connector and a trigger for the flow. Click on a connector icon to see all available triggers for that connector.

445

┌───┐
│ 🔍 Sha│   │
└───┘

All   Built-in   Standard   Premium   Custom   My clipboard

| SharePoint | Office 365 Outlook | OneDrive for Business | EasyVista Service... | GitHub | RiskIQ | Projectwise Share |

Triggers   **Actions**   See more

	Send an HTTP request to SharePoint SharePoint	ⓘ
	Create sharing link for a file or folder SharePoint	ⓘ
	Stop sharing an item or a file SharePoint	ⓘ
	Create item SharePoint	ⓘ

You can also directly search for a trigger or choose one of the suggestions below the connector icons.

When you have selected the trigger you want to use, the Flow Editor will open, and you can continue building the flow.

24.5.4   *Finalize the Flow*

When you have finished creating a flow, you should always test it by performing the trigger action. That way you can make sure it runs and gives the result you wished to achieve when you created it. Therefore, the final steps is the same for all flows. Save the flow by clicking on the 'Save' button below your last step or at the top right.

The Flow checker usually has a red warning if something is wrong in the flow syntax. Click on the button to see an explanation. If the flow has a syntax error, it is not possible to save and test it.

 💾 Save   ⚕ Flow checker   ⚗ Test

If there is no warning message, you can directly click on the 'Test' button and then 'Save and Test'.

For new flows, only the 'Manually' test option is valid.

Test Flow   ×

◉ Manually
   Perform the starting action to trigger it.

○ Automatically

The option 'Automatically' can be used when you need to repeat the testing. That way, you don't have to perform the trigger action (for example create a new test item) for each test run. Select which run you want to repeat.

In the left corner above the Flow Editor, Power Automate will give you a hint what to do to test the flow.

ⓘ To see it work now, modify a list item in the SharePoint folder you selected.

24.5.5   *Flow Activity*

On the Activity page, you can see runs, failures and notifications for all your flows. You can reach the Activity page from the Power Automate Settings icon.

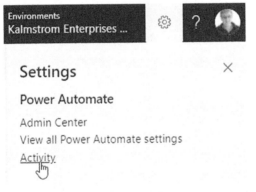

Under the Settings icon there are also links to the Power Automate Admin center and to settings for region and language.

24.5.6   *Dynamic Content*

When you add dynamic content in flow fields, the content in actions changes depending on what happened in the services used in the flow, for example in a SharePoint app. Dynamic content can be selected from a list that is displayed to the right when you click in a flow field.

The dynamic content is fetched from the trigger and the previous actions in the flow. In the image below, the mouse cursor is placed in a 'Start Date' field, so the date options 'Modified' and 'Created' are suggested as dynamic content for that field.

When the screen is narrow, the dynamic content is instead displayed below the field. Sometimes, you might need to click on the 'Add dynamic content' link under the field to display the dynamic content list.

Search, or click on 'See more' above the suggestions, if you cannot find the dynamic content you are looking for.

24.5.7   Custom Value

When you create a flow, you must specify the site and app for each step in the flow. Often, you can select both, but sometimes you need to type in the data. When you do that, you must also select your value as a custom value.

You can either type the name and then select 'Use [NAME] as custom value' or scroll to the bottom of the list first and select 'Enter custom value'.

Sites are mostly possible to select, but with apps it happens in two cases that you need to select a custom value:

- Only lists that can have the modern experience show up in the 'List Name' dropdowns in Power Automate, so if you use a list based on for example the Tasks template, you need add the list name as a custom value.

- In the exercise below, we use the trigger 'SharePoint - when an item is created'. That triggers are primarily intended for lista pps, but they give the dynamic content 'ID', as opposed to the "when a file is created" actions. Therefore, I often use an "item" trigger even if the flow runs in a document library.

In such cases, the document library name will not be displayed in the editor dropdown for 'List Name'. Instead, you must add the library name as a custom value.

24.6   EXPORT AND IMPORT FLOWS

A flow can be exported as a .zip package and imported and re-used as a template. That way, you don't have to start from scratch with a new flow. Instead, you can just change those flow settings that should be different.

24.6.1   *Export a Flow*

When you export a flow from the Power Automate site, you download it to your computer in compressed format.

1. Under 'My flows', click on the ellipsis at the flow you want to export and select 'Export'.

2. Select file format: 'Package (.zip)'. (The .json option gives a logic app than can be imported for example to Microsoft Azure.)

3. Give the package a name and click on 'Export'. Select to download the package to your computer if that does not happen automatically.

24.6.2   *Import a Flow*

When you have received a flow package, you can import it to your 'My flows' page.

1. Under 'My flows', click on 'Import' in the top left corner.

2. Upload the flow .zip package you want to import.

3. When the file has been uploaded, a new page will open.

Package details
Created by Kate Kalmström on 03/28/2020

Name
Skype message at new task

Environment
Kalmstrom Enterprises AB (Upgrade) (orgff0ecebe)

Description
N/A

Review Package Content
Choose your import options.

NAME	RESOURCE TYPE	IMPORT SETUP	ACTION
ⓘ Skype alert at new task	Flow	Update	✏

Related resources

NAME	RESOURCE TYPE	IMPORT SETUP	ACTION
ⓘ kate@kalmstrom.com	Skype for Business Online Connection	Select during import	✏
ⓘ kate@kalmstrom.com	SharePoint Connection	Select during import	✏

Import   Cancel

4. Click on the 'ACTION' icon under 'Review Package Content'. An Import Setup pane will open to the right.

5. Select to create a new flow from the imported one.

Import setup ✕

Setup

Create as new ⌄

Create as new

Update

6. Give the new flow another name than the original flow and save.

7. Click on ACTION under Related resources' to establish the required flow connector(s). Either create new connections or click on the existing ones before you save.

8. Click on 'Import'.

9. Now the new flow will be created, and you can open it directly from the Import page. It is also added under 'My flows'.

The imported flow still has all the settings from the original flow, so you should edit the new flow and make any changes needed so that it works as you wish.

The imported flow is turned off by default, so before you test it you need to turn it on under My flows >the flow ellipsis.

24.7 WORKFLOWS

Workflows are created in SharePoint Designer 2013, refer to chapter 10. The most common workflow designer is the text-based one, where you can find buttons for condition and action in the ribbon.

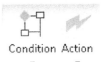

Condition Action

When you have clicked on one of these buttons, you will have this kind of links for the Condition and Action:

If value equals value   Set field to value

Click on the links to select or type in the valid values, fields or what your workflow should be using or doing.

There is also a Visual Designer view for SharePoint 2013 workflows, where you can create workflows by dragging shapes to a design surface.

24.7.1 Start Creating a List Workflow

The most common workflow, the list workflows, are only intended to be used on the items in one app. (Note that SharePoint Designer 2013 talks about lists and libraries and doesn't use the word "app" anywhere: I will continue to use "app" here for consistency.)

List
Workflow ▾

1. Open the site that has the app you want to create a workflow for, *refer to* 10.2, Open a Site in SharePoint Designer.

2. With the site homepage selected in the left menu, click on the 'List Workflow' button in the ribbon, to create a new workflow.

3. Select the app you want to use.

4. Give the workflow a name and a description. Keep the default SharePoint 2013 workflow. 2010 workflows are no longer supported in SharePoint Online.

Create List Workflow - Customers	?	✕

 Add a new workflow to your list

Enter a name and description for your new workflow

Name:

Notifications

Description:

Choose the platform to build your workflow on

Platform Type: SharePoint 2013 Workflow ⌄

OK   Cancel

When you click OK, the summary page will have a new tab with the name of the workflow, and two new pages have been created: the Edit Workflow page and the Workflow Settings page.

The image below shows the tabs when creating a "Set Title" workflow in the Sales site.

Switch between the two workflow pages with the thumbnail links under the tab, or use the buttons Edit Workflow and Workflow Settings in the ribbon.

Edit
Workflow

Workflow
Settings

Before you start building the workflow, open the Workflow Settings page and set when the workflow should be started.

Start Options   ∧

Change the start options for this workflow.

☐ Allow this workflow to be manually started

☐ Start workflow automatically when an item is created

☐ Start workflow automatically when an item is changed

I would recommend that you make sure the boxes are checked, because the checking does not always stick in the box.

24.7.2   Dynamic Content

When you add dynamic content to a workflow, the content in actions changes depending on what happens in the SharePoint app that the workflow is associated with.

In *SharePoint Designer*, dynamic content is called "lookup" content, and it is added via 'Add or Change Lookup' buttons. What is shown as suggestions in the dropdowns depends on the action and the app content.

String Builder   ?   ✕

Name:

Lookup for String   ?   ✕

Field Data to Retrieve

Choose the data source to perform the lookup on, then the field to
retrieve data from:

Data source: | Current Item | ⌄

Field from source: | | ⌄

Return field as: | % Complete | ⌃
                    | Approval Status |
                    | Approver Comments |
Clear Lookup | Assigned To |
                    | Attachments |
                    | Body | ⌄

Add or Change Lookup   OK   Cancel

24.7.3   *Finalize the Workflow*

When you have created a list workflow, you must
publish it. In the same ribbon group as the Publish
button, you can also find buttons to save the
workflow (to continue working with it later) and to
check the workflow for errors.

Save   Publish   Check
                  for Errors

Save

Even if you have checked the workflow for errors, you should also perform
the trigger and see if the action is performed as intended.

24.7.4   *The Workflows Page*

You can see details on running and completed workflows if you right-click on
the ellipsis at an app item and select More/Advanced and then Workflow.

Modern interface:

More   >   Workflow   🖑

Details   Compliance details

Classic interface:

Edit Item

Delete Item

View Item

Advanced   ▸   Manage Permissions

                 Compliance Details

                 Workflows

If you cannot check the workflow directly, because it is activated by a timer and not by a changed or created item, you can start it manually from the workflows page. Select the workflow you want to test and click on the Start button to start the workflow manually.

24.8   EXERCISE: SET TITLES

In two exercises, I will show how to automate updates of title fields in SharePoint libraries. Good document titles are important if you want to get relevant results from searches, but for many organizations it is a problem that titles in SharePoint document libraries are either missing or not accurate.

Therefore, I will suggest a flow and workflow that updates file properties and sets the title to the same as the file name. It is not an ideal solution, but the document name is most often more relevant than an empty title.

I use a "Procedures" SharePoint document library for these exercises. To be able to check the flow smoothly, I suggest that you make the "Title" column visible in the "All items" view. When the flow or workflow runs as it should, you can hide the "Title" column again.

24.8.1   *Set Titles Flow*

Below I will give an example on how to create a simple flow that updates the "Title" column in a new or modified item in a SharePoint document library. Before the update, the flow looks if the "Title" field is empty, and the flow is only run when that condition is met.

We use dynamic content in several places in this flow, and in some cases, you will have two options: content from the trigger and content from the action. In other flows, the source of the dynamic content may be crucial, but here, it does not matter which one you choose – the result will be the same.

24.8.1.1   Actions

To set the title to be the same as the file name, we must get the column values, or properties, of the new or modified file. When we have that, we will know the name, and we can set the flow to perform an update of the "Title" column.

We will use the action 'SharePoint – Get file properties' to fetch column values from the new or modified item. Each item is identified with its ID.

When the values have been fetched by the first action, we will add a 'SharePoint – Update file properties' action to update the "Title" value in the item, so that it becomes the same as the item's "Name" value.

24.8.1.2   Condition

As we don't want to change any existing "Title" values, we will add a condition action after the trigger. This condition limits the actions, so that they are only performed when the condition is met.

A condition is set in three fields, where your selection in the middle field decides the relation between the two other fields.

A condition can be either true (If yes) or false (If no), and you can build different scenarios depending on if the condition is true or not. Often only the 'If yes' option is used, as no action is required when the condition is not met. That is the case in this example flow.

We will set the condition to be true when the "Title" value of the item that triggered the flow is equal to 'null', which means that the field has no value.

This image shows the finished flow. You can see the expanded 'Get file properties' action in the steps below.

24.8.1.3   Steps

This flow starts running when an item in a SharePoint document library is created or modified. If the condition is met, the flow fetches the item's properties, reads the file name, and adds the same value to the "Title" field.

1. Create an automated blank flow.
2. Give the flow a name.
3. Select the trigger 'SharePoint - when an item is created or modified'.
4. Click on 'Create'.
5. Enter your site name and your library name.
6. Click on 'New step'.
7. Add a Condition:
    a. In the left Condition field, add the dynamic content in the Title field of the item that triggered the flow.
    b. Keep the default 'is equal to' in the middle field.
    c. Type null in the right field.
8. Add the action 'SharePoint – Get file properties'.
    a. Enter your site name and your library name.
    b. In the 'Id' field, add the dynamic content 'ID' from the trigger.

9. Click on 'New step'.
10. Add the action 'SharePoint – Update file properties'.
    a. Enter your site name and your library name.
    b. In the 'Id' field, add the dynamic content 'ID'.
    c. In the 'Title' field, add the dynamic content 'Name'.
11. Save and test the flow.

Demo:

https://www.kalmstrom.com/Tips/SharePoint-Flows/Flow-Update-Title.htm

24.8.2   *Set Title Workflow*

The image to the right shows a finished workflow that sets the "Title" value to the same as the "Name" value if the "Title" field is empty.

Stage: Stage 1

If Current Item:Title is empty

    Set Title to Current Item:Name

Transition to stage

Go to End of Workflow

24.8.2.1   Steps

1. Open the site that has the list you want to use in SharePoint Designer.

2. Create a list workflow for the library you want to use.

3. Click on the 'Workflow Settings' button in the ribbon and set the workflow to start automatically when an item is created or modified.

4. Click on the 'Edit the workflow' link.

5. Click on 'Transition to stage' at the bottom of the Stage 1 box.

6. Type 'go' and press Enter.

7. Click on stage and select 'End of Workflow'.

8. Click in the 'Stage 1' box.

9. Click on the 'Condition' button in the ribbon and select 'If any value equals value':

   a. Click on the first value and open the Function Builder.

   b. Keep Current Item and set the field to 'Title'.

   c. Click on equals and select 'is empty' from the dropdown.

10. Click in the box below the condition box.

11. Click on 'Action' in the ribbon and select 'Set Field in Current Item':

   a. Click on field and select 'Title' from the dropdown.

   b. Click on value and open the Function Builder.

   c. Keep Current Item and set the field to 'Name'.

12. Check, publish and test the workflow.

Demo:

https://kalmstrom.com/Tips/SharePoint-Workflows/Title-List-Workflow.htm
(The demo shows how to set the title when it is not the same as the name.)

24.9   SUMMARY

After studying this chapter, I hope you have a general idea on how different kinds of flows and workflows are created and can be used.

We have looked at Power Automate, Microsoft's modern alternative to the classic SharePoint workflows. I have described some important differences between the two automation methods and shown the basics in both flow and workflow creation and management.

I have also explained how the SharePoint built-in flows are configured. Microsoft is currently developing another built-in flow that will let users create simple if/then rules for e-mail notifications, based on changes in list apps. When this feature is implemented, there will be a new option under the Power Automate button: Create a rule.

Finally, I have given two exercises for you to try. I hope they gave you a good overview over how it is to work with the two automation tools.

You can find more automation descriptions in later chapters: 25.11.1.1, Workflow that Switches Content Type, and 30.3, Review Flow.

In the next chapter, I will introduce an important feature that is necessary to understand for more advanced use of SharePoint: the content types.

25 CONTENT TYPES

One of the best ways to make sure that a SharePoint tenant or site will contain the desired content and is managed in a consistent way, is to use content types. A content type is a template for a specific type of item, like a task, a contact item or a library item with a Word document. The content type has the metadata columns and settings that is needed for every item of that kind.

When your company often sends quotations, you can for example create a special content type for quotations and add it to a document library. Such a content type would include a template for the quotation document and metadata columns like client company, contact person and PO number. It can also have settings for retention, *see* below in 25.3.3, Edit Content Type Settings.

When you add such a quotation content type to a document library, people who use that library can select the Quotation content type from the 'New' dropdown each time they want to create a new quotation. That way, all quotations will use the same template for the file as well as the metadata and settings.

Instead of just adding the content type to a document library, you can create a document library that is solely intended for quotations and remove the default content type (which is called Document) from that library. Then all new items will use the Quotation content type.

By default, SharePoint includes many predefined content types, such as Document, Item or Announcement, because all content in SharePoint is created from a content type. You can (and probably should) also create your own content types.

When you create a custom content type, you always start from an existing content type. The new content type inherits all the attributes of its parent content type, for example document template, columns and settings. When you have created your custom content type, you can change any of these attributes, and you often want to add more columns.

In this chapter, I will describe how to create a custom content type that can be used by the whole tenant and how to create a content type for a site.

I will also explain how a content type can be associated with an app and how you can create a template that gives the values of the metadata columns in printed documents.

Finally. we will take a closer look at the built-in Document Set content type, which automatically creates multiple documents based on specified templates for each new library item. We will also create a task entry content type.

25.1 SITE AND LIST CONTENT TYPES

Content types are sometimes called site content types and sometimes list content types. Which term you use depends on how the content type is used.

- A content type is called a site content type when it is created or modified. The site content types can be managed in the SharePoint Admin center >Content type gallery and in each site at Site settings >Site content types, and they are grouped in categories.

- When you add a site content type to an app, it is called a list content type. A list content type can be customized for its specific app, and these customizations are not added to the site content type.

  If the site content type is updated, the list content type by default inherits these changes, and any modifications made to the shared attributes in the list content type will be overwritten.

  If the list content type has attributes that are not shared with the site content type, they will not be overwritten when the site content type is updated.

25.2   The Content Type Gallery/Hub

Content types can be created in the SharePoint Admin center, which connects to a classic site called Content Type Hub. When you create and publish content types in the SharePoint Admin center (or directly the Content Type Hub site), they become available for the whole tenant, and you don't need to create content types for each site. This gives reusability and consistency of information across the tenant.

Earlier, custom content types for the whole tenant could only be created directly in the Content Type Hub. The site is still there, and under its Site settings >Site content types you can find all content types that are available in the tenant.

Today, the SharePoint Admin center has a menu option under Content services >Content type gallery, that connects to the Content type Hub site. The Content Type Gallery shows the same content types as the Hub site, and therefore, you can create and manage the tenant's content types in the SharePoint Admin center.

You might however still need to open the Content Type Hub site for advanced settings and editing, to test the content type and to create list templates.

The Content Type Hub site is not listed in the SharePoint Admin center under 'Active sites'. Instead, it can be reached:

- Via 'go to the classic experience' links in the Content Type Gallery right panes.

- From the Site settings of any root site in the tenant. Click on 'Content type publishing' under the Site Collection Administration heading. On the page that opens, you can find a link to the Content Type Hub.

Taxonomy_hcRL3VioiV2xubyCk0o+0A==

https://m365x446726.sharepoint.com/sites/contentTypeHub/_layouts/15/mngctype.aspx

25.3   CREATE A CONTENT TYPE IN THE GALLERY

These are the steps to create a custom content type from the SharePoint Admin center:

1. Open the SharePoint Admin center >Content services >Content type gallery. Now you can see and edit all existing content types.

2. Click on '+ Create content type' to open the right Create content type pane.

461

3. Enter a content type name and other details. Select first Category and then parent for the content type you wish to build your custom content type on. You should also add your content type to an existing or new category.

4. Click on Create, and your content type will be added to the list of content types in the Content Type Gallery.

25.3.1   Add Site Columns to a Content Type

When you have created the content type, you should add site columns to it. The Content Type Gallery has no "Created" column to sort the content types by, but you can filter by category and/or parent content type and then sort the names alphabetically to find your new content type.

As you have built your custom content type on top of a predefined content type, some predefined properties for that content type are kept, as the "Name" and "Title" columns from the Document content type.

Click on the name of the new content type to open it. Now you can add more columns to the content type. You can either create a new site column or use an existing one. In both cases, a right pane will open where you can add details for the new column.

Content type gallery > **Quotation**

∅ Edit   ⯭ Publish   ⚙ Settings ∨   ⟳ Manage workflows   🗑 Delete

Quotation

Category
Custom Content Types

Parent
Document ⓘ

Content Type ID
0x01010092F18EA21038F94DAA6D432957A73EAE

Site columns
Add and manage the site columns that are a part of this content type.

+ Add site column

Create new site column

Add from existing site columns

Name	Type	Required	Source
Name	File	Yes	Document
Title	Single line of text	No	Item

25.3.2   Edit Site Columns

When you have added a column to the content type, you can edit how it will be displayed in the item form. Open the ellipsis to the right of the column name or use the buttons in the command bar above the column, to open the 'Edit site column settings' right pane.

In the column dropdown, you can also delete the column and change the column order. 'Format the site column' is for addition of JSON code and out of scope for this book.

Site columns

Add and manage the site columns that are a part of this content type.

✏ Edit site column settings   ✏ Format the site column   🗑 Delete

Name	Type
✅ Name	⋮ File
Title	Edit site column settings
Client	Format the site column
	Delete
	Reorder site columns > Move to top
	Move up
	Move down
	Move to bottom

In the Edit site columns right pane, you can hide a column from the form or set it to be required. The image below shows the default settings.

✕

Edit site column settings

Show or hide site column

☑ Show this column in lists

　　⦿ Optional (may contain information)

　　◯ Required (must contain information)

Update sites and lists

☐ Update all site and list content types inheriting from this content type with the settings on this page.

To edit site columns, go to the classic experience.

Save　　Cancel

When you want to have more options, click on the 'classic experience' link. Now, an 'Edit Column' page in the Content Type Hub will open in a new tab. It resembles the page for list columns.

When you update an existing column type, the default setting for the update of inheriting content types is different in the gallery and in the 'Edit Column' page. As you see from the image above, the box for update is *not* checked by default in the Content Type Gallery. When you go to the 'Edit Column' page in the Content Type Hub, there is a radio button for the update, and it is checked by default!

This is of course a bug, but until it has been fixed, I recommend that you make sure that the setting is the same in both places, because when the content type is defined in the Content Type Hub and published, the change is propagated across the tenant.

25.3.3   *Edit Content Type Settings*

Click on the Settings icon in the top command bar to change the content type settings.

25.3.3.1   Add a Template to a Content Type

Under 'Advanced Settings', you can change the default edit permission for the content type if necessary. If you have modified an existing content type, you might want to disable the update of inheriting content types.

When your content type builds on the Document content type, you can also add a custom file template under the Advanced settings for the content type. Enter the path to an existing template or upload a template from your computer.

Word, Excel or PowerPoint files can be added to a site content type. As always in SharePoint, it does not have to be a real template file. Any document with the correct content and layout will do. *Refer to* 25.8, Create a Document Template with Metadata, on how to create a template that has the content type fields in the document body.

Advanced Settings

×

Document template

Specify the document template for this content type:

◉ Use an existing template   ○ Upload a new document template

/_layouts/15/bpcf.aspx

(Edit Template)

Permissions

Choose whether the content type is modifiable. This setting can be changed later from this page by anyone with permissions to edit this type.

○ Read

◉ Edit

Update sites and lists

Update all site and list content types inheriting from this content type with the settings on this page.

◉ Enable

Save   Cancel

25.3.3.2   Policies – Retention and more

When you select 'Policy settings' under the content type settings, a page in the Content Type Hub will open in a new tab. Here, you can make settings for retention, auditing, barcodes and labels, and you can also add an administrative description and a policy statement.

When you check one of the boxes, you will have options to continue.

Site Content Types ‣ Edit Policy

Name and Administrative Description

The name and administrative description are shown to list managers when configuring policies on a list or content type.

Name:

Meeting

Administrative Description:

Policy Statement

The policy statement is displayed to end users when they open items subject to this policy. The policy statement can explain which policies apply to the content or indicate any special handling or information that users need to be aware of.

Policy Statement:

Retention

Schedule how content is managed and disposed by specifying a sequence of retention stages. If you specify multiple stages, each stage will occur one after the other in the order they appear on this page.

Note: If the Library and Folder Based Retention feature is active, list administrators can override content type policies with their own retention schedules. To prevent this, deactivate the feature on the site collection.

☑ Enable Retention

Specify how to manage retention:
Items will not expire until a stage is added.
Add a retention stage...

Auditing

Specify the events that should be audited for documents and items subject to this policy.

☐ Enable Auditing

Barcodes

Assigns a barcode to each document or item. Optionally, Microsoft Office applications can require users to insert these barcodes into documents.

☐ Enable Barcodes

Labels

You can add a label to a document to ensure that important information about the document is included

☐ Enable Labels

The 'Enable Retention' box gives a link, 'Add a retention stage' that opens a dialog. Here, you can decide how long items entered in an app that uses this content type should be retained.

You can also decide what should happen to the item when it no longer should be kept in the app.

Specify the event that activates this stage and an action that should occur once the stage is activated.

Event

Specify what causes the stage to activate:
◉ This stage is based off a date property on the item
  Time Period: [Created ▾] ÷ [   ] [years ▾]
  ○ Set by a custom retention formula installed on this server:

Action

When this stage is triggered, perform the following action:
  [Move to Recycle Bin ▾]
  This action will move the item to the site collection recycle bin.

25.3.4   *Test a Content Type*

Before you publish a content type, you should check how it works. You can try it in the Content Type Hub site, because here, the content type works without publishing. The publishing is just a method to propagate the content type to the other sites in the tenant.

The Content Type Hub is a classic site, and here you can add the content type to an app and try it. *Refer to* 25.4 below to learn how to associate an app with a new content type.

25.3.5   *Publish and Unpublish a Content Type*

When a new content type has been created, it must be published to be available in other sites than the Content Type Hub. And if a change has been made, the content type must be republished. The publication can take an hour or even more to be finished, but it is often quicker.

To publish from the SharePoint Admin center, open the content type in the Content Type Gallery and click on the 'Publish' button in the command bar. A right pane will open where the 'Publish' option is checked, and you only need to click on 'Save'.

When the content type has been published, the default option in the right pane will switch to 'Republish'.

The Publish right pane also has an 'Unpublish' option to select, if you don't want the content type to be available anymore.

If you have been editing or testing the content type in the Content Type Hub, it might be more convenient to publish it there:

1. Under Site settings >Site content types, click on the content type you want to publish to open it.

2. Click on 'Manage publishing for this content type'.

3. Select your option from the new page that opens. It has the same three options as the Gallery right pane.

25.4   ASSOCIATE A CONTENT TYPE WITH AN APP

When you have created a custom content type, you need to associate it with the app where you want to use it. If you don't want to give users a selection, you also need to remove the default content type.

When you have removed the default content type, all new items in the app will be based on the content type you added. This means that they will all have the same columns and settings, and thereby the same kind of metadata information.

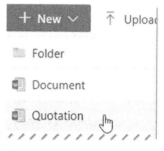

If you don't remove the default content type, users can select the custom content type when needed.

You might find it useful to add several content types to an app, but my preference is usually to create new apps for each content type. There are exceptions, though, and I describe one such case in chapter 30 below.

These are the steps to associate a content type with an app:

1. Open the List settings and click on 'Advanced settings' in the General Settings section.

2. Select the 'Yes' option under 'Allow management of content types' and click OK. (The default setting for this is 'No' in most app types.)

Settings ▸ Advanced Settings

Content Types

Specify whether to allow the management of content types on this document library. Each content type will appear on the new button and can have a unique set of columns, workflows and other behaviors.

Allow management of content types?

⦿ Yes   ◯ No

3. Under the new 'Content Type' heading in the Site settings, click on 'Add from existing site content types'.

Content Types

This document library is configured to allow multiple co
available in this library:

Content Type

Document

___

- □ Add from existing site content types

- □ Change new button order and default content type

4. Select the category and content type you want to use. Click Add and
   then OK.

Select Content Types

Select from the list of available
site content types to add them to
this list.

Select site content types from:

| Custom Content Types | ⌄ |

Available Site Content Types:

Quotation	∧
	⌄

Add >

< Remove

Content types to add:

	∧
	⌄

Description:
None

Group: Custom Content Types

| OK | | Cancel |

Now the content type is associated with the app, but when you look at the
default view, you cannot see the content type columns there. They are not
automatically added to any view, so you need to add them by editing the
view. You probably also need to create some new views.

When management of content types has been
allowed in an app, the **modern** app interface
also gives an option to add the content type
directly from the user interface, under the '+
Add column' command.

+ Add column ⌄

Single line of text

More...

Content type

Show/hide columns

25.4.1   *Delete Default Content Type*

Even if you have added a custom content type to an app, the default content type is still there and gives a possibility to create other kind of items. I would recommend that you remove the default content type from the app. If you do that, all new items will be of the same kind, as there is no other option.

In the Content Types section of the List settings, click on the content type you want to remove and then on the link 'Delete this content type'. (The content type will only be removed from this app. You will always have the possibility to add it again.)

Demo:

https://kalmstrom.com/Tips/SharePoint-Online-Course/Content-Types-Use.htm

25.5   CREATE A CONTENT TYPE FOR A SITE

To see all content types that are available for the site, open the Site settings from the root site and click on 'Site content types' under Web Designer Galleries. You will be directed to a page where you can see a list of all content types that can be used in the site.

You can create and edit custom content types from the Site Content Types page, but these content types can only be used in the same site and its subsites. "Categories" are called "Groups" here, but the process to create a content type is the same as when you create a content type in the SharePoint Admin center or in the Content Type Hub.

You can use the same category/group for your custom content type as when you create from the Admin center/Hub, if you so wish. The content type will only be available for the site anyway and will not be shown in other sites.

Site Settings › Site Content Types ⓘ

📧 Create   Show Group: | All Groups | ⌄ |

Site Content Type	Parent	Source
Display Template Content Types		
JavaScript Display Template	Document	Development
Document Content Types		
Basic Page	Document	Development
Document	Item	Development
Dublin Core Columns	Document	Development

When you create a content type for a site, there is no publication, you only need to associate the content type with an app. You can try the content type in a test app before you associate it with the app where you want to use it.

470

Any changes in the content type are normally propagated to all apps in that site and in any subsites.

25.5.1   *Hide the Title Field*

As mentioned in section 9.6, the "Title" field in library items is often left without a value. I suggested some methods to give it a value, but if you want to hide the "Title" field from the item form in a document library, that is possible. The best way is to create a new content type for the site where you want to hide the title, and then hide the "Title" field in that content type.

1. Create a new content type based in the Document template.

2. When the content type has been created, but still under Site content types, click on the "Title" column to edit it.

3. Select the option to hide the Title column from forms.

Column Settings

Specify settings for this content type column.

This column is:

○ Required (Must contain information)

○ Optional (May contain information)

◉ Hidden (Will not appear in forms)

4. Associate the document library where you want to hide the "Title" field with the new content type.

5. Remove the default "Document" content type.

Demo:

https://www.kalmstrom.com/Tips/SharePoint-Online-Course/Hide-Title.htm

25.5.2   *Add a Template*

You can add a template to the content type created from a site, just as you can when you create the content type from the SharePoint Admin center.

1. In SharePoint, open the Site Settings and click on the 'Site content types' link.

2. Select the content type group and then open the content type that you want to connect the template to.

3. Click on 'Advanced settings'.

4. In the Document Template section, enter the URL to an existing template or upload a template file from your computer.

25.6   EDIT CONTENT TYPES

Site content types created from the SharePoint Admin center can be edited there, and when you created the content type from a site it can be edited from the root site >Site Settings >Site content types.

Changes in a site content type will undo all local customizations of the content type in list content types. Therefore, all changes to a content type should ideally be made before it is used in production.

Demo:

https://kalmstrom.com/Tips/SharePoint-Online-Course/SharePoint-Meetings-Content-Type-Change.htm

25.7   USE LIST COLUMNS WITH A CONTENT TYPE

Sometimes you want to add some different metadata columns to an app. That is no problem even if it is using a custom content type. Editing is allowed by default for content types created for a site, but not for tenant wide content types. For tenant wide content types, you need to allow editing in the List settings of the app where you want to add columns.

1. Click on the link to the content type that the app is using.

2. Click on the 'Advanced settings' link.

3. At 'Should this content type be read only?' select 'No'.

Now you can create new columns. They will be added to the app, but otherwise the app will be like in the content type design. If the content type is updated, any changes in the columns that are included in the content types will be overwritten in your app, but the columns you have added will be kept as they are.

Demo:

https://kalmstrom.com/Tips/SharePoint-Online-Course/SharePoint-Meetings-Flexibility.htm

25.8   CREATE A DOCUMENT TEMPLATE WITH METADATA COLUMNS

When you have added a custom content type to a library app, the metadata entered in the columns will always be displayed in the SharePoint app.

However, the metadata columns can only be seen and set in the Word document if you open its properties, and they will not be included if you print the document.

To include the values of the metadata columns in a printed document, you need to create a template which has the content type fields in a table in the document body. These column values for each document will be filled out automatically when you fill out the properties in the library – and when they are filled out in the document, they will be added to the library item.

Quote Date	2/26/2017
Decision Date	2/24/2017
Value	[Value]
Decision	3. Declined

Create a template by creating a Word document that you connect to your content type:

1. Create a new Word document using the content type you want to add the template to. It opens in Word Online by default.

2. Switch to the desktop application.

3. Insert a table with two columns and as many rows as you have metadata columns in the content type.

4. Enter the column names in the left column cells.

5. Place the mouse cursor in the first row of the right column. Under the Insert tab in the ribbon, click on the Quick Parts icon and select Document Property and then the column name.

6. Repeat step 5 for each row and select the other metadata columns.

7. Save the document as a .docx or .dotx file to your computer.

Now you can connect the Word document to your content type, to be used as a template for new library items, as described above. You should also open the Library settings >Advanced settings and set documents to open in the client application.

You can of course use all other Word features in your template and make it compliant with your company graphic profile as needed.

Demos:

https://kalmstrom.com/Tips/SharePoint-Online-Course/Content-Types-Template.htm

25.9   THE DOCUMENT SET CONTENT TYPE

When you work with projects within an organization, you usually need to create a set of documents for each project. Templates are often used for such documents, to make them consistent.

With a Document Set content type, you can have project documents created and named automatically from your specified templates when you create a new project item. All the documents needed for a project are found in that project item.

If you plan to use folders for project documents or similar, I recommend that you study document sets first. Using document sets is a better option than folders in many ways.

Another way to avoid folders, is of course to use one library for each project. In my opinion, the document sets give a better overview, and separate libraries do not give you the automatic creation and name giving of documents that document sets do.

The Document Set content type works in both the classic and the modern library interface and in modern as well as classic sites.

While simpler content types like Document and Item becomes visible in sites soon after they have been created in the SharePoint Admin center or directly in the Content Type Hub, the Document Set content type can take several hours. Document sets created in sites are quickly available.

25.9.1   Activate the Document Set Feature

In **modern** sites, Document Set content types cannot be selected until you have activated the feature. (In classic sites the feature is activated by default.)

1. Open the site settings from the site collection root site.

2. Click on 'Site collection features' under the Site Collection Administration.

3. At 'Document Sets', click on the 'Activate' button.

4. When the button changes into 'Deactivate' and an 'Active' button is shown to the right, you can create a new Document set content type or associate a library with an existing Document set content type.

25.9.2   Use A Document Set in a Library

When a user creates a new project item in a library and uses a document set content type, the specified set of documents will be created automatically.

The content writer can just open each document and start writing, instead of creating and naming multiple new documents.

In the image from a modern library to the right, some of the default menu entries are kept, and the Document Set content type have just been added as an option.

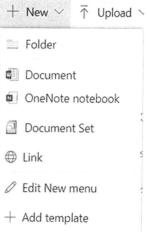

In the image from a classic library below, the default content type has been removed and folders are not allowed.

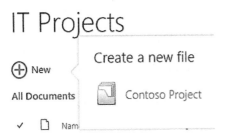

IT Projects

⊕ New

All Documents

✓ ☐ Nam

Create a new file

🗋 Contoso Project

25.9.3 *The Document Set Files*

🗋 Support system

When a new document set item has been created in a library, it has a specific icon.

You can add any templates to the document set, but in the image of the open "Support system" document set below, the specified documents are an Excel cost break-down, a PowerPoint executive overview and a Word specification.

By default, the auto-created documents are named with the name of the project item (Support system) + the name of the template.

Support system

View All Properties
Edit Properties

⊕ New   ⬆ Upload   🔄 Sync   ⟳ Share   More ∨

	Name		Modified	Modified By
✓ ☐				
📊	Support system - Costs ✳	⋯	A few seconds ago	Peter Kalmström
📊	Support system - Executive overview ✳	⋯	A few seconds ago	Peter Kalmström
📄	Support system - Specification ✳	⋯	A few seconds ago	Peter Kalmström

The image above comes from the **classic** library interface, that has a heading, called welcome page. The image shows the default look.

The welcome page is a web part that can be edited, by editing the page. You can also create a welcome page for all instances in the Content Type Hub on the page where you also add the files, *see* below.

The **modern** interface has no such welcome page. It just shows the files, and the open Information pane.

25.9.4   *Create a Document Set Content Type*

Create a custom site content type built on the Document Set parent for the tenant or for a site with columns and settings, in the same way as described for other content types above.

Use the category/group Document Set Content Types and the parent Document.

You can create a new document set content type for the tenant from the SharePoint Admin center as well as from the Content Type Hub, but when this is written, you must use the Content Type Hub to add the templates to the content type:

1. In the Content Type Hub, open >Site settings >Site Content Types., open the document set and click on the link 'Document Set settings'.

2. Show the group where you added the new document set content type.

3. Click on the document set content type.

4. Click on the link 'Document Set settings'.

5. At Default Content, add links to the templates you want to use in this document set.

Content Type	Folder	File Name		
Document ☑		C:\Users\Peter\Desktop\Costs.xlsx	Browse...	⊟ Delete
Document ☑		C:\Users\Peter\Desktop\Executive overview.ppt	Browse...	⊟ Delete
Document ☑			Browse...	⊟ Delete

Add new default content ...

Then you only need to associate the Document Set content type with a library, as described above in 25.4.

Demos:

https://kalmstrom.com/Tips/SharePoint-Online-Course/Document-Set-Content-Type.htm

https://kalmstrom.com/Tips/SharePoint-Online-Course/Document-Set-Use.htm

25.10 CONTENT TYPES IN THE HIGHLIGHTED CONTENT WEB PART

The modern Highlighted Content web part gives a possibility to show content that is associated to one or more content types.

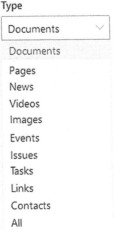

However, custom content types are *not* included among the options you can choose. Neither is the very common Item content type. Hopefully, Microsoft will add more content types in the future.

The image to the right shows the current options. As you see, there are some content types to choose from, even if Item and custom content types are missing.

25.11 TASK ENTRY CONTENT TYPE

In chapter 23 we created a Data Entry view for users who wanted to report an issue. Another option is to create a content type form for the first creation of an item.

Just as with the view, you can hide fields in the Data Entry form that in are not important when users create a new item. I will once again use a Tasks list as example, but entry forms can of course be created for all apps.

When you have added the Entry Form content type to a list, users will have a choice when they create a new item in the modern experience. In the classic experience, users will have the first content type when they create a new item.

When users edit an item, they can select which content type to use in both experiences. The switch to the more elaborate form can also be done automatically with a workflow, *see* below.

25.11.1 *Create an Entry Content Type*

1. Create a new content type, in the site or in the SharePoint Admin center/Content Type Hub. Select the parent content type to be fetched from List Content Types and then select Task.

2. Open each column that you want to modify and hide those of the columns that are not necessary in an entry form.

3. Associate the content type with an app where you want to use the new form.

4. Under Content Types in the List settings, click on the link 'Change new button order and default content type'.

□ Add from existing site content types

□ Change new button order and default content type

Columns

5. Set the new content type as number one.

Now, when you create a new task, it will automatically open with the new content type (as lists built on the Tasks template only have the classic interface).

If you use this tip with an app that has the modern interface, you will have a choice of both content types when you create a new item.

Next time you open the same task in edit mode, there is a dropdown for Content Type above the other fields. Here, you can choose to instead select the elaborate content type, with all the columns.

Content Type	Task Entry Form ˅
	Task Entry Form
Task Name *	Task
Assigned To	Peter Kalmström x

25.11.1.1   Workflow that Switches Content Type

If you want a different form to be shown automatically the second time a task is opened after creation, you can let the full form stay as default and let a workflow show the Entry form when the item is first created.

When the item is changed, no workflow will run. Therefore, the default content type will be used that time.

Stage: Stage 1

Set Content Type ID to Task Entry Form

Transition to stage

Go to End of Workflow

Flows do not work as well with content types as workflows, so it is not possible to use a flow for this automation in the same easy way.

1. Open the site in SharePoint Designer and create a list workflow for the app you want to use.

2. Click on the 'Workflow Settings' icon in the ribbon and select 'Start workflow automatically when an item is created'.

3. Click on the 'Edit the workflow' link.

4. At Transition to stage, end the workflow by entering 'go to End of Workflow'.

5. Click in Stage 1 and select the Action 'Set Field in Current Item'.

6. Click on field and select 'Content Type ID' from the dropdown.

7. Click on value and from the dropdown, select the value to the content type you wish to switch to.

8. Publish and check the workflow.

Demos:

https://kalmstrom.com/Tips/SharePoint-Online-Course/SharePoint-Forms-Content-Types.htm

25.12 SUMMARY

After studying this chapter, I hope that you understand how content types are used and that you feel inspired to create your own content types for lists and libraries.

You have learned to create a content type and associate it with an app, and you can also connect a document template to a content type.

I have introduced the Document set content type and described how you can create a Data Entry form content type to be used when an item is first created.

You will find more information about content types in the two last chapters in this book, but in the next chapter, I will describe how you can add CSS and JavaScript code to SharePoint pages.

26 Add CSS, JavaScript or RSS to a Classic Page

In this chapter, we will see how you can use the **classic** Content Editor web part to add CSS and JavaScript to a page. I will also introduce the RSS Viewer web part, which helps you add an RSS feed to your SharePoint site.

Modern SharePoint pages have a Code snippet web part, but it is only used to display code. It does not do anything - the code is not executed. Currently there is no easy way to customize modern pages with code. Therefore, techniques described in this chapter can only be used in classic pages.

CSS is a language that describes how HTML (or XML) elements must be rendered, for example in a web page. The look of your SharePoint site is decided by CSS code in the background. JavaScript is a programming language for web pages.

How to write CSS and JavaScript is far out of scope for this book, which is mainly no-code, but here I will show how you can do if you have a snippet of code that you want to use on a classic SharePoint page.

I will describe how you can add code to make small changes in a site page. There are three ways to do it, but you cannot do it by directly pasting your CSS or JavaScript code into the HTML source of the page. It will look fine until you save the page, but when you do that your code will disappear. You must use the Script Editor or the Content Editor.

If you want to modify an object on the page but don't know the name for it, press the CTRL + SHIFT + I keys to show the browser's developer tools.

26.1.1   Script Editor

You can paste CSS or JavaScript code to the minimal Script Editor web part in the Media and Content category.

In wiki pages, you can also use the Embed Code button under the INSERT tab, which inserts the Script Editor web part in the page.

<//>

Embed
Code

Embed

26.1.2   Content Editor Source

The Content Editor web part, in the Media and Content category can be used to add code to a page. When you have added the Content Editor web part to the page, the CSS or JavaScript code can be pasted into the HTML source of the web part:

1. Add the Content Editor web part to the page.

2. Click on the Edit Source button under the FORMAT TEXT tab in the ribbon.

3. Paste your code in the HTML source.

4. Apply and save the page.

Edit
Source

Demos:

https://www.kalmstrom.com/Tips/SharePoint-Online-Course/Content-Editor-CSS.htm

https://www.kalmstrom.com/Tips/SharePoint-Online-Course/Content-Editor-JavaScript.htm

26.1.3   *Content Editor Link*

In my opinion, the best method for adding CSS or JavaScript code to a page, is to create a separate .css, .txt, .js or .htm file with the code. Upload it to the Site Assets library and add a link to the file in the Content Editor web part.

This method is good if you often change the CSS code, because you can make the change directly in the file. Another advantage is that you can use the same file in multiple pages.

1. Add the code to a file and upload it to the Site Assets library.

2. Add the Content Editor web part to the page.

3. Edit the web part and type the path to the CSS or JavaScript file in the Content Link field.

4. Apply and save the page

Demos:

https://www.kalmstrom.com/Tips/SharePoint-Online-Course/Content-Editor-CSS-Link.htm

https://www.kalmstrom.com/Tips/SharePoint-Online-Course/Content-Editor-JavaScript-Link.htm

If you want to change the CSS for a site and not just for a page, *refer to* 27.4.2, Link to an Alternate CSS File.

26.1.4   *The RSS Viewer Web Part*

Use the RSS Viewer web part when you want to show content on a SharePoint page from any site that has an RSS feed. When you have added the web part and entered the link to the Atom page of the site you want to display in the web part, it will be updated automatically.

1. Open the site that you want to display in SharePoint.

2. Click on the 'Atom' subscription button and copy the URL to the page that opens.

3. Open a SharePoint wiki or web part page where you want to add RSS content in edit mode.

4. Add the RSS Viewer web part from the Content Rollup category.

5. Edit the web part.

6. Paste the URL to the RSS page in the 'RSS Feed URL' field in the web part panel.

7. Define settings for how often the RSS feed should be updated and how many items should be shown on the page.

8. (To avoid having the title 'RSS Viewer' on the web part, expand the Appearance accordion and set the Chrome Type to 'None'.)

9. Click on 'Apply' and save the page.

Demo:

https://www.kalmstrom.com/Tips/SharePoint-Online-Course/RSS-Viewer.htm

26.2 SUMMARY

In this chapter we have looked at the various possibilities to add CSS and JavaScript to a classic SharePoint page. We have also seen how the RSS Viewer web part can enhance a SharePoint page.

Now I will describe how you can enhance SharePoint by activating the SharePoint Server Publishing Infrastructure.

27 SharePoint Server Publishing Infrastructure

As we have seen earlier in this book, SharePoint Online has various features that are not enabled by default. One of them is the SharePoint Server Publishing Infrastructure, that is available in modern and classic Team sites.

Note: currently there is an entry for SharePoint Server Publishing Infrastructure in Communication sites too, but when you try to activate it you will get an error message. Hopefully, Microsoft has fixed that issue when you are reading this book!

When the SharePoint Server Publishing Infrastructure has been activated, several new features become available in the site. Some of them are immediately obvious, while others are visible only through the links in the Site settings page or in galleries or libraries.

In this chapter, we will have a look at some features that require activation of the SharePoint Server Publishing Infrastructure. You will learn how the options in the Look and Feel group in the Site settings become different after activation and what possibilities the new options give. I will also introduce the classic Content Query web part.

When you have activated the SharePoint Server Publishing Infrastructure for a site, you can also activate the SharePoint Server Publishing feature for that site and any subsite. This feature gives you more powerful layout options, and we will look at them in the last sections of this chapter.

27.1 Activate the Publishing Infrastructure

Activate the SharePoint Server Publishing Infrastructure from the root site of the site collection. In the Site settings, click on the link 'Site collection features' under Site Collection Administration.

Scroll down to SharePoint Server Publishing Infrastructure' and click on the Activate button. The activation might take a few minutes.

When you have activated the SharePoint Server Publishing Infrastructure, the site and any subsites will have the new features that become available, and the navigation settings will also be changed for all sites in the collection.

Demo:

https://kalmstrom.com/Tips/SharePoint-Online-Course/Publishing-Infrastructure-Activate.htm

27.2 Navigation Changes with Publishing Infrastructure

When the SharePoint Server Publishing Infrastructure has been activated for a site collection, the Look and Feel group in the Site settings has become different.

The links to the Site navigation and Top link bar are now replaced with a 'Navigation' link, which give more options than before:

Look and Feel
Design Manager
Title, description, and logo
Device Channels
Navigation Elements
Change the look
Import Design Package
Navigation

- The navigation areas are called Local and Global Navigation instead of Site navigation and Top link bar.

- You must enable 'Show subsites' in the Navigation Settings to display links to subsites. Even if you select 'Use the top link bar from the parent site' when you create a new subsite, the link will not be shown until you enable 'Show subsites'.

- The image below shows the default setting for the Global Navigation. The Current Navigation has similar settings.

Global Navigation

Specify the navigation items to display in global navigation for this Web site. This navigation is shown at the top of the page in most Web sites.

◯ Display the same navigation items as the parent site (This is the top-level site.)

◯ Managed Navigation: The navigation items will be represented using a Managed Metadata term set.

◉ Structural Navigation: Display the navigation items below the current site
(Structural navigation has significant performance impact and is not recommended in SharePoint Online. You can find more details here.)

☐ Show subsites
☐ Show pages

Maximum number of dynamic items to show within this level of navigation: `20`

The default Structural Navigation is easy to maintain, security trimmed and updates automatically when content has been changed.

If you instead enable Managed Navigation, you can add a term set for the navigation.

Find term sets that include the following terms.

[   ] 🔍 📄

▷ 🗂 kalmstrom.com Solutions

▷ 🗂 People

▷ 🗂 Search Dictionaries

◢ 🗂 Site Collection - kalmstromnet.sharepoint.com-sites-demosite

　　📄 Demo site Navigation

　　📄 Wiki Categories

[Create Term Set]

Open the Term Store Management Tool to edit term sets.

Microsoft warns that both these options might influence the SharePoint Online performance. I have not noticed any problem, but you should be aware of the possibility so that you can disable the SharePoint Server Publishing Infrastructure if necessary.

- A bit down on the Navigation Settings page you can find the entry 'Structural Navigation: Editing and Sorting'. Here you can add headings and links, delete links or move them up and down in the navigation more easily than you can do without the Publishing Infrastructure.

Move Up	Move Down	⟲ Edit...	✕ Delete	Add Heading...	Add Link...

🗂 Global Navigation
🗂 Current Navigation
　　▢ Home
　　▢ Conversations
　　▢ Documents
　　▢ Notebook
　　▢ Pages
　　▢ Site contents

- When the SharePoint Server Publishing Infrastructure is activated, you can use the Navigation page to create a mega menu more easily that with drag and drop. Without the Publishing Infrastructure this is only possible in Communication sites, as we saw in chapter 6.

- When you click on 'Add Link...' 'in the top right corner of the Structural Navigation: Editing and Sorting' box, you will have more advanced options than before. You can, for example, set links to open in a new window.

Navigation Link ✕

🔲 Edit the title, URL, and description of the navigation item.

Title:

URL: http://   Browse...

☐ Open link in new window

Description:

Audience:

OK   Cancel

Demos:

https://www.kalmstrom.com/Tips/SharePoint-Online-Course/Publishing-Infrastructure-Navigation-Changes.htm

https://www.kalmstrom.com/Tips/SharePoint-Online-Course/Publishing-Infrastructure-Mega-Menu.htm

27.3   THE CONTENT QUERY WEB PART

The Content Query web part is available for classic pages when the SharePoint Server Publishing Infrastructure feature has been activated. You can find it in the Content Rollup web part category.

The Content Query reminds of the Content Search web part that I have used in several earlier examples, but there is an important difference in how the search is performed: The Content Search can search the index of the entire tenant, while the Content Query only can search the site (default) or specified sites in the site collection.

There is a certain delay before the index is updated, so you will not see your changes right away when you let the Content Search web part search the whole index. With the Content Query web part any changes are shown more quickly, and therefore the Content Query is suitable for content that is often changed, like tasks.

The Content Query is a bit easier to configure than the Content Search, as you don't have to build a query. You can find all options in the Content Query web part properties.

Here is an example of how you can use the Content Query web part to collect tasks from subsites within the same site collection and show them on a page.

◀ Content Query   ✕

Content Query Tool Part   ⌃

⊞ Query   Help

⊞ Presentation

⊞ Appearance

⊞ Layout

⊞ Advanced

OK   Cancel   Apply

486

1. Open a classic page in edit mode and add the Content Query web part from the Content Rollup category.

2. Edit the web part and open the Query accordion.

3. Add site URLs, if you want to restrict the search to certain sites in the collection.

4. Select to show items from the Tasks list type.

5. Expand the Presentation accordion and remove the text in the Link textbox under Fields to display. (If you don't do that, you will have an error message.)

6. Under Presentation you can also group and sort the displayed items, set the number of columns and make other settings.

7. Expand the Appearance accordion and enter a suitable web part title.

8. Make any other web part settings you prefer before you apply the changes.

9. Save and publish the page.

◄ Content Query   ✕

Content Query Tool Part   ⌃

☐ Query   Help

Source:

◉ Show items from all sites in this site collection

○ Show items from the following site and all subsites:

                Browse...

○ Show items from the following list:

                Browse...

List Type:

Show items from this list type:

Tasks   ✓

Content Type:

Show items of this content type group:

<All Content Types> ✓

Show items of this content type:

<All Content Types> ✓

   ☑ Include child content types

Audience Targeting:

   ☐ Apply audience filtering

Demo:

https://www.kalmstrom.com/Tips/SharePoint-Online-Course/Publishing-Infrastructure-Content-Query.htm

27.4 SHAREPOINT SERVER PUBLISHING

Once the SharePoint Server Publishing Infrastructure feature has been activated for the site collection, you can activate the SharePoint Server Publishing feature for each site in the collection.

Enable the SharePoint Server Publishing feature for sites where you want to have more layout options than those I have shown in earlier chapters.

The SharePoint Server Publishing gives you access to the Master page feature from the Look and Feel group in the settings. Here you can specify a master page for the site and use an alternate CSS URL for the entire site and its subsites.

Another SharePoint Server Publishing feature is the Image Renditions, which lets you define different image formats.

The SharePoint Server Publishing feature is activated in the Site Settings >Manage site features under Site Actions. Scroll down to the feature and click on Activate. The activation only takes a few seconds.

27.4.1 *Publishing Pages*

When SharePoint Server Publishing is enabled you can create pages of the publishing type. These are classic pages that resembles wiki pages, but they have more layout and image options.

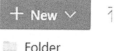

While other site pages are stored in the "Site Pages" library, the publishing pages are stored in a separate "Pages" library that you also can reach from the Site contents. Under the '+New' button in the "Pages" library, you can find a selection of publishing pages.

Folder

Page

Article Page

The check in/check out feature is enabled by default in publishing pages.

Welcome Page

Error Page

The first option in the dropdown, Page, can also be created from pages with the classic interface, if you add a page to the site via the 'Add a page' link under the 365 Settings icon.

You can create other kinds of pages even if SharePoint Server Publishing has been enabled for the site. When you add a page from the modern interface, it will be a modern page, and if you want to create wiki or web part pages, you can do that from the "Site pages" library as usual. The publishing pages can only be created from the "Pages" library.

Demo:

https://kalmstrom.com/Tips/SharePoint-Online-Course/Publishing-Infrastructure-Server-Publishing.htm

27.4.1.1 Image Renditions

Image Renditions is one of the new features you get when the SharePoint Server Publishing feature has been activated. When you create a new publishing page and insert an image, multiple renditions of the image will be created.

The wiki page picture options are present in publishing pages too, and you insert an image in the same way, under the INSERT tab. When you upload an image from your computer, you will first have a chance to add metadata to your image.

Upload Image

EDIT

Save | Cancel | Paste | Cut | Copy | Delete Item

Commit | Clipboard | Actions

ℹ The document was uploaded successfully. Use this form to update the properties of the document.

Content Type	Image ▼
	Upload an image.
Name *	HOSP180x180 .png
Title	
Keywords	
	For example: scenery, mountains, trees, nature
Comments	
	A summary of this asset
Author	
	The primary author
Date Picture Taken	📅 12 AM ▼ 00 ▼
Copyright	

Version: 1.0
Created at 3/7/2016 12:18 AM by Kate Kalmström
Last modified at 3/7/2016 12:18 AM by Kate Kalmström

Save | Cancel

When you have clicked on Save, the renditions will be created, and you can select which format you want to use for your image.

Click on the 'Pick Rendition' button under the IMAGE tab to see the options.

The image below shows the default options, but you can add your own rendition sizes in the Site settings >Image Renditions under 'Look and Feel'.

Click on the 'Add new item' link, give the new rendition a name and specify its width and height in pixels.

BROWSE   PAGE   PUBLISH   FORMAT TEXT

Address: /sites/Communicat

Alt Text: Kanban board

Change Picture ▾   Pick Rendition ▾

Full Size Image

Display Template Picture 3 Lines (100 x 100)

Display Template Picture On Top (304 x 100)

Display Template Large Picture (468 x 220)

Display Template Video (120 x 68)

Edit Renditions

489

If you select 'Edit Renditions', you can see all renditions of the image.

Edit Renditions: KTM-Arabic.png

Display Template Picture 3 Lines

100 x 100
https://m365x446726.sharepoint.com
/sites/Communications
/PublishingImages/Pages/publishing
/KTM-Arabic.png?RenditionID=1

Click to change

Display Template Video

120 x 68
https://m365x446726.sharepoint.com
/sites/Communications
/PublishingImages/Pages/publishing
/KTM-Arabic.png?RenditionID=4

Click to change

Display Template Picture On Top

304 x 100
https://m365x446726.sharepoint.com
/sites/Communications
/PublishingImages/Pages/publishing
/KTM-Arabic.png?RenditionID=2

Click to change

Display Template Large Picture

468 x 220
https://m365x446726.sharepoint.com
/sites/Communications
/PublishingImages/Pages/publishing
/KTM-Arabic.png?RenditionID=3

Click on the 'Click to change' link at the size you want to edit and drag the handles to the portion of the image you want to use.

Demo:

https://www.kalmstrom.com/Tips/SharePoint-Online-Course/Publishing-Infrastructure-Image-Renditions.htm

27.4.2   Link to an Alternate CSS File

When the SharePoint Server Publishing Infrastructure feature has been activated for the site collection and the SharePoint Server Publishing feature is activated for the site, you can use an alternate CSS file for that site. Add the alternate CSS file in the Master Page settings:

1. Upload the CSS file to the Site Assets or to another location on your SharePoint site.

2. In the Site settings, click on 'Master page' under 'Look and Feel'.

3. Expand 'Alternate CSS URL'.

4. Select the 'Specify a CSS file' option and browse to the location where you uploaded your CSS file.

5. Before you click OK, check the box for subsite inheritance if you want all subsites to use the CSS file.

◢ Alternate CSS URL

Typically, Master Pages define CSS styles for your site. If you would like to apply a separate CSS style sheet independent of your master page, specify it here.

○ Inherit Alternate CSS URL from parent of this site
○ Use default styles and any CSS files associated with your Master Page
◉ Specify a CSS file to be used by this site and all sites that inherit from it:

Choose the first option to inherit these settings from the parent site. Choose the second option to rely only on the styles defined in master pages. Choose the third option to apply a separate CSS style sheet.

All Channels [   ] [Browse...]

☑ Reset all subsites to inherit this alternate CSS URL

Demo:

https://www.kalmstrom.com/Tips/SharePoint-Online-Course/Publishing-Infrastructure-Alternate-CSS-URL.htm

27.5   SUMMARY

In the chapter about SharePoint Server Publishing Infrastructure, we have looked at the changes this feature gives in the Site settings 'Look and Feel' group and at the new navigation options they give.

You have also learned how to use the Content Query web part, and you have seen how the activation of SharePoint Server Publishing can give a site more layout options for pages and images.

In the next chapter, I will explain how you can use Excel or Access to create example data for SharePoint testing.

28 CREATE EXAMPLE DATA

When you are trying different solutions and scenarios for SharePoint apps, it is helpful to use example data. In this chapter I will show how to create example data for a SharePoint list in Microsoft Excel and Access.

28.1 COPY AND PASTE EXAMPLE DATA FROM EXCEL

When you don't have too many rows in the SharePoint datasheet grid, it works well to paste values you have created in Excel. In this example, I will add example data to a Number column called "Hours Worked". To create the example data, I will use the Excel RAND function.

1. In the List settings, edit the SharePoint view, so that the item limit includes all the rows you want to use. This way you can open the list in grid view and easily paste example data you create in Excel into the Hours Worked column. In this example we want to create 100 items.

⊟ Item Limit

Use an item limit to limit the amount of data that is returned to users of this view. You can either make this an absolute limit, or allow users to view all the items in the list in batches of the specified size. Learn about managing large lists.

Number of items to display:

100

◉ Display items in batches of the specified size.

○ Limit the total number of items returned to the specified amount.

2. Open a new Excel spreadsheet.

3. Enter a RAND function in the function field to generate 100 random numbers: =int(RAND()*100)

f_x =INT(RAND()*100)

	A	B
1	44	
2		

4. Drag the cell down to copy the formula to as many cells as you need for the SharePoint list column.

5. Copy the Excel column and paste it into the SharePoint "Hours Worked" column.

If you have a long SharePoint list it is safer to open it in Access and paste the values into the "Hours Worked" column there, as Access is more stable.

Demo:

https://www.kalmstrom.com/Tips/SharePoint-Online-Course/HelpDesk-Hours-Worked.htm

28.2 CREATE EXAMPLE DATA IN ACCESS

To create more complex example data, you can open the app in Access, *refer to 22.4.2*, and let a query combine values from various columns.

Here, I will use example data for a "Tasks" list as an example. Multiple selections must not be allowed in the "Assigned To" column.

1. Import the "Tasks" list to Access as a linked table. As it has People or Group type column, we will also have a "User Info" table.

2. Create a new table. It will open automatically in the design area. Give it the name "Priorities".

3. Give the field the name "Priority'.

4. Enter the priority values under 'Priority'. (The ID values will be set automatically.)

ID	Priority	Click to Add
1	High	
2	Low	
3	Normal	
* (New)		

5. Create another table named "Titles" with the field 'Title'. Add some titles to the field.

6. Click on the 'Query Wizard' button under the ribbon Create tab. Keep the default 'Simple Query Wizard' option. Click OK.

7. Select first table and then the fields that you want to include in the query. In this case, it is the 'Title' and 'Priority' fields we created but also the 'ID' and 'Work email' fields from the "User info" table that was added when we imported the SharePoint list.

Simple Query Wizard

Which fields do you want in your query?

You can choose from more than one table or query.

Tables/Queries

Table: UserInfo

Available Fields:

Name
Compliance Asset Id
Account
Work email
OtherMail
Mobile phone
About me
SIP Address

Selected Fields:

Title
Priority
ID

Cancel   < Back   Next >   Finish

8. Click OK to the Relationships message and close the 'Relationship' tab.

9. Click on the 'Query Design' button under the Create tab in the ribbon.

10. Select the 'All' tab in the right pane that opens and drag the tables you want to use to the query design area.

11. Double-click on the four field names we want to use, to add them to the grid area.

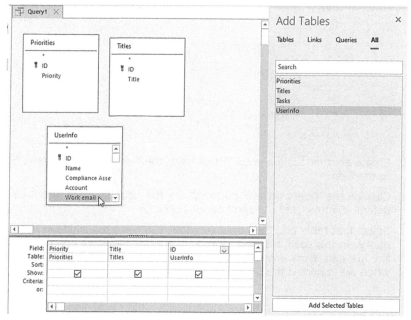

12. Add the parameter 'Is Not Null' to the 'Work email' field, in case there are any blank rows that you want to get rid of. You can also add 'And Not' + any e-mail address you don't want to use in the example date.

13. Click on the 'Run' button under the 'Design' tab in the ribbon to get all possible combinations of the included fields.

14. If needed, click on View >Design View to adjust the query so that you get reasonable values. Then run the query again.

| Work email |
| UserInfo |
| ☑ |
| Is Not Null And Not 'l |

15. Click on the 'Append' button under the ribbon 'Design' tab.

16. From the dropdown in the Append dialog, select the SharePoint list where you want to have the example data. Click OK.

17. In the grid area, append the query columns to suitable columns in the SharePoint list if needed.

18. Click on the 'Run' button under the ribbon 'Design' tab.

Now when you refresh the SharePoint list, you will see the new items created by the Access query there.

Demo:

https://kalmstrom.com/Tips/SharePoint-Online-Course/HelpDesk-ExampleData-Access.htm

28.3   SUMMARY

It is often important to try out different scenarios in SharePoint before you go out in production, and in such cases, it is useful to create example data. In this short chapter, have given tips on how such example data can be created in Excel and Access.

Now, we are getting close to the end of this book. I will just give you two chapters more, and in those I will show how business processes can be enhanced by using the techniques you have learned by studying *SharePoint Online from Scratch*.

We will start with a solution for Meetings management within an organization. It includes creation of a content type, but now I will not give you the creation steps. Go back to chapter 25 if you have forgotten how to create them.

29 MEETING NOTES AND ACTION POINTS

In this last chapter I want to repeat and expand techniques that we have gone through earlier. I will show how you can combine what you have learned to create a SharePoint solution that automates the management of meetings, meeting notes and meeting decisions in general.

I hope my suggestion will inspire you to try something similar for your organization. By now, you should have the knowledge to modify the solution given in this chapter, so that it suits your environment perfectly!

The solution has a "Meetings" list for all meetings. Each meeting will be entered as an item in this list. The list is associated with a content type called Meeting.

The Meeting content type has a Hyperlink column, which is intended for links to an "Action points" list for each meeting. One person will be assigned to creating such an "Action points" list before each meeting, so creating it must be a quick task.

The building of this system involves several steps:

- What to consider?
- Create a content type for the "Meetings" list
- Create a content type for the "Action Points" list
- Add the new content types to the lists
- Manage changes in the content types
- Create list templates
- Copy templates to other site collections
- Create a meetings overview page
- Use list specific columns with content types
- Display "My Action Points" on a page.

29.1 CONSIDERATIONS

Before you start creating a SharePoint solution for meetings management, you should consider your organization's information strategy.

- What do you want to store?
- How many mandatory fields are necessary? In general, you should try to keep them at a minimum!
- How should data be categorized?
- How to best find information?
- What Permissions are needed? Some meeting notes will need strict permissions, others can be open to all users. How to manage that in the best way?

- For how long should we store the meeting notes? How can the retention time be set?

- Should the meeting notes be stored in lists or libraries? Lists are more powerful in general, but if it must be easy to print the meeting notes, you need to use libraries.

Demo:

https://www.kalmstrom.com/Tips/SharePoint-Online-Course/SharePoint-Meetings-Intro.htm

29.2   CREATE CONTENT TYPES

For this meeting management example, I create two content types in the Content Type Gallery: a "Meeting" content type and an "Action Point" content type.

29.2.1   *Meeting Content Type*

We start with creating a Meeting content type for the "Meetings" list.

1. Create a Meeting content type in the Content Type Gallery. It should inherit from the regular Item content type in the List Content Types group.

2. When the new content type has been created, we can start customizing it. As we have built this content type on the Item, there is only one column, the "Title" (besides the created by, modified at and similar auto generated columns).

3. I suggest a "Comments" column from the existing site columns, for meeting notes.

4. Maybe you also have an existing "Department" column of the Managed Metadata type, connected to a "Departments" term store.

   If not, I would recommend that you create a new "Department" Managed Metadata site column and connect it to a term set in the Term Store, before you add the (now existing) "Department" column to the "Meeting" content type.

5. For the rest of the columns, you may have to create new site columns:

   a. Meeting notes – Multiple lines of text. Under 'More options', turn on 'Append changes to existing text'.

   b. Chairperson – Person or Group

   c. Internal Attendees – Person or Group, allow multiple choices

   d. External Attendees – Multiple lines of text, plain text

   e. Action Points – Hyperlink

6. Publish the content type when you have tested it in the Content Type Hub.

Demo:

https://kalmstrom.com/Tips/SharePoint-Online-Course/SharePoint-Meetings-Content-Type-Item.htm

29.2.1.1   Set Retention on the Meeting Content Type

Meeting information should not be kept forever, and when content types are created in the SharePoint Admin Center/Content Type Hub, you can add retention to them.

1. Open the Meeting content type settings and select 'Policy settings'. An 'Edit Policy' page in the Content Type Hub will open in a new tab.

2. Check the box at 'Enable retention'.

3. Click on the link 'Add a retention stage...'

4. In the dialog that opens, set the time you want to keep the item in the list.

5. Select what to do with the item when it no longer should be kept.

29.2.2   *Action Point Content Type*

In the Content Type Gallery, you should also create a content type for the "Action Points" lists. This will be a Task content type, selected from the List Content Types group.

When you base a new content type on the Task content type, you will have multiple columns. Therefore, you probably want to remove some of the columns instead of creating new ones.

Demo:

https://kalmstrom.com/Tips/SharePoint-Online-Course/SharePoint-Meetings-Content-Type-Task.htm

29.3   CREATE APPS AND ADD CONTENT TYPES

When the content types have been published, it is time to create apps for meetings and action points and associate them with the new content types.

29.3.1   *Meetings List*

In my suggestion, one common "Meetings" list is used for all meetings – or all meetings within a department or similar, and each meeting is entered as an item.

1. Create a new custom list. Call it "Meetings" and make your preferred changes to it. You might for example want to add it to the Site navigation and enable version history.

2. Allow management of content types under List Settings >Advanced settings.

3. In the new Content Type group in the list settings, click on the link 'Add from existing site content types' and add the Meeting content type.

4. Remove the default content type.

5. Create views.

Demo:

https://kalmstrom.com/Tips/SharePoint-Online-Course/SharePoint-Meetings-Content-Type-Use.htm

29.3.2 *Action Points List*

The "Action Points" list must be created for each meeting. I suggest that you use a list built on the Tasks template. For the creation, you can follow the steps for the "Meetings" list above.

29.3.2.1 Action Points Template

To make it easier for the people who are responsible for creating the "Action Points" lists, you should create the list as you want to have it. Then you can either save it as a template or give permission to the responsible people to create a new list from it via Microsoft Lists.

Contoso Action Points
App Details

That way the responsible people can either just 'Add an app' and select the "Meeting Action Points" template or create a new list from the Site content and select to create it from the "Action Points" list.

Select an existing list   ✕

Select a list to use as a template for a new empty list on this site.

Columns, views and formatting will copy over to the new list.

Select a Team or site   Choose a list from Benefits3 (this site)

Benefits3 (this site)		Name	Type	Last modified
All Company	○	Contacts	List	10/29/2020 11:44 AM
Ask HR	◉	Contoso Action Points	List	11/10/2020 9:59 AM

You can do the same for the "Meetings" list, if you want to use it in multiple sites.

Demo:

https://kalmstrom.com/Tips/SharePoint-Online-Course/SharePoint-Meetings-Action-Points.htm

29.4 CREATE A MEETINGS OVERVIEW PAGE

It is convenient to have a page that gives an overview of all company meetings. If you only want to include meetings from one site, you can use the modern List web part or add the "Meetings" list as an app part in a classic page.

When the meetings are stored in different pages, we cannot use a modern page. The Highlighted content web part can show content from all sites, but custom content types are not yet displayed in the list of content types to be selected.

In a **classic** page, it is possible to show content from multiple sites with the Content Search web part.

1. In a classic page, insert the Content Search web part and edit it.

2. In the Query Builder, select 'Items matching a content type' and don't restrict by app. Restrict the search to the Meeting content type.

3. Switch to Advanced Mode and click on SORTING, to sort the meetings. When you sort them after creation date, the most recent meetings will be displayed on top.

Build Your Query

BASICS   REFINERS   SORTING   SETTINGS   TEST

Sort results
You can have several levels of sorting for your results based on their managed properties.

Sort by: | Created | Descending |

CrawlLogLevel   Add sort level
CrawlObjectID
Ranking Model
Choose a way of   CrawlUrl
ranking results.
                         CRC
Dynamic ordering   Created
On top of the ranking   CreatedBy   or demote items in the search
results.

4. Make other changes to the web part, like how many items should be shown, how many rows and what should be mapped to the rows.

29.5   SUMMARY

I hope the building of the meeting management system I suggest in this chapter has given a deeper understanding of content types and the Content Type Hub.

In the last chapter, we will have a look at another business solution, this time for rental agreements. Here, I will give the steps for a flow that sends a reminder about contract renewal. This flow runs on a schedule, so you will learn something new in the last chapter too!

30 RENTAL AGREEMENTS

This chapter has rental agreements as the starting point. Such contracts must be stored in a way that gives a good overview over what the organization is renting, and renewals must be taken care of in due time.

My intention is not to give a recipe on how to create the perfect application for rental agreements management. Instead, I want to point to various options that might be useful when you handle similar information sharing situations in your own organization.

We will create a Rental Agreement content type with suitable site columns and associate it with a list app. Then we can create the same type of list in other sites via the 'Add an app' command or by using Microsoft Lists.

We will automate the renewal reminders with a flow that sends a reminder to the person who is responsible for the renewal.

30.1 CREATE A CONTENT TYPE

The first step when building a rental agreements solution, is to create a content type for the rental agreement items.

The content type should be based on the List Content Types group and the Item. That will give you a list with just a "Title" column, which you can rename to "Location Name" when the content type is used in a list. (We cannot rename the column when we create a content type. That would rename all "Title" columns in all content types in the tenant!)

I suggest the following columns: (My comments about new or existing site columns are based on what site columns most organizations have or not have already, so don't take them too literally.)

- Square Meters (of the location that is being rented): a new site column of the Number type.
- Start Date (for the rental agreement): an existing site column.
- End Date (for the rental agreement): an existing site column.
- Department (that is renting the location): an existing site column.
- Renewal Date: a new site column of the Date and Time type. Set the internal column name to, "RenewalDate", because it should be used in a query when we build a flow. *Refer to* 7.13, Internal Names.
- Responsible Person: a new site column of the Person or Group type.

+ New   ⊞ Edit in grid view   ⋔ Share   ▓ Export to Excel   ◈ Power Apps ∨   ⚙ Automate ∨   ⋯

Rental Agreements

| Location Name ∨ | Square Meters ∨ | Start Date ∨ | End Date ∨ | Department ∨ | Renewal Date ∨ | Responsible Person |

When the content type has been created, create a custom "Rental Agreements" list app and associate it to the Rental Agreement content type.

I suggest that you also enable version history in the list (and add an edit button in the views if you are using the classic experience).

Demos:

https://www.kalmstrom.com/Tips/SharePoint-Online-Course/Rental-Agreements-Content-Type.htm (This demo shows creation in a site, but you can of course create the content type in the SharePoint Admin center/Content Type Hub too.)

https://www.kalmstrom.com/Tips/SharePoint-Online-Course/Rental-Agreements-Content-Type-Use.htm

30.2 "RENTAL AGREEMENTS" TEMPLATE

You can of course have all the rental agreements in one list, but if you have multiple lists you can set different permissions on them, and users will not be burdened by many items in one list.

When you have created a "Rental Agreements" custom list and added the views and settings you prefer, it is easy to create new lists for other kinds of contracts or agreements from it.

You can either create new lists from the "Rental Agreements" list via Microsoft Lists or save the app as a template.

Demo:

https://www.kalmstrom.com/Tips/SharePoint-Online-Course/Rental-Agreements-Template.htm

30.3 SCHEDULED REVIEW ALERT FLOW

When you have many rental agreements, it is useful to let a flow send an e-mail to the responsible person when it is time to review the agreement and either renew or cancel it. (Since Microsoft stopped supporting SharePoint 2010 workflows in SharePoint Online, there is no easy way to create a similar workflow in SharePoint Designer.)

Microsoft has given a built-in reminder flow for modern SharePoint apps that contain a column of the type Date and Time, but it only sends a reminder to the person who created the flow. This flow is suitable if all rental contracts have the same responsible person.

With multiple responsible persons, it is still possible to use the built-in reminder flow, if all responsible people create their own flows. That is however an insecure way.

Here, I will explain how you can create a flow that works for all people who are added as responsible for a rental contract in a "Rental Agreements" list. We will use an expression that sets the reminder date to seven days before the contract's expiry date.

The flow is set to run every day. It searches the "Renewal Date" value of each rental agreement for items that will expire in 7 days. When such a rental agreement is found, the flow will generate an e-mail to the responsible person.

The flow should send the reminder seven days before each rental agreement's end date. To find those contracts, we will use the flow action 'Get items' with a filter query. In this query, we need to use the internal column name "RenewalDate".

The query picks items where the value of the "Renewal Date" column is equal to seven days after today. We will use an expression for the "seven days after today" parameter.

30.3.1   Steps

In this flow, we will use a 'Get items' action, and a filter query in that action will help us find the contracts that expire in seven days. In the steps below, I give the formula for the query.

1. On the Power Automate site >My flows, create a 'Scheduled cloud flows – from blank' flow.

2. Give the flow a name and set the 'interval' to '1' and the 'Frequency' to 'Day'. You can also set a start time.

3. Click on 'Create'.

4. Click on 'New step' and add the action 'SharePoint - Get items'.

   a. Enter the name of the site and select the list.

   b. Open the advanced options.

   c. At 'Filter Query', enter the internal name for the "Renewal Date" column + eq. Add an apostrophe (') to start building a string.

   d. Open the Expression tab to build an expression for the rest of the field:

      i. In the function field, start writing "format" and then select 'formatDateTime'.

503

ii. Add a parenthesis for input and start writing "add" inside it. Select 'addDays'.

iii. Add another parenthesis and start writing "utc" inside it. Select 'utcNow'. That will also add a new parenthesis to the function.

iv. After the new, empty parenthesis, enter a comma and 7 (for seven days) inside the addDays parenthesis.

v. Before the last parenthesis, add a comma and a string. Enter the date format, by ISO standard yyyy-MM-dd, inside the single quotes.

You should now have this expression:
FormatDateTime(addDays(utcNow(),7),'yyy-MM-dd').

Dynamic content   **Expression**

f_x formatDateTime(addDays(utcNow(),7),'yyy-MM-dd')

Update

e. Place the cursor after the start of string apostrophe in the 'Filter Query' field and click on 'Update' under the expression.

f. Add an end of string apostrophe in the 'Filter Query' field.

S	Get items	ⓘ ...
* Site Address	Benefits3 - https://m365x446726.sharepoint.com/sites/benefits	⌄
* List Name	Rental Agreements	⌄
Limit Entries to Folder	Select a folder, or leave blank for the whole list	🗀
Include Nested Items	Return entries contained in sub-folders (default = true)	⌄
Filter Query	RenewalDate eq ' f_x formatDateTim... × '	

5. Click on 'New step'.

6. Add an 'Apply to each' action.

7. Add the dynamic content 'value' from the 'Get items' action to the output field.

8. Click on 'New step'.

9. Add the action 'Office 365 Outlook - Send an email (V2)'

a. In the 'To' field, enter the dynamic content 'Responsible Person Email' from the 'Get items' action.

b. For the e-mail subject, type some general text and add the Title of the rented object as dynamic content. (You might find your custom name "Location Name" in the list of dynamic content instead of "Title".)

c. Insert a link in the 'Body' field:

    i. Switch to HTML view.

    ii. Instead of the default <br>, enter <a href="[the dynamic content 'Link to Item']">See Rental Agreement</a>.

10. Click on 'Save'.

11. Click on 'Test' in the top right corner.

12. Select 'I'll perform the trigger action' and then 'Test'.

13. Add a test item that has its Renewal day 7 days from today in the Rental Agreements list.

14. Click on 'Run flow' in the Flow Editor right pane.

15. Check that the e-mail is sent to the person you added as responsible in the list and that the subject is correct and the link to the item works.

Demo:

https://www.kalmstrom.com/Tips/SharePoint-Flows/Flow-Contract-Reminder.htm (The demo shows a library, so another action is used to fetch the items. Otherwise, the steps are similar.)

30.4   SUMMARY

In this chapter we have looked at how SharePoint can be used to facilitate the management of rental agreements. We have created a rental agreement content type that you can associate to multiple lists.

I have also suggested a way to automate the renewal reminders with a flow.

This was the last chapter, and as you have come all this way, I hope you have found my book interesting and useful. If needed, you should now be ready to continue exploring SharePoint Online on your own, with the help of more advanced books and online information.

Good luck!

Peter

31 ABOUT THE AUTHORS

Peter Kalmstrom is the CEO and Systems Designer of the Swedish family business Kalmstrom Enterprises AB, well known for the software brand *kalmstrom.com Business Solutions*. Peter has 19 Microsoft certifications, among them several for SharePoint, and he is a certified Microsoft Trainer.

Peter begun developing his kalmstrom.com products around the turn of the millennium, but for a period of five years he also worked as a Skype product manager. In 2010 he left Skype, and since then he has been focusing on developing standard and custom SharePoint solutions.

Peter has published eight more books, all available from Amazon:

- Excel 2016 from Scratch
- Microsoft Teams from Scratch
- Office 365 from Scratch
- PowerShell for SharePoint from Scratch
- SharePoint Flows from Scratch
- SharePoint Online Exercises
- SharePoint Online Essentials
- SharePoint Workflows from Scratch

Peter divides his time between Sweden and Spain. He has three children, and apart from his keen interest in development and new technologies, he likes to sing and act. Peter is also a dedicated vegan and animal rights activist.

Kate Kalmström is Peter's mother and a former teacher, author of schoolbooks and translator. Nowadays she only works in the family business and assists Peter with his books.

Made in the USA
Middletown, DE
04 June 2021